PETRARCH'S *ITINERARIUM*

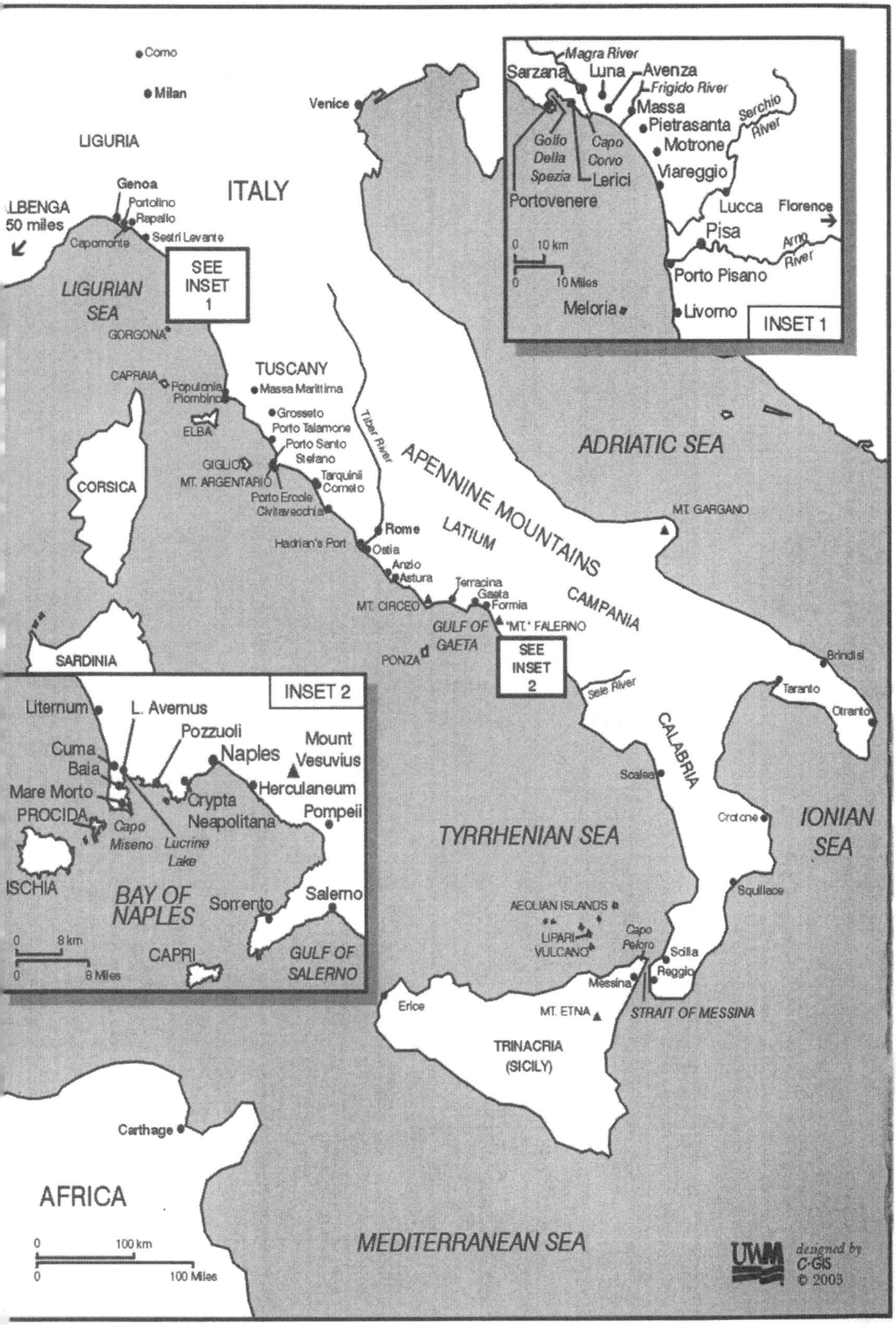

Como
Milan
Venice
LIGURIA
ITALY
Genoa
Portofino
Rapallo
Sestri Levante
Capomonte
ALBENGA 50 miles
SEE INSET 1
LIGURIAN SEA
GORGONA
CAPRAIA
Populonia
Piombino
ELBA
TUSCANY
Massa Marittima
Grosseto
Porto Talamone
Porto Santo Stefano
GIGLIO
MT. ARGENTARIO
Porto Ercole
Civitavecchia
Tarquinii Corneto
CORSICA
Tiber River
APENNINE MOUNTAINS
Rome
Hadrian's Port
Ostia
Anzio
Astura
LATIUM
Terracina
Gaeta
Formia
MT. CIRCEO
GULF OF GAETA
"MT." FALERNO
PONZA
SEE INSET 2
CAMPANIA
SARDINIA
ADRIATIC SEA
MT. GARGANO
Brindisi
Taranto
Otranto
Sele River
CALABRIA
Scalea
Crotone
IONIAN SEA
TYRRHENIAN SEA
Squillace
AEOLIAN ISLANDS
LIPARI
VULCANO
Capo Peloro
Scilla
Reggio
Messina
STRAIT OF MESSINA
Erice
MT. ETNA
TRINACRIA (SICILY)
Carthage
AFRICA
MEDITERRANEAN SEA
0 100 km
0 100 Miles
UWM
designed by C-GIS © 2003
INSET 1
Magra River
Sarzana
Luna
Avenza
Frigido River
Massa
Pietrasanta
Motrone
Serchio River
Golfo Della Spezia
Capo Corvo
Lerici
Viareggio
Portovenere
Lucca
Florence
Pisa
Arno River
Porto Pisano
0 10 km
0 10 Miles
Meloria
Livorno
INSET 2
Liternum
L. Avernus
Pozzuoli
Cuma
Baia
Naples
Mount Vesuvius
Mare Morto
Herculaneum
Crypta Neapolitana
PROCIDA
Capo Miseno
Lucrine Lake
Pompeii
ISCHIA
BAY OF NAPLES
Sorrento
Salerno
0 8 km
0 8 Miles
CAPRI
GULF OF SALERNO

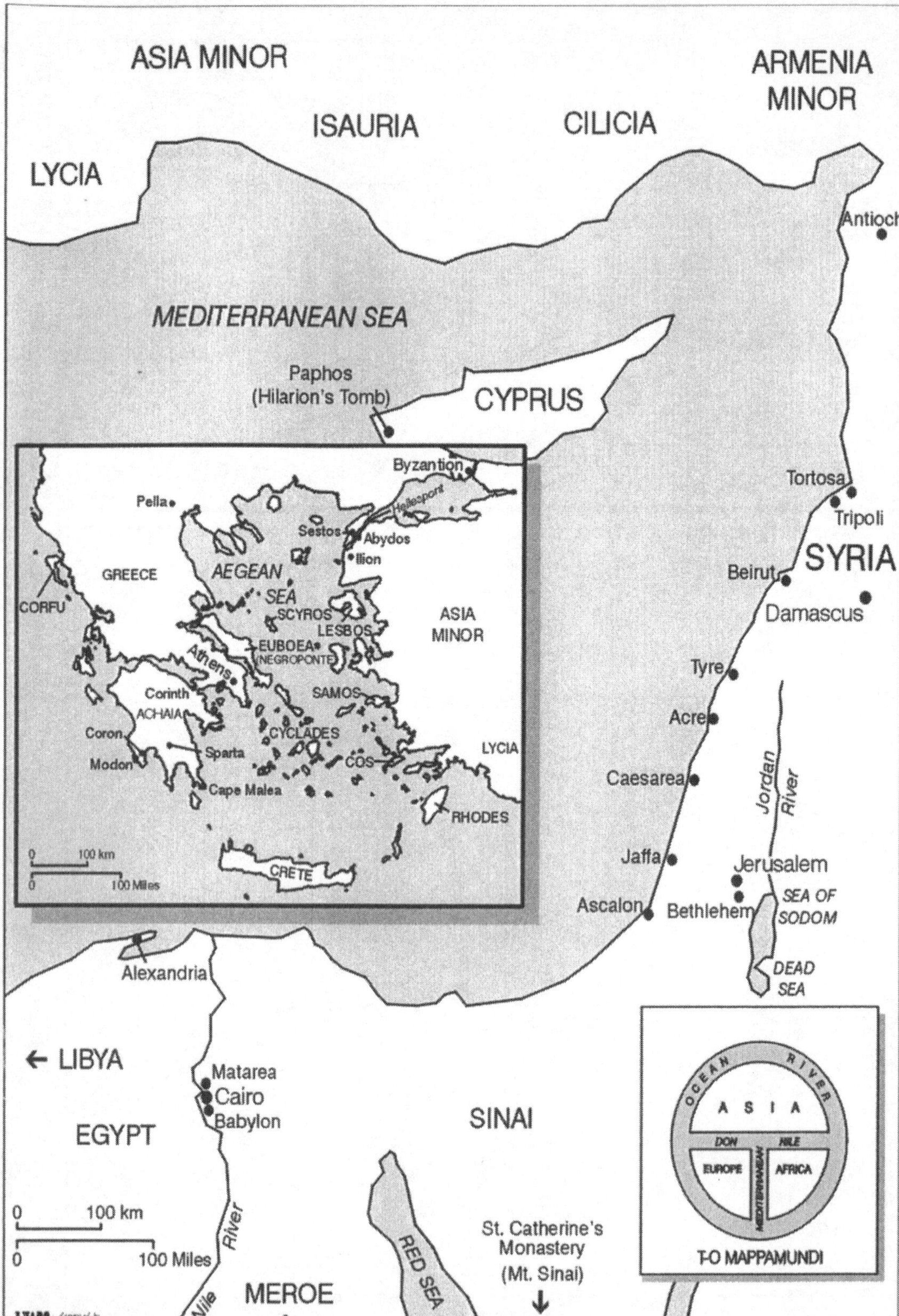
ASIA MINOR
ARMENIA MINOR
ISAURIA
CILICIA
LYCIA
Antioch
MEDITERRANEAN SEA
Paphos (Hilarion's Tomb)
CYPRUS
Byzantion
Pella
Hellespont
Sestos
Abydos
Ilion
GREECE
AEGEAN SEA
CORFU
SCYROS
LESBOS
ASIA MINOR
EUBOEA (NEGROPONTE)
Athens
Corinth
ACHAIA
SAMOS
Coron
CYCLADES
Sparta
LYCIA
Modon
COS
Cape Malea
RHODES
0 100 km
0 100 Miles
CRETE
Tortosa
Tripoli
SYRIA
Beirut
Damascus
Tyre
Acre
Caesarea
Jordan River
Jaffa
Jerusalem
Ascalon
Bethlehem
SEA OF SODOM
DEAD SEA
Alexandria
LIBYA
Matarea
Cairo
Babylon
EGYPT
SINAI
OCEAN RIVER
ASIA
DON
NILE
EUROPE
AFRICA
MEDITERRANEAN
T-O MAPPAMUNDI
0 100 km
0 100 Miles
Nile River
St. Catherine's Monastery (Mt. Sinai)
RED SEA
MEROE
UWM
designed by C-GIS © 2000

PETRARCH'S *ITINERARIUM*

A Proposed Route for a Pilgrimage from Genoa to the Holy Land

Edited and Translated with an Introduction and Commentary

by

H. JAMES SHEY

SUNY PRESS

Library of Congress Cataloging-in-Publication Data

Petrarca, Francesco, 1304–1374.
[Itinerarium ad sepulchrum domini nostri Yehsu Christi. English]

Petrarch's Itinerarium : a proposed route for a pilgrimage from Genoa to the Holy Land / edited and translated with an introduction and commentary by H. James Shey.
p. cm.

ISBN 1-58684-022-3 (pbk. : alk. paper)

1. Italy—Description and travel—Early works to 1800. 2. Palestine—Description and travel—Early works to 1800. 3. Petrarca, Francesco, 1304-1374--Knowledge--Geography. 4. Petrarca, Francesco, 1304–1374—Knowledge—Italy. 5. Petrarca, Francesco, 1304–1374—Knowledge—Palestine. I. Shey, H. James, 1935– . II. Title.
PQ4496.E29I75 2003
263'.042569442--dc22
2003021689

For information, contact
State University of New York Press, Albany, NY
www.sunypress.edu

For Matthew and Michael

TABLE OF CONTENTS

Preface

This edition grew slowly out of a NEH Summer Seminar at the Folger Shakespeare Library in Neo-Latin Archival Sciences in 1985. My interest in Latin Paleography was greatly advanced in another NEH Summer Seminar conducted at Yale by Robert Babcock and Barbara Shailor in 1989. I am very grateful to these scholars for their inspiring professionalism and guidance.

In casting about for a project for this seminar, I found Petrarch's *Itinerarium* a most suitable text: it was at that time in need of a modern edition and it is of a length which a fledgling paleographer would not find intimidating. The work also suited my interest in historical geography and cartography. At the Beinecke Rare Book and Manuscript Library, which owns a Ms. of the *Itinerarium,* I was able to ascertain the whereabouts of over twenty manuscripts and to begin the slow process of acquiring microfilm copies. When Gerhard Rauscher, a colleague in our German Program, told me he would be spending time in Stuttgart, I importuned him to acquire a copy of a manuscript I knew to be there (thank you, Gerhard). Another member of the Yale Seminar, Diane Anderson, who was working at the Hill Monastic Manuscript Library at St. John's University, was able to supply me with copies of two manuscripts in that collection (thank you, Diane).

While thus making myself a pest to friends and colleagues, I discovered that Giuseppe Billanovich had long been scheduled to edit the *Itinerarium* for the National Edition. Such is my admiration for this scholar's work that my project now seemed to me a bootless enterprise. Sometime later, I learned that Francesco Lo Monaco had produced a provisional Latin text in 1990. After examining this new edition, I decided that there was room for another provisional text. By this time, my Commentary was well advanced, but I was able to integrate Lo Monaco's work with my own and to take into account additional material which I found in Alfonso Paolella's critical edition of the early vernacular translations published in 1993.

I owe thanks to the University of Wisconsin-Milwaukee for sabbatical leaves in the fall of 1991 and the spring of 1999. It has been during these periods that I have been able to start the project in earnest and to put the finishing touches to it. I also wish to thank my friends, colleagues, and students for their unfailing interest in my work. I have profited in great and small ways from the advice and criticism of so many that it would be impractical to name them all, but special thanks are due to Thomas Neder, Jennifer Rea, Bonita Forrest, and especially Eugene Jones, who helped me collate the early printed editions and some of the Mss.; to Richard Monti and Jean D'Amato, who provided expert help on the topography of the Bay of Naples; and to Patricia Marquardt, Michael Mikoś, Lynn Leverenz, and Roy Swanson, who read various parts of the manuscript and made invaluable suggestions for improvement.

I am especially grateful to Bruce Precourt, without whose technical assistance this project would not have been completed. Thanks are also due to Doris Hoyer, Lois La Rose and Christi Craig for their cheerful help through the many revisions of the manuscript on its way to the final draft. Donna Shenström of UWM's Cartographic Service, Jovanka Ristić of the American Geographical Society Library, and the staff members of the Interlibrary Loan Service were unfailingly helpful and generous with their time.

December 2000

Multos ex iis qui nunc vivunt eruditos homines veri simile est mihi longe praestare ingenio ac doctrina et fortasse breviore tempore meliorem hac mea editionem effecturos fuisse. sed hi hoc non egerunt. ego ut potui egi: nec multum quidem, at tantum tamen effecisse visus sum quod et indoctis utile nec doctis inutile esset.

Daniel Wyttenbach, *in praefatione Plutarchi Moralium,* vol. 1, xiii (Oxford 1797).

What you call *Rambling Learning,* is to me very agreeable, and fairly allowable.

Thomas Warton (Letter dated 20 October 1767) to J. Toup, contributor of copious notes to Warton's edition of Theocritus (*The Correspondence of Thomas Warton,* ed. D. Fairer, Athens, Ga. 1995).

INTRODUCTION

A PEOPLE WITHOUT HISTORY IS NOT REDEEMED FROM TIME, FOR HISTORY IS A PATTERN OF TIMELESS MOMENTS. . . .
T. S. ELIOT, "LITTLE GIDDING," IN *FOUR QUARTETS*

QUID EST . . . ALIUD OMNIS HISTORIA QUAM ROMANA LAUS?
PETRARCH, *INVECTIVA CONTRA EUM QUI MALE DIXIT ITALIE, PROSE* 790

Petrarch loved to travel and delighted in recounting his adventures in the large number of letters he wrote to his friends. His most extended description of a trip, however, is of one that he did not make. While living in Milan in 1357, he planned a pilgrimage to the Holy Land, and scheduled it for the spring of the following year. At the last moment, he cancelled his plans. Nonetheless, Giovanni di Guido Mandelli, Petrarch's partner in planning the trip, resolved to go ahead without his scholarly friend and asked him to write an itinerary. Petrarch responded with his *Itinerarium syriacum*, as it is commonly called these days. The itinerary takes Mandelli first to Genoa, then down the west coast of Italy by ship, through the Strait of Messina, around Greece and across the Aegean to the Syrian coast, and finally overland to Egypt via Mt. Sinai and the Monastery of St. Catherine. All of this in about 6,100 words, dense with literary and historical references and allusions.

Petrarch says near the end of his itinerary that he wrote it in three days. Although there are reasons for doubting the literal truth of this assertion, he probably did write his guide in a short period. Nevertheless, the result of his hurried labors is a small gem of travel literature, which has been called "the first instance of a literary and historical pilgrimage" (Howard 1980.33). Above all, the guide radiates with Petrarch's enthusiasm for what he is describing. For example, although he never traveled south of the

Bay of Naples, he describes the passage through the Strait of Messina as though he had made it himself. There will come a point during the passage, he promises Mandelli, when Reggio on the north and Messina on the south will both be in the passenger's field of vision almost at the same time; all he has to do is adjust his angle of vision slightly. Petrarch had evidently talked with someone who had told him this vivid detail, and he wanted his friend to see with his eyes what he himself has already seen in his imagination.

Before analyzing the *Itinerarium* in more detail, it will be helpful to discuss what enabled Petrarch to write his guide on such short notice, with so few lapses and with such enthusiasm. Something more needs to be said about his travels, and much more about his scholarly preparation for the task. Petrarch's talents were so many and varied that his lifelong interest in geography and those studies that are implicit in or closely related to the study of geography, such as topography, cartography, geometry, astronomy, and cosmology, are easily overlooked. He himself certainly viewed geography as ancillary to the study of history, literature, and philosophy (if we include his interest in cosmology) and rarely spoke of them except as a means of elucidating these more important (to his mind) subjects.

According to the medieval classification of knowledge, geography did not form a separate science. Indeed, in Weisheipl's otherwise admirable account of the system of classification, the word geography (or equivalent term) does not receive so much as a mention (1978.461–482). Most thinkers of the time considered it a subdivision of geometry, while some preferred to view it as part of astronomy or mathematics. So it is that the long geographical discourse in Martianus Capella's popular *De nuptiis Philologiae et Mercurii* forms part of the section on geometry (*De nuptiis* 6; Stahl 1971.1:125–128 and 2:215–275). In fact, the word geography was scarcely ever used at this time, *cosmographia* or *chorographia* being the terms generally applied if one wanted to distinguish what we mean by geography from geometry (Wright 1925.127–129). *Ymago mundi* (representation of the world), which was the title of an influential compendium of geography by Pierre d'Ailly (1350–1420;

selections in Grant 1974.630–639 with Columbus's marginal notes), is merely a creative rendering of the Greek *cosmographia* into Latin (cf. the more prosaic *descriptio mundi).* The practical consequence of geography's subordinate position in the medieval educational system is that the evidence for Petrarch's interest in geography, topography, and cartography is widely scattered throughout his writings and has at first a miscellaneous or fragmentary quality about it. But once the evidence is gathered together and put in proper focus, it shows that Petrarch's interest was far from casual; he had in a real sense been preparing himself to write the *Itinerarium* his whole life.

Petrarca Peregrinus

A first reading of any biography of Petrarch is likely to be a perplexing experience. Petrarch is a hard man to keep track of whether one is considering his scholarly and artistic activity, his numerous personal and professional relationships, his spiritual life, or merely his physical whereabouts.[1] Compared with the other considerations, this last may appear of small importance. After all travel is something most of us do for economic reasons or for recreation, and we do not attach any particular importance to our comings and goings. But Petrarch's choices of residence and his decisions about what trips to make (or not make) were almost always keyed to his intellectual, professional, and spiritual concerns and were often seen by him as weighted with symbolic meaning at the time or were discovered by him on later reflection to have importance in the pattern of his life. On some occasions, he was apt to represent his travels as aimless wanderings. The son of an exile from Florence, he seemed to behave as though the penalty of exile had been placed on his own shoulders (see discussion of Starn 1982.132–139). In a metrical letter datable to the winter of 1354 (Wilkins 1955.236–240), Petrarch sadly confides that there is no place where he feels at home; he is a visitor wherever he happens to be (incola ceu nusquam, sic sum peregrinus ubique, *Metr.* 3.19.16, *Rime* 798). On other occasions, he senses very strongly the analogy between his own travels and those of that prototypical wanderer with a purpose. "Compare my wanderings with those of Ulysses," he writes to Ludwig van Kempen ("Socrates") in the dedicatory letter to his *Familiares* (Ulixeos errores meis confer, *Fam.* 1.1.21; cf. *Fam.* 9.13.24–25), and proceeds to draw out the analogy at considerable length. Rhetorical exaggeration? Perhaps, but Petrarch gives the impression that he is perfectly serious.

About a half a year after his birth in Arezzo on 20 July 1304, his mother took him to live in Incisa fifteen miles southeast of Florence. In 1311 his family stayed for a while at Pisa before taking ship for Marseilles on their way to Carpentras about 15 miles northeast of Avignon. In 1316 Petrarch, two or three years younger than the average "freshman" of the time, was off to the university at Montpellier some eighty-five miles away; in 1320 he was in Bologna to complete his study of civil law (on medieval education see Kibre and Siraisi 1978.120–144). Back in Avignon by 1326, he devoted himself, not to a legal career, which had never suited him, but to the writing of Italian verse for amusement. On 6 April 1327, while attending Good Friday services in Avignon, Petrarch saw and fell in love with a married woman named Laura. Although she did not return his love, she emerged as the primary focus of his lyric poetry and, henceforth, would dominate his emotional life, at least as he presents it in his poetry. During this same period, he settled into the serious work of editing Livy. The 142 books of this massive history, circulating usually in units of ten books called decades, survived into the Middle Ages with great loss to their number. Petrarch reunited under one cover the first, third, and fourth decades, giving Livy's work the most inclusive and best edited form it had known since the Nichomachean recension of the late fourth or early fifth century.[2] This achievement, remarkable in itself but especially in one so young, set the intellectual tone for the rest of his life both as a scholar and a literary artist.

In 1330, he was invited to spend the summer at Lombez at the foot of the Pyrenees by Giacomo Colonna, recently made bishop of the place. At the end of his stay, Petrarch joined the household staff of the bishop's brother, Cardinal Giovanni, at

Avignon, since 1309 the new headquarters of the Papal See. His position was that of chaplain, his first ecclesiastical appointment, which may have required him to take minor orders and a commitment to celibacy. In the summer of 1333, with the Cardinal's permission, Petrarch undertook a northern journey — Paris, Ghent, Liège, Aachen (Aix-la-Chapelle), and Cologne. Much later, in his *Letter to Posterity*, he admitted that he had fabricated all kinds of good reasons for making the trip, but the real reason had been his desire to see new things (vera . . . causa erat multa videndi ardor ac studium, *Prose* 10). In April of 1336, with his younger brother Gherardo, Petrarch climbed Mt. Ventoux, about a day's ride from Avignon, a short trip but a pivotal event in his spiritual life as he later presented it to the world (*Fam.* 4.1, *Prose* 830–844).

Early in 1337 Petrarch visited Rome for the first time. Soon after his return, he took up residence at Vaucluse on the south side of the Sorgue, his official home for some years to come. In the autumn of the same year, Cardinal Colonna asked him to accompany an important visitor to the Cave of Sainte-Beaume (near Marseilles), where it was believed that Mary Magdalene had lived for thirty years doing harsh penance (*Sen.* 15,15; *Opera* 2.1044–1045). This was a pilgrimage of sorts, but it had been imposed on him and seems to have struck Petrarch as mostly an annoying waste of time.

In 1338 or 1339 in the country solitude of his new home, Petrarch began work on his *De viris illustribus*, in the beginning a series of lives of the great men of the Roman republic. About the same time, he began the *Africa*, an epic poem telling of Scipio's defeat of Hannibal. By 1341, he had made considerable progress and probably read some of it to King Robert of Naples, to whom he dedicated his work, destined always to be in progress. Petrarch had come to Naples to be examined by King Robert as to his fitness to rise to the status of Poet Laureate. While at Naples, he took the opportunity to tour the area extensively. Using Virgil as his Baedeker, he traced the movements of the hero Aeneas in the area, as he later described (*Fam.* 5.4 and *Metr.* 2.15 in Bigi, *Opere*

448–457). In April of 1341, Petrarch left Naples to receive his laurel crown in Rome.

On his way home, Petrarch accepted an invitation from Azzo da Coreggio, sometime lord of Parma, to make an extended visit. Petrarch had earlier represented Azzo in a legal matter at Avignon (Wilkins 1961.11–12), and they were already good friends. Much later, he dedicated to his friend his *De remediis utriusque fortune.* In the summer of 1343, Petrarch began to write a piece on the cardinal virtues, the *Rerum memorandarum libri,* but laid it aside in September to return to Naples on a diplomatic mission. He was shocked to see how badly things had deteriorated at court since the recent death of King Robert. In 1344, we find him again in Parma working hard on the *Africa,* and in the following year in Verona, where he discovered a copy of three of Cicero's epistolary collections, including the letters to Atticus. This important find later inspired him to make collections of his own letters. In 1350 he journeyed to Rome again, this time a pilgrim in the year of Jubilee, an event he himself had helped to promote: the Black Death (1348) and constant wars of the time pointed to a need for universal penance (see Sumption 1975.236–242 on the Jubilee year). On the way, Petrarch visited Florence for the first time, becoming acquainted with some of his admirers there, the most prominent of whom was Boccaccio. This same year he visited Genoa and Mantua. In 1353, he took up residence in Milan, where he lived until 1361, but with frequent trips away from home, sometimes protracted ones: Basel and Prague in 1356 and Paris again in 1360–1361. During this period in the second half of 1357, he joined Giovanni Mandelli in planning what would have been the greatest trip of his life if only he had carried it through, a pilgrimage to the Holy Land. The last twelve years of his life were divided among Venice, Pavia, Padua, and finally Arquà (1370), a small community in the Euganean hills to the south of Padua.

This brief sketch omits mention of numerous other journeys undertaken by Petrarch and still others planned and even begun, but aborted for reasons of poor health or for some other reason (see Frasso 1974 and Paolella 1996.152–176 for more detail). In a letter to Francesco Bruni (*Sen.* 9.2; *Opera* 2.944–952, dated

1367/68), Petrarch reflects on the large amount of traveling he has done over the years. Such has been his desire to see new sights that in his youth he would gladly have traveled to China, or India, or Sri Lanka (Taprobane). But as he grew in years, he began to regret the loss of time away from his library and his writing. And so, he says, he adopted a new policy (*Opera* 2.944–945):

> Itaque consilium cepi: ad eas terras non nauigio: non equo pedibusue per longissimumque iter semel tantum sed per breuissimam chartam sepe libris ac ingenio proficisci: ita ut quotiens uellem hore spatio ad eorum litus irem ac reverterer non illesus modo sed etiam indefessus, neque tantum corpore integro, sed calceo insuper inattrito et ueprium prorsus et lapidum, et luti, et pulueris inscio.

Instead of wasting time going to far away places by ship or horse or on foot, Petrarch decided he would visit them often (not just once), in the space of an hour, in his imagination, using his books and with the aid of a very small map. In this way he could make trips and return home as often as he wanted, not only safe and sound, but with no wear to his shoes since they would have no contact with briars, stones, mud, and dust.

Some of the books especially useful to Petrarch in making his imaginary trips were those of the Roman cosmographer Pomponius Mela (fl. AD 37–44), Pliny the Elder's *Natural History* (especially the geographical books 3–6), and Solinus (c. AD 200), whose *Collectanea rerum memorabilium* was based heavily on Mela and Pliny. The Roman historians (Livy, Sallust, Florus, Justin, and Quintus Curtius) would naturally have taken him on many of his imaginary journeys, as would the Jewish historian Josephus and the later Christian writers like Eusebius (Jerome), Orosius, Isidore of Seville, Macrobius, and many others, not to mention the Bible itself.

Petrarch's primary interest was always reserved for the authors of antiquity, whose works he diligently sought out, recopied, edited, and disseminated among his friends. The eyewitness reporters and chroniclers of his own day he rarely mentions by name, but it would be a mistake to suppose that he ignored them. The Papal Court at Avignon was an irresistible magnet for visitors from all over the world, and quickly became the hub of cultural activity of all sorts (Simone 1965.9–24, Ullman 1973.29–33, and Ross 1970.533–545). Petrarch would eagerly seek out these visitors to learn all he could about the world outside his own experience. For example, when Richard de Bury arrived at Avignon as Edward III's ambassador (1329–1333), Petrarch was particularly keen to hear what he had to say on the subject of Thule, since Richard was known as an extremely well read scholar (see Thomas 1960). Petrarch's trip to the north (*Fam.* 3.1 and 1.4 and 5) had only intensified his long-standing curiosity about the location of the island (Iceland?), first described by a Greek named Pytheas during the time of Alexander the Great. Petrarch had carefully noted the comments on Thule in many ancient sources; to him it represented the extreme limit of the inhabited world. Since most of these authors placed Thule at no great distance from Britain (the Shetland Islands), Petrarch quizzed Richard on the subject but found him irritatingly reluctant to say anything until he had consulted his extensive library back home. After Richard returned to England, Petrarch never heard another word from him, despite his frequent letters to Richard reminding of his promise to send information (quamvis sepe literis interpellatus, *Fam.* 3.1.6).

Some time after this incident, there fell into Petrarch's hands a copy of *De mirabilibus Hibernie (=Topographica hibernica;* see Dimock 1867), written by Gerald de Barri (1146/47–c.1223), also known as Giraldus Cambrensis (Gerald the Welshman). In 1185, Gerald accompanied John, son of King Henry II, to Ireland. Important geographic and topographical information filled the *Topographia,* the fruit of Gerald's investigations. Petrarch was particularly pleased with what Gerald had to say about Thule (Dimock 1867.5:98–100), since his own thinking on the subject was tending in the same direction: Thule is either a mythical place or it is very far from England in the Arctic Sea.

In addition to showing Petrarch's eagerness to gain geographical information from whatever source, *Fam.* 3.1 reveals how carefully he examined each of his sources, ferreting out the improbable and contradictory.[3] In this case he is able to cite Pliny and Claudian in support of Gerald, sources which the Welshman either did not know or failed to mention for some other reason.

Prose authors whose works are straightforwardly geographical or contain a great amount of geographical and topographical material must not be stressed to the exclusion of the poets. Petrarch was fascinated with the works of Virgil, Ovid, Lucan, Claudian, and other learned poets of the Alexandrian school, whose poems glitter with toponyms and topographical descriptions. In his own poetry, he loved the irreducible particularity of real names and places as a solid anchor for his universal themes. This fondness for place-names is best observed in Petrarch's Latin poetry where he is following classical models, as in *Africa* 6.839–918 (*Prose* 684–689), a passage in which Petrarch lovingly enumerates the cities, harbors, rivers, etc., that lay along Mago's route from Genoa to Rome: such catalogues are the staple of epic poems. But even in his Italian lyric poetry, a fragile form ill-suited to such catalogues, Petrarch cannot resist the lure of the toponym. In a sonnet (*Canz.* 148.1–8; *Rime* 214) somewhat reminiscent of a passage in Ovid, *Met.* 2.237–259, where the Roman poet catalogues some thirty rivers and springs, which begin to dry up as Phaethon's chariot plunges towards earth, Petrarch commemorates the planting of a laurel tree (symbolic of his poetic art) on the banks of the Sorgue near his home at Vaucluse. Using the rhetorical structure of the priamel, which he had observed in such diverse authors as Horace and St. Paul, Petrarch extols the beauty of his own little stream and freshly planted sapling by comparing them favorably with much greater and more famous rivers and more impressive trees:

> Non Tesin, Po, Varo, Arno, Adige et Tebro,
> Eufrate, Tigre, Nilo, Ermo, Indo et Gange,
> Tana, Istro, Alfeo, Garona e 'l mar che frange,
> Rodano, Ibero, Ren, Sena, Albia, Era, Ebro —
>
> non edra, abete, pin, faggio o genebro —
> poria 'l foco allentar che 'l cor tristo ange

> quant' un bel rio ch' ad ogni or meco piange
> co l' arboscel che 'n rime orno et celebro.
>
> (Not the Tesin, the Po, the Varo, the Arno, the Adige and Tiber, / the Euphrates, the Tigris, the Nile, the Hermus, the Indus and Ganges, / the Don, the Danube, the Alpheus, the Garonne, and the one that pounds the sea [Timavo], / the Rhone, the Ebro, the Rhine, the Seine, the Elbe, the Loire, and the Hebrus— / not ivy, fir, pine, beech or juniper— / can diminish the fire that torments my heart / as much as a beautiful stream that weeps with me continuously, / and the sapling that I glorify and celebrate in rhyme. (Cf. the trans. of Musa 1996.)

The Sorgue and the laurel surpass the beauty and utility of all the items in the catalogue because they have the power to assuage the fiery pangs of his love for Laura.

A great spur to Petrarch's natural curiosity about the world was his acquisition (by 1335; Billanovich 1956.339) of a manuscript which contained Pomponius Mela's *Chorographia* and Vibius Sequester's *De fluminibus, fontibus* . . . a work that is little more than a gazetteer listing alphabetically under separate headings the world's rivers, springs, lakes, groves, marshes, mountains, and peoples. A partial listing of those items at any rate as are mentioned by Virgil, Ovid, Lucian, and Silius Italicus. Petrarch lavished much care on Mela and Vibius, filling the margins of his manuscript with explanatory and editorial notes.[4] So substantial were Petrarch's scholarly contributions to these texts that no modern editor will fail to mention his work. For example Gelsomino (1967.xxii), Vibius's most recent editor, does not hesitate to say that Petrarch is the most important figure in the history of Vibius's text (Petrarca principem locum obstinet in textus Vibiani historia).

It was through the good services of Petrarch that Boccaccio became acquainted with Mela and Vibius. He must have borrowed Petrarch's manuscript sometime between 1351 and 1355, for it was in 1355 or shortly thereafter that Boccaccio began to write his *De montibus, silvis* etc., clearly modeled on Vibius's work (Stocchi 1963.63–64) and like it designed as a guide to classical poetry (and history), but including numerous references to Biblical sites and to some items of contemporary interest.[5] Boccaccio's *De montibus* in turn inspired Domenico Silvestri (c. 1335–1411) to write his *De insulis et earum proprietatibus*, the aim of which was to fill in on the subject of islands, an obvious omission in Boccaccio's otherwise admirable work (*Prefatio* in Pecararo 1954.29). Silvestri's book is the first known example of an *isolario* (a book of islands), a minor genre that won wide popularity in the fifteenth century. A fellow Florentine, Cristoforo Buondelmonti, who traveled to Rhodes in 1414 to begin his exploration of the Cyclades and to produce his *Liber insularum arcipelagi,* soon took up Silvestri's example. In his book Buondelmonti not only described each island he visited (79 of them), but also produced maps for most of them, which seem to be derived from nautical charts (portolan maps) carried on board the ships in which he traveled (Harvey 1987. 1:482–484). Between Petrarch's scholarly work on Vibius Sequester (and Mela) and Buondelmonti's *isolario* and the others that followed it there is a strong causal nexus, with Boccaccio and Silvestri standing as sturdy intermediate links.[6]

The imaginary journeys Petrarch took in his library were uncommonly well informed, since he was reading geographical sources known to only a few of his contemporaries and he was reading them with a critical acumen unmatched by any of his generation. When he tells us he makes use of maps (per brevissimam chartam, *Sen.* 9.2), that too is quite exceptional, since few people were in the habit of consulting maps in the Middle Ages. Travelers naturally tried to prepare themselves for their journey, but usually not by consulting a map. By preference they would talk to somebody who had visited the place they were going; failing that, they would scout out written accounts made by merchants, missionaries, and pilgrims who had traveled the route before them.

There were in fact relatively few maps in circulation in this period. Of the most common sort of map, the *mappamundi,* only about 1,100 have survived, mostly in book manuscripts dating from the eighth through the fifteenth centuries. The curious thing is that they commonly appear in a relatively small number of authors. Sallust, Lucan, Macrobius, Isidore of Seville, Gautier de Metz, and Guillaume de Conches account for about two-thirds of the surviving *mappaemundi* (see tables in Destombes 1964.21–23). One might expect to find maps accompanying an author like Pomponius Mela, but the first manuscript of the *Chorographia* to contain a map was produced in 1417 (for discussion see Gormley 1984.182–183), a small *mappamundi* painted within the capital letter "O" (the initial letter of *Orbis).* The fact that 46 manuscripts of the poet Lucan dating to this period contain *mappaemundi,* but that only one of the geographer Mela is so adorned ought to alert us that there was a quite different idea of the function of maps in the Middle Ages; although, it must be noted that Lucan enjoyed the privileged status of both poet and historian at this time (Moore 1896.228 and 303–304). As with Mela, so it is with Pliny. The first datable map to accompany the *Naturalis historia* was made in 1465 (Destombes 1964.182).

The *mappamundi* (literally = a linen cloth [on which is painted the shape] of the world) was until the fourteenth century essentially a simple diagram used mainly to illustrate the texts of a very limited number of authors. Most commonly, the *mappaemundi* showed the world as circular in shape and were of four basic varieties: one type shows the round world divided by horizontal lines into zones; another is an O-shape divided by a T-shape (referred to as a T-O map) into three continents (Asia, Europe, and Africa) separated by the waters of the Tanais (the Don), the Nile, and the Mediterranean Sea; the third type is a kind of blend of the first two types, showing a fourth continent in the Southern Hemisphere; and the fourth type shows the influence of the portolan charts (to be discussed below).[7]

Most often, these maps were quite small and schematic, showing little geographical information that might be of practical use, but there were also some large elaborate ones like the Vercelli, Hereford, and Ebstorf maps that were intended for public display in a church or a palace. These were meant to convey historical, theological, and ethical information primarily. Most *mappaemundi* of Petrarch's time were hardly maps in our sense of the term. Although some might contain some reliable geographical information, the map maker saw his main function as that of a teacher of a higher sort, whose job it was to explain man's origin and place in the world and to elucidate his relationship with the physical world and its maker. The map maker's method was that of a medieval painter using the elaborate system of symbols worked out by artists over hundreds of years (Woodward 1987. 1:326–342). Indeed the mapmaker (if not the designer) and the artist who illumined manuscripts were often the same.

Since Petrarch owned copies of many of the authors in whose works *mappaemundi* often appeared, the chances are very good that he owned some maps; but just because we know that he owned a copy of Sallust's *De bello iugurthino,* for instance, we are not justified in concluding that it contained a map. There are more than 200 manuscripts of that work, but only sixty have *mappaemundi* (Destombes 1964.66). Petrarch's copy of Isidore's *Etymologiae,* now in Paris (lat. 7595), does not contain a *mappamundi* (according to Destombes 1964.311).

In July of 1355, Petrarch received a letter from a certain Giovanni da Parma asking on behalf of himself and Luchino dal Verme (an influential friend of Petrarch's) how they could best resist the bad effects of the summer's heat. In his reply (*Variae* 50; Fracassetti 1863.3:440–442), he pretends at first to take the request literally, but then quickly decides that it must have a deeper level of meaning and that the heat refers to the onset of some passion (anger? lust?). He then describes at length a tree whose branches represent various virtues. Let Giovanni and Luchino seek the salutary shade of this tree. Before the end of October, Petrarch received a reply to his letter together with two colored drawings on parchment. In his acknowledgment, Petrarch (*Variae* 61; Fracassetti 1863.3:473–476) tells us that one of these portrayed the tree he had described in his first letter and the other was an *orbis terrarum* (non eam modo . . . arborem, sed totum mihi terrarum orbem in membranis descriptum insigni quidem artificio remisistis . . .). The several terms referring to maps were very fluid in the Middle Ages so that it is hazardous to put much faith in their being used in a consistent way (Woodward 1987.1:287–288 and Campbell 1987.1:375). Here however, it seems safe to say that Petrarch's *orbis terrarum* (a term preferred by classical writers) was a *mappamundi*, very likely a large decorative one suitable for public display (say 50 x 70 cm.). Petrarch was after all a very important man by this time, and anyone making him a gift would want it to be impressive. Since the map was not part of a manuscript, it could be as large as desired.

Can anything else be said about this map? There are a few clues that may justify a bit of speculation; the first regards the allegorical tree. The idea of a Tree of Virtue is not of course original with Petrarch. The metaphor, its origins solidly in the New Testament (e.g., Matt. 7:16–20), was fully blown in the Middle Ages, as may be seen in the *Liber floridus* of Lambert of St. Omer (c. 1120) and the tract of Pseudo-Hugh of St. Victor, *De fructibus carnis et spiritus* of the same period, the earliest manuscript of which contains wonderful illustrations of the Trees of Virtue and of Vice (see Katzenellenbogen 1939.65–68, with plates 64–67).[8] The parchment illustrating Petrarch's Tree of Virtue can hardly have differed much from those found in the texts of Lambert and Pseudo-Hugh: out of Humilitas grow the cardinal virtues (Prudentia, Justitia, Fortitudo, and Temperantia) and the theological virtues (Fides, Spes, and Caritas); and out of these grow still more virtues.

Since Petrarch's *orbis terrarum* was sent as a companion piece to the highly allegorical Tree of Virtue, we may not go far astray if we regard the map itself also as allegorical in its presentation, and view the two as a diptych of sorts. All that Petrarch says about the map is that it showed the "arena of this life where mortals dwell" (huius vitae arenam habitatam mortalibus). If Petrarch is using the term *arena* in its proper sense, there are only two closely related meanings the noun can have here. The first meaning is the more general one: a scene of any struggle or dispute. If we relate this meaning to the Tree of Virtue, we may conjecture that Petrarch's map portrayed a struggle in which virtues struggle with vices for the possession of man's soul. Possibly the map was illustrated at the margins by scenes or vignettes drawn from something like Prudentius's *Psychomachia*, an allegorical epic of the early fifth century in which the opposing forces of Virtue and Vice are represented by female warriors (text in Cunningham 1966). Prudentius's work, owned by Petrarch (de Nolhac 1907.1: 205–206), was very popular and frequently illustrated (see Katzenellenbogen 1939.1–13, with pls. 1, 3, 5, 6, and 7): it might have easily provided a model for the illustrations in the map sent to Petrarch.

The word *arena* also has a more specific meaning of amphitheater. If *arena* was meant in this sense, the map may have shown the world as a vast amphitheater in which a series of Christian heroes (saints) are shown dueling with historical persons who are identifiable with certain vices. In the brilliant second chapter of his *De providentia,* Seneca describes the Stoic hero Cato battling against the wrongs dealt him by Fortuna while all the Immortals look down from above in rapt attention, like spectators in an amphitheater. Such a conception would have greatly appealed to Petrarch.

All of this may seem a heavy burden to place on the term *arena,* but the idea of a map of the world as a place of combat or an amphitheater is not so far fetched considering the allegorical nature of medieval *mappaemundi.* Of the five large display maps from the period 1200–1400 that have survived to modern times one, the Ebstorf map (destroyed in 1943), shows the world as Christ's body: Christ's head in Paradise (east), feet in the west, and hands embracing the world at the equator, with Jerusalem as the navel (Woodward 1987.1:307, 309, 310, 334). Other maps of the period, those of Ranulf Higden (c. 1299–1363) in his popular *Polychronicon,* show the world in an oval shape, thought by some to be derived from the practice of drawing maps in the shape of Noah's ark, as described by Hugh of St. Victor (Destombes 1964.149–160 and Woodward 1987.1:312–313 and 334–335). If Petrarch said his *orbis terrarum* represented the world as an *arena,* perhaps we should take him at his word. There cannot have been many men of his time (or any other) who chose their words more carefully than he.

The map Petrarch alludes to in his letter to Francesco Bruni as facilitating his imaginary journeys he calls a *charta,* which is short for *carta de navegar,* or *carta pro navigando,* or *carta de marear* (for the terms see Campbell 1987.1:375). As the full forms of this word for map show, they were intended to serve as practical guides for seafarers. Frequently these maps are referred to as nautical charts, but most often modern scholars call them portolan charts. The term is derived from the Italian *portolano,* which means a set of written instructions for sailing. Produced at Majorca, Genoa, and Venice beginning in the thirteenth century, portolan charts show a remarkably accurate outline of the Mediterranean basin and the Black Sea, recording some 1200 names of cities (with some names of rivers and the occasional landmark), often including the Atlantic coast from Morocco to Denmark. Generally these maps showed little or nothing of inland features, since these were of no practical use to those traveling by sea, though Italian charts were much more austere in this regard than those of the Majorcan school.

Only 180 of these charts have survived which can be dated from their first appearance in the late thirteenth century to 1500; only about 33 have survived from the fourteenth century (Campbell 1986.69), presumably because the majority of them were "working" maps and were used up aboard ship performing the primary function for which they appear to have been designed. The earliest written reference to a portolan chart occurs in the chronicle of Guillaume de Nangis, where he describes how in the summer of 1270 Louis IX's fleet was scattered by a storm and regained its bearings by reference to such a chart (see Campbell 1987.1:439, and n. 484).

The most striking characteristic of the portolan chart is its realistic portrayal of the Mediterranean area's true shape (see esp. Lanman 1987). Italy is distorted on the earliest surviving chart (the *carte pisane;* two-page reproduction in Harvey 1991.40–41), but on all subsequent maps it is shown very much as cartographers show it today, the familiar "boot" of Italy. It comes as a happy surprise to learn that our conception of Italy's shape is the same as Petrarch's. In a metrical letter sent to Luchino Visconti in 1348, Petrarch celebrates the beauty, fertility, and strength of Italy. In it we find the following verses (*Metr.* 2.11.27–35; *Rime* 760–762):

et terra pelagoque potens ac rite supremum
imperium testata situ, ceu calcibus orbem
concutias; stimulique loco pretendis Hydruntem
Brundusiumque biceps arctois obicis undis.
At matutini qua prospicis ostia Phebi
flexa Crotona tegit Graiumque a stirpe Tarentum
planta pedis; Regium zephyros a pollice frangit,
Neapolis sure medium femur occupat altum
Ianua et exstantes thirreno in flumine Pise.

The lines are addressed to Italy personified. They say that Italy's very configuration (situ, 28), which is likened to a booted human leg poised to deliver a kick to the world, shows her power. Against the storms from the North, Italy opposes Brindisi and Otranto, like spurs (stimuli loco, 29) on the heel of a boot. Crotone and Taranto offer protection with the flexed sole of the foot pointed to the East, while Reggio is positioned to put the toe to the west winds. Naples occupies the middle part of the lower leg on the west coast (Neapolis sure medium, 34); and Pisa and Genoa hold secure positions on the upper thigh (femur occupant Ianua et . . . Pise, 34–35). That Petrarch saw Italy as a *booted* human leg is shown by the reference to Brindisi and Otranto, harbors about 25 miles apart on Italy's "heel," as spurs, equipment normally attached to boots. Golden spurs incidentally were the insignia par excellence of a Christian knight in Petrarch's time (Gautier 1883.198 and 293; and Keen 1984.7 and 65). In *Fam.* 23.11 Petrarch criticizes the practice of conferring these spurs in the Church of the Holy Sepulcher in Jerusalem, but it was still being done in the fifteenth century. In 1413 Niccolò (III) d'Este knighted four of his group of pilgrims as part of their visit to the church by giving them spurs (*lo prefato signore calzòloro gli speroni, dicendo che sempre si ricordassero, dove avevano ricevuto questi ordini di cavalleria,* Ghinassi 1861.125).

Since Petrarch's "Italy" was drawn to resemble a human leg, the map may have been oriented to the north so that the "leg" would be pointed towards the ground as one looked at the map. Portolan charts (from which Petrarch took the shape of his "Italy") usually were designed to be viewed from all directions since place-names have no constant orientation on them (Campbell 1987.1:377–378). In the few surviving portolan charts that were designed to be viewed from one particular direction, the orientation is to the south, as it appears was generally the case on maps made by the ancient Romans (Castagnoli 1975.59–69).

What combination of practical experience, technical innovations such as the compass, and new theoretical sophistication (through an infusion of Greek and Arabic astronomy) produced the portolan charts is the subject of speculation and vigorous debate (Campbell 1987.1:380–390). It is clear, however, that this new and modern shape of the Mediterranean basin in general and Italy in particular quickly won acceptance, so that early in the fourteenth century makers of the old *mappaemundi* (Pietro Vesconte and Paolino Veneto) show in their work the influence of the portolan charts, even though *mappaemundi* of the T-O variety continued to be made almost to the end of the fourteenth century (Woodward 1987.314–318). What makes these innovations even more remarkable is that some of them ran counter to the expressed views of Pliny the Elder, whose *Natural History* was widely known and whose authority was highly regarded in the Middle Ages (Thorndike 1923.1:41–99 and Chibnall 1975.57–78). Specifically Pliny had declared (*Nat.* 3.43 in Rackham 1938) that Italy was shaped very much like an oak leaf ([Italia] folio maxime querno adsimilata). That this was the picture of Italy educated Romans carried in their imagination until the end of the classical period is known from Rutilius Namatianus's *De reditu suo* (2.17–20, Doblhofer 1972):

> Italiam rerum dominam qui cingere visu
> et totam pariter cernere mente velit,
> inveniet quernae similem procedere frondi,
> artatam laterum conveniente sinu.

If one wants to form an idea of what Italy looks like as a whole, says Rutilius drawing on Pliny, he will find it most like an oak leaf. Rutilius's testimony is valuable because he is obviously interested in geography and topography.[9] In addition, he has a good command of Greek, occasionally using Greek toponyms in place of the Latin equivalent. This means he had access to Greek sources unavailable in the Middle Ages. He clearly preferred Pliny's description of Italy to those of Strabo (5.1.2; Jones 1917) and Polybius (2.14 and 24.11, commentary in Walbank 1957), who both waver lamely in their descriptions of the shape of Italy (sometimes, they say, it is triangular, sometimes quadrilateral). Pliny's oak leaf had evidently carried the day as far as Rutilius was concerned, and there is no reason to suppose that the well-educated person of the Middle Ages would have thought otherwise. Tucked away at Bobbio until discovered by Galbiato in 1493, Rutilius's little poem was virtually unknown in the Middle Ages, but Pliny's *Natural History* circulated widely, often in epitomes such as the one made by Richard of Crichlade (c. 1150) for his students, which compressed the thirty-seven books into nine, or it was incorporated piecemeal into the works of encyclopaedists like Vincent of Beauvais. Especially important for the dissemination of Pliny's work is Solinus's *Collectanea rerum memorabilium (Collection of Remarkable Facts)*, in which the author has stitched together well over eleven hundred extracts from Pliny (Mommsen 1895.238–243). Virtually an epitome of Pliny's geographical sections, Solinus's work was itself epitomized and thus received even wider distribution.[10] Pliny's description of Italy as resembling an oak leaf appears in Solinus at 2.20 (similis querneo folio).

If one considers that as late as c. 1505 the Portuguese navigator, Duarte Pacheco Pereira, who had traveled very extensively, chose to quote Pliny before, and sometimes instead of, reporting his own eyewitness testimony (Chibnall 1976.73), he will form a clearer notion of the boldness of the portolan chartmakers in altering the shape of Italy. Petrarch himself stood second to no one in his admiration for Pliny, quoting on one occasion with approval a source (Aulus Gellius, 9.4.13 and 9.16.1) which called him the most intelligent and learned man of his generation *(Invective contra medicum*, 1.202–203 in Ricci 1978). Firsthand knowledge of Pliny had come surprisingly slow to Petrarch, who first read the *Natural History* in 1343; but he had certainly read Pliny's description of the shape of Italy by the time he composed his metrical letter in 1348 (Billanovich 1945.xcviii–cii and Rico 1974. 170–

174, 401–403, and 456–457), and he had read Solinus much earlier than that. Petrarch does not waver for even a flicker of an eye: to him Italy has the shape of a booted human leg. That was the shape he saw on his *charta* and he believed it. What compelled his acceptance is an intriguing question that cannot delay us here; but considering the kind of man Petrarch was, one supposes it was a reasoned acceptance.

Undoubtedly as soon as Italy began to resemble a human leg on portolan charts, everyone with a bit of imagination recognized the similarity. Opicinus de Canistris (1296–c. 1350) for example, beginning in 1335, produced a number of maps in which the whole Mediterranean area took on human and animal shapes.[11] Inspired by the resemblance of Italy to a human leg, Opicinus saw the whole of Europe as an oddly shaped man. When he viewed his map west side up, he saw Spain as the very large head of a man, southern France as the chest, Lombardy as the belly and Italy as the right leg (he describes Rome as being *tibialis*, on the shin). Using the basic outline of a portolan chart that he had acquired, he proceeded to construct his own maps for his own purposes: Europe-man was paired with Africa-woman, their faces almost touching at the Strait of Gibraltar. They represent Adam and Eve, Opicinus tells us (Salomon 1953.48). Between them stands the Mediterranean Sea, which is made to resemble the Devil (map in Almagià 1944.1:pl. 48).

Opicinus's cartographic antics would not detain us here, if it were not for the fact that he was in the papal service at Avignon at the same time as Petrarch worked there. It seems altogether likely that Petrarch would have met Opicinus on one of his many visits to the papal palace either on official business during the 1330s and 1340s or merely spending time in the papal library (it was here that Petrarch first read Pliny) where Opicinus also was accustomed to spend time, since he was a *scriptor* in the Penitentiaria Apostolica and considered himself moreover a *philosophus*, an intellectual (Salomon 1953.55). Although the two men were vastly different in temperament and talent, they did have certain interests and attitudes in common.

The two collections that contain Opicinus's rather bizarre maps of the Mediterranean basin are filled with notes that provide insight into the development of cartography in the early fourteenth century (Almagià 1944.1:95–98; Salomon 1953.50). Opticians tells us that he had access at Sauvignon to both Genoa and Majorcan maps of the portolan variety, saying that he first learned about maps from studying those made at Genoa, where he had trained as an illuminator of manuscripts as a young man (Salomon 1953.48). This shows that portolan charts had quickly made their way inland from the great shipping centers to be used by anyone for whatever reason. Since Opicinus shows little interest or talent for the technical side of map-making, it is supposed that he taught himself how to copy the outline of the Mediterranean area from preexisting maps. His example shows that Petrarch, who had some artistic skills (Chiovenda 1953 reproduces a number of his sketches), could have easily taught himself the same technique of copying, for he is credited with having made a map (for known copying techniques see Campbell 1987.1:391).

Flavio Biondo (1392–1463; see Fubini 1968.10.536–559), the greatest geographer and topographer of his time, says that Petrarch made a map of Italy. In his *Italia illustrata*, composed between 1448 and 1453, Biondo twice refers to a *pictura Italiae*, which he says is the work of King Robert of Naples and Petrarch. Since these important texts are brief and difficult of access, it will be helpful to set them forth here as de Nolhac (1907.1:152) quoted them from pages 353 and 355 of the rare 1531 Basel edition:

> Pictura Italiae quam imprimis sequimur Roberti regis Siciliae et Francisci Petrarcae eius amici opus . . .
>
> (The map of Italy, which we are primarily following, [is] the work of Robert, king of Sicily, and his friend Francesco Petrarch . . .)
>
> Hunc vero Ficarolo ramum intra centum proximos annos inchoasse ideo non dubitamus, quia Roberti regis Neapolitani et Francisci Petrarcae pictura Italiae, quam nos sequi supra diximus, ipsum non habet ramum.

> (But we do not doubt that this Ficarolo branch [of the Po] was formed within the last one hundred years, because the map of King Robert of Naples and Francesco Petrarch, which we said above we were following, does not show this branch.)

Concerning the authorship of the map Biondo could not be more positive or explicit. The context in which the two references appear has to do with the Po delta. The second passage supplies a significant detail about the map, which will be discussed below.

Since many modern scholars have been reluctant to accept Biondo's testimony (Caesareo 1904.219–225, whose arguments are accepted by Billanovich 1947.71), it is fortunate that we also have that of Giovan Battista Aleotti. Trained as a hydraulic engineer and architect, but with more than a touch of the humanist in him (see Quintavale 1960.2:152–154), Aleotti discusses in a technical essay published in 1601 at Ferrara the configuration of the Po delta as it was in antiquity. The details of this description, as Almagià has shown (1929.5), prove that Aleotti is relying on Polybius's *Histories* (2.16), the earliest account of the Po valley (c. 150 BC).[12] According to Polybius the Po of his time flowed into the Adriatic through two channels, which had divided at a place called Trigaboli, six miles south of Ferrara. Aleotti confirms what he has been saying about the geography of the Po delta by citing a map which shows the main course of the Po dividing south of Ferrara: *come si vedea nell' Italia fatta dipingere da Roberto re di Sicilia e dal Petrarca* (cited by Almagià above). Aleotti's testimony confirms the existence of Petrarch's map, and the use of the verb *dipingere* disposes of the possibility that Biondo's *pictura* may have been some sort of written account, a "picture in words" rather than an actual map.

Aleotti saw Petrarch's map in the palace library of the Estense signori, which is where Biondo had probably seen it. How the map came to be in Ferrara may be explained by an incident late in Petrarch's life. In 1370, he set out for Rome though he was in precarious health. He got as far as Ferrara when he fainted and lay in a coma for some time (rumor that he had died circulated widely, *Sen.* 11.17). The young Marquis Ugo d' Este was especially solicitous in his care for Petrarch. A while later, while still convalescing, Petrarch heard that young Ugo had died quite suddenly. This moved Petrarch to write his brother Niccolò (II) d' Este, Lord of Ferrara, a letter of condolence (*Sen.* 13.1) in which he recalls the wonderful care taken of him as he lay seriously ill. It may be that Petrarch had given the Este family his map as a token of his gratitude. He almost certainly would have had the map with him as he set out for Rome, whose topography had fascinated him since his first visit in 1337, and it would have been one of the few things of any value he would have been carrying.

In his second reference to Petrarch's *pictura Italiae,* Biondo says that the map does not show the *Ficaroli ramum,* the channel that the Po takes just south of Ficarolo (north-west of Ferrara). Until c. 1150 the Po flowed into the Adriatic through two main channels, which divided south of Ferrara. In the middle of the twelfth century the people of Ficarolo dug a new channel near Sellata to the south of their town and diverted the main flow of the Po so that it now passed about three miles north of Ferrara (Nissen 1883.1:190–191 and Philipp 1942.2180).

In saying that Petrarch's map does not show the branch at Ficarolo, Biondo is in effect saying the same thing Aleotti says about it (the map shows the Po delta as it was prior to the construction of the channel at Ficarolo). Such is Biondo's confidence in Petrarch and King Robert's authority that he cannot believe that they would have been ignorant of the Ficarolo branch if it had existed. Biondo therefore is led to the mistaken conclusion that the diversion of the Po's waters at Ficarolo must have occurred after Petrarch's map was completed (c. 1341), about 190 years after it actually took place.

Petrarch's and King Robert's "Italy" belongs to the cartographic tradition of the regional map, which is independent of the *mappaemundi* and portolan charts (Harvey 1987.1:464–501). Only two regional maps of Italy have survived from the early fourteenth century, both by Paolino Veneto (1275–1344). The earliest example (c. 1323), found in Paolino's *Chronologia magna* (an universal history) in Venice (Bibl. Marc. lat. 399), shows the Po delta in some detail, with the branch at Ficarolo (rota Ficaroli = rotta di

Ficarolo) clearly labeled (Almagià 1929.4–5 and pl. 4). The map in Rome (Bibl. Vat. Lat. 1960), accompanying a later edition of Paolino's chronicle, also shows the Ficarolo branch but does not name it.

If Petrarch and King Robert produced a map of Italy, which showed the Po delta without the branch at Ficarolo, it is difficult to believe that this was anything other than a deliberate choice. Petrarch knew the area well since his school days at Bologna,[13] and there was every reason to suppose that King Robert was equally well informed on the Po delta. The king had known Paolino Veneto since 1316 when he came to Naples as a papal nuncio for a year. After Paolino returned to the area in 1326 as bishop of Pozzuoli, he served Robert as *consiliarius* and was his close personal friend (*familiaris et fidelis noster*, Robert's own words quoted by Ghinato 1951.57). Since both Petrarch and Robert knew very well of the branch at Ficarolo, Almagià's suggestion (1925.5) — that Petrarch and King Robert set out purposely to show Italy as they thought it was in antiquity — is hard to resist. The hypothesis would neatly explain the omission of the Ficarolo branch from their map, while allowing for the fact that both certainly knew of the branch's existence.

If Biondo and Aleotti had reported that they had seen a map made by Petrarch alone, no one would have doubted their testimony. It is their insistence that King Robert collaborated on the project that causes serious doubts. We have Petrarch's own words (*Fam.* 4.2.15) that he and the king had not met as of January 1339 or 1340. Whether one accepts the historicity of this letter, and *Fam.* 4.3 which also must be taken into consideration, or not (Billanovich 1947.196–198; Wilkins 1951.320–323), it seems unlikely that their friendship could have proceeded to a stage in which scholarly collaboration by correspondence might have taken place. It is also difficult to believe that the cartographic project could have been undertaken and substantially completed in the short span of Petrarch's visit to Naples in 1341 (about a month), which was filled with various activities leading up to his three day examination for the laurel crown (Wilkins 1961.24–27). In addition, Petrarch, who in various places reports extensively on his activities in Naples, never mentions any such collaboration.

If Petrarch produced an historical map of Italy (that is, compiled it from historical data) in collaboration with King Robert, the inspiration for the undertaking must have come from Petrarch. King Robert's scholarly interests lay primarily in the direction of rhetoric, philosophy, scripture studies, law, and the physical sciences (mechanics and medicine), as Petrarch informs us (*Rerum memor.* 1.37; *Prose* 280). The scholars who enjoyed King Robert's patronage at Naples were not noticeably interested in antiquity (Weiss 1969.27). These scholars no doubt reflected the interests of King Robert. Petrarch's interests, on the other hand, were largely antiquarian at this time. His creative activities (the *De viris illustribus* and the *Africa*) were the direct outgrowth of his earlier editorial work on Livy's *Ab urbe condita.* For example in his *Africa* (8.862–951), Petrarch attempts to reconstruct the Rome of the second Carthaginian war. Petrarch knew that the Septizonium and Trajan's column did not exist at that time, so they are excluded from the scene. He still believed however that the Pantheon was the Temple of Cybele, so the Carthaginian envoys are treated to a view of it under that name. On the whole, Petrarch's attempt to reconstruct second-century Rome is not very successful, but that is less important than the fact that he was trying his best to reconstruct a historically authentic Rome (Trompeo 1943. 254–264 and Weiss 1969.34–35).[14] It was in a similar spirit, it appears, that Petrarch set out to make his map.

Let us suppose that as an aid to his scholarly and literary labors Petrarch had been working on an historical map of Italy already before his trip to Naples in 1341. Petrarch would certainly have brought the map with him, for it would have been a fine opportunity to add to the map or revise it in the very place where Virgil had composed most of his *Georgics* and the *Aeneid.* Naturally, he would have shown such a map to King Robert, who would have been able to supply many details regarding the bay of Naples, southern Italy, and Sicily. If this were the extent of King Robert's contribution to the map, the collaboration, about which Biondo and Aleotti are so positive, could easily have taken place in a short period. If these were the circumstances, Petrarch might have happily granted full authorial rights to his royal host and patron.

The cartographic work of Paolino Veneto may have had some influence on the map by way of King Robert's contributions, but it is unlikely that the influence was very profound; after all Petrarch was making an historical map. Nor is it likely that Petrarch's and King Robert's map had influence on Paolino's maps of Italy for the same reason (cf. Degenhart and Schmitt 1973.81–85, who think otherwise). In any case, Paolino's cartographic endeavors were undoubtedly completed several years before Petrarch appeared in Naples.

One more element must be added to this reconstruction of the genesis of Petrarch's map. On several occasions, Petrarch refers to some very old maps (charte vetustissime). These "very old" maps would not have been portolan charts, since this sort of map has not been discovered to exist prior to the second half of the thirteenth century. Even the oldest portolan chart would hardly qualify as "very old" in Petrarch's vocabulary. Nor would these maps have been *mappaemundi,* since Petrarch's "very old" maps yielded detailed regional information not found in any *mappamundi.*

In his copy of Virgil's works, which contained the fourth-fifth century commentary of Servius (facsimile in Galbiati 1930), Petrarch often wrote comments, adding material when Servius failed him or correcting him when he thought he was wrong. In commenting on Virgil *A.* 3.411 (where Virgil describes the Strait of Messina), Servius says that the distance from Capo del Faro on the south to Columna on the north is three miles (Quia a continenti, id est a Columna usque ad Pharon tribus millibus distat). In an attempt to qualify this statement, Petrarch says that Servius is referring to a place called "Columpna regia, a place not far from Reggio, which Pomponius [Mela] and very old maps mention": *est . . . Columpna regia in adverso Ytalie, non procul a Regio, cuius est Pomponius in Cosmographia et carte vetustissime meminerunt;* quoted as transcribed by de Nolhac 1907.1:150.

Columna Rhegia or Regia, about six miles north of Reggio, was not a town, but a column which marked the spot where the crossing of the Strait of Messina most commonly took place. It is mentioned, as Petrarch says, by Mela (2.68), Pliny (*Nat.* 3.73), Strabo (6.1.5) and some other ancient sources. In the medieval period the ancient name gave way to Villa San Giovanni, a small town near the place of crossing: one fifteenth-century *portolano* calls the town Fossa de San Zoune (Kretschmer 1909.617).

The fact that Petrarch's "very old map" used the ancient Roman name Columna suggests that it was a Roman itinerary map. Vegetius, whose military manual *De re militari* or *Epitoma rei militaris* of about AD 400 was well known to Petrarch (Tristano 1974), provides the basic text regarding these maps (3.6; text in Önnerfors 1995):

> Primum itineraria omnium regionum, in quibus bellum geritur, plenissime debet habere perscripta, ita ut locorum intervalla non solum passuum numero sed etiam viarum qualitate perdiscat, compendia deverticula montes flumina ad fidem descripta consideret, usque eo, ut sollertiores duces itineraria provinciarum, in quibus necessitas gerebatur, non tantum annotata sed etiam picta habuisse firmentur, ut non solum consilio mentis verum aspectu oculorum viam profecturus eligeret.
>
> (In the first place [the good commanding officer], when he is in a war zone, ought to have itineraries of the whole area, written out in such excruciating detail [attempt to translate the pleonasm of *plenissime*, *per*scripta, and *per*discat] that he knows distances not only to the yard, but also by the condition of the roads, and takes fully into account the shortcuts, trails, mountains, and rivers — all accurately described, the attention to detail being so intense that the more skillful commanders are said to have had not only annotated [annotata] itineraries for the provinces where there was trouble in hand, but cartographic [picta] ones as well, so that upon setting out he [shift from plural to singular] might choose a route not only with an informed plan in mind, but at a

> glance of his eye. Cf. the translations of this passage by Dilke 1987a.1:236-237; Stelton 1990.139 and 141; Podossinov 1991.120; and Milner 1996.71. The proper translation of *itinerarium pictum* [lit. painted or drawn itinerary] remains problematic.)

This passage shows the importance of written itineraries for the Romans. It contrasts the usual sort of written itinerary with the kind kept by the careful commander. Normally an itinerary provided a list of places between two termini, together with the number of *mansiones* or staging posts along the way. Vegetius recommends that a commander provide himself with itineraries packed with much more information than the usual. A number of written itineraries dating from the late empire and early Christian period have survived which describe journeys both by land and by sea (see Dilke 1987a.1:236–238).

The context supplied by Vegetius seems to suggest that only the most conscientious commander might provide himself with a map (itinerarium pictum) and that its chief value might be for quick reference in an emergency. Vegetius conveys the distinct impression that written itineraries rather than "drawn" ones were the usual thing (cf. Podossinov 1991.113–123, esp. 120 for criticism of Dilke; see also Brodersen 1995.186–190). If this assumption is so, it would help to explain why there are relatively few unambiguous references to itinerary maps from ancient Rome and why only one *itinerarium pictum* has survived, the famous Peutinger Table (tabula = map), dated to the middle three decades of the fourth century.

In its original form, the Peutinger Table was intended to show the approximately 70,000 miles of main roads in the Roman Empire. It marks distances between cities, staging posts, rivers, and forests, placing them in linear space with little regard for orientation and in a grossly distorted fashion. One of the many important features of the map is that it shows even relatively insignificant places like villas and large bathing establishments. This magnificent parchment roll, originally over 22 ft. long, is obviously the best product that the art and science of cartography had to offer at the time (see description and bibliography in Dilke

1987a.1:238–242). In conception and design, it is altogether grander than the sort of *itinerarium pictum* alluded to by Vegetius, who is talking about a regional map of a single province or at most country. It was the later sort of map, more modest in scope, which Petrarch must have acquired. As his note on Servius's reference to Columna shows, it was perhaps a regional map of Italy or more likely one limited to southern Italy and northern Sicily.

Petrarch makes a second reference to his "very old maps" a few folios after the first in his copy of Virgil. At *A.* 3.531 Virgil says that the first thing that the Trojans could identify as they approached the eastern coast of Italy was the temple of Minerva (templum Minervae). Servius informed Petrarch that the temple was also called *castrum vel castra Minerve.* This is not enough for Petrarch. Making use of *scriptores cosmographos,* whom he does not name except for Pomponius Mela [2.66–67], something he calls *descriptiones terrarum* (probably these are contemporary written descriptions or *portolani*), and certain very old maps that had fallen into his hands (*quibusdam cartis vetustissimis que ad manus nostras venerunt,* quoted from de Nolhac 1907.1.150–151), Petrarch is able to place *Castrum Minerve* close to Otranto (supra sive ultra Ydruntem), i.e., approximately where the modern town of Castro stands (about ten miles south of Otranto).

This same note contains Petrarch's reflections on the status of geographical research in his time. He says that mistakes in geography are being made for a wide variety of reasons (Errorem sane circa locorum notitiam multa pariunt): sometimes places are at a great distance and difficult to access at the present time; sometimes the names of places have been changed; sometimes places are rarely mentioned, and when they are, the reference is obscure; and sometimes there is disagreement among authorities regarding a place. Most of all (super omnia), Petrarch finds a widespread lack of interest and sheer laziness in geographical matters (*incuriositas ingeniorum* and *segnities*). As a result, not only ordinary readers (communes lectores) but also the commentators themselves simply "tiptoe" around the problems (ipsi glosatores suspenso gressu ista pretereunt, de Nolhac 1907.1:150).

The final reference Petrarch makes to "very old" maps is found in a letter (*Misc.* 1 in Wilkins and Billanovich 1978.202–203) he wrote in the middle of 1355 (possibly in 1357).[15] Petrarch wrote the letter to accompany a copy of his *Invective contra medicum,* which Boccaccio had requested. Near the end of the letter Petrarch says that he is also sending him a book worn out with old age and torn by the jaws of dogs (librum illum senio victum et canum morsibus lacerum) and a very old map Boccaccio has requested (vestustissimam quam postulas cartam). As Boccaccio seems to have undertaken the composition of his *De montibus* by this time and since Pliny is a major source for the work, Stocchi (1963.64–73) has reasonably argued that the old book in question is Pliny's *Natural History.* Petrarch's copy (Paris lat. 6802, with some notes in Boccaccio's hand; see Billanovich 1952.383–388), made in the thirteenth century and hardly old in a physical sense as books were judged by Petrarch, is overcome by old age in the sense that the text is burdened with numerous mistakes made by ignorant copyists over a long period of time. These are the "dogs" who have mutilated Pliny's book, as he specifically complains in his *De remediis* 1.43 (Rawski 1991.1:141; on Petrarch's many complaints about scribes see Rawski 1967.135–138). The "very old" map Boccaccio has asked for (more help with the *De montibus*) is one of Petrarch's old Roman maps, which he had used to settle several geographical puzzles in Virgil. From a note written in the margin of his Pliny (transcribed by de Nolhac 1907.2:77), it is clear that Petrarch also used portolan charts as he read along in the geographical section on southern Greece (Attendendum in cartis cosmographis quod . . .).

The image Petrarch carried on his mind of the configuration of the Mediterranean basin was surprisingly modern. Here it should also be noted that he believed in the sphericity of the earth like the vast majority of ancient medieval and Renaissance thinkers and probably the majority of ordinary people of his time since even the popular works in the vernacular assume a spherical earth, such as Dante's *Divine Comedy* and John Mandeville's *Travels* (Woodward 1987.1:318–321). Petrarch never expressed himself in writing on the subject, but we know that he was certainly taught in school that the earth is round.

In 1896, Leopold Delisle published a list of books found in a manuscript once owned by Petrarch; Petrarch himself wrote the list. Delisle, and several other luminaries including de Nolhac who studied the list, concluded that it merely represented some books which Petrarch owned, but Ullman (1973.113–133) has successfully argued that it is in fact a list of Petrarch's favorite books drawn up between 1333 and 1343 with an earlier dating the more likely. Experienced readers of Petrarch's works are not surprised to find that among the prose authors Cicero heads the list. As Ullman remarked, "If Petrarch was the father of humanism, Cicero was its grandfather" (1973.118–119, where the list is printed). Nor does it come as a surprise that Seneca, Livy, Florus (the epitomizer of Livy), Suetonius, and Justin are on the list as well as the poets Virgil, Lucan, Statius, Horace, and Juvenal, and the Christian writers St. Augustine (*The City of God, Confessions,* and *Soliloquia*) and Boethius (*Consolation of Philosophy*).

The various authors are neatly grouped in categories, only one of which occasions some surprise. Petrarch has labelled it "Astrol[ogia]." At the top of the short list of three is a work he calls *Spera,* which stands for *Sphaera (The Sphere).* As there were a number of works circulating during the Middle Ages under that title, Ullman (1973.124) is not quite sure what work Petrarch is referring to, but he mentions the work by Johannes de Sacrobosco (John of Holywood, d. 1256) as possibly the book in question. Sacrobosco is indeed the most likely prospect for the authorship of Petrarch's *Spera.* Composed c. 1220, around the time Robert Grosseteste composed his *De sphaera* (Southern 1992.142–146), Sacrobosco's work was intended for use at schools and served the purpose so well that it became the standard text on astronomy, along with the anonymous *Theorica planetarum* (translations of both with notes conveniently collected in Grant 1974.442–465).

It is easy to see why Sacrobosco's work had such wide appeal. It is written on a rather elementary level thought suitable for first or second year university students. Amid the sober and lucid presentation of materials derived primarily from Claudius Ptolemy (fl. AD 127–148) and his Arabic commentators on the motion of the planets in a geocentric universe Sacrobosco charmingly quotes Virgil, Ovid, and Lucan. It is undoubtedly here that Petrarch first read in a scholarly and academic context (he had already read this same thing in Ovid, *Met.* 1.32–36) that the earth is a sphere: says Sacrobosco, "That the earth is round is clear from the following considerations . . ." (*Quod terra . . . sit rotunda sic patet . . .* ; text in Thorndike 1949.81, who also supplies the translation printed in Grant 1974). Sacrobosco also provided his students with Eratosthenes's measurement of the earth's circumference, 252,000 stades. Despite the uncertainty of modern scholars as to the exact length of a stade (Clagett 1963.118, Engels 1985. 298–311, and Dilke 1987.148 n.3), Eratosthenes's figure is considered amazingly close to the real number (Sarton 1959.105).

Almost certainly Petrarch was required to read the *Spera* in his first or second year at Montpellier since by the fourteenth century Sacrobosco's work had gained almost universal sway in university curricula (Thorndike 1949.42–44). Because it was one of his favorite books, he may well have attended the lectures on Sacrobosco's work still being given at Bologna by Cecco d'Ascoli (Francesco Stabili). Cecco's commentary on the *Spera* (Latin text printed by Thorndike 1949.343–411) is fascinating. It manages to introduce into Sacrobosco's elegantly restrained astronomical text all sorts of astrological and necromantic considerations. In 1324, while Petrarch was still a student at Bologna, an inquisitor forbade Cecco ever again to teach astrology at Bologna or elsewhere. For reasons that might have been more political than doctrinal, Cecco was condemned by the Inquisition at Florence three years later and burned alive at the stake along with copies of his books (for an account see Thorndike 1932.2:948–968, 1946.293–306, Guidubaldi 1976.5: 404–405 and Tester 1987.193–196).

Intriguing on many accounts, Cecco's case reminds us how easily the distinction between astronomy and astrology could be blurred in the Middle Ages. While some like Hugh of St. Victor (d. 1141) carefully maintained a distinction (*Didascalicon* 2.10), others like Domingo Gundisalvo (fl. 1140) reversed the usual understanding of these terms (see selections in Grant

1974.56 and 74). As a practical matter, Cecco seems not to have maintained the distinction at all. Cecco's fate is eloquent testimony that it could be very dangerous to stray from the path of orthodoxy, especially if the freedom of man's will is in question. Sometime in the late 1340s (Wilkins 1961.122–123), the troublesome charge of necromancy was aimed unofficially at Petrarch himself (*Fam.* 9.5). This he naturally worried about but always managed to stay well within the proper limits regarding the forms of astrological inquiry, which had been set down by various orthodox thinkers like St. Ambrose in the fourth book of his *Hexameron (PL* 14, 123–274), St. Augustine (*De civ. Dei* 5.6 and *Conf.* 4.3 and 7.6), and his contemporary Nicole Oresme (c.1325–1382) in a number of works (selection in Grant 1974.488–494). Given the fact that Petrarch lists Sacrobosco's work under the heading of "Astrology," he may not have been always clear on the distinction between astronomy and astrology. This is entirely excusable inasmuch as even the most orthodox writers allowed a certain amount of legitimate overlapping: one could believe in the influence of the stars on one's physical being (e.g., on health), provided man's free will and God's omnipotence are preserved.

Petrarch maintained an interest in astronomy / astrology throughout his life. In c. 1360 he acquired a manuscript which contained the Pseudo-Aristotelian *De pomo* (Paris lat. 8500; remarkable for its miniatures), patterned on Plato's *Phaedo.* On his deathbed, holding in his hand an apple from which the work takes its name, Aristotle speaks of the creation of the stars and of man's mistaken belief in their divinity and influence on his life until the time when humans first realize the true creator of the stars (bibliography in Schmitt and Knox 1985.51–52).

As he entered his sixty-third year (in 1366), Petrarch wrote a long letter to Boccaccio (*Sen.* 8.1) in which he dwells on the ancient belief that this year of one's life is filled with danger, especially as regards health (for a technical discussion of this idea see Mosshammer 1976.291–306). Petrarch quotes several authorities, but his chief informant is Firmicus Maternus, author of the fourth-century astrological treatise *Mathesis* (4.20 in Kroll 1897; translation by Bram 1975), which he puts third on his short list of astrological favorites (though there is some doubt about the reading of Firmicus's name on the list). Petrarch scoffs at the whole idea, but all the same he did not send the letter until he was well (and safely) along in his sixty-third year. Having survived his *annus climacterius* unscathed, Petrarch wrote Boccaccio once more on the subject (*Sen.* 8.8) claiming with apparent relief that the year had turned out very well indeed. One senses that Petrarch was genuinely concerned about the prediction despite his ridicule of it. To put this curious little episode in some kind of perspective, we may note that Samuel Johnson, who bestrode the literary scene in eighteenth-century England much as Petrarch did in fourteenth-century Italy, seems to have arranged his famous trip to the Hebrides to coincide with the year of his "Grand Climacteric" in 1773 (Rogers 1995.10–29). The lion of English letters regarded the journey as a kind of rite of passage to old age.

Four years later (in 1370), Petrarch's health was not good, and he had received medical advice from his friend Giovanni Dondi, professor of medicine in Florence and of astronomy at Padua. An odd combination it may seem, but the two disciplines were always closely allied in antiquity and the Middle Ages (see Tester 1987.23–24, 60–64, 149–150, and 186–187). Cecco d'Ascoli's lectures on Sacrobosco's *Spera* had been required for medical students at Bologna; and long after the Inquisition's unpleasant dealings with Cecco, Sacrobosco's work continued to be required for a medical degree (Thorndike 1944.281), though Cecco's commentary remained forbidden reading. In his reply to one of Dondi's letters in which Ptolemy had been cited as an authority (*Sen.* 12.2), Petrarch rejects Dondi's advice, saying that Ptolemy and medical doctors are natural allies when it comes to making predictions (una est . . . huius [Ptolemy] et medicorum causa . . . ubi de iudiciis sermo est, *Opera* 2.1000). Here Petrarch is talking about judicial astrology (de iudiciis), predictions made on the basis of current celestial configurations, as distinguished from horoscopic astrology, predictions made on the basis of the celestial configurations at the time of one's birth.

We gather from what Petrarch says that he is quite familiar with the works by Ptolemy mentioned by Dondi. De Nolhac

(1907.2:150) thinks that Petrarch is referring to the *Almagest (Syntaxis mathematice)*, a masterpiece of clear and orderly astronomical exposition, using calculations worked out with the aid of trigonometry and solid geometry. Certainly, the work was widely available in the Latin translation made by Gerald of Cremona in 1175, but it was very technical and did not deal with astrological matters.[16] It is much more likely that Petrarch's letter is referring to the *Centiloquium*, a very popular collection of one hundred aphorisms falsely attributed to Ptolemy. The Greek text, entitled ὁ Καρπός, "Fruit" (Greek text in Boer 1961), had been circulating widely in Latin translation since the early twelfth century. Cecco d'Ascoli is known to have lectured on the *Centiloquium* at Bologna from several references he makes to it in his lectures on Sacrobosco's *Spera* (Thorndike 1949.381 and 382), so that it is probable that Petrarch was familiar with the work. Many of the sayings (varying from two to eight lines) are concerned with καταρχαί or "beginnings," that is, the astrological circumstances under which enterprises may be undertaken or begun with success, or if begun how they will turn out, and many of these are concerned with the astrological circumstances under which sickness may or may not be likely to occur. The position of the moon is of special importance since physical changes in the human body (indeed in all living things) mirror the changes in the moon's position (*Centiloquium* 61). The *Centiloquium* is often found in manuscripts in the company of Ptolemy's equally popular *Tetrabiblos* (ed. Robbins 1940), a work that sought to lay the scientific basis for the various practices of astrologers. This work, available as early as 1138 in a Latin translation (from the Arabic) by Plato of Tivoli under the title *Quadripartitum*, was unquestionably the most influential book on astrology for centuries, and it would be very surprising if Petrarch had not read it.

In his letter to Dondi Petrarch rejects his friend's medical advice insofar as it may be based on the authority of Ptolemaic astrology. Nevertheless, Petrarch remained interested in the alliance between medicine and astrology, if only to condemn it, as in his letters to Francesco Bruni (*Sen.* 1.7, 1362/63), Boccaccio (*Sen.* 3.1, 1363), and elsewhere. According to evidence cited by Thorndike (1923.3:217), Petrarch's library contained a treatise on astrological medicine (*Compendium medicinalis astrologie*) written in c. 1330 by a friar named Niccolò di Paganica. Niccolò's work discusses the configuration of the stars and planets and their influence on inferior creation in general and the human body in particular.

Second to Sacrobosco's *Spera* on Petrarch's list of astrological favorites is Macrobius's commentary on Cicero's *Somnium Scipionis,* a short piece firmly but loosely modeled on Plato's Myth of Er at the end of the *Republic*. Apart from some quotes found in St. Augustine, Lactantius, Nonius Marcellus and others, this section from the end of the sixth book is all that the Middle Ages knew of Cicero's *De re publica* until about one third of the whole was recovered early in the nineteenth century (the lower script of a palimpsest). Macrobius's commentary (text in Willis 1963 and translation in Stahl 1952; discussion in Gersh 1986.2:500–595), about sixteen times the length of Cicero's ten-page text, has a long cosmological and geographical section (1.14.21 to 2.9, about half of the whole) which was frequently bound and circulated separately, with notes from commentators and works of a similar nature (notably Pliny, *Nat.* 2.1–88). Until the works of Greek astronomers and geographers began to be studied in Latin translations in the twelfth century, Macrobius was the primary source of knowledge on such matters. From Macrobius's commentary, the early Middle Ages learned that the earth was a sphere and knew the remarkably accurate measurement of the earth's circumference provided by Eratosthenes. It was in Macrobius that Petrarch read, and no doubt believed, the tedious computations (1.20, 20–32) showing that the sun is eight times the size of the earth (the true ratio of volumes being 1,300,000:1) and read (1.20.21 and 2.3.14) that the sun was twice the distance from the earth as the moon (4,800,000 stades), whereas the true value is 400 times. Certainly there were other numbers floating about (Michael Scot's commentary on Sacrobosco's *Spera* said the sun was 166 times the size of the earth; Thorndike 1949.305), but we can be fairly certain that Macrobius's numbers were the ones believed by Petrarch. Finally the description of the earth given at 2.9 is known to be the basis of 150 surviving *mappaemundi,* about 14% of the total number surviving (Destombes 1964.43–45 and 85–89). Petrarch probably owned one of these, perhaps several if he owned more than one copy of Macrobius, as he often did with favorite authors.

One of Macrobius's important sources for his commentary was Porphyry's commentary (now lost except for some fragments) on Plato's *Timaeus,* large parts of which are given over to cosmological and astronomical considerations. Petrarch knew Plato's dialogue in the partial Latin translation and commentary of Calcidius, a Christian of the fourth (?) century (text by Waszink 1962; discussion by Stahl 1962. 142–150 and Gersh 1986.2:421–492). Having read through his copy of the *Timaeus* (Paris lat. 6280) once again in November of 1355, Petrarch was moved to jot in his manuscript a note to Plato: "Oh happy man, yet miserable: you had all this knowledge of the universe, but you did not know its Creator" (Felix miser, qui hec sciens unde ista nescisti, de Nolhac 1907.2:142).

Petrarch had studied geometry as part of his university training, and geometric principles were implicit in whatever understanding he had attained of astronomy: geometry as the science of quantity at rest was studied in the quadrivium as a prerequisite to astronomy, the science of quantity in motion (see Boethius, *De institutione arithmetica,* 1.4 in Guillaumin 1995.7 and 182–183). Euclid has an honored place as "il nobil geometra" on Petrarch's select list of famous intellectuals, at the top of which stands Plato's name (*Triumphus fame,* 3.59; *Rime* 545; translation Wilkins 1962). He probably had not studied all of the fifteen books which the Middle Ages believed constituted Euclid's *Elements* (books 14 and 15 are pseudepigraphical), but he had been required to study at least a substantial number.

According to tradition Plato had inscribed above the door of his Academy the minimum requirement for entrance to his school: "Let no one without a knowledge of geometry enter here" (ἀγεωμέτρητος μηδεὶς εἰσίτω; for the late origin of the motto see Saffrey 1968.67–87). Had Petrarch been there, he would not have failed to gain admission, though he may have looked for an unobtrusive spot in the back row of Plato's lecture hall. Had he heard Plato say, as tradition says he often did, "God is always doing geometry" (Πλάτων ἔλεγε τὸν θεὸν ἀεὶ γεωμετρεῖν, Plutarch, *Ques. conviv.* 8.2), he would doubtless have been charmed by the idea. Perhaps Petrarch had seen contemporary engravings intended to illustrate Prov. 8:27–30 that show God with a geometer's compass in hand "drawing a circle on the face of the deep" (see pl. in Rawski 1991.1:129).

One final note on Petrarch's interest in geometry. In one of his letters to Pasquino de' Capelli (dated 24 September 1392 by Novati 1891.2:392), Coluccio Salutati says that Francescuolo da Brossano, Petrarch's son-in-law and trusted executor of his last will and testament, had told him personally (ex ore) that Duke Gian Galeazzo Visconti of Milan was in possession of a book that had come from Petrarch's library. Brossano says that the book was entitled *De mensuris orbis terre (Concerning the Measuring of the Earth)* and that its author was Marcus Terentius Varro (116–27 BC), a Roman polymath much admired by Petrarch and one whose lost works he doggedly searched for and with some success (*Fam.* 24.6). According to Brossano, his book was quite large (librum quidem magnum), written in a very old script (in antiquissima littera), and contained geometric diagrams (in quo sunt quedam geometrice figure). This book, now lost, has excited a good deal of speculation.

Until Euclid's *Elements* became available in its entirety in Latin translations of the twelfth century (by several different authors), all that was available for instruction in geometry was a collection called the *Corpus agrimensorum romanorum*, a set of treatises (some 35 in number) in which geometry is put to the practical use of surveying land (see list and description of contents in Dilke 1971.227–230). Written by various hands and at various times (beginning in c. AD 80), this collection was periodically revised in later antiquity to serve as a school text. Eventually Boethius's partial translation of Euclid and excerpts from Isidore and Casiodorus were included. In this new form, the collection circulated as the *Ars geometriae* in five books under Boethius's name. Once all of Euclid was available, the *Ars geometriae* fell into disuse (for an account see Ullman 1964.263–285 and Reeve in Reynolds 1986.1–6).

It looks as though Petrarch's book may have been composed of a number of treatises taken from the *Corpus agrimensorum*, especially the ones with geometric diagrams (see Dilke 1967.9–29 and facsimiles in Butzmann 1970), and perhaps introduced by an essay on geometry by Varro. He is known to have written an encyclopaedic work on the liberal arts, areas of learning (artes) essential to a freeborn (liber) man. Varro's work, called *Disciplinarum libri ix (Nine Books of Disciplines)*, included a section on geometry. Being a self-contained essay, the section may have circulated independently of the rest and ended up as the general introduction to Petrarch's book, where Brossano mistook it to be the first of many chapters on geometry, all of them by Varro.[17] Petrarch may have been interested in the book principally for antiquarian reasons (was the script rustic capitals?) or simply because it contained something done by an author he greatly admired, but his interest in geometry ought not to be overlooked or discounted.

Petrarch stood at an exciting juncture in the history of man's thinking about the world and of graphically representing it on a map. Space began to be viewed in a more abstract way, with no part of the world being seen as more important than another. During this period problems relating to a map's alignment with the earth's axis, projection, and scale began to be addressed in a new way (Harley and Woodward 1987.1:504–506). When Petrarch made his map of Italy, he began presumably by tracing its outline from an already existing portolan chart, on which Italy looked to him like a booted human leg. This task required only a modicum of draftsmanship; but if he wanted his outline of Italy shown on a larger scale to accommodate more interior detail, as seems likely, he would have resorted to his mathematical training to produce a larger map in proper proportion.

Everything points to the likelihood that Petrarch's map was constructed as an historical map, to aid in his studies in Livy especially and to help him in the composition of his epic poem. Historical cartography cannot of course be said to have been Petrarch's invention since Christian scholars like Eusebius and St. Jerome had long ago tried to reconstruct the geography and topography of the Holy Land. St. Jerome, for example, devoted much of his scholarly energy to topographical investigations (Wilkinson 1974.245–257) and produced important maps of Palestine and Asia Minor (Woodward 1987.1:288–289, 299, 322, and 324–325). But Petrarch must have been the first of his time to attempt to reconstruct the Italy of antiquity, not only in his writing, as in the *Africa*, but also in a map.

In this work, he resorted especially to the Roman geographers Pomponius Mela and Pliny the Elder. Besides Boccaccio and Domenico Silvestri mentioned above, Guglielmo da Pastrengo (1290–1362) and Domenico di Bandino (d. 1418) came to know Mela and Vibius Sequester ultimately through Petrarch. In 1379–1381, Coluccio Salutati located Petrarch's own manuscript in Padua and had a copy made for himself (Gormley 1984.302–311). Thus in fourteenth-century Italy, only a handful of scholars had any knowledge of Mela, all of them through Petrarch's leadership. A somewhat similiar story could probably be told about Pliny, though the later manuscripts tradition remains to be explored for Pliny (Chibnall 1975.74–75; Reynolds 1986.316; and Eastwood in French 1986.197–235).

Petrarch's interest in astronomy was not that of a pure scientist since it was compromised by his running battle with the practitioners of astrology, whose work he unfailingly and warmly condemned, but in whose work he maintained a lively interest. Probably the distinction between the two studies meant very little to him, as was the case with most of his contemporaries. Nevertheless, he was keen to know how the world stood in relationship with the rest of the universe. It is much to his credit that he counted Sacrobosco's *De Sphaera* among his favorites. For this we are inclined to forgive him Firmicus Maternus, as bad as he is (Tester 1987.132–142).

Scholar though he was and resolved in his later years to make his journeys in his armchair with the aid of books and maps, Petrarch never really lost his taste for travel. Writing to Boccaccio in the fifty-ninth year of his life (*Sen.* 3.1) to console his friend and himself on the recent deaths of two of their dearest friends, Petrarch impulsively proposes that Boccaccio come to visit (he was in Venice at the time) and the two of them would track down the source of the Timavo. There is much confusion on the matter, he says, owing to some verses in Lucan (7.192–194) that put the source in the Euganean hills. But Virgil (*A.* 1.242–246) says the source is in Aquileia (east of Venice), correctly Petrarch thinks, and it is time to settle the matter finally. Petrarch, advanced in years and with a bad leg (*Fam.* 5.10), is ready for the open road. We know that the proposed expedition never took place (*Sen.* 3.2), but the fact that Petrarch proposed it gives an insight into the man. In addition to Virgil's testimony, Petrarch was able to cite Pliny (*Nat.* 2.225 etc.) and Mela (2.61) on the location of the Timavo in Aquileia, but the weight of all this authority was still not enough for Petrarch: he had to see for himself.

There were many of Petrarch's time, like Giovanni di Piano Carpini, William of Rubruck, Marco Polo, Francesco Balducci di Pegolotti, and the indefatigable Ibn Battuta of Morocco (born in the same year as Petrarch), who could claim with greater justice than he to have matched or exceeded the travels of the legendary Ulysses, but none was more truly the Greek hero's successor, if full credit is given to the desire to see *and* understand.[18]

Petrarca Cosmographus

In Petrarch's introduction to the *Itinerarium,* we learn the circumstances of its composition. Rather at the last minute, Petrarch had withdrawn from the trip, pleading that he would be unable to endure the seasickness to which he was prone (see Commentary). Mandelli, who had apparently organized the trip, had been counting on Petrarch to supply a running commentary on the various sites they were planning to visit and so he asked his friend to write a guidebook, to substitute for the loss of his presence. Specifically Mandelli wanted Petrarch to direct his attention to places and historical events which might improve him as a Christian, an educated man, and a professional soldier and diplomat (lines 73–76 of the Latin text). Thus neatly enumerated, Mandelli's requests appear to make the aim of the *Itinerarium* three-fold; but the division is more a logical one than real, for Petrarch saw the aim of his work as a conceptual whole. At a time when the crusading spirit was very much alive, he thought of his ideal Christian as a well-educated soldier / diplomat, whose skills should be directed against Christendom's real enemies rather than against Christians.

In line 78 Petrarch refers to the quality of *magnanimitas*, a translation of the Aristotelian μεγαλοψυχία (loftiness of spirit). That quality, defined and described by Cicero (*De officiis* 1.19–20), is true nobility of thought and action dissociated from self-interest. It implies a large number of constitutive virtues: courage (moral and physical), self-control, generosity, and devotion to public service are chief among them. In short, the complex quality best defines the heroism of such Romans as Aeneas and Scipio Africanus. It is not necessary to assume that Petrarch is trying to flatter Mandelli by ascribing the perfection of the virtue to him. Rather he is holding that virtue out to his friend as one to be striven for or cultivated, if already attained in some measure.

In fulfilling the charge given him by Mandelli, Petrarch says that he intends to recall to his friend's mind *exempla*, patterns of behavior for imitation or avoidance. Modern readers, taught to search for the subtle catachresis or the fashionable metonym, may smile at his reference to this forthright and all too obvious rhetorical device, which many handbooks and treatises fail even to mention (Lyons 1989. 241–242). The *Itinerarium* merits the attention of scholars for the way it combines classical sources, many little-known in Petrarch's day, with the new research reflected in the portolan charts, but the *exempla* raise the little work above its stated utilitarian function and animate it with a spirit that gave it remarkable moral authority among his contemporaries.

Aristotle defined example (paradeigma) as one of the two basic kinds of rhetorical argument: the enthymeme, a kind of abbreviated syllogism, is a method of deductive reasoning; example is a method of inductive reasoning (*Rhetoric,* 1.2.1356b and 2.20; see studies of Price 1975 and Benoit 1980.182–192). The aim of both is persuasion. Roman writers typically did not concern themselves with the logical status of the *exemplum*, but all of them strongly recommended its use. Quintilian, Rome's great schoolmaster, defines *exemplum* as the narration of a real or imaginary deed (action), which is useful in persuading people of what you have in mind *(Institutio oratoria*, 5.11.6). Since speaking is an action, Valerius Maximus, a rhetorician of Tiberius's reign, chose *Facta et dicta memorabilia* as the title of his large collection of *exempla* (on *exempla* in Latin literature see Price 1975 and van Moos 1988.69–187). This miscellany became hugely popular in the medieval period and circulated even more widely in the fourth-century epitomes of Julius Paris and Januarius Nepotianus (see Bloomer 1992 for a modern appreciation). Petrarch used Valerius's book as a model for his own *Rerum memorandarum libri* and quotes from it often in his other works.

The classical *exemplum* developed in two directions in the later period (Scanlon 1994.54–134). The sermon *exemplum*, founded on the scriptures, the church fathers, and on hagiographical writings, urged the faithful to religious and moral improvement. The secular *exemplum*, founded primarily on the Roman historians, advised on the proper behavior in attaining and exercising temporal power in numerous Mirrors of Princes, a genre which originated early in the ninth century in the court of Charlemagne. Machiavelli's *Prince,* saturated with *exempla* drawn from Livy (Whitfield 1971.73–96 and Lyons 1989.35–71), is an excellent later specimen of the type. Although both the sermon and the secular *exempla* are usually didactic in tone and form, their primary function is not primarily to enlighten the mind, but to move the will (persuade).

Petrarch often uses sermon *exempla* in his various works (e.g., in *De otio religioso* and *De vita solitaria*) with apparent reverence and appreciation, but they are few in number in the *Itinerarium,* while secular *exempla* abound, drawn from many classical sources. In his history, Thucydides (1.23) wrote of "the events which have happened and of the like events which may be expected to happen hereafter, given human nature." It was precisely the exemplary nature of his narrative that gave it meaning and value for future generations. Dionysius of Halicarnassus, commenting on Thucydides's thought, later formulated his ideas more abstractly as "history is philosophy from examples" (ἱστορία φιλοσοφία ἐκ παραδειγμάτων, *Ars rhetorica,* 11.2 in Usener 1892). If pressed for a definition of *exemplum,* Petrarch probably would have endorsed Quintilian's, but *exemplum* has proved exceptionally difficult for many scholars to define. From medieval and Renaissance collections of *exempla,* it is quite clear that many *exempla* were not in narrative form (see Banks 1904; Little 1908; Welter 1926; and Bremond 1982). Desiderius Erasmus, in his extended treatment of *exemplum* in his *De duplici copia verborum* (1512), says that under "examples" he includes stories, fables, proverbs, opinions, parallels or comparisons . . . and anything else of the same sort (Knott 1969.1, 6:232–258). Welter's definition (1927.1) says that among other things an *exemplum* may be a description; Crane (1890.xlvii) says it may be a moral reflection or a mere reference to a biographical or historical fact. Even the simple mention of a name may have exemplary value. Cato is often named in classical and medieval texts as the "image" (*imago, eikon*) of virtue or Amyclas as an exemplary figure of contented poverty (Curtius 1953.59–61), very much in the way that an actor or an actress may appear in the popular media of today as an "icon," of cool sophistication, or rebellion, or whatever. If we may adapt Dionysius's definition of history to the *Itinerarium,* Petrarch's "philosophy," the spirit which saves the *Itinerarium* from being a collection of loosely related bits and pieces, will emerge from the examples he has chosen to present to Mandelli for his consideration. Only a limited number are in narrative form.

The *Itinerarium* is a set of written instructions for a friend setting out on a voyage to the Holy Land. The Greeks called such sailing directions *periploi,* "sailings around," sc. the coasts of the Mediterranean. When considering those produced in the Middle Ages, scholars have agreed to call them by their Italian name, *portolani,* "port books." The earliest of them to survive, entitled *Lo Compasso da Navigare,* dates to the middle of the thirteenth century (see Campbell 1987.1:382–383). We know that Petrarch owned at least one portolan chart, but did he also own a *portolano*?

The main purpose of a *portolano,* sparse and unpretentious as they are, is to record the distances between landmarks (coastal towns, harbors, islands, the months of rivers etc.). Petrarch starts his *Itinerarium* as if he intends to record distances. The mileage between Genoa and Portofino, he says, is twenty miles. His next statement of distance is a little imprecise. He says that Piombino is "50 miles or not much more" from Livorno. Progressing further south along the coast, he comments that Civitavecchia is ten miles from Corneto. After this, Petrarch virtually dispenses with any attempt to give distances.

It seems likely that Petrarch derived such figures as he gives for distances from a *portolano.* The Portolan Parma-Magliabecchi, for example, gives exactly those mileages for the distances between Genoa and Portofino and between Corneto and Civitavecchia (Kretschmer 1909.294 and 298). But Livorno is a name that does not make an appearance in any *portolano* or portolan chart until 1426 (Campbell 1987.1:427). The *portolani* do however give the distance between Porto Pisano, a few miles north of Livorno, and Piombino as sixty miles. Petrarch's "50 miles or so" is probably an estimation based on the information given him by his *portolano.* When Petrarch gives up recording distances and contents himself occasionally with vague phrases like "not much farther on" and "in a few miles," the reason is not that he lacks the information but that he is in a hurry and does not want to take up time recording something that Mandelli could easily ascertain on board ship, if he were interested. Perhaps he knew that Mandelli owned a *portolano* or intended to acquire one.

The subscript of the Cremona Manuscript says that Petrarch handed his *Itinerarium* over to one of Mandelli's messengers on 4 April 1358 (Novati 1904.45). Shortly after that, within a few days at most, Mandelli must have set out for Genoa, with how many in his entourage we do not know. On horseback Mandelli could expect to cover the approximately 75 miles which lie between Milan and the port city at the rate of about 20 miles per day (see "Speed of travel" in Ohler 1989.97–101). He could have been in Genoa and ready to put to sea by the middle of the month at the latest, but there is good reason to think that he did not set sail as planned, as we shall see.

Petrarch's treatment of Genoa is representative of the relative weight he will give to matters of religion, culture (literature, art, etc.), and history, ancient and modern. After reminding Mandelli of Genoa's recent domestic problems, Petrarch quickly moves on to Genoa's ancient past. While touching on the spelling of the city's name, he records his interest in the inscriptions to be seen on the city's monuments. He alludes to Genoa's rather inglorious role in the second Carthaginian war, her rather more glorious resistance to Rome's domination, her great harbor and mole, and her present-day navy, which he compares to the Carthaginian navy of old. Almost as an afterthought, he recommends that Mandelli visit San Lorenzo to see the "emerald" dish, which some claim was used by Christ at the Last Supper. Even if the piece is not authentic, he says, the workmanship is very fine and worth seeing. At Genoa the lessons of history predominate, with only the slightest attention given to his friend's spiritual edification. Livy and Florus's epitome are his major sources, though he had some acquaintance with the local chronicles he mentions.

Of the 525 surviving accounts written by pilgrims to the Holy Land between 1100 and 1500 (listed in Röhricht 1890 and Atiya 1938), only a very few extend their narratives to describe the return home in any detail at all. Likewise, until the fifteenth century, pilgrims, with their minds focused on the holy places to be visited and not wanting to display undue *curiositas* (Zacher 1976), give few and imprecise details about the geography of the outward journey. Some of these accounts were written as the journey progressed or, perhaps more commonly, constructed from memory with the help of notes upon return. Petrarch's account is unique in that it was written in advance by one who had never traveled much of the route he so accurately describes. Having gotten his man to Egypt, Petrarch abruptly abandons him there in Alexandria, trusting him to book passage on whatever ship was available. His account, like most pilgrim texts of this period, shows no interest in the details of the return, but it is quite otherwise regarding the outward journey.

The stretch of Italian territory between Genoa and Naples (almost 400 sea miles) Petrarch knew well. This part of his *Itinerarium* therefore is enlivened by personal observation, as in his comments on the beauty of the Italian *riviera*, which he had traveled both by land and sea: in 1312 on his way to Provence, in 1341 and 1343 on his way to Naples and in 1337 and 1350 on his way to Rome. In 1343 he followed the shore route overland from Genoa to Lerici, where he boarded ship, only to be forced ashore again at Motrone because of bad weather. From there he proceeded via Siena and Perugia, first to Rome and then on to Naples (*Fam.* 5.3.3–4). Although Petrarch knew many of these coastal towns and landmarks from experience, he certainly relied on his portolan chart to keep them all in their proper order and for the names of many places he had not visited.

Almagià (1929.67–72) provides a useful transcription of Italy's coastal place-names as they appear on seven portolan charts, mostly of the fourteenth century. Among the maps in Almagià's collection are the celebrated *carte pisane,* two by Vesconte, and ones by Paolino Veneto and Angelino de Dalorto (Dulcert?). In five of the seven charts, the first toponym mentioned after Genoa is "codemonte," which appears in Petrarch's Latin version as *caput montis,* likewise the first name after Genoa. This is what the sailors (naute) call the promontory, he says. One could hardly wish for a more explicit reference to a portolan chart. Next in order on the charts is "rapal(l)o," and Portofino, which follows, appears in a variety of spellings. Dalorto's "por dal fim" is close to Petrarch's Latin "Portus Alfinus," which he again says is what the sailors call it. In all but two of the charts the next in order is Petrarch's Siestrum (modern Sestri Levante), which three of the charts spell "sestre" and two "siestri(-o)." If Sestri Levante is Pliny's Segesta (*Nat.* 3.48), as Petrarch probably thought it was and as it probably is, his Latinized form of the vernacular name is an obvious clue as to what source he is following: his nautical chart, not Pliny's classical version of the name. Kretschmer (1909. 594–595), drawing on many sources of the fifteenth century, some of them charts and some *portolani,* produces the following somewhat expanded list of names for the same coastal area: Zenoua,

Nervi, Lecco (= Recco), Codemonte (Punta Chiappa), Porto Dolfin, Sancta Margherita, Rapallo, Chiauari, Lauania (= Lavagna), and Sestri. Petrarch's list corresponds exactly with Almagià's list, produced mainly from fourteenth-century sources, as is to be expected.

None of the charts collated by Almagià mentions Lerici. Only in one *portolano,* that of Bernadino Rizo, dated 1490, is this place mentioned as "Castello alerisi" (Kretschmer 1909.222 and 596). But Petrarch had personal experience of this port, and besides he mistakenly connected its name (Erix) with the famous ancient city and mountain of the same name in Sicily. This connection was important to him because the city was founded by Aeneas's half-brother Eryx and because of the celebrated temple of Venus that stood on the mountain's summit, founded by the Trojans to honor the mother of their hero Aeneas (Virgil, *A.* 5.759–760). Four of Almagià's charts give the correct modern name for Italy's largest harbor (speza or spezia = La Spezia). Very likely Petrarch knew this name, but he preferred to call the great harbor Portus Veneris (a small harbor at the entrance to La Spezia), because that name has powerful Virgilian associations and harmonizes well with Erix (Lerici).

The description of the harbor has an epic quality about it: *nomine Veneris insignem portum, securum ventorum omnium et omnium que sub celo sunt classium capacem* (the harbor famous for the name of Venus, free of all winds and able to accommodate all the fleets that are under the heavens). No one can read this sentence aloud and remain insensible to the fact that Petrarch has shifted his rhetoric into a higher gear: *-em, -um, -rum, -rum, -ium, -ium, -um, -em:* the sonorous word-endings sough gently like the lapping waves of the great harbor. Then one notices that the adjective phrases describing the harbor are patterned chiastically:

securum ventorum omnium
et
omnium . . . classium capacem

The dependent genitive phrases with their modifiers are themselves in a chiastic formation that is accomplished by the repetition of *omnium*, in a rhetorical figure called anadiplosis.

But Petrarch is just warming to his task. He continues: *In medio sinus est, maris oportunus fatigatis puppibus* (Lying open to all, the bay welcomes ships tired of the sea). Except for one wrong quantity, the line would scan as eight dactyls, the rhythm of heroic verse. *Puppis* (stern) as metonym for *navis* (ship) was confined to poetry in Latin of the classical period (Quintilian, *Inst.* 8.6.20), as Petrarch was well aware. There is in the sentence a remarkable incidence of patterned rhyme: *-us, -is, -us, -is, -us.* In addition, the words of this short sentence are "mixed together" in the rhetorical figure called synchysis, much in favor with Roman poets. In a particularly elegant double chiasmus, the two predicate adjectives are enclosed by both the nouns they modify and the nouns they govern. *Oportunus* looks backward to *sinus*, the noun it modifies, and *fatigatis* looks forward to *puppibus;* and *oportunus* looks forward to *puppibus*, which it governs, and *fatigatis* backward to *maris.* Finally, we note the attribution of a human quality (tiredness) to the ships, a figure of speech called prosopopoeia, as Petrarch had observed in Virgil, *A.* 1.168 (fessas . . . navis). The rhymes, the snug interlocking of words, and the spondaic heaviness towards the end of the sentence reinforce its meaning.

The Virgilian associations and reminiscences in the description of La Spezia were intended to set the tone, so to speak, for the *exemplum* of the city of Luna, which follows immediately. The city fell in recent times, so the story went (see Commentary), because of an adulterous love affair, just as Troy of old. Whether Petrarch believed the story or not is irrelevant. Ostensibly, he is cautioning Mandelli against sins of the flesh: illicit sex can bring down wealthy, powerful men and indeed whole civilizations, as the examples of Luna and Troy show. Paris seduced Helen and the result was catastrophic. Perhaps Petrarch believed that his friend was overly susceptible to the charms of women. Certainly, he seems quite serious when he cautions Mandelli in similar vein regarding Cyprus: pass the island by quickly, he says; it is a place dear to Venus and soft with sexual allurement. The *exempla* of

Luna and Troy were probably intended to preach the moral lessons they so obviously proclaim, but the mention of Troy would also serve to cast Mandelli's mind to the East and to the great heroes of old. The whole of the *Itinerarium* is fundamentally a call to heroism, meant for Mandelli and any who might read it.

As palpable as is Virgil's presence in this section of the *Itinerarium,* it is ghostly compared with the presence of Petrarch himself as poet of the *Africa.* In that poem (6.856–884), he describes these same places, in rather labored hexameters it is true (for the peculiarities of the prosody, see Corradini 1874.92–93), but with an energy and spirit that would have pleased the man he refers to as the Poet. In the passage Mago, Hannibal's youngest brother, is sailing from Genoa back to Africa towards the end of the second Carthaginian war, contemplating the Italian coastline as he goes. Coastal toponyms common to the *Africa* and the *Itinerarium* are: Genoa, Portofino, Sestri Levante, Portovenere, Lerici, Capo Corvo, the Magra, Luna, the Arno, Pisa, Piombino, Monte Argentario, Porto Ercole, Porto Talamone, the Tiber (Ostia), and Rome. Names of islands common to both are: Gorgona, Capraria, Elba, Corsica, Sardinia, and Giglio. The *Itinerarium* substitutes Meloria for Palmaria, a small island near Portovenere. Some names are peculiar to the *Itinerarium*: Capomonte, Rapallo, Sarzana, Avenza, the Frigido, Massa, Pietrasanta, Motrone, Viareggio, the Serchio, Lucca, Florence, Livorno, Populonia, Massa Marittima, Grosseto, Porto S. Stefano, Corneto, Civitavecchia, and "Hadrian's" Port. Of these twenty names, nearly three quarters of them were excluded from the *Africa* because they would have been anachronistic in a poem describing events of the third century BC.

The *Itinerarium* shows all the names of this coastal area in their proper order except one. Petrarch places Populonia south of Piombino, whereas it should be placed several miles north. Mentioned by Virgil and Livy most notably, Populonia (or Populonium) was a town of some consequence in Rome's early history, a fact that explains Petrarch's interest in the place. In the late Republic, however, the town faded badly and by the medieval period was obscure to the point of invisibility. Petrarch's determination to fix the location of this now obscure place is revealed in a marginal note in a manuscript of Livy (Paris 5690), which he bought at Avignon in 1351. At 30.39 Livy describes how in 201 BC the consul Titus Claudius Nero got caught in a storm, was driven into the port at Populonia (or Populonium, as Livy spelled it), and then later sailed to Elba. In his note Petrarch wrote, "Populonium was what is [now] Massa [Marittima]." There is an unintelligible bit followed by "From there Elba is 12 miles away." Later he added another note right below the first: "I made a mistake in writing this" (*Erravi hec scribens;* transcribed by de Nolhac 1907. 2:29, n.1). The information that Populonia was twelve miles away from Elba must have come from Pliny (*Nat.* 3.81) because no *portolano* or any chart mentions Populonia. The fact that Pliny gives the distance as ten miles instead of twelve does not mean much since Petrarch was probably quoting from memory when he jotted his note. But the piece of information about the distance and the fact that Pomponius Mela (2.72 in Silberman 1988) locates Populonium (as he spells it) north of Porto Talamone allow Petrarch to fix the town's position fairly well, but not well enough to save him from a mistake. Somehow, he figured out that Populonia was not Massa Marittima by the time he wrote the *Itinerarium* in 1358. The map of Italy made by Petrarch in collaboration with King Robert no doubt tried to place Populonia, but we can be sure that it was mistakenly put south of Piombino.

While Petrarch's description of the Italian *riviera* in the *Itinerarium* is mostly indebted to his own *Africa,* another epic, Lucan's *De bello civili* (often called the *Pharsalia*), gives first sign of its important influence. Mago's flight from Italy, the Carthaginian wounded and soon to die, is modeled on a passage in Lucan in which the Roman poet describes Pompey's flight to Egypt, where he dies (details in Bruère 1961. 94). It is because of Lucan that both the *Africa* and the *Itinerarium* have a reference to Meroë, an exotic region in Nubia (modern Sudan) between the Nile, the Blue Nile, and the Atbara rivers, which was famous for its wine. The reference is pertinent because this area of the *riviera,* the Cinque Terre region, is still famous for its wine.

The reference to Meroë however is not simply copied from the *Africa,* but serves an additional function. Like the reference to Troy in the Luna *exemplum,* it casts Mandelli's thoughts ahead to his destination. Specifically it reminds him of Egypt, which Petrarch felt very strongly should be included in the pilgrimage. To judge from what Petrarch says towards the end of the *Itinerarium,* his friend may not have been keen on the idea of an overland excursion to Egypt via St. Catherine's. Such a trip would certainly be particularly hard and dangerous in the summer's heat, as well as expensive and time consuming. In 1384 Frescobaldi and his Florentine friends took nearly two months (October and November) to duplicate Petrarch's itinerary from Jerusalem to Alexandria, though in reverse order (Bagatti 1948.1). Petrarch's later exhortation to go to Egypt, disproportionately long and a trifle shrill, appeals first to the example of the archetypal wanderer Ulysses and then to the Holy Family itself, in flight from the mad Herod. Then he alludes to the example of Lot's wife, who looked back to her home when she should have kept looking forward. Next he invokes Aeneas's heroic entrance into the underworld. Turning to Lucan, he cites Cato's heroic march through the African desert. Finally, he tries to shame Mandelli: look at the example of the Jews of the exodus. They wandered for forty years in the desert, he says, burdened by their women and children, their old and infirm. This accumulation of *exempla,* drawn both from the Bible and from classical sources, speaks clearly to Mandelli's resistance to the proposed excursion to Egypt, perhaps because of the physical hardships involved or perhaps time was the critical factor. Here at the beginning of the *Itinerarium,* Petrarch is already suggesting that Egypt may be a place of quiet pastoral beauty and pleasure by linking the Italian *riviera* with Meroë. A place so famous for its wine cannot fail to be inviting to the weary Italian pilgrim.

At the end of this section of the *Itinerarium,* Petrarch makes explicit mention of his *Africa,* not to cite it as his source, but to give the impression that the passage from which he has just been paraphrasing is yet to be composed in its final form. In fact we know that it was already substantially set in the form we have it now before Petrarch visited Naples in 1343 after the death of King Robert (*Sen.* 2.1). While in Naples he allowed, much to his later regret, Marco Barbato da Sulmona to make a copy of the passage immediately following the one we have been considering, namely Mago's dying soliloquy as he neared Rome (*Africa*, 6.885–918; *Rime* 686–688). The poetic lines on the beauty of the Italian *riviera* he promises someday to write for Mandelli's perusal, if he can find the time, have been tucked away among his papers for over fifteen years, destined to remain unread by anyone except perhaps Boccaccio until after his death. This cagey behavior regarding the status of the *Africa's* progress is typical for Petrarch, even with his good friends.

The toponyms found in the *portolani* and portolan charts for the coastline between Rome and the Bay of Naples are few: Capo d'Anzio, Astura, Monte Circeo, Terracina, Gaeta, the Garigliano, Mondronge, Lago di Patria, Capo Miseno, Baia, Pozzuoli (on one fourteenth-century chart), Naples, Castellamare, Sorrento, and Capo di Minerva. Most of the charts collated by Almagià mention Formia, but they call it by its medieval name, Mola (omitted from Kretschmer's commentary). Formia was important to Petrarch because it was here that Cicero was murdered by Mark Antony's henchmen; Astura was also associated with Cicero, who maintained a favorite villa on the little island (now joined to the mainland). Petrarch does not mention the Garigliano (the ancient Liris), rather oddly since it is one of the principal rivers of central Italy and well known to Roman poets.

Petrarch knew the Bay of Naples quite well from his two visits in 1341 and 1343, during which he managed to tour the area with good guides (Barbato da Sulmona and Giovanni Barrili). Most of the places he recommends to Mandelli's attention he had described earlier in a letter written to Giovanni Colonna on 23 November 1343 (*Fam.* 5.4) and in a metrical epistle written soon after to Rinaldo Cavalchini (*Metr.* 2.15 in Bigi's edition). During his depressing second visit, Petrarch planned a rather arduous overland excursion to Mt. Gargano and down the coast to Brindisi, but Queen Sancha, widow of King Robert, talked him out of it (*Fam.* 5.4.2). Petrarch makes it sound as though the projected trip was merely an excuse to get himself away from Naples for a while and to take a look at the Adriatic coast.

Despite Petrarch's dismissive comments, the planned trip to Mt. Gargano, about 120 miles north of Brindisi, was probably in the nature of a pilgrimage. Michael the Archangel, for whom Petrarch seems to have had a special reverence (*Sen.* 2.8), had been venerated there since his appearance on the mountain in the fifth century (*ODCC*, s.v. Michael the Archangel). The shrine (Santuario di San Michele), with a thriving monastery nearby, was a very popular place of pilgrimage throughout the Middle Ages, often combined with Rome in a sort of packaged tour (see Petrucci 1963.145–180).

Modern studies of Petrarch's life do not usually give him much credit for religious piety, nor do they award high marks to his so-called devotional works. Apart from the *Secretum*, which has won almost universal praise, his other works (*De otio religioso, De vita solitaria, De remediis utriisque fortune,* and *Penitential Psalms*) are often described as pedantic, arid, perfunctory, artificial, etc., as if Petrarch had little personal feeling for his religion (Whitfield 1965.52–59 and Bergin 1979.119–134). But in the words of his most authoritative biographer (Wilkins 1961.254),

> Petrarch's personal religion consisted essentially in acceptance of the beliefs and the observances then held and prescribed by the Church. He never questioned any article of the creed; he never explored the field of theology; and after his youth he conformed regularly and willingly with the practices of confession, of fasting, and of daily and nightly prayer.

Very much in the same vein is Rico's evaluation (1986.56):

> In spite of his weaknesses and shortcomings, Petrarch was always a Catholic, not only absolutely orthodox but even extremely devout. Certainly he did not wish to be an expert in theology: he wanted to be a specialist in the philology of antiquity. However, as both a Christian and an intellectual he had a good knowledge of the Bible, of the Church Fathers and of the *doctrina communi*. . . .

It is hard to imagine why Petrarch would have wanted to go to Mt. Gargano if it were not as a pilgrim. Certainly there was little or nothing of historical or antiquarian interest to attract him there. And it would be quite in character for him to keep his pious motive private.

The same letter to Colonna reveals that he was also frustrated in his efforts to make what might be described as another pilgrimage, to Liternum to see where Scipio Africanus, the hero of his epic poem, had spent his final unhappy days. The town, deserted in the early Middle Ages, was now difficult of access, and Petrarch never made the trip for lack of a guide (*Fam.* 5.4.9). Petrarch does not of course recommend that trip to Mandelli, but he seems to assume that he will have time to visit the Virgilian sites he proceeds to describe. Here we may note parenthetically that if Mandelli and his friends had been traveling in a merchantman, as would likely be the case in the fourteenth century (Hyde 1993 b.93), the ship's business would have allowed them a few days to do some touring. Genoese merchants, at least in the thirteenth century, limited the number of pilgrims to no more than a hundred, none of which could be female (Byrne 1930.8). Other types of ships, catering to the pilgrim trade, had different rules (on types of ships see also Scandurra 1972.205–224, Savage 1977.4:45–50, and Ashtor 1985.197–223).

In this section of the *Itinerarium,* more than in any other, Petrarch seems fully aware of the triple injunction laid upon him by Mandelli. His friend is a Christian, but he is also a well-educated one and a career military man and diplomat. His needs, as he outlined them to Petrarch, are not those of an ordinary pilgrim. If we keep Petrarch's assigned task clearly in mind, we will not be inclined to criticize the section on Naples as being disproportionately long nor in any way irrelevant. This whole section is a good illustration of how topographical and biographical descriptions may have exemplary value. Petrarch's descriptions of the places and monuments associated with Aeneas's visit to the area, and with his descent into the underworld at Avernus in particular, will be seen to have special exemplary value, as discussed below.

The fourteenth-century portolan charts collated by Almagià show more than fifty names on the western coast of Italy between Genoa and the southern tip of the bay of Naples. Thirty-five of these names appear in Petrarch's *Itinerarium*. At the same time, Petrarch is far from slavishly following his portolan chart. He adds over fifteen names of modern towns and landmarks (e.g., Livorno and the Arno), many of which do not make their appearance on any *portolano* or portolan chart until the next century as can be seen from Kretschmer's *Kommentar* (1909.594–599). In addition, he includes the names of numerous places of historical or literary interest that never find their way into the *portolani* or the charts, particularly as regards the topography of the Bay of Naples. For the coastline between the southern end of the Bay of Naples and Reggio, Almagià's fourteenth-century charts show over thirty names. For this same stretch Petrarch mentions only Salerno, the river Sele, Scalea, Scilla (the promontory to which the mythical monster gave her name), and Reggio. Salerno is mentioned because of Petrarch's backhanded interest in the medical profession. Although the river Sele traditionally marked the boundary between Campania and Lucania, it is mentioned on only one fourteenth-century map, that of Paolino Veneto who spells the name "cela." Petrarch probably mentions it because he is remembering his Virgil (*G.* 3.146–151) and Lucan (2.426). It is the latter's spelling (Siler) he adopts rather than Virgil's (Silarus). "Siler" is the spelling also given by Vibius Sequester (*flum.*140 in Gelsomino 1967).

The mention of the name Scalea tells us that Petrarch had his eye on his portolan chart because the name appears in no ancient source known to him, nor in any other ancient source for that matter. Petrarch probably felt obliged to record the name because he saw that it was written in red on his map. Out of the many hundreds of names on portolan charts, a rather select few were rubricated, an indication of their importance. Along Mandelli's route as described by Petrarch, the following names besides Scalea's are usually written in red: Genoa, Pisa, Piombino, Corsica, Sardinia, Rome, Gaeta, Naples, Salerno, Reggio, Messina, Crotone, Taranto, Brindisi, Corinth, Kyllene, Modon, Coron, Mo-

Monemvasia (southeastern tip of the Peloponnese), Candia (Crete), Rhodes, Fethiye and Antiocheta (southern Turkey), Cyprus, Curcho (Armenia Minor), Latakia (Syria), Tortosa, Tripoli, Beirut, Sur, Acre, Jaffa, Damietta, and Alexandria (see Campbell 1987.1:379). Many of these places were important ports of call, and their names will be familiar to almost everyone, but a sizeable number of places whose names are rubricated were relatively insignificant even in Petrarch's day. Why Scalea's name, or Crotone's, should be thus distinguished, while Otranto's is passed over, is unclear.

Scilla appears in only one late fifteenth-century portolano, spelled "Ziglio," but Petrarch knows that it is a promontory (saxum) at the entrance of the Strait of Messina. The word he uses to describe it *(undisonum*: full of the sound of waves) is borrowed from the epic vocabulary of Statius (*Ach.* 1.198) and heralds the reappearance of allusions to the *Aeneid* as Mandelli is guided through the Strait and up the east coast of Italy to Otranto. The mention of Mt. Pelorus, which the Romans mistakenly thought was named after Hannibal's helmsman, renews thoughts of the second Carthaginian war introduced at Genoa. The mention of Taranto evokes the names of Pyrrhus and Hannibal. With characteristic obliquity, Petrarch mentions only the names of the defeated. He knew that Mandelli would easily supply the names of the Roman victors, Fabricius and Scipio. Today few are familiar with Fabricius's name, but he was an "icon" of Roman austerity and incorruptibility from late Republican times through the Middle Ages for his refusal to accept bribes from Pyrrhus, though he was a poor man. In Petrarch's great "Roman" *canzone*, (*Canz.* 53, Spirto gentil) Fabricius, along with the Scipios and Junius Brutus, rejoices at the prospect of restoration of Rome's past glory: "My Rome will be beautiful again," he says (Roma mia sarà ancor bella, 53.42).

Petrarch carefully notes a number of islands that Mandelli will see. His sources, ancient and modern, could have supplied him with the names of many more. Aside from the ones in the Tuscan Archipelago already noted, he mentions one island in the six counted as part of the Ponza group, all the islands in the Bay of Naples except Nisida, two out of the seven or eight reckoned as part of the Lipari Islands, and of course Sicily. For the rest of the journey he mentions only the following: Corcyra, Crete, Euboea, Scyros, Cos, Lesbos, Samos, Rhodes, and Cyprus. To name all the islands of the Cyclades he says would be like trying to count the stars. Only Corcyra, Crete, Rhodes, and Cyprus actually lay on Mandelli's proposed route. The rest are mentioned because of their historical or literary associations.

Petrarch expected that Mandelli's ship would take him to Otranto before crossing the Adriatic to the west coast of Greece. This route seems out of the way, but the Adriatic was much feared because of its sudden storms, and it seemed prudent to cross the sea at its narrowest point at Otranto. Besides, if Mandelli were traveling on a merchantman, there would be business in Otranto. Corinth is mentioned because of its ancient fame: Mandelli would not see it. Modon and Coron were regular stops for pilgrims and merchants. Although these two towns were not far apart, there might be stops at both, if the ship were a merchantman. As Mandelli sails in the southern Aegean, Petrarch casts his mind to the north: to Athens and Sparta, to Euboea, to Scyros, to Sestos and Abydos on the Hellespont, and to Troy. This excursus, an imaginary journey within a journey, is presented in a leisurely fashion and includes stops at various other places famous for their literary and historical interest. Is there any principle governing Petrarch's selection of places on this imaginary tour?

All the places except one are ones mentioned by Lucan when the action of his epic moves to Greece and the Aegean area in books 6–9. He mentions most of them in books 8 and 9 after Pompey has been defeated at Pharsalus and is fleeing to Egypt with Caesar giving chase. Petrarch's use of the name "Byzantion" is a small clue to his source. It is naturally the name that Lucan uses (9.958), but the city's name had long since been changed to Constantinople. Another clue is a verbal echo of Lucan in the description of Sestos and Abydos (see Commentary). The only place Lucan does not mention is Scyros, which Petrarch identifies as the place where Achilles tarried before being tricked into joining the expedition against Troy by Ulysses. The inclusion of Scyros with its reference to Troy alerts us to Petrarch's thought process. This is the second reference to Troy in the *Itinerarium,* soon to be followed by a third, in which the city is called "Ilion," thus recalling the title of Homer's famous poem. Petrarch has in mind Lucan's description of Julius Caesar's visit to the ruins of Troy at 9.964–999, a brief delay in his pursuit of Pompey. In visiting Troy, Caesar was imitating Alexander the Great's visit after his victory at the Granicus, with intentions analogous to those of the Greek. Caesar was fully aware of the symbolic value of his visit for his imperialistic dreams, as Lucan describes it and as modern scholars have documented (Gelzer 1968.244–245).

But there is much more to Caesar's visit than that. From Virgil we have the following account: Dardanus left Italy and founded Troy; Aeneas, his descendant, fled a burning Troy and returned to Italy, the land of his ancestor (*A.* 3.161–171). Aeneas's descendants would found Rome and create the Empire. Julius Caesar himself believed that he was descended from Aeneas (Suetonius, *Jul.* 6), and when in Lucan (9.990–999) Caesar vows to rebuild the walls of ancient Troy, he is speaking as a remote descendant of the original founder. Rome and Troy are linked in an unending reciprocity that produces great nations. On the authority of Virgil, many thinkers in thirteenth and fourteenth century Italy took these considerations very seriously, as has been documented in the case of Dante (see Davis 1957.106–113 and MacKail 1921.105–131). Although Petrarch realized, as few of his contemporaries did, that there were elements in the *Aeneid* that were pure fiction (*Sen.* 4.5), this much of Virgil's story he accepted as historically founded (at least). When Petrarch provides Mandelli with an imaginary trip to Troy, we can be sure that he meant it to be taken with rather more seriousness than modern readers might be inclined to allow. He probably intends to remind him, as he does so often in the *Itinerarium,* how sadly deficient modern Italians are, compared with the ancients. All we can manage, he says, is an imaginary trip to Troy, because it is now in the possession of the Turks.

The evidence for Lucanian influence on this section of the *Itinerarium* would seem less than compelling if it were not for the section that immediately follows. As Petrarch guides Mandelli towards the southern coast of Asia Minor, the imaginary excursion completed, he suddenly breaks into a lengthy description of Pompey's defeat of the Cilician pirates, one of his most famous military successes. The story of Pompey's victory turns out to be timely because merchants and pilgrims traveled in constant fear of Turkish freebooters, particularly in the eastern Mediterranean, and all efforts to eliminate the problem had long been ineffective (see Commentary). Here we have an *exemplum* in the form of a short narrative, but Petrarch has greatly abbreviated the argument. The piracy problem of today can be dealt with, he says, if we had leaders of the caliber of Pompey the Great. The feckless leaders of today should study the reasons for his success. Ultimately Pompey's success was due to the unity and strength of the Roman state, which had the good sense to give him the power necessary to do the job (see Cicero's *De imperio Pompeii*).

As relevant as this story about Pompey might be to current affairs, it may be incorrect to suppose that Petrarch first thought of the contemporary problem of piracy and then cast about for a suitable *exemplum*. Improbable as it may seem, Petrarch's train of thought appears to have been the other way round. The *exemplum* came first to Petrarch's mind, from his reading of Lucan, but he immediately saw its modern application. To return to book 8 of the *De bello*, as Pompey, in flight from Caesar, approaches the southwestern coast of Asia Minor, he reflects that his journey has been safe from pirates because of his earlier victory over them (8.257–258: Cilicum per litora tutus / parva puppe fugit). Lucan's influence can be felt again in Petrarch's brief description of Rhodes and in the rather longer description of Cyprus (see Commentary). Pompey sailed past these places on his way to Egypt. Once Petrarch's itinerary leaves Italy, and Virgil and Livy fail him as sources, Lucan emerges as the dominant influence. Petrarch returns to the *De bello* whenever he can.

Lesser Armenia was a small Christian kingdom under great pressure from the Turks to the north and from the Mamluks to the south throughout the first three quarters of the fourteenth century. Though there were serious doubts about the Armenians' orthodoxy, they were always an important factor in formulating crusader and trading policy throughout this period (see Boase 1978 and Housley 1986.9–11, 21–23, 30–31 and *passim*). The Mamluks overran the country finally in 1375. Petrarch refers to Lesser Armenia in full knowledge of its strategic importance for the recovery of the Holy Land and as a conduit for trade with the Far East (*Sen.* 2.3; *Opera* 2:841).

When Mandelli's ship turns south along the coast of Syria, Petrarch lists eight maritime cities, in five cases using forms of names he could have found only on his portolan chart or at least in some modern source: Tortosa, Baruth, Sur, Acon, and Jaffa. It also appears that he got the name "Sea of Sodom" (= Dead Sea) from his portolan chart. Since he gives the names from north to south and speaks of "doing down" the list of names, he appears to be reading a map oriented to the north, or at least to be viewing his chart with north at the top when he wrote. The few regional maps of Palestine that exist from this period usually have east at the top but one thirteenth-century map by Matthew Paris is oriented to the north (Harvey 1987.1:475).

There are indications that Mandelli was not completely decided on how much of the Holy Land he should try to see. It was apparently still unsettled when the *Itinerarium* was written whether he should debark at Beirut and see Damascus or proceed to Jaffa and thence directly to Jerusalem. Likewise, as suggested above, the excursion to the Sinai and Egypt was still very much open to question. To do all the land touring recommended by Petrarch would normally take about three months. Longer stays seem to have been in favor in the fourteenth century, but Hyde (1993b.93–94 and 110) lists the length of stay for six fifteenth-century pilgrims: the average length is twenty days, including one stay of forty days. If this last example is omitted, the average would be about two weeks, which was the usual length of stay according to Ashtor (1984.214–218).

Petrarch does not concern himself much with the details of Mandelli's land tour of Jerusalem and environs. As he indicates at the beginning of the *Itinerarium*, the essential minimum of every pilgrim's journey was his visit to the Holy Sepulcher, which many visited more than once (Savage 1977.4:57, n.57). It is most shameful that the tomb of Christ is now under the control of the Muslims, and he specifically asks Mandelli to reflect on the example of Titus, son of the emperor Vespasian, who breached the walls of the city in AD 70 and soon restored the whole of Palestine to Rome's possession. He recommends that his friend read the eyewitness account of the historian Josephus, whose *Jewish War* and *Jewish Antiquities* Petrarch had studied very carefully. These works along with the Bible are the main sources for this section.

As soon as there is reference to the possibility of extending the pilgrimage to Egypt, Lucan reappears prominently as a source. Petrarch paraphrases a verse from his epic and cites Cato as an exemplary figure, as we have seen. Petrarch thought the *Aeneid* was the supreme poem, but when he set out to write his own epic, he followed Lucan's example in choosing to write about an historical theme, and there was much about Lucan's view of the world that he found compelling. The concepts of Fate and Fortune, which intrigued Petrarch throughout his life, hover in the atmosphere of the Roman's poem — largely malignant powers beyond man's control or understanding. When Caesar crosses the Rubicon, he says, "Lead on, Fortune" (Te, Fortuna, sequor, 1.226). This begins a long journey that brings him finally to Egypt. When he arrives, he is presented with the severed head of Pompey, his former friend and son-in-law, whom Fortune has also led to Egypt. Alexander and Pompey, both Fortune's darlings for a time, lie buried in Egypt, where their greatness has been brought to nothing. Petrarch is playing on the exemplary theme of the vanity of human existence and the inexorability of death, so popularly illustrated in the Middle Ages by reference to Alexander's fate, both in religious and secular contexts (Cary 1956.143–225).

To Alexander's fate Petrarch adds the example of Pompey and draws the usual moral: "Where is their glory now?" In this last section however Petrarch gives equal emphasis to Julius Caesar and his adopted son Octavian, afterwards Augustus. Their exemplary value, operating on an entirely different level, stems from the way that each was able in turn to reduce Egypt to

Rome's control, Caesar in the summer of 47 BC and Augustus in 31 BC. As Petrarch said explicitly in the *De vita solitaria* (2.6; *Prose* 494–496), if Caesar or Augustus were alive today and were Christian, as they surely would be, they would not tolerate Muslim control of Egypt and the Holy Land. It shamed and angered Petrarch that Christians of his day had allowed the Egyptian Mamluks to retake Jerusalem in 1244 and to reestablish their complete control of Judea and Syria with the capture of Acre in 1291.

These disastrous reverses in the East gave birth to a new literary genre, beginning to fade somewhat in Petrarch's day, but still very much part of the literary scene. Some of the best minds in Europe devoted their energies to devising strategies for regaining what had been lost, which they circulated in tracts often called "recovery literature." Special interests and embryonic nationalism played their roles in the formulation of the various plans, as one might expect. Peter Dubois's plan, for instance, was openly motivated by his desire to extend French power by establishing a second Empire in Egypt (Atiya 1938.48–62; cf. Schein 1991.209–212). Ramón Lull of Majorca, whose strategy evolved over time, argued at one point that the initial movement should come against the Muslims in southern Spain. Crusading armies could then drive across North Africa to secure Egypt (Atiya 1938.74–94; cf. Schein 1991.102–107, 207, and *passim*). Whatever the ulterior motive and whatever the strategy, everyone understood that the problem of Egypt had to be addressed. After the failures of the Crusades of Louis IX (Strayer 1969.2:487–518), most were ready to admit that Egypt was too strong to take by direct assault and proposed a "softening-up" process. Fulk of Villaret, Hayton of Armenia, Henry of Cyprus, and others advocated a program of economic warfare. The most influential proponent of this strategy was Marino Sanudo (the Elder), whose lengthy and comprehensive *Secreta fidelium crucis* (text in Bongars 1611; partial trans. by Stewart 1896) took fifteen years to write. In 1321 he traveled to Avignon to present his work to Pope John XXII, who impaneled a blue-ribbon committee to study the document, Paolino Veneto among its members. Sanudo's main thesis was that all trading with Egypt should be suspended: the necessary supplies of spices from the

Far East could be routed through Persia and Lesser Armenia (Atiya 1938.114–127). Not least of the many virtues of Sanudo's book was its contribution to the study of geography, its text being enhanced by the inclusion of five maps of Pietro Vesconte (two regional, two city plans, and a *mappamundi),* three of which are reproduced by Stewart (1896).

While cynical politics may have compromised some of these "recovery" tracts, most authors had traveled in the Holy Land and Egypt as pilgrims and wrote out of disinterested motives. In fact at least part of some "recovery" texts could just as well be described as pilgrim texts, as in the case with Sanudo's work. The crusaders themselves were often referred to as pilgrims; and if they fell in battle, they were said to suffer martyrdom (Daniel 1989.6:44). If every spy who came to the Holy Land to gather information for a possible crusade was a de-facto pilgrim, every pilgrim had at least a bit of the spy in him. The pious Giacomo da Verona, who made his pilgrimage in 1335 purely out of religious devotion, carefully recorded the condition of each harbor he visited and from his chats with local merchants estimated that about 20,000 army regulars were stationed in Cairo (Röhricht 1895.3:239 and 245). In 1349 Niccolò da Poggibonsi and his friends were detained in the Sinai, accused of being spies (Bacchi della Lega 1945.1:119); and in 1494 Pietro Casola tells how in Jerusalem a Jewish doctor falsely accused six pilgrims of spying. They were released from prison only after paying a heavy fine (Newett 1907.271–274; Italian text in rare ed. of Porro 1855). As Atiya notes (1938.155), "Pilgrimages and Crusades were closely associated in the Middle Ages."

By the second half of the thirteenth century, it was customary to plan a crusade in two stages. A preliminary expedition (passagium particulare), if successful, was to be followed by a full-scale crusade (passagium generale). A number of preliminary expeditions were sent out, but after Pope Gregory X's full-scale crusade failed even to leave the harbor in 1276, no great crusade was ever again successfully mounted (Schein 1991.17–50). Some preliminary expeditions met with encouraging results, but something always prevented the second phase of the operation. Like everyone else, Petrarch was enthusiastic when the newly crowned Philip VI of France took the cross in 1333. This action inspired Petrarch to write a poem in the grand manner (*Canz.* 28), in which the prospective crusade is viewed as a continuation of the victories of the Greeks and the Romans against the Eastern foe. Two of the three triumphs which Petrarch says Augustus celebrated (28.80–81) were for his victories over Mark Antony and Cleopatra at Actium and Alexandria (Suetonius, *Aug.* 22). As always, Philip's crusade came to nothing.

Like so many in northern Italy (Housley 1986.146–149), Petrarch was no doubt encouraged by the Christian victory against the Turks at Smyrna in October of 1344, but again this advantage led to no further victories. By this time, England and France were enmeshed in the Hundred Years' War and the Italian communes were as usual at each other's throats. In a letter of 1351 Petrarch deplores the current hostilities between Genoa and Venice, saying that Venetian arms might be better aimed at Memphis and Smyrna (*Fam.* 11.8.14). It is in this context that the references to Julius Caesar and Augustus acquire their exemplary value. These Romans were victorious over Egypt certainly, but Petrarch is careful to record that these victories came even as they were engaged in great civil wars: Caesar against Pompey and Augustus against Mark Antony. Even Alexander has exemplary value in this connection. To this end, Petrarch relates Augustus to Alexander by recording an anecdote taken from Suetonius about his visit to the Greek's tomb in Alexandria. Petrarch was no great admirer of Alexander (see Commentary), but everyone knew that his victory over the Egyptians was absurdly easy: he simply marched unopposed into Egypt where he was hailed as a liberator and a god (Quintus Curtius, 4.7). There is no need to signal the meaning of these ancient icons of military prowess with a "moraliter" as in the *exempla* of Jacques de Vitry or in the *Gesta Romanorum*. Their deeds are loud reproaches for Christian kings, as are the deeds of Titus at Jerusalem and Pompey's against the Cilician pirates.

In the course of writing the *Itinerarium*, Petrarch insistently reminds Mandelli of three different eras of Rome's heroic past by alluding to three different epics: Virgil's *Aeneid*, which traces the beginning of Rome's rise to greatness; his own *Africa,* largely based on Livy's *Ab urbe condita,* which focuses on Rome in the most glorious days of the Republic; and Lucan's *De bello civili,* which describes the sad disintegration of the Republic, but adumbrates (ironically, it is true) a recovery under Augustus, the beginning of the Empire and the famous *Pax Romana.* Just as Lucan's epic provided the appropriate *exempla* for the eastern Mediterranean, the first two serve a similar function of exemplarity for Italy, the section of the *Itinerarium* to which we must now return. The example of Aeneas, Scipio, and the others are not usually advertised as *exempla,* as was the case with Luna, but Petrarch is constantly and subtly reminding Mandelli of the example of their noble deeds, as he sails down the west coast of Italy. Seneca (*Ep.*6.5) says that "instruction is the long road around, the short effective road is through example" (longum iter est per praecepta, breve et efficax per exempla). Petrarch shortens the short road even more by frequently using elliptical and iconic *exempla*—a deft allusion, a name, or sometimes a description. As he himself put it, "Compact brevity is memorable" (brevitas memorem succincta relinquit, *Metr.* 2.10. 249 in Bergin 1983.183–229).

Even the earliest "recovery" texts (for partial list see Schein 1991.269–270) argued that the necessary condition for a successful campaign to regain the Holy Land was rededication to the cultivation of virtue, for it was sin that brought Christians defeat. The phrase "nostris peccatis exigentibus" (since our sins deserve, sc. punishment) was the often-repeated formula used to explain both the loss of the Holy Land and the failure of Christians to reclaim their rightful inheritance. Fidenzio of Padua, whose *Liber recuperationis Terre Sancte* was published in 1290, analyzes the various sins that brought on disaster and lists the necessary virtues needed for success (Schein 1991.95–96; cf. Atiya 1938.36–43). Above all Christians must curb their greed and stop fighting among themselves. In sad reflection Giacomo da Verona enumerates a number of cities in Palestine and says, "we have lost them all because of our sins" (proper nostra peccata omnes amisimus, Röhricht 1895.3:225).

Petrarch would have heartily endorsed what the authors of "recovery" books were saying about the prerequisite need for moral reform both in individuals and in various Christian states, and indeed often said the same things in much the same language. In the *Itinerarium* Petrarch takes a different tack, for his little work is indeed both a pilgrim and a "recovery" text. He foregoes the usual exhortations to Christian virtue, but rather aims at energizing those who read his *Itinerarium* by holding up as examples for imitation the achievements of the old Romans. By the cultivation of natural excellence (virtus) and by devotion to his gods and country (pietas), Aeneas set the Italians on their way to greatness; in like fashion Scipio rescued them in the hour of their greatest peril. Petrarch hopes to ally this antique *virtus* and *pietas* with Christian reform. As it is now, he says in the beautiful *Italia mia*, petty war lords tear Italy apart, using northern mercenaries, descendants of people defeated by Marius and Caesar of old (*Canz.* 128). If the princes of today show some sign of *pietas* (segno alcun di pietate), [old Roman] *virtus* (virtù) will take up arms against irrational behavior (furore); for the ancient courage [of the Romans] is not yet dead in Italian hearts (l' antico valore / ne l' italici cor non è ancor morto, 95–96). Petrarch's hope for renewal flickers but dimly in this famous poem of 1345 (for background see Wilkins 1961.48–50), but his love of Italy and his pride in her ancient glory shine through brightly. This loving pride explains in part his extended treatment of Italy in the *Itinerarium*. More to the point, he feels that this loving pride, patriotism we would call it, can be an essential ingredient in the needed moral reform of his countrymen. Accordingly, we should bear in mind that Petrarch meant something rather more complex and important by "love of country" than we mean by the term "patriotism."

Petrarch's *De viris illustribus* contains the lives of thirty-six distinguished figures from the past, but there are no Christians among them. Elsewhere he expressed admiration for some Christian heroes, but only a few. To judge from *Fam.* 23.11.6–8, he was quite familiar with the notion of the Nine Worthies (Neuf Preux), first introduced by Jacques de Longuyon c. 1312 in the popular

Romance *Voeux du Paon* and best known to English speakers from William Caxton's preface to *Morte d'Arthur* and Shakespeare's *Love's Labour's Lost* (v.2). The nine famous heroes were ordered in groups of three: Hector, Alexander, and Julius Caesar (pagan); Joshua, David, and Judas Maccabbeus (Jewish); and Arthur, Charlemagne and Godfrey of Bouillon (Christian). No modern Italians here.

In his *Triumphus fame* (2.137–144 in *Rime* 542), Petrarch bestows great praise on Godfrey, hero of the first and only successful Crusade, in which he took Jerusalem from the Muslims and was elected "Defender of the Holy Sepulcher" in 1099. By the fourteenth century, two different epic cycles, composed in Old French dodecasyllables, sang of Godfrey's noble deeds and those of his ancestors and descendants (see Foulet 1989.6:98–115). Of these often crude and sometimes silly stories Petrarch was undoubtedly aware, but he confines himself to saying that Godfrey built a "nest," which was badly guarded and is now abandoned (= the loss of Jerusalem in 1244). Wretched Christians are consuming one another (consumando l'un l'altro), he says, and "do not care that the Tomb of Christ is in the hands of dogs" (miseri Cristiani . . . non vi caglia / che 'l sepolcro di Cristo è in man de' cani). The image of the "nest" is a deadpan allusion to Godfrey as descendant of the Swan-knight, as told in the epic cycles, and the "dogs" that have chased the swan away from its nest are Egyptians. Petrarch does not deny Godfrey's real achievements, but faults him and his successors in the end for not maintaining control of the Holy Land. There is similar criticism in *Fam.* 23.11.

Petrarch might have appealed to the heroic example of Godfrey in the *Itinerarium,* but his anti-French sentiments were too strong to permit it. These sentiments are most violently expressed late in his life (1373) in his *Invectiva contra eum qui maledixit Italie (Prose* 768–807), but with barely more restraint in his *Sine nomine* letters (written between 1343-1359; text in Piur 1925 and trans. in Zacour 1973), and in three famous sonnets of the *Canzoniere* (136–138). The misogallism surfaces in the *Itinerarium* when Petrarch refers to "French arrogance" in his section on Cyprus and indirectly when he refers to Christian cowardice in giving up Acre and Jerusalem. Even if Petrarch were not anti-French, a French hero did not suit his purpose. Petrarch wanted exemplary heroes connected with both Italy and with Africa. Africa, because the Holy Land was now controlled by Egypt, an African country. Aeneas had been distracted from his duty temporarily by his dalliance with Dido the Carthaginian (African) queen; but he recovered himself, led his followers to Italy, and defeated the impious Turnus. His spiritual descendant Scipio defeated Rome's most dangerous enemy, the Carthaginian Hannibal, first on Italian soil and then in Africa. The series of events begun by Aeneas leads to Scipio's victory, as a consequence of which Rome flowers into a world power. As it happens, Petrarch did not believe in the historicity of the Dido episode in the *Aeneid* (the chronology is all wrong; *Sen.* 4.5), but no matter. The fiction embodied an allegorical truth that Petrarch did believe in. Following Origen, Eusebius, and to some extent Augustine, Paulus Orosius (fl. AD 420) in his *Historiae adversum paganos* (text in Zangemeister 1889) argued that God intended Roman rule to provide the law and order so necessary for the spreading of Christ's message. According to Orosius (6.20), for example, it was providential that Augustus celebrated his triumphant victories on 6 January 29 BC (actually in August of that year), the day on which future Christians would celebrate the Epiphany, when Christ "manifested" himself as king to the gentiles in the persons of the Magi. When Augustus received tribunician power *in perpetuum*, a spring of oil flowed for a whole day in Rome. Under the peaceful rule of Augustus, Orosius says, Christ (the "Anointed One") appeared, and from Him Christians came forth in abundance and without cessation. The idea that the establishment of the Roman Empire was an essential part of God's plan for mankind became a cornerstone of medieval historiography. Evidence of this Orosian view of history in the *Itinerarium* may be seen in the statement that Christ brought Titus to Jerusalem to avenge His death at the hands of the Jews (Orosius, 7.3) and in the iconic reference to Augustus as conqueror of Antony in Egypt.

Rome's providential rise to power, culminating in Augustus's defeat of Antony, began according to Dante with the journey of Aeneas into the underworld, as described by Virgil in *Aeneid* 6.

In Dante's view (*Inferno*, 2.25–27; text in Grandgent 1972), Aeneas learned from his journey the things that were the *cause* both of his victory over Turnus and of the papal office (intese cose che furon cagione / di sua vittoria e del papale ammanto). Dante immediately links Aeneas's journey with another, St. Paul's elevation to the third heaven (2 Cor. 12:2–4), whence he brought back "confirmation of that faith which leads to salvation" (*Inferno*, 2.27–30). Aeneas and St. Paul had to travel to "Other Worlds" to bring back knowledge, temporal and spiritual, for mankind. Both journeys were essential to God's plan.

There were many challenges to Rome in her divinely guided progress through history, but Dante and others of the fourteenth century including Petrarch felt that the threat posed by Hannibal constituted another of Rome's defining moments. After Scipio defeated the Carthaginian on African soil, Rome's future was all but guaranteed. At *Paradiso*, 27.61–62, St. Peter speaks of "that high providence which through Scipio defended for Rome the glory of the world [Rome's powers] and will soon bring help" for Italy's woes, presumably the restoration of Rome's power (Davis 1993.73). Scipio's enemies, the Carthaginians, are seen as forebearers of the enemies now facing Christians. In *Paradiso*, 6.49–51, the canto of Imperial Rome, Hannibal leads over the Alps followers whom Dante calls "Arabs." The providential nexus between ancient and modern Italians exists also between their ancient and modern foes. Dante took quite seriously Jupiter's words of prophecy to Venus in the *Aeneid*. "I set no limit of place or time on them [the Italians]; I have given them rule without end" (his ego nec metas rerum nec tempora pono: / imperium sine fine dedi, *A.* 1.278–279). This and other similar passages in the *Aeneid* Dante cited as if they had the force of Scripture. The histories of the Romans and the Jews were both sacred because God intended both people to prepare the way for Christianity (Moore 1896.27 and 167–168). For Dante it was no accident that David was born just as Aeneas was making his way to Italy (Scott 1972.129–134).

In the Orosian view of history, the last serious challenge to Rome's supremacy came during the final years of the republic's existence in the great civil wars, victoriously waged by Julius Caesar and Augustus. As Dante often stressed, Christ willed to be born at the time of the general peace established by Augustus and to be enrolled as a Roman citizen (Luke 2:1). Indeed Christ's redemptive act on the cross was efficacious partly because it was accomplished under the legitimate authority of Roman law (Davis 1993. 71).

For Dante Aeneas's journey to the underworld was apparently an event as historical as the victories of Scipio and Augustus, but Petrarch's views on the matter are not quite so straightforward. He certainly believed that the settlement of Italy by the defeated Trojans had a basis in historical fact, but it would be difficult to say how much of the *Aeneid* he considered historically true. Yet Petrarch believed that all of the *Aeneid* was poetically true, as he tried to explain on more than one occasion (e.g., *Metr.* 2.10.215–226 and *Sen.* 4.5). Working in the best allegorizing tradition of his friend Pierre Bersuire of *Ovide Moralisé* fame, he says that in Virgil you will find no verse without a hidden meaning (nullum invenies sine tegmine versum, *Metr.* 2.10.227). For Petrarch the story of Aeneas's catabasis is true, perhaps not historically speaking, but certainly in a philosophical sense. As he puts it, "Plato, Socrates, and the other philosophers merely teach what we poets sing" (*Metr.* 2.10.244–246). In the underworld, Aeneas "dies" to the concerns of his past and embraces his destiny as progenitor of the Roman people, whose future heroes are then revealed to him as in a vision. These future Romans are foreordained "to spare the conquered and to bring low the haughty" until the end of time (*A.* 6.853). It is a story beautifully consonant with Petrarch's philosophy of history. When he provided Scipio with a vision of the future in his own epic (most of books 1 and 2; see Bernardo 1962.110–126), he turned primarily to Cicero's *Somnium Scipionis* as interpreted by Macrobius. Virgil's *Aeneid* 6 however, also influenced him. Just as Virgil's vision shows a victorious Augustus and the establishment of a Golden Age (aurea ... saecula, *A.* 6.792–793), so likewise does Petrarch's. But his vision extends beyond Virgil's, showing Titus's "revenge" on Jerusalem (*Africa*, 2.271–273) and eventually fourteenth-century Rome. Sadly fallen on evil days, old and decrepit, Rome nevertheless will remain queen of the world until the end of time (2.244–246).

In such a context, we understand that the recurring references in the first part of the *Itinerarium* to Scipio's exploits against Hannibal, the lengthy description of Lake Avernus and environs in particular, and the place of Aeneas's catabasis are to be viewed as attempts to put Mandelli in touch with the historical and philosophical sources of Italy's former greatness. Petrarch sincerely believed in the power of these exemplary figures to renew Italy's spirit, however badly weakened it may be at present. He never gave up hope in Italy's potential to reassume its providential role in history.

Several years after Petrarch wrote his *Italia mia* (*Canz.* 128), there emerged at Rome a man who also believed that Italy's ancient glories could be reenacted. Cola di Rienzo (1313–1352; see Wright 1975) overthrew Rome's kakistocratic government, long torn by factional strife, and promulgated a republican form of rule appointing himself head of state with the ancient title of tribune of the people. By June of 1347, the news of these events in Rome reached Petrarch at Avignon, and he reacted with the utmost enthusiasm. At long last, here was a man who wanted as much as he to restore Rome to its former power. He immediately wrote a long letter of exhortation (*Variae* 48; trans. in Cosenza 1913.15–47) to the Roman people and to Cola, who is compared to Brutus, famous liberator of ancient Rome. He urges Cola, whom he had met in Avignon in 1343, to maintain his resolve by reading the histories of ancient Rome. At first Cola's suppression of the tyrannical nobles was well received at the papal court, but soon Cola began to alarm everyone including Petrarch by his grandiose proclamations and personal affectations. Petrarch must have winced when he heard that at his installation ceremony Cola had himself crowned in quick succession with six different crowns: oak, ivy, myrtle, laurel, olive, and silver, each with its own significance. As a final touch Cola arranged for the mayor of Rome to present him with a terrestrial globe, a symbol recognized since Roman times as indicating world domination (Arnoud 1984.53–116). Petrarch publically defended Cola against rising criticism and privately offered him stern advice, but nothing could slow Cola down. On 15 December 1347 Cola was forced to resign (Wilkins 1961.63–73).

Petrarch was bitterly disappointed by Cola's failure, but he never gave up hope of a strong and united Italy, in which both the Pope and the Holy Roman Emperor resided in Rome. His campaign to persuade the Popes to return to Rome began with the election of Benedict XII (1334). He soon wrote the new Pope a metrical epistle (*Metr.* 1.2) in which he portrayed Rome as a distressed and dishevelled matron pleading for the Pope's return, a topos derived from Jeremiah's *Lamentations*, 1.2: [Jerusalem] *the queen of nations has become like a widow*. Another such letter followed when Clement VI was elected in 1342. Again a piteous Rome pleaded for the Pope to come to her aid (*Metr.* 2.5). When Guillaume Grimoard, a Benedictine Abbot whose personal integrity Petrarch respected, was elected Pope in 1362, Petrarch was pleased. When the new Pope took the name Urban (V), the choice of name suggested to Petrarch that at last there may be a Pope who was inclined to return to Rome (the City, *Urbs* = Rome). Rumors to that effect reached Petrarch, and so he wrote the Pope a lengthy prose letter (*Sen.* 7.1; written in 1366) to encourage the move. When Urban did bring the Curia to Rome the following year, Petrarch was elated and wrote him another long letter to encourage him to stay (*Sen*, 9.1). In this letter, Petrarch predicts that with the Papacy back in Rome "everything is possible, including the recovery of the Holy Land" (nihil penitus non sperandum usque ad recuperationem . . . sacrae telluris; *Opera* 1554.2. 938). Despite Petrarch's pleading, Urban returned to Avignon in 1370.

In February of 1351 Petrarch wrote his first letter to the still uncrowned Holy Roman Emperor Charles IV (Charles of Bohemia) urging him to reestablish order in Italy and to restore Rome to its former glory by taking up residence there (*Fam.* 10.1; *Prose* 904–914). As in the letters to Popes Benedict, Clement, and Urban, Rome is presented as a destitute matron pleading for help. When he received no answer, he wrote another letter, in which he repeats his earlier appeals and speaks of a formulation of plans for a Crusade (*Fam.* 12.1). Petrarch finally met Charles in 1354 when he came to Italy to be crowned King of Italy and to receive the imperial crown from the Pope's representative in Rome (5 April 1355). Petrarch hoped to persuade Charles to stay, but conditions were so unsettled that he quickly withdrew from Italy. A bitter Petrarch reproached the Emperor saying, "You call yourself an emperor, but you are only King of Bohemia" (*Fam.*19.12.4).[19] It is no accident that the rhetoric of Petrarch's exhortations to the Popes and to Charles are virtually interchangeable. Petrarch believed that it was essential for both the Pope and the Emperor to live in Rome to insure the city's restoration to its former glory as "mistress of the provinces" of a new empire, as he had put it in a letter to Cola di Rienzo (*Sine Nomine* 2; Zacour 1973.83). As Foster observes (1984.12–13), Petrarch's "Christian piety may seem at times hardly separable from his Italian patriotism."

In 1348 Petrarch's disappointment over the Cola di Rienzo affair and his extreme vexation with life in Avignon prompted him to take over personal management of his canonry in Parma, which was now controlled by the Visconti of Milan. In March of that year, Petrarch received a letter from Luchino Visconti requesting that he send some shoots from his fruit trees and some of his poetry. Petrarch quickly responded to both requests, sending the shoots with a short poem bidding them to flourish for the great lord to whom they are being sent (*Ad arbores suas, Metr.* 3.6 in *Rime* 758). The poem is replete with Virgilian echoes to the effect that Visconti has introduced a new Golden Age to Italy. The following fall he sent to Luchino a gift of some fruit, along with a metrical letter celebrating the fertility of beautiful Italy (*Metr.* 2.11; *Rime* 760–762). This is the letter that contains the description of Italy as a booted human leg, "poised to give the world a kick" (ceu calcibus orbem / concutias, 28–29). Petrarch's hopes for a united Italy, disappointed by Cola di Rienzo and Charles IV, begin to orbit the magnetic strength of the Visconti of Milan.

By the summer of 1351, Petrarch was back in Provence. Although he spent as much time as he could at Vaucluse, he was inevitably drawn into the activities at the papal court. The state of affairs in Italy, especially the hostilities between Genoa and Venice, concerned him deeply. Above all his disgust at the corruption of the papal court seemed to overwhelm him. In the early summer of 1353 Petrarch made a move he had been planning for some time. Packing up most of his books and his work in progress, he set out for Italy. Apparently, he had not yet decided where to live when he made a stop in Milan to pay his respects to Archbishop Giovanni Visconti, now in sole control of Milan since the death of his brother Luchino in 1349 and the most powerful ruler in Italy. Possessed of great charm and diplomacy, the archbishop persuaded Petrarch to stay in Milan, promising him a residence near Sant' Ambrogio, solitude, and freedom to pursue his work. He in turn expected nothing from Petrarch but the honor of his presence. Most of what the archbishop promised was delivered, but Petrarch was frequently asked to serve in an advisory or diplomatic capacity (see Cognasso 1966.217–220 for a summary account; at greater length Wilkins 1961.129–179), a service Petrarch seemed rather to enjoy.

Soon after Petrarch had notified his friends of his plans to settle in Milan, letters of protest came pouring in, particularly from Boccaccio and his other Florentine friends, who regarded the Visconti as tyrants. Since 1311, the Visconti family had been pursuing an expansionist policy in northern Italy, using any method that worked. In 1350, Archbishop Giovanni actually bought control of Bologna for 170,000 florins. When Pope Clement VI, who regarded the city as a papal possession, excommunicated him, the archbishop restored himself to the sacraments by contributing another 100,000 florins to the papal treasury (Tabacco 1988.310). Most often, the Visconti took what they wanted by force of arms. It will be recalled that in 1343 when Petrarch was making his way to Naples, he encountered Milanese soldiers conducting operations against Pisans at Motrone and Avenza. In their endeavors to control Pisa, Milan came into prolonged conflict with Florence, which had been temporarily concluded by the treaty of Pietrasanta in 1353, shortly before Petrarch arrived in Milan.

Petrarch mildly turned aside all criticisms of his move to Milan (Boccaccio's was particularly harsh), calling the archbishop "the greatest of Italians" in an open letter to his Florentine friends (*Variae* 7 in Fracassetti 1863.3). Petrarch naturally saw the signs of tyranny that his friends complained of, but he saw more danger in the civil strife and constant wars between communes, which had been tearing Italy apart for a very long time. If the works of the Roman historian Tacitus had been available, he would have found them very congenial reading ("if the emperor is good, government is good"). In the late summer of 1353, news reached Milan that the Venetians had inflicted a terrible defeat on Genoa off the coast of Sardinia. Genoa's reaction was to seek the strength of Milan and to deliver their city and its territories (from La Spezia to Monaco) to the archbishop for protection. Petrarch was present at the final session at which the transfer of power was arranged and conveyed his impressions in a letter to his old friend Guido Sette, archdeacon of Genoa (*Fam.* 17.4). The letter gives high praise to the archbishop's statemanship and desire to bring about peace between Genoa and Venice. Peace of course was not the result of this new arrangement. Venice and Florence immediately formed a league directed against the Visconti.

Petrarch certainly realized that the Visconti were using his scholarly and literary celebrity to lend a certain luster to their activities, but he seems to have believed in the justice or at least the necessity of their policies. Certainly under the rule of the Visconti Lombardy enjoyed more stability and peace than the rest of Italy at this time (see Cognasso 1955.5). The "political" crusades preached by the Popes against the Visconti during the fourteenth century were probably viewed by Petrarch not as a black mark against the Visconti, but as another example of Christians warring against Christians when they should be directing their combined energies against their common enemy (for a summary account of the "Italian" crusades see Riley-Smith 1987.222–224; more at length Housley 1982 and 1986.74–81). The fact that the Popes paid mercenaries like John Hawkwood to take the cross on these occasions was just another sign of Avignon's corruption. Petrarch never tired of complaining about the malignant presence of these hired killers in Italy.

It is clear that the Visconti controlled a large territory, but their rule always lacked well-defined boundaries and in some cases lacked territorial continuity. Pavia, a mere twenty miles from Milan, for example, did not belong to Milan in 1355, though it certainly did just four years earlier when Giovanni Mandelli was governor there (see Commentary). At the time Petrarch moved to Milan, the Visconti were contending for possession of Pisa by whatever means, certainly not excluding diplomacy. It was in this latter capacity that Petrarch played a significant role during his eight years at Milan.

Others in the service of the Visconti, like Mandelli, were required to play multiple roles. Related to the Visconti by blood, Petrarch's friend served them as soldier/judge, and administrator in Savoy, Piedmont, and Lombardy. Given the Visconti's interest in Liguria and Tuscany, it is hardly surprising that in 1358 Mandelli would choose to begin his pilgrimage in Genoa rather than Venice, the usual port of departure for pilgrims, and would be quite interested in detailed information about the western coast of Italy, at least as far as Florence's and Pisa's traditional territory extended. These considerations help explain one of the most distinctive features of the *Itinerarium,* namely the disproportionately large number of place-names between Genoa and Rome.

The high concentration of toponyms in this section of the *Itinerarium* is surely due to a request from Mandelli the military man, who was also called upon in his later years to serve the Visconti as a diplomat. Thus on 6 June 1358, a scant two months after Petrarch gave him the *Itinerarium* in Milan, we find "Iohanni Mondelli [= Mandelli] de Mediolano" being greeted with official fanfare at Pisa (see Commentary). His stay at Pisa was short, because just eleven or twelve days later we hear of his presence in Novara, 28 miles west of Milan. There on 18 June he met Galeazzo Visconti, who had arrived in the company of Petrarch. This confluence of Milanese dignitaries was intended to mark the auspicious return of the Novarese to Visconti control after a short defection. On this occasion Petrarch delivered a speech (still extant) in the cloister of the cathedral, in which he welcomed the people of Novara back to the protection of their benevolent lord and bade them resume their former sense of security (Wilkins 1958.167–169). In July of the following year Mandelli was once more in Tuscany on diplomatic business for the Visconti at Florence and Pisa

(Billanovich 1947.224–225). On 8 December 1359 he was to be installed as young Gian Galeazzo's deputy minister in Milan.

The *Itinerarium* in Context

If Petrarch delivered the *Itinerarium* to Mandelli in Milan on 4 April 1358, it is hard to see how he could have traveled to Genoa and prepared his group for departure much before the middle of the month. Since we know he was in Pisa 6 June, this leaves a scant two months in which to make his pilgrimage, an impossibly short time. Until the fifteenth century most pilgrim texts paid little attention to the outward or homeward journeys, the entire attention being focused on the Holy Land and the places visited there. Giacomo da Verona, who started his pilgrimage from Venice in 1335, gives enough detail about his eastward voyage to Jaffa for us to gather that his trip took between 31 and 35 days, if his three weeks' stay at Cyprus to visit shrines is excluded (Hyde 1993b.89). This accords very well with the more detailed information available for the fifteenth century. Gleaning clues from six pilgrim accounts of voyages from Venice to Jaffa and back between 1413 and 1494, Hyde finds that the outward journey averages 36.6 days and the return voyage 64 days (see table in Hyde 1993b.96). The information for the sixteenth century (derived from Braudel 1972.1:265) is more plentiful. The average length of the outward voyages of twenty ships between 1507 and 1608 is 43 days, and for the return 93 (see Hyde 1993b.97). These are rather surprising numbers, but the great difference in time must be due to longer and more frequent delays in harbors in the sixteenth century. The average sailing speed remained fairly constant, between 12 and 15 mph, though information on this subject is sparse (Hyde 1993b.94 and 110 n.21). From June to September the winds are prevailingly from the north in the Mediterranean. This means that ships traveling from Italy to the southern ports of Syria and Egypt could count on a "downhill" run, but the return had to be made in the face of a northerly wind. This explains why the return voyage took about twice as long as the outward, even as it did in antiquity (see Casson 1971.270–299).

Near the end of the *Itinerarium* Petrarch says that Mandelli's journey will take him three months. If Petrarch is referring to sailing time alone or to the land tour alone (a remote possibility), then his estimate for traveling time is quite accurate. If Petrarch meant to include in this estimate both the land tour and the sailing time, the estimate would be off the mark by about half. Niccolò da Martoni, who set out from Gaeta in June of 1394 and returned in May the following year, took over three months to do almost the same land tour as described by Petrarch; earlier in the century Giacomo da Verona took a few days over two months to do the same land tour (Savage 1977.4:59–60). The only way that Mandelli could have completed the trip as outlined by Petrarch would have been if he had delayed his outward voyage until after his appearance in Novara in June of 1358 and returned in the spring of the following year before his diplomatic mission in Tuscany in July of 1359. If carried out as planned, the schedule of Mandelli's trip would have to resemble Niccolò da Martoni's, described above.

Drawing on Röhricht (1890) and Golubovich (1909), and with supplements of his own, Atiya lists 107 pilgrim texts for the late thirteenth and fourteenth centuries (1938. 490–496). Some of these should more properly be designated as examples of recovery literature, but most of them are indisputably pilgrim texts, many of which argue for another crusade to recover the holy places in Palestine. The Italian contribution to pilgrim literature however is notably on the light side. As Hyde comments (1993 c.139), "Between Bernard the Wise in 868–69 and the early fourteenth century, not a single Italian author of a pilgrim book has been identified." This remarkable statistic may be even more remarkable, if Bernard the Wise was not an Italian, but in fact a Breton, as Runciman thinks (1969.1:72) and as seems likely: the Rheims Manuscript includes a statement to the effect that Bernard was born in France (Wilkinson 1977.141). In Bernard's place it appears that we shall have to substitute the "Piacenza Pilgrim" (c.

570) and enlarge the interim period of which Hyde speaks by three hundred years (see Wilkinson 1977.79–89).

In the late thirteenth and fourteenth centuries, the Italians began to make some very significant contributions to pilgrim literature (Atiya 1938.155–186 and Hyde 1993c.136–161). Ricoldo da Montecroce (1242–1320), a Dominican friar, spent a considerable amount of time living in the East, during which he toured the holy places and wrote an account of his pilgrimages, perhaps in 1294 (see Laurent 1873.105–141 and Monneret de Villard 1949). He was in Baghdad when Acre fell in 1291. In Mosul, he bought a copy of St. Gregory's commentary on the Book of Job, part of the loot from Acre. As he read it Ricoldo realized that it was insufficient to say that the sins of Christians caused their recent defeats. Christians, like Job, must accept failure as part of God's inscrutable design (Daniel 1989.6:88 and Schein 1991.124–127). Because Ricoldo had been living in the East for some time when he made his visits to the holy places and continued to live there for some time afterwards, travel to and from the Holy Land is not described in his *Itinerarium*. The account was written with an eye to both the pilgrim and the crusader. Ricoldo believed, as did many of his time, that the key strategy must be the economic strangulation of Egypt (Schein 1991.83).

The two Italian pilgrim texts next in order are the short ones of Francesco Pipino, a Bolognese Dominican, in 1320, and Antonio de' Reboldi, a Franciscan based on Cyprus, who visited Palestine in 1327 and Mt. Sinai and Egypt in 1330 (see texts in Tobler 1859.400–412 and Golubovich 1906.3:331–342). Pipino's account of his visit in the Holy Land resembles Ricoldo's in that he gives little or no information about his movements, the distances traveled, or the time involved.[20] In Reboldi's text we see the form of a sketchy itinerary emerging, which allows the reader to follow along from place to place and to share in a few of his personal reactions to things other than the holy places. Focused entirely on reliving the events recorded in the Bible, neither Pipino nor Reboldi gives an account of the outward or return voyage. Giacomo da Verona's account of his pilgrimage in 1335 therefore begins a new trend in pilgrim literature, which views the whole journey as worthy of reportage. Thus Giacomo's narrative allows us to follow his outward journey from Venice in fair detail. He remarks, for example, on the large Jewish population in Otranto (he preached to them) and he noticed the women of that port city wore earrings, a custom he apparently found unusual (Röhricht 1895.3:173). There are some details in Giacomo's account which suggest that he hoped it might be useful to potential crusaders, but he wrote it primarily for the edification of his fellows back home, as an aid in their prayers and meditations. Even so the narrative begins to show traits that are characteristic of the modern travelogue. Giacomo was an incurable relic and souvenir hunter, carrying two iron chisels with which to extract pieces of rock, as he breezily confesses (Röhricht 1895.3:158, 186, and 187). As interesting as Giacomo's book is, it did not circulate widely outside his own monastery. Röhricht made his edition from one surviving Latin manuscript, a copy made in 1424, and from two German translations dated to the end of the fifteenth century.

This trend towards the recognizably modern travelogue continues with Niccolò da Poggibonsi, a charming Tuscan Franciscan, who wrote the notes for his rather substantial book between 1346 and 1350, while on tour. Striving for a new standard in accurate reporting, Niccolò provided himself with two measuring sticks (one a yard, the other a foot long) and carefully recorded the dimensions in tablets as he went from monument to monument, describing and perhaps sketching architectural styles and works of art and copying or paraphrasing inscriptions which have long ago disappeared. He says (Bacchi della Lega 1945.1:13) that he undertook his tedious labor as a service for those who would never be able to visit the holy places for themselves, but often he seems to envision that future pilgrims will have his book in hand as they make their way from place to place. Accordingly, Niccolò is the first to provide a detailed list of indulgences attached to the holy places. To make his book as accessible as possible, he wrote it in Italian, also a first.

In his introduction, Niccolò displays his pride in his accomplishment when he says that he has worked his name (twice), his father's name, and his place of origin into the text by means of acrostics extending over eighty-six chapters, so that "no one may attribute to himself the labor I alone had for this book." The book indeed became enormously popular, but its first edition was published in 1500 and thereafter over a period of three hundred years sixty-three times, either anonymously or under the fictitious name of Fra Noè of the Order of St. Francis. The good friar paid a heavy price for his authorial vanity.

Next in chronological order is Petrarch's *Itinerarium*, exceptional in every way, in part because of the circumstances of its composition. There is good reason to believe that Boccaccio brought a copy of it back to Florence after his lengthy stay with Petrarch in the spring of 1359, and that once in Boccaccio's hands, it began to circulate widely among Petrarch's many admirers there: Coluccio Salutati, Domenico Silvestri, and Guido del Palagio, all of whom were most eager to acquire anything written by Petrarch. The last named, Guido del Palagio, is important at this juncture in our survey because in 1381 he inspired Lionardo Frescobaldi to undertake with him a pilgrimage to the Holy Land.

Although Guido was unable to meet Petrarch before his death in 1374, he became friends with Petrarch's son-in-law Francescuolo da Brossano in the hopes of gaining access to Petrarch's writings (Billanovich 1947.374–375; see Commentary). Thus there can be no doubt that Guido had any number of ways of gaining access to the *Itinerarium*, and very little doubt that he actually had a copy of it. Guido, who had been the moving force behind the idea of the pilgrimage, suddenly withdrew because of important business and personal considerations, but not before he and Frescobaldi had recruited Giorgio Gucci, Simone Sigoli, and four others for the trip. On 4 September 1384, the seven (with six servants) set sail for Alexandria from Venice. After their return to Florence in the late spring of 1385, Frescobaldi, Gucci, and Sigoli all wrote accounts of the trip in the vernacular. Andrea Rinuccini, who had been a late addition to the group, died in Damascus, but may have left a diary, which Frescobaldi and Gucci are conjectured to have incorporated into a second edition of Frescobaldi's account. In all, twenty-eight manuscripts have survived of the various versions (Defiol 1982.145–176), testimony to their popularity.

It must have been through Guido del Palagio that Petrarch's *Itinerarium* exerted its influence on the other Florentine pilgrims, and that mostly on the level of inspiration and initial planning. It is probably not a coincidence that they carried out, though in reverse order, the route recommended by Petrarch, including a visit to Damascus and especially the visit to Egypt, the key objective in most fourteenth-century strategies to recover the Holy Land. Frescobaldi forthrightly informs his readers that he was in fact recruited by Charles III of Anjou-Durazzo and King of Naples (1382–1386) to carry on military espionage. Charles, Frescobaldi tells us (Angelini 1944.40–41), had vowed to mount a crusade, and as a sign of his commitment, he and his followers wore gold and silver images of a ship on their chests. Frescobaldi's assignment was to scout out a good port for landing (many had been blocked up by the Mamluks), to study the rivers and places good for making camp, and identify good battlegrounds. Frescobaldi considers that he is a good man for the job because he has fought in seven battles. His account is proof that Frescobaldi took his commission seriously, for it shows a greater interest in geographical and topographical detail than most pilgrim books (Cardini 1986.196–203).

Gucci and Sigoli, aware of Frescobaldi's spying activities, seemingly try in their accounts to supplement his efforts, so that these too show more precise detail than usual. Sigoli, in his description of the bitter / sweet water of Matarea (see Commentary), is the only one of the three who shows explicit knowledge of Petrarch's *Itinerarium*. Although many pilgrims mention their visit to Matarea (associated with the flight of the Holy Family to Egypt), Petrarch and Sigoli are the only ones who have yet been found to mention this curious story, with the possible exception of Antonio de' Reboldi. Since Sigoli's story matches Petrarch's in all essential points, it seems likely that he had read it in the copy of the *Itinerarium* presumed to be in Guido del Palagio's possession.

These three Florentines, inspired by Petrarch, it would seem, are the first laymen from Italy to write accounts of their pilgrimage to the Holy Land. They are wealthy upper class merchants who travel with servants and all the amenities their money can buy. They are all exceptionally alert to details, recording their routes and means of travel, the time it takes to get from place to place and what things cost; and at least one of them considered himself a spy, making straight the path of crusaders to follow. All three, but especially Gucci, kept a sharp eye on their Muslim hosts, recording their customs and behavior not without some hostility, but with a grudging effort to understand. A Saracen by the name of Said (Saetta or Saeto in Italian) guided them from Alexandria to Cairo. Now in his seventies and accompanied by his son Elias, Said told Frescobaldi that he had served as guide and interpreter to sixty-six pilgrim groups in his career. In fact this same Said had served Niccolò da Poggibonsi as guide to the Sinai. Niccolò tells us that Arab brigands seized Said in the desert because he had resisted their attempts to extort money from the Italian pilgrims. Niccolò was overjoyed when Said managed to give his captors the slip and rejoin the group. Both Niccolò and the Florentines call Said "a good and just man" according to his light (Bacchi della Lega 1945.1:xv–xvi).

In the fourteenth century, the pilgrims' natural curiosity about things other than holy places begins to throw off the restraints imposed in earlier times. In Reboldi's account (Golubovich 1906.3:336), we find a description of a giraffe, the first of many to come in subsequent pilgrim books. A few years later, Giacomo da Verona is fascinated by his first look at an elephant; Niccolò da Poggibonsi is amazed by an ostrich. But it is not until the end of the century that we find in a pilgrim text, Italian or otherwise, more than the slightest interest in classical antiquity, a defining characteristic of the Renaissance. Although Petrarch cannot be said to have influenced Niccolò da Martoni directly, interest in Graeco-Roman antiquity, which Petrarch did more than anyone else to foster in the fourteenth century, is beginning to bloom in Niccolò's book, written in 1395–1396 (text in Legrand 1895.3:566–669).

The vast majority of all extant accounts of pilgrimages to the Holy Land were written by members of the clergy, as might be expected. After the start of the crusades and the establishment of the Latin Kingdom in Palestine and Syria, many others besides the clergy made pilgrimages, but few of them wrote accounts of their experiences. This scarcity of pilgrim books written by laymen makes those of the three Florentine merchants all the more valuable. In the words of Frescobaldi and the others, we gain valuable insights into an important stratum of medieval society. In the account of Niccolò da Martoni we are able to view fourteenth-century Italian society from yet another perspective, that of a university-educated layman engaged in the rather lucrative practice of the law.

Niccolò was a notary, a diploma'd expert in business and administrative law. A notary was rather like an English solicitor, whose duties included drawing up contracts and statutes, handling estates, and advising judicial magistrates. Notaries were often deeply involved in the cultural and political life of their communities, as was the case in Florence with Brunetto Latini and Ser Petracco, Petrarch's father. Niccolò hailed from Carinola, a small town at the foot of Monte Massico, but he mentions nearby Capua and Naples several times and probably conducted a considerable amount of business there. Although notaries elsewhere in Europe were turning to the vernacular languages for official use at this time, they still preferred to do business in Latin in southern Italy and Sicily because of the polyglot composition of the population and the consequent high rate of foreign correspondence (Setton 1948.216–221). It was perhaps out of ingrained habit that Niccolò used Latin to write his account of his pilgrimage, though in doing so he nearly condemned it to extinction. It survives in one copy made of the original (now lost) in March of 1397 and in an epitome of this copy, both now in Paris.

It is a wonder that as practised in writing Latin as he was, Niccolò wrote it so barbarously by classical standards and so badly even by the debased standards of his time (cf. McGovern 1972.227–239 on the Latinity of Italian notarial prose). The more is the wonder, since he shows ample sign of having read beyond the technical materials of his notarial profession, in areas of literature we would describe as belletristic. All pilgrims know the Bible and numerous lives of the saints; many of the better educated quote St. Jerome, Eusebius (in Jerome's translations), Josephus's *Jewish War* and *Jewish Antiquities* (in various translations), and occasionally St. Augustine and Isidore. Quite exceptionally Burchard of Mt. Sion (c. 1280) quotes the Roman poet Horace (both the *Epistles* and *Odes*; Stewart 1896.102 and 103). Whether Burchard had actually read Horace himself or whether he had lifted these eminently quotable verses from another author (e.g., Jerome) or some *florilegium* is impossible to say with certainty, but the chances of the latter being the case are strong, especially since the *Odes* were so little known in the Middle Ages (Moore 1896.200–206). Niccolò's quotation from Boethius's *De consolatione Philosophiae* (2 m.3.17) may also come from a commonplace book since it is a rather famous statement of the "all must die" topos (Legrand 1895.3:668).[21]

Elsewhere Niccolò shows firsthand knowledge of non-religious or devotional texts of a surprising sort. On the outward journey he notes as they pass Cythera (medieval Latin, Citrinus; modern, Cerigo), an island 8 miles S of Cape Malea, that it was here (not in Sparta) that Paris, son of Priam, seduced and abducted Helen (Legrand 580). This unusual version of the story, as well as the less well-known story of Hesione, Martoni clearly got from Guido delle Colonne's *Historia destructionis Troiae* (also known in the manuscripts as *Historia Troiana*), where these stories are fully elaborated (text in Griffin 1936.42–44 and 67–79; trans. in Meek 1974).[22]

Niccolò's firsthand knowledge of Guido's work is confirmed by his fumbled attempt to quote from it (certainly from memory) in his description of his visit to the Parthenon in Athens, now architecturally modified and called St. Mary's. In the church there is a column on which the sign of the cross has been emblazoned, it is said by the hand of Dionysius the Areopagite, who was holding on to the column at the very moment when Christ died on the cross. As scripture tells us, there was an eclipse of the sun and an earthquake, which naturally could be felt and seen in Athens. According to the story, Dionysius exclaimed, "Either the god of nature is suffering or the structure of the world is falling apart" (*aut deus nature patitur aut machina mundi dissolvitur*, Griffin

1936.17). Niccolò remembers the line as "Either the structure of the world will be destroyed or the Son of God will suffer something" (*aut machina mundi destruetur, aut Filius Dei aliquid patietur,* Legrand 651).

Dionysius the Areopagite was by the ninth century identified with St. Dionysius, patron saint of France (St. Denys), and the theological writings of another Dionysius, the Pseudo-Areopagite (c. 500), were also attributed to the saint about this time (Paton 1951.20–26). A somewhat different version of the anecdote from the one told by Guido delle Colonne and Niccolò may be found in these writings, widely read in the ninth-century Latin version of John Scotus Erigena. Guido himself seems to have lifted the story from Sacrobosco's *De Sphaera* (see Meek 1974.276–277). The appearance of the story in Sacrobosco's textbook on astronomy / astrology (see above) insured that anyone who attended a university for a year or two would have known it. Niccolò was undoubtedly acquainted with the story from both sources, but he is thinking of Guido's book, as the references to the Paris / Helen and Hesione stories show.

Although Martoni is chiefly interested in the spiritual treasures of St. Mary's, he notes that the doors of the church had once stood in the gateways of Troy, brought to Athens as booty. His keen interest in anything relating to the "history" of Troy is very much characteristic of the Middle Ages and the Renaissance. As late as 1613 the English antiquarian John Selton, in his notes to Michael Drayton's *Poly-Olbion,* feels it is necessary to denounce as misguided "that universall desire, bewitching our Europe, to derive their bloud from Trojans" (Hebel 1933.4:22). Indeed not only Italians, but also most Europeans believed that their various countries had originally been colonized by Trojan refugees: Francus, a companion of Aeneas, settled France; Antenor founded Venice; Brutus, Britain, and so on. The history of Troy was not known from Homer's epics, which did not have Latin translations until Boccaccio and Petrarch arranged it, or even from Virgil's *Aeneid* or the last few books of Ovid's *Metamorphoses,* but from the short prose fictions of Dares Phrygius and Dictys Cretensis, supposedly eyewitnesses to the events they describe (texts in Eisenhut 1958 and Meister 1873).[23] For the early Middle Ages these works, fifth or sixth-century Latin translations of Greek originals of about the first century AD, were considered authentic history, whereas Homer, Virgil, and Ovid offered poetic inventions (Griffin 1936.3–4, Frazer 1966.3–15, and Merkle 1996.563–580). When Benoit de Saint-Maure translated and greatly expanded Dares and Dictys into French verse in c.1160, his *Roman de Troie* became hugely popular. When Guido delle Colonne turned Benoit's French into Latin prose and further expanded it, the story enjoyed international success and was soon turned back into many vernacular languages, including French by Raoul Lefèvre as *Le Recueil des Histoires de Troie,* which Caxton in turn translated into English and printed in 1475, the first English book to come off the press. Petrarch's devotion to Virgil's version of the Trojan War and of Aeneas' heroic role in it is rather exceptional in the Middle Ages, especially outside Italy. In the counter-tradition of the more popular treatments of Troy's history by Benoit and Guido delle Colonne, Aeneas is depicted not as a hero but as a betrayer of the Trojans to the Greeks and as the one who was bribed to lead the murderous Pyrrhus to the aged King Priam (Griffin 1936.217–228 and 233–234). Worst of all in the view of many, Virgil portrayed Aeneas as a necromancer, a dangerous thing to be accused of, as Petrarch himself had occasion to learn.

Niccolò also reveals his interest in Arthurian legend. As he crosses the strait between mainland Greece and Negroponte (Euboea), an informant points to an old castle on a small island in the strait and tells him that the castle belonged to Morgan Le Fay, whom Niccolò calls the mother of La Pulzella Gaia (the "Merry Maid") and seems to identify with the Lady of the Lake. He is told that Morgana held Gawain captive in the castle: *hedificium . . . quod dicitur fuisse castrum Fate Morgane, domine Laci* [*sic;* for *Lacus*], *matris Pozelle Gage; in quo castro dicitur fuisse captivum dominum Calvanum* [*sic;* for the classically correct nominatives], Legrand 654). Niccolò is alluding with obvious recognition to a *cantare* dating to 1350–1375 called *La Pulzella Gaia* (text in Levi 1914.31–58; see summary in Gardner 1930.242–247), in which Gawain wins the love of La Pulzella, but later betrays it. Morgan Le Fay punishes her daughter's indiscretions by imprisoning her in a castle, which Gawain eventually finds and from which he rescues La Pulzella by the improbable method of disguising himself as the Lady of the Lake. Niccolò has the names of the principal characters of the story correct, but seems confused about the plot. Morgan Le Fay is not to be identified as the Lady of the Lake, and it is La Pulzella who is imprisoned, not Gawain.

It is not at all surprising that Niccolò is an enthusiastic (if somewhat careless) reader of Arthurian legend, because various romances built on the legend were popular in Italy from their very beginning (see Gardner 1930; Kleinhenz 1986 s.v. "Italian Arthurian Literature"; and Hoffman 1990.1:170–188). Only Petrarch stands out among his contemporaries as labeling the Arthurian stories as humbug, dreams that lead the common folk astray (*Triumphus cupidinis,* 3.79–82 in *Rime* 497; see also de Nolhac 1907.2.230–231). What may be surprising is that Niccolò would record his interest in such works in an account of his pilgrimage, but we must remember that although the stories of Troy and Arthur are romantic fiction to us, they were for Niccolò history, imaginatively elaborated and sometimes in need of allegorical interpretation perhaps, but history nevertheless. He cites from these works much in the same spirit that a scholar like Petrarch might cite Livy and Justin, out of deeply felt connection with the Graeco-Roman past, or in the case of the Arthurian stories, with the early Christian past. "For the Middle Ages and even well beyond," as Fleischman says (1983.305), "historical truth was anything that belonged to a widely accepted tradition." History was what most people believed was true, even if there were little or no basis in fact for it. Petrarch believed much less of accepted tradition than many others.

The most notable feature of Martoni's pilgrim book is his keen interest in classical antiquity, not as he found it in the texts of ancient authors, but in the ruined monuments. On the outward voyage, he gives a paragraph to Crete in which he seems well informed on current events on the island and on its relationship to the Duchy of Archipelago headquartered on Naxos to the north (for a brief account see Newett 1907.395–396), but he concludes his remarks by reminding his reader of the famous Labyrinth in which "there used to live the Minotaur" (Legrand 581). Likewise at Rhodes, he gives a paragraph to the famous Colossus. Our Niccolò is the first to record the belief that the statue once bestrode the entrance to the harbor later known as Mandraki, a span of some 1300 ft. This belief inspired many illustrators of atlases of the Renaissance to produce engravings which might well have inspired Shakespeare to write of Julius Caesar that "he doth bestride the narrow world / Like a Colossus." Niccolò adds that St. Paul addressed the people of Rhodes as Colossians because of this great statue (Legrand 585–586). He is by no means the only pilgrim to make this howler.

But it is on his return voyage that Niccolò gives full reign to his interest in the ancient monuments, particularly and most importantly at Athens. Petrarch mentions Athens in his *Itinerarium* purely out of deference to the city's famous past, not because it has any current cultural, political, or economic significance. After an edict of Emperor Justinian closed the schools of philosophy in 529, Athens had quickly sunk into an insignificant town, whose very name is virtually unrecognizable in the various Western vernaculars: Setines, Sitines, Cetines, Senes, Selline etc., all approximations of εἰς Ἀθήνας pronounced ee-Satheénas, the locative form in the demotic Greek of the day. For most of the fourteenth century the Duchy of Athens languished under the control of Catalan mercenaries, but in 1388 it passed into the hands of the Florentine Nerio Acciaiuoli. As Nerio felt death approach in September of 1394, he provided in his will that the city of Athens with all its possessions be left to the Church of St. Mary of Athens, and then he entrusted the Church and all its possessions to the protection of the Venetians who controlled nearby Negroponte (Setton 1948.195–196).

In late February of 1395, shortly after the Venetian occupation of Athens and while Nerio's heirs were still squabbling over the will, Niccolò arrived for a two-day visit. Having come in the early morning of the 24th after an all-night hike in the rain, Niccolò immediately asked some locals to show him the notable buildings and some "old stuff" (aliqua antiqua). His description of Athens is the first Western report in nearly nine hundred years (Legrand 648–653).[24] He looked upon a city of about one thousand hearths (focularia), he thought, huddled under the protection of the Acropolis, with an estimated population of 8,000 to 10,000.

Niccolò's guides proceeded to show him Aristotle's School (studium), really the ruins of a Roman aqueduct. Next he was shown the great palace of the Emperor Hadrian, really the temple of Olympian Zeus. Then he was led to the entrance of the Acropolis, the Propylaea, which he does not describe except to say that it compares well with the entrance way of the city of Capua. Within lay the Church of St. Mary, so huge Niccolò could not imagine how it could have been built, and many wonders besides the column of Dionysius the Areopagite. Niccolò speaks only briefly of the exterior in his eagerness to tell of the jewel-encrusted portrait of the Virgin painted by St. Luke the Evangelist and of the New Testament written in Greek letters of gold by the hand of St. Helena, mother of the Emperor Constantine. From Niccolò's account and from other later sources it is clear that the Parthenon is still in near perfect condition and remained so until that fateful Venetian bomb fell through the roof on the evening of 26 September 1687 (Paton 1951.8–19).

Great historical changes are usually the result of a long process, but it is the spectacular precipitating event that often claims our attention. Petrarch's dramatic entrance onto the intellectual scene is often seen as the event that brought on the cultural movement recognizable as humanism, heralding the arrival of the Renaissance. Patient study has shown however that Petrarch's way had been prepared by precursors, people like Lovato Lovati (d. 1309), enthusiastic collector of ancient texts, and Albertino Mussato (d. 1329), author of the first tragedy to be written in classical meters since antiquity. Niccolò da Martoni's pilgrim book is fascinating because it shows how far the humanistic spirit had filtered down to the lower strata of Italy's intelligentsia by the end of the century. In Niccolò we find a man still very much of the Middle Ages, but also one just making tentative, but eager entry into a new world.

Niccolò's outlook can most easily be detected and illustrated in his descriptions of Athens, particularly the Acropolis. He calls it "Castrum Acthenarum," the common designation of Athens's citadel in the Middle Ages. For him the Parthenon is an "ecclesia," a church called St. Mary's since the Latins took it over from the Byzantines. He casually estimates the number of exterior columns at sixty, omitting any mention of the sculptured frieze and pediments, but he carefully provides a list of relics he saw in the church's treasury: bones from the skull of St. Macarius, from the arm of St. Denys, from the arms of Sts. Cyprian and Justin etc. Only the church's doors briefly claim his attention because of their association with Troy.

Niccolò's description of the antiquities of Athens is not matched again until the visit by another Italian, Ciriaco d'Ancona (d. 1452) about forty years later (see Setton 1948.232–235; MacKendrick 1952.131–145; Weiss 1969.138–142), but the two descriptions stand in bold contrast. Instead of the term "Castrum," Ciriaco used the word Acropolis. It is a quite familiar term nowadays, but quite unknown in the West during the Middle Ages. Ciriaco is the first writer of Latin to use the word in about a thousand years, its only other occurrence in all of Latin letters being found in the fifth-century commentary on Statius's *Thebais* (*ad* 12.632), according to the *Thesaurus linguae latinae*. For Ciriaco the beautiful building on the Acropolis is not St. Mary's, but the noble temple of Pallas Athena. He correctly puts the number of exterior columns at fifty-eight and rhapsodizes about the sculptured exterior frieze and the pediments, some of whose scenes he is able to identify correctly. This is no small thing, since scholars are still debating the subject matter of the interior frieze. There is nothing about the Christian modifications to the Parthenon that seems to interest Ciriaco. Indeed one scholar (Paton 1951.175) doubts that he even entered the church, though that is hard to believe. Elsewhere in Athens the remains that Niccolò accepted as Aristotle's School Ciriaco is able to identify correctly from an inscription as an aqueduct begun by Hadrian and finished by Antoninus Pius. Even after we allow for the considerable differences in talent and interests between the two men, Ciriaco must be considered altogether a man of the new humanism, whereas Niccolò is still very much a man of another age, but definitely intrigued by the new world he has glimpsed.

The last Italian pilgrim book to be considered reveals yet another stratum of society. In 1413 Niccolò III d'Este, *signore* of Ferrara, set out with a retinue of about fifty, which included a physician, a chaplain, two cooks, a tailor, a barber, two trumpeters for ceremonial occasions, and a personal secretary. His travel time is the fastest on record: leaving Venice on 15 April, he made his outward journey in twenty-six days and the return in forty-three. With only two weeks in the Holy Land, he was back in Ferrara exactly three months after he had set out (6 April to 6 July). Almost certainly, he had chartered a ship for the occasion, as did Henry, Earl of Derby (later Henry IV of England), for his pilgrimage to the Holy Land in 1392 (Newett 1907.34–35). Bolingbroke's travel time incidentally was remarkably good, considering that he traveled in the middle of winter (early December to the end of March). Winter crossings, admittedly unpredictable and dangerous, were far more common than generally supposed (Hyde 1993b.104–106).

Luchino dal Campo, Niccolò's *cancelliere*, is responsible for the account which has survived (text in Ghinassi 1861). With his account one notices a new precision in recording time. Before Luchino the time of day, if it is indicated at all, is given by reference to the canonical hours of terce, nones, and vespers. Informed presumably by the ship's hourglass, fifteenth-century pilgrims begin to use the 24-hour system, counting the hours from sunset to sunset in the Italian way. Thus Luchino writes that they left Venice early in the morning on Saturday, 15 April, boarding their ship at S. Nicolò al Lido, with Pietro Contarino as captain. One hundred and twenty miles later at 22 hours the following day, they landed one mile from Pola (Pula) in Croatia. Since there were two hours of daylight left, the *signore* decided to take a look at the town and the "old things" he had heard were there (*si deliberò . . . andare a videre Pola e quelle cose antiche, che si dice esservi,* Ghinassi 107): a Roman amphitheater and triumphal arch most notably. Local dignitaries appeared on the scene with a welcome for the distinguished visitors and offerings of food. Whereupon, Niccolò ordered tables to be set up *sopra all'erba fresca*. After a pleasant picnic, everyone retired to his berth aboard ship.

Niccolò's eager search for antiquities at Pola is just about the last time we hear of them on the whole trip. The only other detectable interest in classical antiquities occurs in connection with the island of Cerigo (= Cythera), which they pass during the night of 28 April. Luchino writes that *signore* expressed regret at not being able to land on the island since it was the place where Paris abducted Helen. He would have liked to see the places about which he had read.[25] Niccolò, a man of considerable education (Gundersheimer 1973.66–91), had access to the family library, which an inventory dating to 1436 tells us contained 279 volumes, or at least that many were in the library when the inventory was made (Cappelli 1886.12-30). Item 239 is described as "la destrution de Troia," which must be Guido delle Colonne's version of the story. Item 175 lists "el Troiano in vulgare," which may be an Italian translation of Guido's book, and item 237 records a "Troiano, in francexe," which may be Benoit de Sainte-Maure's work. As Niccolò has read the story of Paris and Helen, the books were in the Estense library before 1413, the date of Luchino's book.

The inventory shows that of contemporary writers Petrarch is the most popular, with Boccaccio a very close second. Item 15 describes a "libro chiamado lo itinerario de Messere Francesco Petrarcha al sepolcro," apparently a vernacular version written on parchment and covered in red leather. There is no sure way to know whether the *Itinerarium* was in the library for Niccolò and Luchino to read prior to the pilgrimage, but there is a good chance that it was. Benvenuto da Imola, who quotes Petrarch's *Itinerarium* in his great commentary on Dante (see Commentary), probably obtained his copy of Petrarch's work while in Florence attending Boccaccio's lectures on the *Commedia*. In about 1375, Benvenuto moved to Ferrara to continue work on his own commentary. The *Itinerarium* may have been introduced into the court library through Benvenuto's good services. According to the inventory, Petrarch's *Bucolicum carmen* (item 125) and Benvenuto's commentary on that collection of pastoral poems (item 130) were both in the library. Or if it was not Boccaccio who brought the *Itinerarium* to Ferrara, then it was surely Donato degli Albanzani, great friend and admirer of Petrarch, who came to Ferrara in 1382 and in the later 1380s became tutor to young Niccolò III (Novati 1890.365–385 and Paolella 1993.xxiv–xxv). A copy of the *Itinerarium* is still in the Estense library at Modena (Kristeller 1963.1:370), but this is a Latin manuscript of the fourteenth century and is found bound with another of Petrarch's shorter works, and Mussato's classical tragedy *Ecerinis*. The manuscript does not appear in the inventory of 1436, but it may have been on loan when the inventory was made. The vernacular version has been lost.

If Petrarch's *Itinerarium* was in the court library before 1413, as seems likely, and since Petrarch was greatly admired at Ferrara, Niccolò and Luchino undoubtedly read Petrarch's work before setting out. Courtly interest in geography is evident in the following: two copies of Marco Polo's *Description of the World (Divisament dou Monde*, one copy in the vernacular (item 180) and the other perhaps in the Latin translation of Francesco Pipino (item 52); three copies of Pomponius Mela's *Chorographia*, one "in vulgare" (item 170);[26] Albert the Great's *Liber cosmographicus de natura locorum* and Isidore's *Imago mundi* (perhaps a *mappamundi* from the *Etymologies* or the *De natura rerum*; item 42); Fazio degli Uberti's *Dittamondo*, an encyclopedic poem in *terza rima* in which the author travels through the world, guided by Solinus (item 164); and other works such as Orosius's *Histories* and Isidore's *Etymologies* that contain important geographical information. Shortly after the inventory was compiled, Guarino da Verona, who had come to Ferrara to supervise young Leonello d'Este's education, undertook his Latin translation of Strabo's *Geographia*. As we have seen, it was in Ferrara that Flavio Biondo (born about fifty miles south of Ferrara) consulted Petrarch's map of Italy while working on his *Italia illustrata* (1448–1453), in which the foundations of modern historical geography were established.

Niccolò's initial display of interest in antiquities faded quickly. Luchino, reflecting no doubt the signore's dominant tastes, dwells in his account on the picturesque and on the pleasurable experiences they enjoy. On the island of Cherso off the Illyrian coast, they watch members of the crew catch some fish no one had ever seen before, a prelude to an impromtu fish fry (Ghinassi 107). On Corfu, after a fine lunch, they rested until they all went to hear the Greek monks sing their vespers. Afterwards, they proceeded to a beautiful garden shaded by some orange trees, which dropped sweet-scented blossoms onto their tables as they ate (Ghinassi 110). As they round "Canomaglio," Cape Malea, the most southerly point in Greece, Luchino offers a panoramic view of the Aegean Sea, casting his reader's imagination over the entire Cyclades, to Negroponte, and the Black Sea and to the corresponding cape on the southeastern coast of Turkey (*ad un altro cavo, che si chiama crio in Turchia*, Ghinassi 113). This is the only section in Luchino's account which is reminiscent of Petrarch's *Itinerarium*: it is just at this point in the journey that Petrarch gives a similar panoramic survey of the Aegean, taking Mandelli on an imaginary trip to Athens, Negroponte, Scyros, the Hellespont, Troy etc., with a well-gauged didactic purpose absent in Luchino's text. It is a passage such as this that reminds us that both Petrarch and Luchino were undoubtedly glancing at their portolan charts as they wrote. Making good time, but with some rough weather, the *signore* arrived on 4 May about midday at Rhodes, where Hospitallers greet them all and offer lodging and everything they might need. Some of the group were put up at St. Catherine's near the harbor, but Niccolò was lodged at the governor's place, where he dined in a beautiful garden.

While Luchino's narrative of the outward voyage takes up nearly fourteen pages, only ten rather perfunctory pages are given to the pilgrimage proper (Ghinassi 119–128). Luchino describes the usual "holy circuit," of Jerusalem and environs, with Franciscan friars, as was now the custom, acting as guides. Here let us follow the poet Ezra Pound's summary of Luchino's account (*The Cantos* XXIV, 111–112 in Pound 1975; see Hugen 1974.229–238 on Pound's use of the pilgrim text).

> Donkey boys, dust, deserts, Jerusalem, backsheesh
> And an endless fuss over passports;
> One groat for the Jordan, whether you go there or not,

> The school where the madonna in girlhood
> Went to learn letters, and Pilate's house closed to the public;
> 2 soldi for Olivet (to the Saracens)
> And no indulgence at Judas's tree; and
> "Here Christ put his thumb on rock
> Saying: hic est medium mundi."
> (That, I assure you, happened.
> Ego, scriptor cantilenae.)

The group did visit the Holy Sepulcher of course, but Niccolò spent a good deal of time there dubbing a few members of his entourage "cavalieri" and making speeches (Ghinassi 125–126). A quick two-day jaunt to Bethlehem (17–18 May) effectively concluded the pilgrimage.

A leisurely narrative of twenty pages is devoted to the delightful return home. Although they had stopped briefly at Cyprus on the outward journey, Niccolò decided to make a more extended stay at the Lusignan court, arriving 26 May and departing 31 May. The visit was a long round of sightseeing, feasting in beautiful gardens, and enjoying local entertainments like the Turkish juggler and sword-dancer (four-page description). Towards the end of their stay, after they had enjoyed a sauna bath followed by lunch and a game of ball, King Janus impressed them with a display of his armaments and bested some of their number in a shot-putting contest. Much of this section is reminiscent of the descriptions of elegant courtly life at Ferrara which Angelo Decembrio will soon depict in his *De Politia litteraria*, a tribute to Niccolò's son Leonello (Gundersheimer 1973. 104–120). The temporal interests in Luchino's book, and those mostly of a sensual kind, greatly overbalance spiritual concerns. Only on a few brief occasions on the return voyage is there any attention paid to religious matters, as when on Rhodes the group inspects some relics at St. John's near the palace of the Grand Master of the Hospitallers. But as Hyde observes (1993c.155–156), the fashionable sophistication displayed in Luchino's book is not at all typical of other later fifteenth-century pilgrim books, such as those of Mariano da Siena (c. 1431), Gabrielo Capodilista and Roberto da Sanseverino

(1458), and Santo Brasca (c. 1480), where the proper balance between the temporal and the spiritual is seen in edifying abundance.

Concluding Thoughts

Dante, for all his interest in geography, never mentions the word *mappa*; the word *carta* appears eight times in the *Commedia*, but always in the sense of "page" of writing, as Hyde points out (1982.134). While Dante had certainly seen a *mappamundi*, there is no sign in any of his work that he had ever seen a portolan chart. In 1335 Giacomo da Verona becomes the first pilgrim to consider his outward voyage worth reporting in some detail, though he says nothing of his return trip, and he too gives no sign of consulting a portolan chart. Fifteen years later Niccolò da Poggibonsi, who describes both his outward and return voyages in detail, mentions that he looked at a *carta* to discover the name of the island of Sapienza (Bacchi della Lega 1945.1:151).

Sometime between 1336 and 1338 in Naples Boccaccio wrote his *Filocolo*, the first Italian prose romance, telling the story of Florio and Biancifiore. Although Boccaccio is often heedless of geographical reality in the story, in the scenes set in the eastern Mediterranean he is clearly relying on a portolan chart, apparently the first sign in belletristic writing of the use of such maps. Boccaccio's cartographic source was likely to have been a copy of a map made by Pietro Vesconte for Marino Sanudo's *Secretum fidelium crucis*, which had come into the hands of Boccaccio's early mentor Paolino Veneto (Bertolini 1968.211–225, Degenhart 1973.1–137, and Hyde 1982.135–137). A few years later (1339–1341) Boccaccio wrote his *Teseida*, a torpid vernacular epic in twelve cantos, to which he obligingly supplied notes. In his *chiosa* or gloss to stanza forty of book one, Boccaccio clarifies the geography of the Dardanelles by referring to a portolan chart: "As one can plainly see on a nautical map (sopra la carta da navigare)," one has to pass through a strait to get from the Aegean to the Black Sea (Marti 1969.2:665). A few lines later in the same gloss, he speaks of

Abido (Abydos) in connection with the Hero and Leander story. He adds that nowadays sailors call the place "Aveo," exactly the name that is found on early portolan charts (Kretschmer 1909. 652). Meanwhile in Avignon, no later than the mid-1330s, Petrarch also was using portolan charts. We know that the eccentric Opicinus de Canistris began to produce maps which he had copied from portolan charts in 1335, and so we may be confident that Petrarch had them by this time as well. We can see evidence of his use of them by 1338 or 1339 in the composition of his own epic, the *Africa*. He also must have been working on his map of Italy during this period.

Thus by the middle of the century portolan maps were in the hands of pilgrims, poets, and scholars. To the new cartographic precision, Petrarch brought an infusion of knowledge from ancient authors like Pomponius Mela. Some seem to view Petrarch's scholarly efforts in a negative way. By introducing ancient sources to Boccaccio, Petrarch is viewed as something of a corrupter. Says Hyde (1993d.201–202),

> Indeed, by the time he began his literary gazetteer *De montibus, silvis, fontibus, etc.* around 1355–57, Boccaccio had retreated so far from an interest in the modern world that he omitted any material derived from Paolino or Hayton as well as from Marco Polo, whose book he does not seem to have known.

This followed by,

> Thus we find in Boccaccio's later years the same withdrawal from the facts of contemporary geography and ethnography which is to be found in Petrarch's *Itinerarium Syriacum*. Petrarch's passing interest in the Canaries, which are mentioned once in his letters and once in the *De vita solitaria*, clearly arose from his reading about the Fortunate Islands rather than from any serious concern with contemporary exploration.

Although Hyde and others who make similar observations know quite well that Boccaccio set out in his *De montibus* to write a handbook or gazetteer for students studying literature and history, they seem not to be able to forgive him for excluding things not likely to be found in the students' reading assignments, and they insist on holding Petrarch responsible for Boccaccio's unfortunate retreat from reality.

Hyde's mention of the Canary Islands raises some interesting issues. These islands, known in antiquity as the Fortunate Islands or the Islands of the Blest, were endowed with a special status by many poets and declared to be a place for departed Heroes (Hesiod, *Works and Days,* 161–173) or for purified souls (Pindar, *Olympian Odes,* 2.61–76). These islands kept their fairyland status in the Middle Ages until their actual existence was rediscovered in 1336, and Dulcert added them to his portolan charts three years later (Campbell 1987.1:410). In 1346, in his *De vita solitaria,* 2.7 (*Prose* 522–524), Petrarch refers to the recent discovery in a rather dismissive way, saying that from what he has heard the natives found on the islands were primitive savages who lived like animals. The Fortunate Islands of the ancients turn out to be not so fortunate after all, he drily adds. Petrarch's disillusionment about the Fortunate Islands did not diminish his interest in the whereabouts of Thule or the Hyperboreans or in the Brahmins of the Far East, whom Petrarch idealized and had spoken of at length earlier in *De vita solitaria.*

In about 1351–1353, Boccaccio entered into his commonplace book, a collection of material now called *Zibaldone Magliabechiano,* a brief essay entitled *De Canaria,* his Latin translation of some letters written by certain Florentine merchants reporting back to Florence on an expedition to the Canaries in 1341 (see text in Stocchi 1959.143–156; see also Padoan 1964.264–277). Among other things, the essay describes the customs and behavior of the natives. Simple they are, but strong, brave, intelligent, respectful of authority, generous, fair, and knowing nothing of money or spices.

These two texts of Petrarch and Boccaccio, written independently, constitute Europe's first literary response to exploration into the Atlantic and to encounters with indigenous people to the West (Fernández-Armesto 1987.223–252). These antithetical statements provide the divergent models which will guide later European encounters during the coming age of exploration and conquest of American Natives: the indigenous people of the New World are seen either as primitive savages who must be tamed, civilized, and converted, or as noble savages from whom we "civilized" ones can learn virtue and true happiness (see Cachey 1991.45–59 and 1995). Boccaccio does not refer to the Canaries in his own *De montibus* because he omits the names of all islands from his gazetteer, a lacuna Domenico Silvestri later rectifies with his *De insulis et earum proprietatibus*. Sometime later, in his commentary on Dante, *Inferno* 5 (Padoan 1964.6: 334 and 872), Boccaccio uses the simple goodness of the Canary islanders in the matter of clothing their nakedness to castigate the moral degeneracy of the "smart set" in Florence. Drawing on his own *De Canaria*, Boccaccio seizes upon its exemplary value and uses it much as the Roman Tacitus made use of the noble Germans and as Montaigne will make use of the cannibals and Voltaire of the Hurons later on. Sticks with which to beat contemporary decadence.

How odd that Petrarch's and Boccaccio's interest in historical geography should be considered retrograde and counted against them. Together these two did more in their time than others did, both on a scholarly and on a popular level, to advance the study of geography. It is also apparently counted against them that neither shows any sign of having read Marco Polo's *Description of the World* (*Divisament don Monde*). But apart from the Paduan scholar Pietro d'Abano (fl. c. 1320; see Benedetto, 1928.cxxii–cxxiv and Randall 1961.26–35), there is no sign among the fourteenth-century humanists that any of them had read Marco Polo's work until Domenico Silvestri and Domenico di Bandino at the end of the century, and the earliest surviving map to make use of Marco Polo is the Catalan Atlas, which dates to c.1375 (Destombes 1964.203–204). The reason for this apparent neglect is that the book seemed to serious scholars to be largely fiction, as indeed one of its alternative titles (*Le livre des Merveilles*) seems to suggest (Critchley 1992.137). A book that announces itself as a book of marvels is not likely to be taken very seriously by somebody like Petrarch. He and others of like mind were right to be suspicious of Marco Polo's book, even as some scholars are to this day (Wood 1995). It would not have escaped Petrarch's notice that Marco's recollections of his travels were set down in writing by Rustichello da Pisa, who was also the well-known author of *Roman de Roi Artus*, the first Arthurian romance written by an Italian (Gardner 1930.44–63). Indeed there is a certain appropriateness about this circumstance since here we see the beginning of a trend whereby the new travel writing of the fourteenth century bears the same close relation to the rise of the modern novel as the old did to the romances of antiquity and the Middle Ages (Rennie 1995). We recall that Europe's first romance, Homer's *Odyssey*, is also the first travel book. The coordinates set by Ulysses are the ones that all who would tell a good story must follow.[27]

In his *Itinerarium* Petrarch, soberly turning his back to the enticements of paradoxography (with one exception), blends the new knowledge of his day with a knowledge of the ancient geographers unparalleled by any of his time. It is this mixture of the old and the new that gives the book its resonance. The echoes from Livy, Virgil, and Lucan in particular endow it with exemplary value and mark it as a piece of "recovery" literature quite out of the ordinary, for Petrarch is urging the "recovery" of an heroic spirit which must precede any attempt to recover the Holy Land. As a travel guide it is so sharply focused that Petrarch might seem to have made the journey himself. Indeed so vividly authentic did it seem to Aziz Atiya, author of the enduring classic of modern crusade literature *The Crusades in the Later Middle Ages* (1938; rev.1965), that he wrote,

> Ogier d'Anglure was only one of numerous pilgrims of noble origin who flocked to the Holy Land from many countries of Europe during the latter half of the fourteenth century. Others from France include three great crusaders — Jean II le Maingre, dit Boucicaut, Marshal of France, and the comtes d'Eu and de la Marche; while England is represented by Henry Bolingbroke and the Duke of Norfolk, and Italy by Thomas III Marquis of Saluces, Francesco Petrarca the poet . . . (183).

Habent sua fata libelli.

From his study in Milan Petrarch knew not only what Giovanni Mandelli would see, but also what was important to see. As Whitfield put it (1965.88), "His glance takes in securely the physical and spiritual features of the landscape." The *Itinerarium*, far from being a "little-known work . . . [which] can hardly have influenced the pilgrim-book tradition" (Hyde 1993c.153), was read by Boccaccio, Benvenuto da Imola, Coluccio Salutati, Guido del Palagio and the other Florentine pilgrims, Domenico Silvestri, Domenico di Bandino, Niccolò III d'Este and Luchino dal Campo, not to mention Mandelli and his companions, surviving in well over twenty manuscripts. Besides the lost vernacular translation in the Estense library and another lost manuscript in Naples, there are six extant anonymous Italian translations, five of the fifteenth century and one of the sixteenth, which constitute the strongest possible evidence for the popularity of the *Itinerarium* outside of antiquarian circles (edited by Paolella 1993). Benedetto di Falco's often reprinted sixteenth-century guide to Naples and environs (edited by Morisani 1972) often quotes or paraphrases the Latin text on topographical matters such as the location of Virgil's tomb. Petrarch in fact created a much-admired example of what would later be called the *methodos apodemica*, a systematic approach to travel (on which see Monga 1996a.645–684; esp. 647–648). Not a bad record for a pilgrim book that was written by a non-pilgrim for someone who probably was unable to make his pilgrimage to the Holy Land. In miniature form the *Itinerarium*, one of the most readable and modern of Petrarch's Latin works, shows how he strove in all his work to link Italy's Roman past to the present and beyond. In it the poet, scholar, and militant Christian are in a fine balance.

ENDNOTES

1 Before approaching Wilkins's biographical studies (preferably in the following order: 1961, 1958, 1959, and 1955), one would do well to read Mann 1984. Also to be consulted are Dotti 1992 especially, Bishop 1963, and Bergin 1970.

2 For Petrarch's important role in the transmission of Livy's text see Billanovich 1951 and 1981–85, together with the dissenting views of Reeve 1989.97–112. Petrarch's text of Livy, completed between 1326–1329, is preserved in the British Library (Harley 2493). Petrucci 1967. 115–129 provides a convenient list of manuscripts owned by Petrarch and still in existence (with useful bibliography). For other books once owned by Petrarch but now lost (e.g., his manuscript of Pomponius Mela) one must still consult de Nolhac 1907, Sabbadini 1905–1914, and Billanovich 1947. For samples of Petrarch's handwriting see especially de la Mare 1973. 1–16.

3 For the interesting problems of dating *Fam.* 3.1 see Billanovich 1947.50–51. It looks as though the letter is one of Petrarch's "fictional" ones, composed or at least heavily revised in 1352.

4 Petrarch's manuscript has not survived, but it can be reconstructed (along with his marginal notes) from a fifteenth century manuscript which is its descendant and almost certainly a direct copy; see Gormley 1984.297–299 and 302–311, with references to Billanovich's earlier work.

5 Branca's characterization of Boccaccio's *De montibus* as "a catalogue, or rather an inventory, of cultural geography . . . conducted out of literary curiosity rather than in a spirit of exploration and discovery" (1976.110) seems needlessly negative in view of what Branca himself has to say about Boccaccio's keen interest in geography in the *Decameron* (1976.276–307). Until recently there was no modern edition of the *De montibus*, the best being that printed 1473 in Venice, according to Wilkins (1978b. 357). Now one may consult the annotated edition of Stocchi 1998.7–8:1817–2122. On all aspects of the work see Stocchi 1963.

6 Although Petrarch's influence on Silvestri's *De insulis* was largely indirect, it should be noted that Silvestri was a great admirer of Petrarch's work and was in direct contact with him. In c. 1385 or earlier Silvestri made a copy of Petrarch's *Itinerarium* (Mann 1974.364–366) and cites it five times in his *De insulis* (Pecararo 1954.278). For more on Silvestri's relationship with Petrarch see the introduction and bibliography of Jensen's edition of Silvestri's Latin poetry (1973.ix–xviii). Metrical epistle ix is addressed to Petrarch, urging him to publish the long-awaited *Af-*

rica. Silvestri also translated into Italian Petrarch's *Invective contra medicum*, which Ricci (1978) edits along with Petrarch's Latin text (see Wilkins 1961.114, 123–124, and 157 on the origin and evolution of this work). For more on Silvestri's life and literary activity see Ricci 1950.13–24.

7 The classificatiion of *mappaemundi* and the nomenclature may vary from scholar to scholar; see Destombes 1964.8–23 and Woodward 1987.1:294–299, who outlines the current state of affairs. The fourth kind of *mappamundi* is that proposed by Woodward, who calls it the Transitional Type.

8 The image of the Tree of Virtue (and of Vice) became so popular that it found its way into the vernacular literatures of the day; see for example Jackson 1985.218–225.

9 Rutilius Claudius Namatianus, a Gallic provincial most likely from Toulouse, held important offices in Rome under Honorius. In 416 or 417 he decided to return home by the sea route to look after his estates, which were being threatened by barbarians. Upon arrival he began a poem in elegiac couplets describing his return *(De reditu suo)*, but the poem breaks off just at the point when Rutilius has reached Luna, some sixty-five lines into book 2. If Rutilius ever finished the poem, some five or six hundred verses may have been lost. A Latin text with English translation may be found in Duff 1935.753–829, text and French translation in Vesseroux 1961, and a German translation with Latin text and full commentary in Doblhofer 1972.

10 The 153 extant manuscripts of Solinus's work are eloquent witnesses of its popularity during the Middle Ages. It was a handy source for many of the "marvelous facts" that made their way into the encyclopedias and *mappaemundi* of the day. For discussions of Solinus see Beazley 1897.1:248–273 and Stahl 1962.136–141. Those wishing to consult a translation may do so in the facsimile edition of Golding 1587, the only English version available.

11 Between 1335 and 1341, after suffering some kind of emotional or mental collapse, Opicinus produced two collections of some rather fantastic drawings, maps, and notes. The first collection (Cod. Vat. Pal. 1993), discovered in 1927, was edited with a commentary by Salomon 1936. The second collection (Cod. Vat. lat. 6435) was discovered and briefly described by Almagià 1944.1:95–98 and pl. 48 (one of Opicinus's maps as described). More on Opicinus and both collections may be found in Salomon 1953 and Tozzi 1990 and 1992.

12 Niccolò Perotti translated Books I–V of Polybius's Greek into Latin for Pope Nicholas V in 1452–1453. The translation was first published in 1473 and was reprinted before the end of the century. See Momigliano 1974.347–372. Aleotti was probably using Perotti's translation.

[13] Petrarch himself frequently traveled by boat on the Po, as the numerous references to the river in his *Familiares* and *Seniles* indicate. Indeed one of his most successful sonnets (Po, ben puo' tu portartene la scorza, *Canz.* 180) appears to have been composed while sailing on the Po from Parma to Verona, perhaps in 1345 (for brief analysis see Foster 1984.129–130). Probably in the fall of 1349 (Wilkins 1961.85), Petrarch again visited Ferrara. On this occasion Petrarch fell in love with a beautiful Ferrarese woman and wrote at least one lyric about his new love (one of the *rime disperse* in *Rime* 605) and possibly several others (another of the *rime disperse* in *Rime* 596 and *Canz.* 270 and 271). On these poems see Hainsworth 1988.24 and Barber 1991.xliii–xliv. On these visits, Petrarch undoubtedly traveled by boat on the Ficarolo branch.

[14] When Petrarch had visited Rome in 1341 for his coronation, he had been given an archeological tour by the Dominican Giovanni Colonna, who was himself an aspiring historian and shared Petrarch's interest in Livy. Some months later he wrote Colonna a letter in which he recalled in detail the pleasure of that tour, which included visits to some eighty sites, both ancient Roman and early Christian (*Fam.* 6.2; some date this letter to 1337). There are numerous examples of misidentification of sites, which Petrarch was able to correct later on. For example, Colonna told him that the Pantheon was the temple of Cybele. Thanks to his careful reading of Suetonius (*Aug.* 97.1), Petrarch is able to correct this mistake in the *De remediis* 1.118. Incidentally Petrarch was an enthusiastic reader of Suetonius at a time when he was not well known in Italy; eventually he acquired three copies of the *Lives of the Caesars* (Billanovich 1960.28–58).

[15] There has been much debate on the dating of this letter. See Wilkins 1958.142–146, where the various arguments are summarized. Wilkins himself believes that the letter was written in 1357.

[16] For a succinct account of the transmission of Greek and Arabic technical and philosophical learning into medieval Europe, primarily in the twelfth and thirteenth centuries, see Lindberg 1978.52–90. A large number of texts were turned into Latin during this period, but a considerable number were translated into the various vernaculars, including Hebrew.

[17] The contents of Varro's *Disciplines* can be somewhat reconstructed from paraphrases in later authors such as Pliny, Aulus Gellius, Cassiodorus, and Martianus Capella. For recent discussions see Simon 1966.88–101, Stahl 1971.44–53, and Rawson 1985.158–164. The section on geometry can be reconstructed in rather more detail than many of the other sections of the *Disciplines*. This could be an indication that this section was pressed into service as a school text. There always remains the

possibility that Varro wrote a separate treatise called the *De mensuris orbis terrae*, and that it was this lost work that Petrarch had owned.

18 For summary accounts of these and other notable medieval travelers see the relevant chapters in Newton 1926, Labarge 1982, Dunn 1986, Phillips 1988, Ohler 1989.

19 The letters Petrarch wrote to Charles sound very much like those Dante wrote in 1310–1312 to Charles's grandfather Henry VII (*Epistolae* 5, 6, and 7; text and translation in Toynbee 1920) to encourage the Emperor to come to Italy and restore it to its former glory (see Ferrante 1984 and Armour 1989).

20 Pipino's pilgrim text is a minor production compared with his *Chronicle* and especially with his Latin translation of Marco Polo's *Divisament dou Monde*. For more on Pipino's career see Manzoni 1894 and for more on his connection with Marco Polo's book see Critchley 1992.137–157. Pipino thought that Marco's book would be useful to missionaries to the East.

21 We are used to thinking of Boethius's *De consolatione Philosophiae* as readily available and well known to anyone with even a bit of university education, but Dante says in his *Convivio* (2.12.2 in Vasoli 1988) that it is a book "not known to many" (quello non conosciuto da moltis libro). This is another reason for thinking that Niccolò had the quote from Boethius from a *florilegium*.

22 This version of the myth is little known to modern students of Greek myth, but it was the most popular one in the Renaissance. Antoine Watteau's *Pilgrimage to the Island of Cythera* (1717; in the Louvre) is based on this version, as well as another similar painting of 1718 now in Berlin.

23 Petrarch, perhaps the best-read man of his time, of course knew the works of Dictys and Dares, and he made use of them, but sparingly and reluctantly (see de Nolhac 1907.2:43, 177, and 240). In a partial revision of the third part of his *Triumphus fame*, undertaken in 1371 and only discovered in recent times (see *Rime*, 571–578), we find the fullest statement of his views on Dictys and Dares: they often contradict one another (naturally, the one being Greek and the other Trojan) and there is no one to decide who is telling the truth (Dare e Dite / fra lor discordi e non è chi 'l ver cribri, 577.107–108). In cases where they disagree, and independent witnesses are lacking, their work is of no value to someone looking for the truth (le certe notizie son fallite, 577.111). Petrarch had high standards, but he did not suspect that their works were fictions.

24 Ludolf von Suchem [Südheim], on pilgrimage from 1336–1341, wrote his account of it around 1350. During the first part of his journeys he spent some time in the Morea (Peloponnese). He was close to

Athens, but did not actually visit there and has nothing believable to say about the place. See Setton 1948.224–225 and Paton 1951.26–30.

25 Of Luchino's reference to the rape of Helen in connection with Cythera Ghinassi's note says (154), "non so onde abbia tolto l'autore che il ratto d'Elena avvenisse a Citera." Hyde (1993 c.154) says, "By now it would seem that travelers were being told it was from Kithera that Paris had abducted Helen," as if the story were something that mischievous sailors had recently cooked up. We note that Petrarch does not so much as mention the island though it lay directly on Mandelli's route. If he had believed that the rape of Helen had taken place there, he surely would have mentioned it. Dares's *De excidio Troiae Historia* (10) is the earliest source for the story; Dictys (1.3), in contrary fashion, keeps the rape at Sparta. Since Dictys's version could be corroborated from other sources, Petrarch would have accepted his account in this case.

26 Item 170 in the inventory says, "Libro uno chiamado Pomponio in vulgare," followed by a description of the book's appearance. Bolgar (1954.530–531) does not record any vernacular translation of Mela until the sixteenth century.

27 In this connection, we should recall that the most popular travel book in the Middle Ages and the Renaissance, Sir John Mandeville's *Travels*, written c.1356–1366, is also the most fraudulent, being a cento of marvelous tales and accurate information drawn from a wide variety of authors such as Vincent of Beauvais and Jacques de Vitry: see Deluz 1987.205–220 and Phillips 1988.206–211. Over 300 manuscripts survive in all the major European languages; the French and English texts with notes on the sources may be consulted in Warner 1889. The definitive English edition is that of Seymour 1967. The book was taken quite seriously by Christopher Columbus, Sir Thomas More, Sir Walter Raleigh, and many other worthies well into the nineteenth century. The book however should probably not be viewed as a "hoax," but a very skillful work of fiction, heralding many more (Howard 1980.52–76). The identity of the author, a scholar like Petrarch, remains a topic of debate.

NOTES ON THE LATIN TEXT

The textual history of the *Itinerarium* can only be written when the census of Petrarchan manuscripts is completed. In the introduction to his recent edition, Lo Monaco speaks of some 40 manuscripts of the work known to him, but remarks that more are likely to be discovered in large miscellaneous collections that have been poorly catalogued, if at all. Undoubtedly, only a few of this number will prove to be of any great authority when the definitive text is established; some of the least valuable of those now known to us will turn out to have played very important roles in the text's history, for fate has on occasion singled out representatives of very humble branches of the manuscript family for special service in the text's transmission and reception.

The *Itinerarium* did not find a place in Johann Amerbach's limited collection of Petrarch's Latin works (Basel 1496), but it did appear in the first volume of the collected works published by Andrea Torresano da Asola, father-in-law of Aldo Manuzio the Elder (*Librorum Francisci Petrarche impressorum annotatio*, 3 vols., Venice 1501; pages unnumbered). The title is given in the table of contents simply as *Itinerarium*. The text of this edition shows most of the distinctive features of the important Cremona Manuscript, to be described below, along with numerous errors of its own and unmistakable signs of contamination or horizontal transmission. The text of the 1501 edition is closely related to that found in the only Latin manuscript of the work to make its way to the United States, Manuscript Marston 17 in the Beinecke Library of Yale University (= Y), written in 1434 and bound later with Boccaccio's *De Montibus* (described by Dutschke 1986.174–176). Y has "Imeniosius est maris," for example, for the correct "In medio sinus est maris" of lines 135–136 of this edition, while the 1501 edition has "immeniosius est maris." Both have the rather spectacular *saut du même au même* at lines 601–603: the scribe's eye wandered from *rubi* (601) to *rubri* (603) causing him to drop nearly three lines from the text. These and numerous other conjunctive errors show that a close relative of Y supplied the text of the 1501 edition, reprinted in 1503 with only a few minor changes.

The *Opera omnia* edition published in Basel in 1554 prints the *Itinerarium* in vol. 1 at 618–626. It recognizes the epistolary nature of the work, which the 1501 edition failed to do, by beginning "Franciscus Petrarca amico suo, s." and by printing the first 61 lines, which are directed narrowly at the unnamed addressee, in small print. The rest of the text, the itinerary proper, is presented in larger print and is introduced by an elaborate made-up title: *Francisci Petrarchae v. c.* Itinerarium Syriacum, *in quo, quidquid per Europam vel Asiam peregrinis Hierosolymitanis memorabile occurrit, diligentissime describitur.* The text is based, unfortunately, on the 1501 edition. It still has the gaping lacuna at 601–603, which is enough to proclaim its lineage, but it has made an attempt to do something with the nonsensical "Immeniosius est maris" by writing "Imminens mare," which improves nothing, but the words are at least Latin. Although weighed down by more than enough inherited sins, it manages to commit a great sin of its own by losing the last twelve lines of the text, ending with "O fortune fides, o rerum finis humanarum" (lines 664–665).

Since this edition, reprinted in 1581, became the most widely known version of Petrarch's collected works, it gave the world an amazingly corrupt text and the spurious title by which the work is still known today — *Itinerarium Syriacum.* One of the few things to be said in its favor, the edition preserved the epistolary form. The fact that the work is embodied in the form of a letter has important stylistic consequences, as Lo Monaco rightly stresses (1993.366–367).

Giacomo Lumbroso (1888.390–403; repr. 1889.16–49) provided the first modern edition, a great improvement on the previous ones, but far from satisfactory. He composed the text from three manuscripts in Rome, whose relationship to the original and to one another was quite unclear to him. No one manuscript was clearly superior to the other two and all of them in serious error in various different places. Therefore, he made the best text he could, with only his linguistic and literary ability to guide him when all the divergent readings were grammatically acceptable. This eclectic version suffered also because of its classicizing orthography and eccentric punctuation, eccentric by modern standards at any rate. Lumbroso resorted to emendation several times, disastrously on one occasion (*habueris* for *habens* at line 412), but two of his conjectures deserve serious consideration.

In 1904, Francesco Novati published notice of a manuscript of the *Itinerarium* in Cremona (BB 1.2.5 in the Biblioteca Statale), whose *explicit* establishes it as a direct descendant of the copy which Petrarch gave to Giovanni on 4 April 1358: *Explicit Itinerarium Francisci Petrarce laureati extractum ab originali manu sua scripto, in cuius fine sic notatum erat: Datum domino Iohanni de Mandello seu nuncio eius iiii Aprilis 1358*. Copied at the end of the fourteenth century according to Novati, the manuscript (= C) belonged in the sixteenth century to Gerolamo, a member of the distinguished Mandelli family. Although this manuscript was clearly the most important witness to the text as it was when it first left Petrarch's hand, its contents were not reported for another 70 years.

Michele Feo (1974.179–183) finally provided a rather extensive description of the manuscript and partially collated its readings with Lumbroso's text and some Florentine manuscripts, which he does not identify. His work provided a solid basis for an authentic text for the first time. Although C had its own errors, Feo was able to restore a number of correct readings, in several places simply by repunctuating. In addition, Feo noted that Lumbroso's text showed several expansions or additions absent from C and two abbreviations or deletions, as follows:

1. After *exhorreo* in line 46, Lumbroso's manuscripts have: *quem non sic iunior horruissem; horrui autem semper, sed in dies magis*. In line 47, *vel* is added in consequence of the addition in line 46 and presumably contemporaneous with it.
2. After *restat* in line 153, Lumbroso's manuscripts have the sentence: *Progrediamur ad reliqua*.
3. After *immanitate* in line 263, Lumbroso's manuscripts have: *ut quidam putant; res enim ambigua est valde.*
4. After *nulla* in line 293, Lumbroso has the phrase "que noverim."

5. In line 529, Lumbroso has "ubi cecos illuminavit," where C has the expanded "ubi egros curavit, cecos illuminavit."
6. In line 530, Lumbroso has "mortuos suscitavit," which is expanded in C to "mortuos suscitavit, quatriduanos iam fetentes verbo vivos eruit e sepulcro."

Feo accepted these additions and deletions as authorial revisions and argued that they were made, in one case (#3) at least, in the late 1360s, after Petrarch had gained access to Homer's *Odyssey* in the Latin translation of Leontius Pilatus. Even if Feo is right about the dating of this one addition (see commentary to lines 258–263), it cannot be assumed that all revisions were made at this same time. Since we know that Petrarch's admirers were constantly asking permission to make copies of his various works, it is likely that Petrarch revised the *Itinerarium* in minor ways, on an irregular basis, whenever he had to dig it out of his files for some visitor to copy or read.

The case for progressive revision is best demonstrated by the example of the sentence "Progrediamur ad reliqua," a short transitional expression of no great importance, but the sort of thing a tinkering author might insert (line 153). The sentence is not in C, but is found in many manuscripts, such as the ones on which Lumbroso based his edition, and is accepted by Feo as a revision. The same sentence is in Y and the *Opera omnia* editions of 1501 (1503) and 1554 (1581), but there are none of the other additions or deletions accepted as authorial revisions. It appears then that "Progrediamur ad reliqua" was the first of the minor changes made by Petrarch, with the others to follow at irregular intervals. Petrarch rarely thought of anything he had written as finished, as the multiple forms of the *Canzoniere* and *Bucolicum carmen* illustrate. When he read in his Pliny (*Nat.* 35.80) that the Greek painter Protogenes was criticized because he was forever retouching his portraits, Petrarch wrote a note to himself in the margin to take heed (*Attende, Francisce, dum scribis,* de Nolhac 1907.2:74): too much revision can be counterproductive.

In 1990, Francisco Lo Monaco published his new edition, with translation and commentary. As the basis of the text, he used the Cremona Manuscript (as improved by Feo) and added the testimony of an equally important manuscript in Florence, Pluteo xxvi 9, 100r–111v in the Biblioteca Mediceo Laurenziana. The manuscript (designated T by Lo Monaco) is an autograph of Tedaldo della Casa, who made his copy from a text he found among Petrarch's papers in Padua, where the poet had moved much of his library in 1372 for safekeeping. Probably about four years after Petrarch's death in July of 1374, Tedaldo set out from Florence for Padua with the intention of making copies of as many of Petrarch's works as he could find. Among the copies made by him at this time, is an important manuscript of the *Secretum*, with its controversial marginal notes, one of the *Rerum memorandarum libri*, and one of the *Invective contra medicum*. The *explicit* of this last work, dated 6 October 1378, says that the copy "was written in haste and without much correction" (festinanter scriptus nec multum correctus, Ricci 1978.13). Tedaldo's scribal skills, described by Billanovich in his edition of *Rerum memor. libri* (1943.xi–xvi; esp. xiv n. 2), were of a high order, but for reasons Tedaldo does not explain, he was on this occasion forced to work long hours in less than ideal circumstances. The copy he made of the *Itinerarium* suffered from these same constraints.

Based as it is on C, a copy of Petrarch's autograph given to Mandelli, and on T, a hastily made copy of the exemplar found in Petrarch's library at the end of his life, Lo Monoco's edition presents a secure text wherever C and T agree. Both C and T have a number of singular errors, however, and T shows the additions and deletions accepted by Feo and Lo Monaco as authorial revisions, as described above. Perhaps T is a copy of the draft, with changes made subsequently at various times, of the version which Petrarch handed over to Mandelli in 1358 and was later recopied (= C). On the other hand, it may be that original draft was recopied several times at different stages of revision. Confronted with more than one version of the *Itinerarium*, Tedaldo would have selected one manuscript as his exemplar and used any others to spot-check unclear readings, as time permitted.

Given Tedaldo's haste in copying the *Itinerarium* and the uncertainty as to whether his exemplar in fact represented Petrarch's final wishes regarding the text, Lo Monaco is right to describe his edition as provisional. As a sign of his caution, he refers to the title of the work given in T (*Itinerarium Francisci Petrarchae de Ianua usque Ierusalem et Alexandriam*) as problematic and prefers to use the title as given by C: *Itinerarium ad sepulcrum Domini nostri Ihesu Cristi*. The title given in C may not be the one Petrarch decided upon eventually, but until all the manuscripts are accounted for, it has the merit of being indisputably Petrarchan and it catches the primary and essential motivation of all pilgrimages to the Holy Land, namely to visit Christ's tomb above all else. The title adopted in this edition follows Lo Monaco's conservative example.

In 1993, Alfonso Paolella published a critical edition of six Italian translations of the *Itinerarium*, all of them but one made in the fifteenth century. Five are written in the south Italian *koine* of the period, one of which now resides in the Pierpont Morgan Library in New York City (Manuscript 973; described by Dutschke 1986.233–237). The sixth and most trustworthy, Manuscript 948 in the Biblioteca de Catalunya of Barcelona (here designated Bv), was written after 1459. According to Paolella, Bv is a copy of an original Tuscan translation (= O), now lost, either of Vat. Lat. 3357 itself or a copy of it. The five manuscripts in the southern or Neapolitan dialect show many signs of being related to one another and to Bv and to Vat. Lat. 3357 (see Paolella 1993. L–LIII), though the lines of descent are far from clear.

The history of Vat. Lat. 3357, composed of Petrarch's *De vita solitaria* and the *Itinerarium*, is very complex and interesting (see Ullman 1973.135–175). Once bound in the fourteenth century with a number of other manuscripts still in Florence, the Vatican Manuscript was separated from the rest around 1500 and subsequently came into the possession of Bernardo Bembo, who "discovered" that Petrarch himself had copied the manuscript. This unfounded claim was passed on to posterity by Fulvio Orsini who acquired the manuscript from Bernardo's son Pietro (see description of Vattasso 1908.29–30). Lumbroso, who uses Vat. lat. 3357 for his edition of the *Itinerarium*, easily saw through Bembo's claim, citing in his Introduction the many gross errors in the text.

Such are the correspondences between Vat. lat. 3357 and the vernacular translations, especially Bv, that Paolella prints the Latin and Italian text of Bv facing one another. It is unlikely, however, that the original translator was looking at the text of Vat. lat. 3357. For example, the correct reading at line 106 is "cotem illam alteram," the reading which Vat. lat. 3357 gives. But the Bv translator produced from the Latin he saw "quella altera città." Clearly, he was looking at a Latin text which read "civitatem illam alteram," as many manuscripts in fact do. The five Neapolitan translations likewise have "quell' altra cità." Why none of the vernacular translations show any sign of "cotem" (whetstone) is a problem Paolella does not address. The original translator must have been looking at a copy of Vat. lat. 3357 which had introduced readings from another source. Nevertheless, it remains true that the six vernacular translations edited by Paolella are closely related to Vat. lat. 3357.

Thus, despite their manifest unworthiness, the Yale Manuscript and Vat. lat. 3357 must be viewed as important representatives of the manuscript family. These manuscripts, or copies of them, have largely dictated how Petrarch's work has been received by subsequent ages. Until Lumbroso's edition of about a century ago, the *Itinerarium* had to be read in printed editions which were lacunose and filled with the sort of egregious errors illustrated by Y. The vernacular translations, unedited and unprinted until quite recently, reflected most of the weaknesses of Vat. lat. 3357 and added many mistakes of their own.

For this edition, the early printed editions of 1501 (1503) and 1554 (1581) have been examined, and Lumbroso's text of 1889 has been compared with Lo Monaco's of 1990. In addition to the Yale Manuscript, three other manuscripts have been collated. The first, selected more or less at random from the 22 known to this editor, is Cod. poet. et phil. fol. 2, 35 (103r–110r) in the Württembergische Landesbibliotek in Stuttgart (= S; description in Sottili 1978. 356–358). Of German provenance and written in 1456–1459 in a well-practiced bastarda hand, S provides an interesting comparison with Y. They both agree with C, the representative of the earliest version of the text, insofar as they do not show most of the signs of authorial revision. Both Y and S, however, have the sentence "Progrediamur ad reliqua" at line 155. Y shows no other sign of revision, but S shows the abbreviated versions of lines 529 and 530 described above. Since S shows no other revisions, the manuscript may show Petrarch's text in the second stage of revision. S is certainly not closely related to Y, because it has the correct "In medio sinus est maris," where Y has "Imeniosius est maris," and it does not show Y's lacuna at lines 601–603 (rubo . . . rubri). On the other hand, S has its own large lacuna (*Quamvis* . . . through *Damascus*, lines 498–501) and several shorter ones, where Y's text is whole, if not always sound.

The other two manuscripts were selected for examination because both were associated with men of considerable literary accomplishments of their own and because both were great admirers of Petrarch's poetry and scholarship. The first, Manuscript Bodley 588, is an autograph of Domenico Silvestri (c. 1335–after 1411). Holder of numerous offices in the service of Florence, Domenico was a good friend of Boccaccio and Salutati, and he was well enough acquainted with Petrarch to correspond with him. In this spare time he wrote Latin poetry (eclogues and metrical epistles) and labored for many years on his *De insulis*, intended by him as a supplement to Boccaccio's *De montibus*. Sometime after 1359, he translated Petrarch's *Invective contra medicum* into Italian (ed. by Ricci 1978).

According to Mann's description (1974. 364–366), the manuscript was written about 1400. Domenico, however, was already working on his *De insulis* in 1385 (Pecararo 1954. 22). Since he quotes the *Itinerarium* at widely scattered places throughout (pp. 67.2, 82.6, 112.25, 148.5, and 187.4 in Pecararo's edition), a significantly earlier date for his copy of the *Itinerarium* seems likely.

Written in a rather sloppy gothic hand, Domenico's copy shows all the authorial revisions described above. Tedaldo della Casa's copy was probably in Florence when Domenico made his copy (c. 1385), but numerous divergent readings make it certain that T was not his exemplar. A comparison of Domenico's copy with Vat. lat. 3357 presents a somewhat confused picture. In the matter of lacunae, Domenico's copy matches those in Vat. lat. 3357, of which there are some eleven instances, almost but not quite. In line 12, Vat. lat. 3357 omits the parenthetical "fateor," but it is there in Domenico's copy. The most extensive lacuna in Vat. lat. 3357 is that of "et quoniam ita vis, his etiam comitabor scriptis" at lines 54–55; the same clause is missing from Domenico's copy.

Apart from lacunae, there are numerous conjunctive errors. For the correct *tibi . . . licebit* at lines 60-63, both copies have the ungrammatical *tu . . . licebit*, but just a few lines earlier at line 58, Domenico has the correct "in dies" where Vat. lat. 3357 has "in die." On the other hand, Vat. lat. 3357 has the correct "cotem," whereas Domenico has "civitatem." But in this case, someone, probably not Domenico by the look of the hand, has written "cotem" in the margin. At line 86, both manuscripts have "multum" for the correct "multis." Again, Domenico's copy has been corrected in the margin, apparently not by Domenico. At line 454, Vat. lat. 3357 has the blatantly ungrammatical "Asiam Minorem," but Domenico writes the correct "Asia Minor." One of the worst mistakes in Vat. lat. 3357 is at line 288, where the text reads "filoris alterius . . . forsam" for the correct "furoris alterius . . . fossam." Domenico nearly duplicates this mistake, with *forsan* replacing *forsam*. Someone has supplied the correct "furoris" in the margin but realizes that the text still falls short of intelligibility and adds a crux in the margin to signify his despair. More than any other, it is this error, absent from all the manuscripts and printed editions examined here, that links Domenico's copy and Vat. lat. 3357. There is a close family relationship between the two, but it is also clear they stand removed from one another by at least one intermediary.

The last manuscript appears to be an autograph of Jacopo Sannazzaro (1451–1530), also known as Actius Syncerus. He was born in Naples and spent most of his life there in the service of the House of Aragon and in his literary and scholarly pursuits. In Latin, he wrote elegies, epigrams, eclogues, and a religious poem on the birth of Christ (*De partu Virginis*). In Italian, he wrote Petrarchan sonnets and *canzoni,* and an influential prosimetric romance called *Arcadia* between 1480–1485. Sannazzaro's copy of the *Itinerarium* is now in Vienna in the Österreichische Nationalbibliotek (Cod. Vind. Pal. 9477). The manuscript (here designated V) is described in *Tabulae codicum manu scriptorum . . .* (Vienna 1873) as a *repertorium* or commonplace book similar to the *zibaldoni* of Boccaccio. Besides the *Itinerarium,* the manuscript contains two fairly substantial works on geography which appear to be composed by Sannazzaro himself: *Epitome geographica* (53r–70v) and *Adversaria antiquitatum romanarum et geographica praesertim de Latio et Italia* (71r–94). The *Itinerarium,* following after a few blank pages at 99v–110v, is written in a confident humanistic hand, with somewhat more care and neatness than the *Adversaria* (Journal) which precedes it. The text shows almost all of the revisions accepted by Feo and Lo Monaco as authorial, but curiously it omits the *vel* before *tangere* at line 47. A noteworthy characteristic of the manuscript is the numerous word transpositions throughout, such as *quidem illa* for *illa quidem, se res* for *res se, consuetudo naturam* for *naturam consuetudo,* all within the first 40 lines of the text. Sometimes compound verbs are simple (*monstrari* for *demonstrari*); sometimes the prefix of compound verbs varies (*complecti* for *amplecti*); and sometimes there is the substitution of a synonym or near-synonym (e.g., *navium* for *classium; legerim* for *viderim*). More serious are the lacunae, only some of which can be paralleled in the manuscripts or printed editions examined here. Omitted are: *fugimus,* line 26; *cura est,* line 79; *prius,* line 97; *videas,* line 119; *Inde Rapallam,* line 132; *nunc nichil preter nudum nomen ac ruinas,* lines 206-207; *belli quoque temporibus inviolatum, si vera populi vox est,* line 319; and *numero ac decore memorabiles. Militem ad militie,* a good example of a *saut du mēme au mēme* (from *militie,* line 339, to *militie,* line 340). There are a half dozen other similar lapses, some of them relatively innocuous, but some of them impairing the sense to a serious degree, as is the case with the lacuna at line 339. V is a frustrating manuscript because high initial expectations inspired by its provenance are often disappointed. Sannazzaro's copy, however, cannot be better than his exemplar, unless he was able to consult other manuscripts or improve it by conjecture. Nevertheless, V preserves what appears to be the original reading on several occasions where C and T do not.

The text presented here preserves the epistolary form of the original. It also preserves the formal divisions of the original as they are found in C and in T, in nearly identical form, for they must be presumed to be those of the author himself. The proemium was introduced by an ornate initial colored blue and was set off from what follows by a blank line. The rest, the itinerary proper, was divided into sense units by paragraph signs alternately colored blue and red, 21 in C and 20 in T. Although Lo Monaco has chosen to divide and number the sections to suit his convenience, it seemed worthwhile in this edition to display the text as Petrarch arranged it.

The manuscripts reviewed for this edition do not have anything like the authority of C or T, but even so, they may point the way to the original when these two falter. Until the history of the manuscript tradition is unraveled completely, the text of the *Itinerarium* will remain a bit unsettled at its margins, so to speak, but a high level of confidence in its essential soundness is entirely justified.

The readings adopted for this edition are listed first after its line number. The reading of Lo Monaco's edition, founded as this one is on C and T, is shown for comparison, along with the number of the text division adopted by him in parentheses. Eight presumed typographical errors are noted as well. The four additional manuscripts consulted for this edition are listed in their probable chronological order, with the sigla assigned to them and to Lumbroso's edition as follows:

Manuscripts

B=Bodley 558; copied by Domenico Silvestri c. 1385. In the above discussion, it has been assumed that B post-dates Vat. lat. 3357, though that has not been proved.

Y=Marston 17 at Yale; copied in 1434. What is true of Y is generally speaking true of the early printed editions.

S=Cod. poet. et phil. 2.35 in Stuttgart; dated to 1456–59 by its watermarkings.
V=Codex Vindobonesis Palatinus 9477 in Vienna; copied by Sannazzaro c. 1475–80?

Printed Editions

L=Lumbroso (1889).

This Edition	**Lo Monaco**
42 metum] manuscripts, L	metuum (5); sic
50 metum] manuscripts, L	metuum (6); sic
112 commeatuum] manuscripts, L *Commeatum* is an acceptable form of the genitive plural only in verse.	commeatum (15)
116–117 (ne) . . . discesseris]	non . . . discesseris (16)

Ne is the usual negative with the perfect subjunctive expressing negative command (cf. the construction in line 330: *ne . . . omiseris*). Negatives other than *ne* are seen in this construction (nemo, nihil, nullus, numquam, nec), but not the simple negative *non*. If *non* is preserved (the reading of all manuscripts and early editions), then the verb would naturally be felt as a future (the perfect for the simple future, as often in the Latin of this period) in an imperatival sense (you shall not leave). But this form of the imperative is formal and solemn, inappropriate for the epistolary style of the *Itinerarium*.

162 sit] the reading of B, Y, S, V	fuit (20)

B has *fuit* in the text, but *sit* is written in the margin. The subjunctive is the ordinary mood after *licet*, in the primary sequence in Classical Latin (present or perfect). In the early Empire, *licet* begins to be followed by subjunctives in the secondary sequence (imperfect or pluperfect), as in line 513 (licet magna convivantibus viderentur), and to acquire all the characteristics of an adversative conjunction (= although). Here, however, *licet* is best taken as an independent verb in the present tense and so is followed by the present subjunctive.

189 Meliora] C, V Meloria (23)

Here the correct form of the name (Meloria) is incorrect, because Petrarch is telling Mandelli what the islet is commonly (and incorrectly) called (cf. Petrarch's remarks on Comum and Cumum). On portolan charts and in *portolani* the tiny island is called variously Meriora, Menora, Minora, Meloro, Melloro, and Meliora (Kretschmer 1909.609). This last is the reading of V; it is also the reading of C, but Feo rejects it as a mistake (1974. 181).

204 Argentari (us)] Argentarie (25)

The adjectival form of the word is conjecturally restored. Petrarch uses this proper form in *De vita solitaria,* 2.6 (Argentarii montis habitatore), a work written in rough draft 12 years before the *Itinerarium.* The form *Argentarie* would be the genitive of a noun *Argentaria.* This proper noun is found among a few late authors (Ammianus Marcellinus, Orosius, and Aurelius Victor), but it refers to a place in NE France (Alsace).

243 (ruine)]L arene (28)

Lumbroso writes *ruine,* which he marks with an asterisk. Whether this reading is his conjecture or a reading of one of his manuscripts, he does not say. In noting that C has *arene,* Feo declares that he is uncertain which is the correct reading (qui resto incerto nella scelta, 1974.182). But Lumbroso's reading is preferable, whether it is a manuscript reading or a conjecture. It makes no sense for Petrarch to say that there are two or three large sand dunes (arene) *still* (adhuc) to be seen at Formia. Are we to imagine that Petrarch is keeping track of the condition of the sand dunes at Formia?

256 fallaris] V falleris (30)

The subjunctive form of the verb is needed in the negative purpose clause introduced by *ne*. The future *falleris* is grammatically indefensible. Lumbroso's *fallereris* (the reading of Y and early printed editions) is at least in the subjunctive mood, but in the wrong sequence of tenses, since *dixerim* is a prospective subjunctive and requires the primary sequence after it.

291 fodiend (am)]L fodiendas (34)

Lumbroso's conjecture is surely correct. Feo reports *fodiendas* as the reading of C, and Lo Monaco prints the same thing, presumably also the reading of T, but the other manuscripts examined here have *fodiendos*, making the gerundive modify *montes*. Feo approves of *fodiendas*, saying that it refers to *Neronie piscine*. But this phrase is not nominative plural; it is genitive singular, dependent on *exordia*. If the gerundive is *fodiendos*, then it would indeed modify *montes*. But the phrase *per tot montes* is only one of seven adverbial phrases that need a verb to depend on. That verb must be *fodiendam*, which must modify *fossam* (Nero determined that a canal should be dug, etc.).

297 me] B, S, V omitted

It is easy to see how *me* could have dropped out before *me*moria.

300 Puteoli] V Puteole (36)

Petrarch certainly knew the correct form of the name. He writes the masculine plural accusative form (Puteolos) at *Metr.* 2.16.8 (*Rime* 764), written in December of 1343.

375 Lipar(a) Liparis (42)

Petrarch knew the Lipara form of the island's name from Mela (2. 120) and Pliny (*Nat.* 3. 93). He knew the Greek form *Lipare, -es, en* from Virgil (*A.* 8. 417) and the plural form *Liparae* (-arum) from Livy (5. 28.3), Florus (1. 18. 9 = 2. 2. 7.), and Valerius Maximus (6. 9. 11). He also knew from Pliny (*Nat.* 5. 93 and 31.17) that Liparis was the name of a small river in Cilicia with miraculous properties in its water and that, according to Theophrastus, there was a spring of the same name in Aethiopia with similar qualities. At 347 Petrarch would have written one of two forms, Lipara or Lipare, which in Petrarch's orthography could either be the Greek singular form or the Latin plural form, but not Liparis.

According to Festa, the manuscripts of the *Africa* at 8.312 have *Liparimque,* which implies a nominative case *Liparis,* evidently a latinization of the vernacular form of the name (Lipari). Festa keeps the manuscripts' reading, but Corradini (1874) emends to *Liparamque,* correctly in this editor's view. It seems unlikely that Petrarch would latinize a vernacular form whose proper Latin equivalent was well known to him, especially if he knew the latinized vernacular form would result in a Latin word which already had a meaning entirely different than the one he wanted (Liparis = a miraculous river in Cilicia or a miraculous spring in Aethiopia).

412 proterit] L, S poterit (45)

The reading of Lumbroso's text and of S is clearly superior to the weak *poterit*. All the early vernacular translators were looking at *proterit*, which they correctly translate *disfa* (Paolella 1993.33 and 93). The corruption is perhaps the result of misreading the abbreviated writing of *pro-* (*pterit*, with a curl through the p's downstroke), as may be seen in the Stuttgart Manuscript

438 Eubeam] manuscripts, L	Euberam (49); sic
488 consensus] manuscripts, L	consesus (53); sic
503 utrisque] manuscripts, L	utriusque (54); sic
505 demetur] V	demitur (55)

Latin idiom wants the future here. The verb *demetur* is preceded and followed by verbs in the future or future perfect tense. Only V preserves *demetur*.

522 preterea] manuscripts, L	pretera (57); sic
524 imperavit] manuscripts, L	impetravit (57)

The verb *impetrare* means "to get by entreaty"; the meaning requires *imperare* (command; which is how Lo Monaco translates). *Imperare* is the verb used at Matt. 8:26 and Luke 8:25, the texts to which Petrarch alludes.

552 virtutis] manuscripts, L	virtutum (60)

Since *virtus*, in combination with *species*, is close to being personified, the singular form of the noun is preferable. The Neapolitan vernacular translations have "la bellezza de la virtù" (Paolella 1993. 43).

561 incunabula] Y, S, V	inunabula (61); sic
579 discamus] manuscripts, L	dicamus (64)
614 necessitas] manuscripts, L	necessitate (71); sic
529 multis] V	multa (73)

Recorded research into the source of the Nile is known to many readers (multis legentibus), i.e., to any like

Petrarch who are interested in such things. Extensive reading in general (multa legentibus) is not a requirement. The present participle (legens) is common in post-Augustan prose for the noun *lector* (e.g., Quintilian, 3.1.2).

658 Pelle] L Pelles (77)

The classical spelling varies between *Pella, -ae* and *Pelle, -es*. Lumbroso correctly writes *Pelle,* V has *Pela*. *Pelles,* the Latin version of the Greek genitive, is grammatically unworkable.

Everything about the written word claimed Petrarch's interest. As he grew older, for example, and less able to see as he once did, he complained of the angular gothic style of lettering fashionable in his day and lobbied for a more rounded and legible style, showing the way by the example of his own writing (Ullman 1960.12–16). Although he did not write on punctuation as once supposed (Novati 1909.83–118), copies exist in his own hand which illustrate his meticulous attention to its proper use. The survival of two holographs of his *De sui ipsius et multorum ignorantia,* one now in Berlin (written in 1368) and the other in the Vatican Library (1370) enable Ricci (1943. 258–291) to analyze his use of punctuation in detail. Parkes has recently set Ricci's fundamental study in a broad historical context and presents his findings in a summarized and somewhat revised form (1993.81–83, with glossary at 301–307).

Within a sentence, Petrarch used four punctuation marks. The *punctus* or period he used to end a major division within a sentence, as well as to mark the end of the sentence. Within subordinate and main clauses, he used the *virgula* or slash to separate smaller sense units like prepositional phrases. He used two other marks, the *punctus elevatus* (rather like a period set below a raised reversed comma laid on its side) and a pointed *virgula* (a slash with a period in the middle), rather like parentheses, which did not make their appearance until the end of the fourteenth century.

The following sample of Petrarch's practice is taken from Parkes in a simplified form:

> quod / etsi rhetorici siue oratoris officium sit / apposite dicere / ad persuadendum / finis persuadere dictione / multis tamen indoctis contigisse / aiunt.
>
> which / although it be the function of a *rhetoricus* or orator / to speak appropriately / in order to persuade / the end to persuade by speaking / has nevertheless been achieved by many untaught people / they say.

The frequency of the pauses, to limit the discussion to that alone, argues that Petrarch wanted to show how his written words should be spoken with the proper emphasis. One may see similarly frequent pauses marked in a manuscript someone has prepared for delivery before a large audience. But for Petrarch, punctuation was much more than marking pauses. His use of the *punctus elevatus* and the pointed *virgula* (not indicated in the sample above) shows that he wanted to make clear to his readers subtle logical and semantic relationships between the various parts of his sentence (see Parkes's analysis). These last two marks, though in use by others, were used by Petrarch in a fairly experimental and idiosyncratic way. Question marks in several different forms had been in common use for centuries, but the exclamation mark (*punctus admirativus* or *exclamativus*) was not in use until the end of the century, his friend Coluccio Salutati being among the first to use this mark as well as parentheses.

To attempt to transpose Petrarch's style of punctuation into a modern printed edition, intended only for silent reading, would be distracting and could easily cause confusion. Lumbroso's punctuation of the text, eccentric by modern standards and misleading to read for that reason, is probably closer to Petrarch's actual practice than might at first be supposed. Accordingly, the text of this edition follows in general the modern minimalist practices established by various modern editors of Petrarch's Latin works such as Rossi and Bosco in their edition of the *Le Familiari*, as well as well as Ricci, Martellotti, Dotti and others.

There are seven passages in which punctuation assumes an especially important role in establishing the correct understanding of Petrarch's text, as follows:

1. At line 87, a comma is needed between *officit* and *iugis* to alert the reader to the correct meaning of the word *iugis*. Without hearing the word pronounced, one could take it either as the noun *iugum* (yoke, bond, ridge, mountain heights, etc.) in the ablative plural or the adjective *iugis* (continuous) in the nominative singular. Lo Monaco does not punctuate and understands *iugis* as the noun dependent upon *officit*, translating "la danneggia con imposizioni," whereas it is a predicate adjective modifying *materia*, emphatically placed outside the relative clause to which it belongs. The Tuscan translation (Bv) has it nearly right: *per la sua potenza contrasta e nuoce a se medesima: la qual cosa ha molto già nociuto alle cittade, donde continua* [= *iugis*, the adjective] *materia prorompe lite di cittadinesche discorde* (the Neapolitan version ignores *iugis*, Paolella 1993. 63 and 9). *Iugis* in the sense of "continuous" is also used at line 113 with the noun *labor* (*la continua fatica*, in all the vernacular translations). Lo Monaco (1990.45) misunderstands *iugis* again and translates "la durezza delle catene montuose."
2. Lines 135–136 is properly punctuated as: *In medio sinus est, maris oportunus fatigatis puppibus*. It is a mistake to take *sinus* as genitive dependent on *in medio*. *Sinus* is the subject and *in medio* is an adverbial predicate: the bay is "in the middle," i.e., of easy access (cf. a similar use in line 383: *In medio Pharus est*). The noun *sinus* is modified by the predicate adjective *oportunus* and the noun *maris* is a genitive dependent on the adjective *fatigatis* (see Introduction). Compare Lo Monaco's punctuation and translation: *In medio sinus est maris, oportunus fatigatis puppibus = Nel mezzo de golfo c'è uno specchio di mare addato alle navi che hanno viaggiato a longo*. This makes *sinus* genitive after *in medio*

and takes *maris* as dependent on a noun (specchio), which has no parallel in Latin.

This simple little sentence has caused problems from the beginning, as the early Italian translations show. In the Neapolitan version, we have the unintelligible: *è nel mezzo de uno oportuno golfo de mare affatigato da le navi;* the Tuscan version is virtually the same (Paolella 1993.13 and 66). A comma after *est* makes the structure clear (Petrarch would have used either a *punctus elevatus* or a pointed *virgula*). Recognition of the fact that *fatigatis* (like its synonym *fessus*) may govern the genitive case (maris) is also crucial to correct understanding. This, of course, is a poetical use, but epic poetry is what Petrarch has in mind at this juncture in his *Itinerarium*.

3. At lines 327–328, the correct punctuation is: *sedet ipsa Neapolis inter urbes litoreas, una quidem ex paucis*. Lo Monaco punctuates: . . . *Neapolis, inter urbes litoreas una quidem ex paucis,* which yields in his translation: *si stende Napoli stessa: una delle poche città costiere*. Failure to set off properly the phrase "una quidem ex paucis" results in a significant loss of meaning (see Commentary).
4. At line 421, the correct reading is: *Hydruntem attigeris, pedem habens obvium, Adriacum* . . . Lo Monaco has "Ydruntem attigeris pedem, habens obvium Adriacum." Editors have had serious problems with this passage, primarily because the technical meaning of the noun *pedem* has escaped their notice (see Commentary).
5. At lines 565–576 Petrarch writes one of the longest sentences in the *Itinerarium*. If properly punctuated, it is also one of the simplest. Urging Mandelli to go to Bethlehem, Petrarch says that he will contemplate (contemplabere) a long series of things. *Contemplabere* is the solitary main verb, governing a series of nouns in the accusative case, each noun except the first modified by one or two participles, which are, in turn, modified by various adverbial and prepositional phrases. Each noun / participle phrase is linked only by asyndeton (no conjunctions such as *et*, *ac*

[*atque*], or *-que*), but *et* (and *-que*) is used within some groups to link participles and noun phrases.

Since the sentence is quite long, it will not be reproduced here. If the reader will compare the punctuation of this edition with Lumbroso's or Lo Monaco's, little further comment would be necessary. Just three points may be mentioned here. A comma is needed after "Virginem matrem," otherwise the reader will think that Petrarch is asking Mandelli to contemplate the Virgin Mother as she lies in the manger, as indeed Lo Monaco evidently does, "contemplerai la vergine madre distesa nel presepe." But we have it on good authority (Luke 2:22) that it is the infant who lies in the manger (Invenietis infantem . . . positum in praesepio). The *et* after *contemplabere* (line 566) connects *iacentem* and *vagientem* (both participles modify *infantem*). Secondly, the *pastores* in the next line are both *attonitos* and *stupentes*. The *-que* of *stupentesque* links the two participles and not the two nouns *pastores* and *reges*. To make *stupentes* modify *reges* would be to destroy the careful rhetorical configurations, which link the Magi (reges) with King Herod (regem), in a fine array of balances and contrasts. Note the chiasmus *reges aliengenas* (Magi) . . . *indigenam regem* (Herod); the Magi are "flowing" with gifts, while Herod's sword will render the earth "wet with blood and tears." Finally, it should be noted that the last image of contemplation, St. Joseph (sanctum altorem), does not begin a new sentence. *Altorem*, like all the other preceding nouns, is the object of *contemplabere* and is modified like all the other nouns (except *Virginem matrem*) by a participle (querentem), which incidentally governs the infinitive *ire; latebras* is in apposition to *Egyptum* and not the object of *querentem*, as Lo Monaco would have it.

6. Aside from the textual problem (*discamus* vs. *dicamus*) at line 579, there is a punctuation problem, which is linked to a proper understanding of the participle *quesitum*. In Latin, *quesitum* is a past *passive* participle modifying the pronoun

eum and the punctuation should be: *discamus eum sequi et, ubi aliquando habitavit diu quesitum, tandem . . . invenire . . . .*

Diu modifies *quesitum,* not *habitavit* as Lo Monaco's translation has it (dimorò a lungo). Petrarch is making a case for the long journey to Egypt where the Holy Family once lived. Mandelli's difficult journey to salvation was prefigured by Christ's journey to Egypt. By actually retracing His steps, Mandelli will learn how to do the difficult things necessary for his salvation.

7. At lines 666–667, the correct punctuation is: . . . *docilis, facile, tantis ac talibus magistris, quantum sit fidendum disces.* Thus punctuated, the grammatical structure is clear: the phrase "tantis ac talibus magistris" is in the ablative absolute construction and is quite unconnected to the *quantum* which follows. *Quantum* introduces an indirect question dependent on *disces* ("You will learn how much faith one ought to put in prosperity"). Cf. Lo Monaco's punctuation: *docilis, facile tantis ac talibus magistris, quantum prosperis, sit fidendum disces.* This punctuation makes things very difficult, as Lo Monaco's translation shows: *c'è da sperare* (an attempt at dealing with *sit fidendum* which disregards the subjunctive) *che da maestri di tal valore e tanto favorevoli* (taking *prosperis* with *magistris*) *tu possa facilmente imperare.* It is necessary to punctuate before and after *facile* to make clear the adverb's connection with *disces* at some distance away.

Latin orthography, unlike that of English or French, closely followed the phonetic development of the language. Consequently, spelling evolved to reflect the way words were actually pronounced at any given time. By the medieval period, spelling had wandered considerably from the ancient forms. In addition, local pronunciation varied so greatly that spelling was far from regular. Early in the fifteenth century Poggio Bracciolini, calling medieval spelling of Latin a sin (nefas), set out to restore ancient orthography, but Petrarch was content to follow the practice of his time. For this edition, great effort has been made to follow the standards established by recent editors of Petrarch's Latin prose works such as Martellotti, Ricci, and Dotti. The orthography of this edition, though very similar to that of Lo Monaco's edition, will be found to differ in not a few places.

ITINERARIUM

FRANCISCI PETRARCE ITINERARIUM AD SEPULCRUM DOMINI NOSTRI IHESU CRISTI

Ad Iohannem de Mandello:

Raro admodum spei nostre rerum exitus respondent. Sepe premeditata destituunt, insperata contingunt; neque id mirum cuiquam esse debet, mirum potius si quid aliter accidat. Siquidem ratio principia rerum regit, eventum fortuna moderatur; nichil autem magis adversum rationi quam fortuna. Itaque sepe telam quam ingeniose illa quidem ordita erat, hec impetuose ante tempus abrumpit. Quod probatione utinam egeret neque his querelis adeo vita hominum plena esset ut iam fere nil aliud ingemiscat. Sed ut ad rem nostram veniam, decreveras quidem me volentem, fateor, optantemque vie comitem habere. Nam que usquam optabilior aut sanctior via est, que iustior peregrinatio quam ad sepulcrum ubi ille iacuit, cuius temporalis mors immortalitatem nobis et eternam vitam peperit? Sepulcrum ubi, si dici fas est, et victa mors simul et victrix vita sepulta est. O beatum iter et invidiosum Cristiano animo spectaculum. Hinc ego nunc nescio quibus peccatorum vectibus arceor uncisque detineor. Infans quidem, ut Flaccus ait, pudor loqui prohibet, sed imperiosa veritas fari iubet et ut paream cogit. Cum multe igitur me teneant cause, nulla potentior quam pelagi metus, non quod aut vite cupidior aut timidior mortis sim quam ceteri mortales aut terrestrem mortem maritime preferendam rear: neque enim in loco sed in animo est quod felices facit et miseros, et cum ubique moriendum sciam, ubi sit mori melius ignoro. Frustra bellum et maria vitamus, frustra labores fugimus perituroque parcimus corpusculo; in medias voluptuosorum latebras inque ipsos regum thalamos invisa mors penetrat, et sepe quam forte labor et exercitium distulissent, iners luxus anticipat. Semel utique moriendum est, et hanc mortem ut arcessere vetitum, sic evitare velle dementia est, procrastinare mollities; at equanimiter expectare, tamquam ubique proximam et horis omnibus affuturam, ea virtus eximia est verumque viri opus. Secundam mortem omni nisu fugere consilium erat, sed ita res se habet: ad impossibilia studium omne conversum est. Non mori, non egrotare, non laborare, non dolere, non servire, non egere volunt omnes; non peccare vult nullus, cum ea vera et maxima mortis et egritudinis et laboris et doloris et servitutis et penurie causa sit. Michi vero nunc forte dicat aliquis: si mortem ergo non metuis, quid metuis? Longam mortem et peiorem morte, nauseam; non de nichilo quidem, sed expertus metuo. Quotiens putas illud monstrum retentavi, si forte naturam consuetudo vel vinceret vel leniret? Si quid profecerim queris, non metum minui, sed geminavi potius cum navigatione supplicium. Hoc forsan animo vago et rerum novarum visione inexplebili oculo frenum posuit natura. Congressum itaque nunc noti hostis exhorreo, quem non sic iunior horruissem; horrui autem semper, sed in dies magis, cuius prospectu tamen adeo delector ut quem vel tangere abhominor quam cupide videam stupor ingens sit. Iste me nunc metus hic detinet. Exoptatum michi comitatum tuum invidet fortuna. An unquam vero posthac metum hunc victura sit caritas subdifficilis coniectura est. Ibis ergo sine me et multa conspicies, quorum tibi, dum vixeris, memoria voluptatem renovet. Ego interim dum tu redis, quod ut celeriter feliciterque sit cupio, Europe Italieque finibus contentus agam. Nichilominus te animo comitabor et, quoniam ita vis, his etiam comitabor scriptis que tibi brevis itinerarii loco sint. Morem enim secutus amantium, cuius presentia cariturus es, imaginem flagitasti qua utcunque tuam absentiam solareris, non hanc vultus imaginem, cuius in dies mutatio multa fit, sed stabiliorem effigiem animi ingeniique mei que, quantulacumque est, profecto pars mei optima est. Hic tibi ergo non amici domicilium corpus hoc, quod videntes quidam totum se hominem vidisse falso putant, sed amicum ipsum internis spectare luminibus licebit, quoniam, ut ait Cicero, 'mens cuiusque is est quisque, non ea figura que digito demonstrari potest.' Sed iam nimium te moror quem socii expectant, quem tranquilla veris facies faventesque vocant aure, quem nos omnes, qui te suspiramus abeuntem, iamiam reducem exoptamus.

Poscis ergo, vir optime, quoniam me non potes, comites has habere literulas, in quibus que oculis ipse tuis mox videbis, ex me, qui ea certe necdum vidi omnia nec unquam forte visurus sum, audire expetis, mirum dictu nisi quia passim multa que non vidimus scimus, multa que vidimus ignoramus. Parebo equidem, eoque promptius quo iustius cupis, primum scilicet ut que ad salutem anime, dehinc que ad notitiam rerum et ingenii ornamentum, postremo que ad memoriam exemplorum excitandumque animum pertinere videbuntur explicem iterque longissimum brevi stilo metiar. Prima quarum, nisi fallor, religiosi prorsus ac fidelis, alia ferventis ac studiosi, tertia militaris ac magni animi cura est. Quid vero non possit amor? Certius te visurum speras que calamus meus hinc quam que oculus tibi tuus inde monstraverit. Ingrediamur vero iam tandem iter hoc, et media pretervecti que assidue subiecta oculis inculcare auribus supervacuum est, nondum tibi visam, ut ais, Ianuam veniamus.

Videbis ergo imperiosam urbem lapidosi collis in latere, virisque et menibus superbam, quam dominam maris aspectus ipse pronuntiat. Sua sibi potentia, quod multis iam fecit urbibus, obstat atque officit, iugis unde materia civilium simultatum scatet. Auctorem urbis et nominis Ianum ferunt, primum ut quibusdam placet Italie regem. Quod an ita sit, an ipse situs urbi nomen dederit, quod nostri orbis quasi ianua quedam esse videatur, incertum habeo. Prima ibi celebrior opinio est et in chronicis eorum scripta et publicis insculpta monumentis. Utrique autem illud obstat, quod apud veteres non Ianue sed Genue nomen in usu est. Huius sane multa recentia et memorabilia dici possunt, que pretereo, neque enim scribo nunc historiam, sed loca describo; antiqua autem pauciora, quod non semper hoc sed, quantum intelligere est, prius caput gentis Albingaunum fuerat. Ipsa quidem de qua loquor Ianua, temporibus belli punici secundi a Carthaginensibus eversa, a Romanis ducibus restituta est. In qua tu nunc et populi habitum et locorum situm et edificiorum decus atque in primis classem, quod de Tiria scriptum vides, cuntis terribilem tremendamque litoribus; tum molem pelago obiectam portumque mirabere manufactum, inextimabilis sumptus, infinite opere, quem quotidiane nequicquam feriunt procelle. Quid multa? Cum sedulo civitatem hanc et dextra levaque circumfusum litus ac montes fluctibus impendentes, ad hec corpora, mores, animos, et victum gentis aspexeris, scito te vidisse cotem illam alteram, que Romane virtutis aciem longo exercitio multos olim annos exacuit, quod si quid Livio creditur, nulla provincia magis fecit ut cui scilicet essent omnia que vigilem ac sollicitum Romanum exercitum haberent: locorum montana durities, hostis prompta velocitas, commeatuum difficultas, insidiarum oportunitas, communitio castellorum, labor iugis, periculi plurimum, prede minimum, otii nichil. Itaque cum ubique terrarum cum singulis, hic cum multis difficultatibus uno tempore pugnandum erat. Hinc tu, tametsi socii properent et naute de litore funem solvant, <ne> tamen ante discesseris quam pretiosum illud et insigne vas solido e smaragdo quo Cristus, cuius te tam procul a patria amor trahit, pro parapside usus fertur, videas, devotum si sic est, alioquin suapte specie clarum opus.

Hinc digressus ad levam, totum illum diem ne oculos a terra dimoveas caveto. Multa enim illis occurrent que multo tibi facilius sit mirari quam cuiquam hominum stilo amplecti: valles amenissimas interlabentes rivulos, colles asperitate gratissima et mira fertilitate conspicuos, prevalida in rupibus oppida, vicos amplissimos; et marmoreas atque auratas domos, quocunque te verteris, videbis sparsas in litore et stupebis urbem talem decori suorum rurium delitiisque succumbere.

Viginti nisi fallor passuum milia emensus, extentum in undas promontorium, Caput Montis ipsi vocant, obvium habebis, et Delphini sive, ut naute nuncupant, Alphini Portum, perexiguum sed tranquillum et apricis collibus abditum; inde Rapallum ac Siestrum, et nomine Veneris insignem portum, securum ventorum omnium et omnium que sub celo sunt classium capacem, nostrum prope Hericem; habet enim alterum Sicilia. In medio sinus est, maris oportunus fatigatis puppibus. Et hoc quidem litus omne, palmiferum atque cedriferum, ut adversum Cereri, sic Bacho gratissimum ac Minerve, nulli usquam terrarum cedere certum est. Quo magis id priscis rerum scriptoribus, et presertim vatibus, pretermissum miror. Sed adducor ut extimem non invidiam neque desidiam causam dedisse silentio, sed quod nondum tentata ideoque nondum nota fertilitas locorum erat. Hinc est ut, cum claris sepe carminibus Meroen Falernumque concelebrent terrasque alias, hanc cuntis hac laude prestantem omnes indictam preterierint. Id me movit, omnium qui scripserunt et ingenio et stilo et etate novissimum, ut in *Africe* mee loco quodam, ydoneam nactus occasionem, loca ista describerem, charactere dicendique genere longe alio. Qui liber, nisi vel vite brevitas vel ingenii tarditas vel aliorum librorum unum in tempus cura concidens vel, quorum nullus est modus, fortune impedimenta vetuerint, aliquando forte sub oculos tuos veniens, in horum te atque aliorum, que multa nunc visurus es, locorum memoriam revocabit. Sed multum nobis vie restat. Progrediamur ad reliqua.

Non procul hinc, circa extremos fines Ianuensium, Corvum famosum scopulum et nomen a colore sortitum ac, paululum provectus, Macre amnis ostia, qui maritimos Ligures ab Etruscis dirimit, supraque litus maris sinistramque ripam fluvii ruinas Lune iacentis aspicies, si fame fides est. Aliud enim hac in parte nichil habeo magnum exemplum fugiende libidinis, que sepe non modo singulorum hominum, sed magnarum urbium et locupletium populorum ac regum opes fortunasque pessumdedit. Licet huius rei exemplum maius et antiquius Troia sit.

Hinc iam sensim cedentibus montibus, aliquandiu planum et absque scopulis, lene litus, portus rari, castella procul in collibus, plaga maris inhospita, Sarzanum paulo submotum a litore, novum frequensque oppidum, inde Laventia, vicus ignobilis; fluvius deinde re ac nomine frigidus, aquis arenisque perlucidus, secus Massam amenissimam terram descendit in pelagus. Prope oppidum est, Petramsanctam dicunt, cuius auctor, ut audio, concivis quidam tuus fuit, illius tunc provincie preses et vir domi clarus et nobilis. Itaque familie sue nomen transtulit in suum opus. Ultra iam preter duas Pisanorum arces nichil memorabile, quarum alteram Mutronem, alteram vero Viam Regiam appellant. Nec multo post Sercli atque Arni fluminum fauces sunt, quorum alter Lucam preterlabitur, alter patrie mee muros primum, tandem Pisas interfluit. Et de Luca quidem dubius sum, Florentia prorsus extra conspectum latet. Pisas autem ex ipsa puppe gubernaculi tibi rector ostendet, civitatem pervetustam sed recenti et decora specie et, licet in plano sitam, non tamen, ut magna pars urbium, paucis turribus sed totam simul eminentissimis edificiis apparentem, quondam quoque maris potentissimam, donec patrum memoria non modo vires equoreas sed animos navigandique propositum, magno victi prelio Ianuensium, amisere. Post hec paucis passuum milibus, portus et ipse manufactus, Pisanum vocant, aderit, et fere contiguum Liburnum, ubi prevalida turris est, cuius in vertice pernox flamma navigantibus tuti litoris signum prebet. Hinc si ad dexteram te deflectas, Gorgon atque Capraria, parve quedam Pisanorum insule, presto erunt, nec non turris exigua pelagi medio, que Meliora vulgo dicitur, infausta illi populo, quod scilicet illic ipsa, cuius paulo ante memini, pugna commissa est. Sin pressius intenderis, videbis et Corsicam, incultam insulam et armentis silvestribus abundantem. Quinquaginta inde, vel non multo amplius, passuum milibus, Plumbinum, insigne oppidum, ad levam fertili sedet in colle; portus subest, neque multarum capax navium et securitatis ambigue. Ad dexteram, exiguo spatio, Ilva est, 'insula inexhaustis Chalybum generosa metallis,' ut Maro ait. Perhibent qui longiores ibi traxerunt moras, omnia illic ad victum optima provenire, denique post Sardiniam amissam, Pisanarum opum illam precipuam sedem esse. Haud procul inde Populonia, Massa Maritima, Grossetum, Thelamonis Portus; an ab Aiacis patre an unde dictus, profiteor me nescire. Inde rursus ad dexteram Igilium insula, vino et marmore nobilis; ad levam Sancti Stephani, quem dicunt, et mox Portus Herculeus; Argentari<us> Mons medius. Post Cornetum, turritum et spectabile oppidum, gemino cinctum muro et ab alto colle maria longa despiciens. Huius in finibus Tarquinii fuerunt, olim civitas, nunc nichil preter nudum nomen ac ruinas, unde qui Rome regnarunt Tarquinii prodiere. Post hec illa que Civitas Vetus dicitur decem, nisi fallor, passuum milibus sita est. Deinde quem Hadriani portum vocant, opus inter cunta mirabile, quod ne inter septem illa famosissima numeretur, nichil sibi nisi etas et iactantia Graia defuerit.

His exactis Tyberine fauces ad levam sunt, ad dexteram remanente Sardinia. Supra Tyberis ripam Ostia est, Anci Marcii colonia, quarti Romanorum regis, quam 'in ipso maris fluminisque confinio posuit,' ut ait Florus, 'iam tum videlicet presagiens animo futurum ut totius mundi opes et commeatus illo velut maritimo urbis hospitio reciperentur.' Illic sane cum fueris, scito te a regina urbium Roma non nisi duodecim passuum milibus abesse, de qua si tam parvo in spatio loqui velim, intolerande nimis audacie sim, cuius gestis ac glorie totus terrarum orbis angustus est, cuius nomini libri lingueque omnes non sufficiunt. Post ostia Tyberina Caput Antii apparet; ita enim vocant naute. Civitas ibi Antium fuit, Vulscorum caput, que cum multa olim bella cum Romanis gessisset, capta demum et cum tota gente subacta est. Proxime Astura est, inde mons prealtus, cui carminibus potens Circe nomen imposuisse creditur. Ibi enim, ut aiunt, habitavit atque ibi Ulixis socios convertit in beluas, quae transformatio quid misterii vellet nosti. Locus est autem et fama celebris et scriptorum ingeniis. Hinc ad dexteram Pontie remanent, brevis insula et olim carcer illustrium.

Progredienti tibi Terracina nunc, olim Anxur, primum aderit, mox Caieta, nutricis Eneie nomen servans ubi, quo prosperior navigatio sit, sacrum Erasmi tumulum adire ne pigeat, cuius opem multis iam in maritimo discrimine profuisse opinio constans est. Hic flexus litorum et pelagi sinus ingens, saltusque lauriferi cedriferique et odoratum ac sapidum semper lete virentium nemus arbuscularum. In hoc tractu Formie seu Formianum et Liternum sunt, dicam verius fuerunt: alterum Ciceronis infanda cede, alterum Scipionis indigno exilio nobilitatum et cineribus patrie negatis. Sed hec duo loca extimatione magis animi quam oculis assequeris, alter enim iacet, alter et latet, nisi quod apud Formias adhuc due seu tres magne supereminent <ruine>. Ipsa sed in oculis erit Inarime que se se obviam dabit, insula poetarum nota preconio, Isclam moderni vocitant, sub qua Iovis edicto obrutum Typheum gigantem fama est fecitque locum fabule vapor, velut hominis anhelantis, et Ethneo more estuare solitum incendium. Vicina huic Prochita est, parva insula, sed unde nuper magnus vir quidam surrexit, Iohannes ille qui formidatum Caroli dyadema non veritus et gravis memor iniurie et maiora, si licuisset, ausurus, ultionis loco habuit regi Siciliam abstulisse. Simul et ad levam Cumas colle humili Sibille patriam videbis, ubi Tarquinius Superbus, regno pulsus tandemque Tuscorum et Latinorum destitutus auxiliis, exul obiit. Nam hoc Mediolano proximum,

Lario imminens, Alpibus adiacens, Comum est, non Cume, quod ne forte cum vulgo fallaris dixerim. Hinc iam Misenus collis in mare porrigitur, illic humati tubicinis Frigii nomen habens, cuius rei meminit Virgilius. Sunt qui putent Misenum ibi peremptum ab Enea diis infernis sacra facturo que, ut asserunt, absque humana cede fieri nequeunt, atrocitatemque facinoris Maroneo eloquio excusatam; illic sane sacrificatum ab Enea narrasse Virgilium ubi sacrificasse Ulixem Homerus ante narraverat, pari ritus immanitate (ut quidam putant; res enim ambigua est valde); esse autem huiuscemodi sacris apta loca, quod ibi sint Avernus atque Acheron, Tartarea nomina; ibi Ditis ostia, limen irremeabile, et illic facilis descensus Averni, de quo loquitur poeta, quem patentem diebus dixit ac noctibus, sed laboriosi atque operosi reditus, de qua re quia quod scriptum est legisti, si quid ipse preterea viderim atque audierim sequar, extra propositi metas eam. Hic Sibille Cumane domus maxima super horrentem Averni ripam cernitur, iam senio semiruta, habitatore quidem nullo, sed variarum volucrum nidis frequens. In eodem flexu fontes calidi tepentesque insignius quam in alia parte nostri orbis erumpunt, quidam vero sulfureum ac ferventem cinerem eructantes. Est ubi terra sine igni visibili, sine aquis ex se ipsa salubrem vaporem et medentem corporibus fumum profert; denique iisdem in locis et humane vite remedium convenisse dixeris et mortis horrorem. Et sub Miseno quidem semper in ancoris Romanarum una classium stabat ad occurrendum repentinis incursibus, alia equidem Ravenne erat. Idque alto consilio Augustus Cesar instituit ut Mare Superum atque Inferum, quibus insule instar Italie magna pars cingitur, hoc gemino presidio tuta essent. Intra Misenum Baie sunt, ab illic sepulto Baio quodam socio Ulixis appellate, situ longe amenissimo, ut non immerito hiberne Romanorum delitie videantur fuisse, quod et marmoree testudines calidis fontibus superiecte et murorum reliquie indicant, amplissime urbi etiam satis multe, et scriptorum etiam astipulatur fides. Hic Neroniane piscine ingentia monstrantur exordia; nam furoris alterius quo fossam ab Averno usque Ostiam, tanto terrarum spatio, per tot montes, non impensa rei publice sed iactura, non labore populorum sed exitio, fodiend<am> destinarat, ut humano victa studio natura tuto et libere tantum iter, non aperto quidem mari sed marinis aquis ac navibus ageretur, nulla que noverim nisi in literis vestigia remanserunt. Hic angulus et Lucrinum habet et undam illam Iuliam atque equor indignans, quorum et poeta recordatus est dum *Georgica* scriberet; opus autem a Iulio exstructum, ab Augusto Cesare immutatum, et aut me memoria frustratur aut Mare Mortuum appellant: sic maris ferociam atque impetum compressere hominum manus.

Contra Misenum et Baias, Puteoli tribus aut quatuor passuum milibus procul apparent. Hoc maris intervallum Gaius, Romanorum quartus imperator, pessimorum vero post Neronem primus, per inanem sumptuosamque iactantiam terrestri ponte connexuit, quem ipse idem equestri primum habitu, mox triumphantis in morem, magno procerum comitatu fastuque plus quam Cesareo permeavit. Non longe a Puteolis, Falernus collis attollitur, famoso palmite nobilis. Inter Falernum et mare mons est saxeus, hominum manibus perfossus, quod vulgus insulsum a Virgilio magicis cantaminibus factum putat. Ita clarorum fama hominum, non veris contenta laudibus, sepe etiam fabulis viam facit. De quo cum me olim Robertus, regno clarus sed preclarus ingenio ac literis, quid sentirem multis astantibus percuntatus esset, humanitate fretus regia qua non reges modo sed homines vicit, iocans nusquam me legisse marmorarium fuisse Virgilium respondi, quod ille serenissime nutu frontis approbans, non illic magie sed ferri vestigia esse confessus est. Sunt autem fauces excavati montis anguste sed longissime atque atre, tenebrosa intus et horrifica semper nox, publicum iter in medio, mirum et religioni proximum, belli quoque temporibus inviolatum, si vera populi vox est, et nullis unquam latrociniis attentatum patet. Cryptam Neapolitanam dicunt, cuius et in epystolis ad Lucilium Seneca mentionem facit. Sub finem fusci tramitis, ubi primo videri celum incipit, in aggere edito, ipsius Virgilii busta visuntur, pervetusti operis, unde hec forsan ab illo perforati montis fluxit opinio. Iuxta breve sed devotissimum sacellum supra ipsum Crypte exitum et mox ad radicem montis in litore Virginis Matris templum, quo magnus populi, magnus assidue pernavigantium fit concursus. Proxima in valle sedet ipsa Neapolis inter urbes litoreas, una quidem ex paucis. Portus hic etiam manufactus, supra portum regia, ubi si in terram exeas, capellam regis intrare ne omiseris, in qua conterraneus olim meus, pictorum nostri evi princeps, magna reliquit manus et ingenii monimenta. Non audeo te hortari ut extantem in colle urbi proximo Cartusie domum adeas. Scio ut navigatio fatigationem et fastidium parit. At Clare Virginis preclarum domicilium, quamvis a litore parumper abscesserit, videto, regine senioris amplissimum opus. Illud nulla festinatio, nullus labor impediat quin duos illius urbis vicos, Nidum scilicet et Capuanam, videas, edificiis supra privatum modum et, antequam pestis orbem terre funditus exhausisset, vix cuiquam credibili militie numero ac decore memorabiles. Militem ad militie pelagus, opus professioni tue debitum, te mitto, non studiosum veritatis ad fabulas, et idcirco Castrum Ovi titula cognitum eminus aspexisse satis fuerit. Hec est civitas ubi Virgilius noster liberalibus studiis operam dedit, cum iam ante patria illum tua Mediolanum tenerioribus annis discipulum habuisset. Hic se carmen illud georgicum scripsisse, hic se ignobili otio floruisse verecundissime memorat. Hanc dulcem vocat ille Parthenopem, id enim est aliud de nomine conditricis civitati nomen. Demum peregre moriens, inter extrema suspiria sue meminit Neapolis et huc revehi optavit ut, quam vivus amaverat, vita functus incoleret.

Hinc tandem digresso, biceps aderit Vesevus (vulgo Summa monti nomen), et ipse flammas eructare solitus. Ad quod olim spectaculum visendum cum experiendi noscendique cupidine perrexisset Plinius Secundus, vir scientie multiplicis et eloquentie floride, vento cinerem ac favillam excitante compressus est, miserabilis tanti viri exitus. Sic Neapolis hinc Mantuani, inde Veronensis civis ossa custodit. Mons est autem multarum rerum sed in primis vini ubertate mirabilis, quod Grecum ideo dicitur quia pars illa Italie a Grecis possessa olim Magna Grecia dicebatur. Hinc ad dexteram Capree insula linquitur, asperrimis rupibus circumsepta, secessus infamis senilium Tiberii voluptatum et officina sevitie. Pulcherrimus terrarum tractus ad levam Pompeios atque Herculaneum habuit, celebres olim urbes, nunc inania nomina, quas terremotibus eversas Seneca inter ceteros teste didicimus. Superest adhuc Surrentum et ipsum mellifluo palmite generosum.

Tota regio Terra Laboris hodie, pars olim Campanie fuerat, utraque precipue ubertatis appellatio. Quo pretextu Cereris hic Liberique certamen incerta victoria statuere.

Post hoc gremium maris ecce mox aliud ex ordine panditur, in quo Salernum videbis et Silerim. Fuisse hic medicine fontem fama est, sed nichil est quod non senio exarescat. Hinc utinam tu secundis ventis et cursu tam facili proveharis ut ego ad Italie finem facili provehor stilo. Leva itaque perpetuo tractu Calabrum litus extenditur. Dextera autem longe Trinacria et Vulcanus ac Lipar<a> minoresque insule et ipse fumum flammamque fundentes, ventoseque adeo ut Eoli, ventorum regis, hic regiam fuisse vel fabulosum certe vel historicum sit; utrumque enim lectum est. Hinc quod convenit Eolie dicte sunt. Ubi angustissima Italia est, Scaleam vocant, nescio quam vetus oppidum, sed nomen hauddubie modernum. Unde cum ad extremum Italie angulum perveneris, eum scilicet qui ad occasum vergit, hinc Regium Calabrie metropolim, hinc Sicilie Messanam parvo admodum oculorum flexu et fere simul aspicies. In medio Pharus est qui Messanensis dicitur, in quo sunt infamia illa portenta, multum formidata navigantibus, Scilla et Caribdis. Scillam saxum esse constat ad levam undisonum, procellosum, Caribdim contra aquarum magnam quandam rapidamque vertiginem. Neque te moveat quod libro tertio divini poematis locate aliter a Virgilio videantur. Ille enim venientis, ego autem euntis iter prosequor. Causa vero tante vertiginis apud poetas et historicos una est. Ferunt enim hunc nostrum, qui nos ambit ac dirimit, Apenninum in Trinacriam protendi solitum, donec multis seculis duo maria velut ex condicto, geminum latus montis hinc illinc sine intermissione tundentia, undis succumbere coegerunt. Ideoque illic amoto obice maria suo impetu acta concurrere; Apennini autem ultima, sic a toto corpore montis exsecta, nomine etiam amisso, concessisse in nomen montis Siculi Pelori, unius scilicet ex his tribus unde Trinacrie appellatio sumpta est, qui mons Messane proximus est, cui quod nomen ante fuerit incertum habeo. Hoc enim a Peloro gubernatore Hanibalis, quem ille sive tota cum classe Italiam linquens, ut Valerio placet, sive ut alii volunt et similius vero est, patriam suam puppe unica repetens et Romanos fugiens victores, propterque locorum angustias dum eminus exitum non intelligit, falli ratus occiderat ibique tandem errore recognito terre mandaverat, accepisse notissimum est.

Et Scalea quidem digressis, usque Regium ferme, rectus in meridiem est cursus. Inde rursus ad orientem, relicta procul a dextris Ethna, flammantium principe montium. Inde brevi flexu in septentrionem versus et Scyllaceum naufragiis infame transiliens, Crotonem venies, civitatem quondam inter Italie populos et animorum robore et corporum et forma et opibus ac gloria precellentem, nunc (quid non proterit longa dies?) vix ipsis Italicis bene notam. Hic Iunonis Lacinie templum fuit, toto orbe percelebre. Inde in intimo quodam pelagi recessu Tarentum tibi monstrabitur, Ennio natalis, Virgilio fatalis locus, quamvis alii Brundusium dicant, magni quoque cum Romanis belli causa, Pyrro rege in Italiam accersito adiutoque armis ac menibus, post longum tempus Hanibale, quos hostilium ducum primos Romane historie omnibus seculis numerabunt.

Iam ad finem orbis Italici ventum est, in quo ultimum cum Hydruntem attigeris, pedem habens obvium, Adriaticum equor emensus, primam insularum ab adverso litore Corcyram ignobilesque alias invenies, donec ad Achaie primum angulum perveneris. Illic quidem optabis Isthmum, quod quibusdam venit in mentem, esse perfossum quo cum rectior tibi tum brevior cursus sit. Mons est duo maria dirimens, qui si loco cederet, insula esset Achaia. Eius in vertice Chorintus est, situ inexpugnabili. Id sibi, cum a Romanis capta esset, eversionis prebuit materiam, secutis 'oportunitatem loci maxime,' ut ait Cicero, 'ne posset aliquando ad bellum faciendum locus ipse adhortari.' Cum vero limes equoreus ille preclusus sit, parendum nature et, pretermissa Chorinto, Malee flexus ille longior obeundus est videndumque litus Achaicum atque urbes in litore, Mothona, Corona, et quicquid terrarum mare illud alluit, usque ad extremum regionis angulum. Ut vero alter Italiam, sic ille Cretam respicit, nunc possessionem Venetorum (ut humana omnia volvuntur), olim Iovis regnum, superstitionum fere omnium fontem atque principium. Hanc a dextris, Eubeam, quam Nigropontum vocant, a sinistris habens, inter Cyclades, Egei maris insulas, que siderum in morem pelagus illud illustrant, crebris portibus tutum iter ages. Hic Scyros Achillei amoris atque adolescentie prima sedes, unde Ulixeo tortum astu fulmen illud venit ad Troiam. Hic Cous Ypocratis, Lesbos Theofrasti, Samos Pithagore patria, qua ille deserta in has nostras terras venit et Italicus philosophus dici meruit, cum philosophie nomen, quod primus invenerat, summo studio atque ingenio exornasset. Sed quid ago? Non multo facilius Cyclades omnes quam celi stellas enumerem. Per has ergo navigans, et procul a tergo linquens illa duo Grecie lumina, Lacedemonem et Athenas, ad levam vero Hellesponti fauces Sextonque et Abydon, infaustis amoribus notas, et Bizantion atque Ylion, illud emulatione Romani imperii, hoc propriis famosum malis, recto tramite Rhodon petes, olim Soli, nunc Cristo (verius scilicet soli) sacram, et militie domicilium Iohannis.

Iam hinc Asia Minor ad levam iacet, olim provinciarum mitissima, post Troie ruinam Grecis referta cultoribus, nunc Turcorum veri hostium ferox regio. Huius partes, ad austrum verse et itineri tuo proxime, sunt Licia atque Cilicia, et caput regionis Isauria, arx olim omnium pyratarum, qui summis tunc viribus maria cunta pervaserant ita ut ipsis quoque Romanis classibus aperta acie decertarent. Summa tamen Pompeii Magni virtute ac prudentia superati abductique maritimis latrociniis et terre cultibus restituti, ac ne qua unquam occasio illos ad consueta retraheret, a conspectu maris procul abstracti sunt. Ex his inter ceteras Laudensem Coloniam, patrie tue proximam, constare et de Pompeii laudibus sumptum nomen traditur. Que quidem non tantum a mari sed a fluminibus etiam longe erat, donec nuper eversa, dum resurgeret, ut sibi casus ad aliquid profuisse videretur, translatis sedibus, ripam pulcherrimi amnis obtinuit. Sed nondum tempus est in patriam redeundi. Ad ea que restant procedamus. Ante Cilicie frontem Cyprus est, terra nulla re alia quam inertia ac delitiis nota, quam merito Veneri sacram dixere, et nunc quoque Veneri magis quam Marti seu Palladi sacra est. Raro ibi seu nunquam vir aliquis clarus fuit, neque enim in molli agro voluptatis virtutum rigida semina coalescunt. Libidinem incolarum terre celique fervor indicat. Cum enim regiones tractu maximo soli viciniores grata temperie perfruantur, hec prope contra naturam intolerandis ardoribus estuat, quasi hominum complexio ad elementa transierit. Noli ibi multum immorari. Non est enim militaris certe neque virilis habitatio; fastus Gallicus, Syra mollities, Grece blanditie ac fraudes unam in insulam convenere. Quod optimum atque pretiosissimum habent, illic dissimillimis moribus aliunde veniens, iacet Hilarion.

Contra Cyprum in extremo maris angulo, Minor latet Armenia, cui tergum puppis obvertens in dextrum latus agenda est. Sed iam, quasi tecum periculi fastidiique particeps, ad terram pervenisse gaudeo. In quam ubi descensurus sis nescio, neque enim unus tantum portus patet accessui. Magistri sententia, comitum consensus, ventus, mare, dies, locus, oportunitas quid te agere oporteat dicent. Nam ut antiquo proverbio monemur, consilia capiuntur pro tempore. Sunt autem in litore illo, ut ab aquilone in austrum descendam, maritima oppida, Tortosa, Tripolis, Baruth, Sur, Cesarea, Iaffa, Ascalon, horumque in medio nobilis olim, nunc eversa et in cinerem versa iacet Acon, summum et inexpiabile dedecus ac turpissima cicatrix Cristianorum regum, nisi aliquanto turpior esset ipsa Ierusalem. Sane si altius descendas, id habebis amplius ut videas caput Syrie Damascum. Sic enim vocat eam non quicunque cosmographus sed clarissimus prophetarum Ysaias. Quamvis non ignorem apud alios Antiochiam Syrie primam ac metropolim haberi, cui sententie accedit Hegesippus libro tertio *Historiarum* Iosephum secutus, aliquanto tamen nobilior, ut puto, et certe multo vetustior est Damascus. Videbis civitatem et forma spectabilem et etate, de qua quidem ab ipsis temporibus regum Israel, multis seculis ante urbem conditam, crebra in utrisque literis sacris ac secularibus est mentio. Si infra magis applicueris, quantum spectaculo defuerit, tantum demetur labori; minus terrestri calle lassaberis, quod in terram egresso vicina Ierosolima est, itineris propositique tui terminus. Itaque tametsi multa tibi in medio querenda et visenda monstraverim, que poteras improvisus forte solumque vie finem cogitans preterire, hic quid te moneam non habeo. Omnia enim iam hinc antequam pedem domo moveas, preconcepta animo et diu agitata sunt tibi, quoniam finis rerum, ut philosophis placet, sicut in executione ultimus, sic in intentione primus est. Neque vero tu aliam ob causam tantum laboris ac negotii suscepisti, nisi ut in illa morte Domini sacra urbe locisque finitimis videres oculis, que animo iam videbas: amnem scilicet quo lotus est Cristus; templum seu templi ruinas in quo docuit; locum ubi summa cum humilitate passus est corpore ut nos animi passionibus liberaret; sepulcrum ubi sacratissimum corpus illud substitit, dum ipse mortis et inferni victor ad regna hostis spolianda descenderet, unde etiam reversus idem corpusque iam immortale recipiens, pressis gravi sopore custodibus, resurrexit; Syon preterea et Oliveti Montem: ad hec et unde in celum ascendit, quo ad iudicium reversurus creditur; ubi ventis et fluctibus imperavit; ubi cibo exiguo maximam turbam pavit, ubi aquam vertit in vinum, que licet magna convivantibus viderentur, facilia erant illi qui cibum et vinum et aquam et ipsos de nichilo creaverat convivantes; ubi denique elegit indoctos atque inopes piscatores, quorum hamis ac retibus piscarentur imperatores ac reges gentium; ubi cecos illuminavit, leprosos mundavit, paraliticos erexit, mortuos suscitavit, quodque his omnibus maius esset, nisi quia omnia eque facilia sunt Deo, demonibus ac peccatis oppressam sepultamque animam restituit libertati. Multa etiam que persequi michi longissimum et nequaquam necessarium tibi est, cui omnia ex Evangelio nota sunt, que fixa mente cernentis per singulos passus devotam animam pius horror invadet. Unum quod elabi posset admoneo, videre te urbem illam quam vicisse victores gentium Romani tam clarum opus esse duxerunt, ut Titus, tunc exercitus post imperii gubernator, in ipso ingressu menia urbis admirans, tantam victoriam non humane virtutis sed divine gratie fateretur. Et profecto sic erat. Cristus ipse, quem erasisse de terra viventium existimabant, adversus suos hostes suis merito favebat ultoribus, licet adhuc illis incognitus, noscendus tamen eorum successoribus et colendus. Itaque cum sepe alias, tum in ea vastatione precipue impletum est, quod ex persona eius in psalmo dicitur, 'Resuscita me et retribuam eis,' ea hominum strages, ea fames miserorum, tam mesta necessitas, que si ex ordine nosse cupis, Iosephum lege, non audita sed visa et comunia sibi cum ceteris referentem.

Quid vero nunc cogitas? An nondum te desiderium nostri cepit, ut domum, ut patriam, ut amicos invisere animus sit? Credo id quidem, imo ne aliter fieri posse certus sum. Sed nullus est acrior stimulus quam virtutis. Ille nunc per omnes difficultates generosum animum impellit nec consistere patitur nec retro respicere, cogitque non voluptatum modo sed honestorum pignorum atque affectuum oblivisci, nichil aliud quam virtutis speciem optare, nichil velle, nichil denique cogitare. Hic stimulus qui Ulixem Laertis et Penolopes et Thelemaci fecit immemorem, te nobis nunc vereor abstrahet diutius quam vellemus. Video tibi faciem esse longius euntis. Nec immerito. Ubi enim dimitteres Bethleem, civitatem David, quam celesti ortu claram fore divini vates presago ore cecinerant? Illic prima incunabula nostri regis aspiciens, cogitabis quantum Deo grata fuerit semper humilitas, quam in filii sui unigeniti primordiis evidentissime consecravit; cogitabis ineffabilem Salvatoris originem, qui ante principium genitus, in fine temporum, si ad etatum numerum attenditur, natus est. Virginem matrem, in presepio iacentem contemplabere et divinum infantem in cunis vagientem, angelos ab ethere concinentes, pastores attonitos stupentesque, reges alienigenas cum muneribus affusos, indigenam vero regem gladio sevientem, terram innocuo sanguine beatorum infantium et miserarum genitricum lacrimis madentem et mestis resonans celum omne gemitibus; inter hec, monitu angelico, sanctum altorem, cum intemerata matre celestique alumno, clam ex ingrata patria in Egiptum ire tanto pignori tutas latebras querentem, iam tum gentibus spe iniecta, primogenito propter ingratitudinem abdicato, summi patris hereditatem ad minorem filium, hoc est ad populum gentium, esse venturam.

Sed tu quoque nunc, ut auguror, Ioseph, imo Mariam, imo Cristum profugum sequi vis, sacrum profecto teque dignum iter. Sequendus in terris querendusque nobis Cristus est ut vel sic discamus eum ad celum sequi et, ubi aliquando habitavit diu quesitum, tandem ubi habitat invenire. Iam vero non longe hinc mare quod Sodomorum dicitur, Iordanis influit, ubi consumptarum urbium vindicteque celestis aperta vestigia apparent. His deserti solitudo proxima est. Durum iter fateor, sed ad salutem tendenti nulla difficilis via videri debet. Multas ubique difficultates, multa tibi tedia vel hominum vel locorum hostis noster obiciet, quibus te ab incepto vel retrahat vel retardet vel, si neutrum possit, saltem in sacra peregrinatione hac minus alacrem efficiat. Hic vero preter cetera nativam locorum ingeret asperitatem penuriamque rerum omnium. Sed meminisse conveniet omne optimum magno pretio constare, et Virgilianum illud in tuos usus transferre, ubi ait, 'Vicit iter durum pietas,' et illud Lucani paululum immutare, 'Durum iter ad leges animeque ruentis amorem.' Nichil tam durum quod virtus ardens et pietas intensa non molliat. Equidem si per Syrtes Lybicas et arenosa loca serpentium M. Cato mite Cesaris imperium fugisse laudatur, tu per desertum non fugies immite feroxque iugum Sathane, per quod tantus olim populus fugit sevitiam Pharaonis? Et quod senes ac pueri et muliercule potuerunt, tu vir fortis ac iuvenis non poteris? Deus cum illis erat et tecum erit. His autem in locis legem datam Moysi, colloquium cum Deo habitum, visionem rubi, delapsum celo manna, ceterasque erga carum sed ingratum populum divinas blanditias ac divina iudicia tecum volves. Incidet forte cupiditas Maris Rubri videndi, quod proprie a poeta non Mare sed Litus Rubrum dictum est; non enim ab aquis sed a colore litoris nomen hoc trahitur. Quo cum perveneris, non odores Indicos et Eoas merces, illis faucibus in Egiptum atque inde nostrum in mare convectas, sed populum Deo adiutum per medios fluctus, sicco pede, transvectum meditabere. Illud enim humane cupiditatis et inopie, hoc divine pietatis ac potentie est. Hic Katherine Virginis corpus cernes ubi angelicis manibus collocatum fertur, nec indignum fuit ut que pro lege Dei usque ad mortem decertaverat, in eo ipso monte requiesceret ubi lex divinitus data erat. Per hec loca formidabiles esse solent Arabum incursus, sitis, fames, labor, sed nichil fere periculosius errore vie, nullis indiciis ad rectum referentibus. Ideo vigilanter cave ne ulla te necessitas seiungat a sociis.

Iam tandem in Egiptum laborioso et ancipiti calle perventum est. Ibi ergo supra Nilum videbis Babilonem novam, Cambissis opus, et Carras Egiptias, frequentissimam urbem et immensam, que Babilonem veterem trans Eufratem et Carras Assyrias representant. Spectabis insignem Asie atque Africe limitem, adversum Tanai, flumen ingens stupendumque, de quo et philosophi et poete et cosmographi multa sunt opinati, Aristotiles vero libro integro disseruit, flumen et estivi mirabilis incrementi et inundationis uberrime et infiniti alvei et fontis incogniti, cuius certitudinem et Egiptiorum et Persarum et Macedonum reges, ad postremum Romani quoque imperatores, sed frustra omnes, quesiere. Fons hactenus ignoratus manet; opiniones atque inquisitiones hominum et historie de hoc scripte multis legentibus note sunt. Clarum quiddam et relatu dignum, quod ab illustribus viris accepimus, locus hic exigit. Ferunt fontem esse perlucidum illic ubi ab Herodis rabie Cristum occultabant, quem puer omnipotens e terra arida in refrigerium anxie matris eduxerit; ex illo Cristianos iucundissime bibere, Saracenis absinthio amariorem esse ita ut degustare illum vel summis labiis pena sit, nostrosque inde tam cupide haurientes ceu monstrum aliquod admirentur. Nec sane magnum fuit illi qui fontem fecit, eidem quoque quas voluit leges dare et pro varietate bibentium fidei varium saporem aquis immittere.

Nil iam restat memorabile quod quidem non meminerim, preter Alexandriam, Alexandri opus, Alexandri nomen, Alexandri bustum. Ad quod Iulius Cesar, post Thesalicum diem mortemque Pompeii, cum Alexandriam venisset, ambiguo turbati vulgi murmure permotus, per speciem religionis descendisse legitur. Et Augustus Cesar, post victoriam Actiacam Antoniumque devictum et coactum mori, eodem veniens, Alexandri corpus reverenter aspexit, cumque ex eo quereretur an et Ptholomeum vellet aspicere, elegantissime 'regem ait se videre velle non mortuos.' Cui dicto illa procul dubio sententia inest, virtute animi et rerum gloria, non regno, non sceptro, non dyademate regem fieri. Hoc tu dictum eatenus inflectes ut sanctos cupias spectare, non mortuos. Quia tamen vetustas et fama clarorum hominum non sine quibusdam facibus animos tangunt, poteris et hoc bustum, si nondum senio cesserit, spectare nec minus urnam que Pompeii cinerum ostenditur. Illum enim Greci, hunc Romani scriptores Magnum vocant (Galli autem hoc cognomen ad suum Carolum transtulere). Illos duos habet una urbs, quorum alterum Arthos, alterum miserat Occidens, illum Pelle, hunc Roma. Videbis ubi iniquo marte preventus et circumventus illa magnalia et vix credibilia gessit Cesar. Videbis Pharum unde hoc phari nomen per alias terras usquequaque diffusum est. Spectabis multifidas Nili fauces, ubi fortuna populi Romani truncum sui ducis et lacerum cadaver, abscisumque trunco caput flens victor aspexit, sic cum genero partitus orbem ut illum Nilus, Tybris hunc abluat. O fortune fides, o rerum finis humanarum. Certe ut es ingenio promptus ac docilis, facile, tantis ac talibus magistris, quantum prosperis sit fidendum disces perpetuoque memineris.

Sed iam satis itum, satis est scriptum; hactenus tu remis ac pedibus maria et terras, ego hanc papirum calamo properante sulcaverim, et an adhuc tu fessus sis eundo, certe ego iam scribendo fatigatus sum, eoque magis quo celerius incessi. Quod enim iter tu tribus forte vix mensibus, hoc ego triduo consummavi. Hic utrique igitur vie modus sit. Tibi domum, michi ad mea studia redeundum. Quod ego confestim fecero, tibi vero plusculum negotii superest peragendum Cristi ope feliciter. His spectaculis et hoc duce, doctior nobis ac sanctior remeabis.

FRANCIS PETRARCH'S ITINERARY TO THE TOMB OF OUR LORD JESUS CHRIST

To Giovanni Mandelli:

Very rarely do things turn out the way we expect. Often the best laid plans come to nothing, and something unforeseen happens. Nor should that come as a surprise to anyone; rather it would be remarkable if it were otherwise. If indeed it is our reason that governs the beginning of an enterprise, it is Fortune that controls its outcome. Nothing however is more at variance with reason than Fortune. And so a plan that the former has cleverly designed is often violently unraveled by the latter before it is carried out. I wish that statement required proof and that the lives of people were not so full of such complaints that they bemoan almost nothing else. But to turn to our own situation, you had decided to have me as a companion for your trip, a willing and eager one I confess. For what journey anywhere is more desirable and holy, what pilgrimage more fitting than one to the tomb where He lay buried whose temporal death brought forth immortality for us and eternal life? If it is not forbidden to say so, it is the tomb where both vanquished Death and victorious Life were buried together. Oh, what a blessed journey and enviable sight for a Christian soul! I am now being held back from there and detained by the contemptible bars and hooks of my shortcomings. "Childish embarrassment forbids me to speak," as Horace says, but imperious truth commands it and forces my obedience. So while there are many reasons that keep me back, none is more powerful than my fear of the sea, not because I am more desirous of life or more fearful of death than other men or because I think death on dry land is preferable to death at sea. For what makes men happy or unhappy is not a matter of location but of the soul; and while I know that one must die wherever he is, I do not know where it is better to die. In vain do we avoid war and the seas, in vain do we run from hardship and spare our frail bodies, which are destined to perish. Death makes its way unseen into the hideaways of voluptuaries and the very bedrooms of kings. Often idle self-indulgence brings on an early death which perhaps hard work and exercise might have put off. Certainly everyone must undergo death once. And just as it is wrong to seek after death, so it is madness to wish to avoid it, and cowardice to want to delay it. But to wait calmly for death as though it is everywhere close at hand and may come to us at any time, that is exemplary virtue and the true work of a man. The plan was to flee with all one's strength a second death, but this is what really happens: all energy is focused on the impossible. Everyone wants not to die, not to be ill, not to suffer hardship, not to grieve, not to be subservient, not to be in need; but no one wants not to sin, although that is the true and greatest cause of death, sickness, hardship, sorrow, servitude, and poverty. But now someone may perhaps say to me, "Then if you do not fear death, what do you fear?" I fear a death which is prolonged and one worse than death — seasickness. I do not say this for no good reason; I have experienced it. How often do you think I have checked my monstrous fear on the chance that habit might either overcome or soothe its nature? If you ask what good this has done — I have not lessened my fear, but rather have added a punishment to sea travel. Perhaps nature has imposed this as a restraint on my wanderlust and my insatiable desire to see new things. And so I now dread to do battle with a familiar enemy, whom I would not have so dreaded as a younger man, but whom I have always dreaded and do so more as time goes by. Nevertheless I am so pleased by the prospect of meeting him that I am astonished how eager I am to look upon something I shrink from having the slightest contact with. That fear now holds me here. Fortune begrudges me your company, which I had so hoped for. It is rather difficult to conjecture whether in the future my love will ever overcome this fear. You will go therefore without me and you will see many things, the memory of which will renew your pleasure as long as you live. Meanwhile until you return, and may that be quickly and happily, I shall live content in the confines of Europe and Italy. Nonetheless I shall accompany you in spirit; and since you wish it, I shall also accompany you in this manuscript, which may serve as a short itinerary. As lovers are accustomed to do, you have asked for a picture of me, whose presence you are going to miss, so that by that means you might somewhat console yourself while you are away — not an actual picture of my face, which changes greatly as time goes by, but a more substantial representation of my soul and personality; however insignificant it is, it is certainly the best part of me. You will not be able to look upon this body here, the dwelling place of your friend, which some look upon and mistakenly think they have seen the whole man, but you may look upon your friend with the eyes of your soul. For, as Cicero says, "the true self is one's spirit, not that form which can be pointed to with the finger." But now I am delaying you too much. Your comrades await you; the calm face of spring and warm breezes call you. All of us who sigh for you as you leave already long for your return.

Well then, my dear man, you ask to have these few pages as a companion since you cannot have me with you. In them you want to hear from me, who have certainly not yet seen all these places and perhaps never shall, what you will soon see with your own eyes. This would be a strange thing to say, except for the fact that we generally know many things we have not seen and do not understand many things we have seen. I indeed shall comply, and that with a promptness which matches the appropriateness of your wish, namely that I explain first of all things that seem relevant to the salvation of your soul, secondly matters that have something to contribute to your knowledge of facts and your intellectual development, and finally things that may recall patterns of action and stimulate your spirit; and that I take the measure of a very long journey in succinct fashion. The first matter, if I am correct, is a concern for one who is sincerely religious and devout, the second for one who is an avid intellectual, the third for one who is a high-spirited soldier. But what may love not accomplish? You hope that you will see more clearly what my pen will reveal to you from here than what your eye will show you there. But now at last let us begin this journey. Passing over the intervening territory, which it would be pointless to din into your ears since it is constantly before your eyes, let us go to Genoa (Janua), which you say you have not yet visited.

You will see then an imperial city perched on the side of a rocky hill, proud of its courageous men and fortifications, whose very appearance proclaims it to be mistress of the sea. Its very own power hinders and impedes the city, as it has already done in the case of many others, for from this power issues fuel for civil discord in unending supply. They say that the eponymous founder of the city was Janus, the first king of Italy according to some. I am uncertain whether that is the case, or whether the site itself gave the name to the city since it seems to be a kind of doorway (ianua) to our part of the world. The first view is more popular there, since it is recorded in their chronicles and carved on their public monuments. Against both views, however, there is the objection that among ancient writers the name Genua, not Janua, is used. Of this city, of course, many current and noteworthy things could be said; but I pass over them because I am not writing a history now, but describing places. And indeed there is not much to say about its remote past, because Genoa was not always the capital city of the clan, but Albenga served that purpose in an earlier time, as far as I can tell. Genoa itself, about which I am speaking, was overthrown at the time of the second Punic war by the Carthaginians and was restored by Roman leaders. In this city you will marvel at the character of the people, the geography of the area, the beauty of the buildings, and especially the fleet which is intimidating and awesome to every shore, as has been written of the Tyrian fleet. Then you will marvel at the breakwater put up against the sea and the man-made port, built at incalculable expense and infinite pains, which storms strike in vain every day. What more is there to say? When you have carefully examined this city, the shoreline spread out both on the right and on the left, the mountains overhanging the water, and, in addition to these things, the physical attributes, the character, the spirit, and the way of life of the people, know that you have looked upon that other whetstone which once sharpened the cutting edge of Roman courage for many years with extended training, because if one can believe Livy at all, no province did more to see to it that the Roman army had everything to keep it alert and wary — the ruggedness of the mountainous area, the swift movement of enemy troops, difficulty for supply lines, the opportunity for ambush, the fortification of strongholds, the constant struggle, the maximum of dangers, the minimum of booty, and no time to rest. And so while it had to contend with each of these many difficulties one at a time everywhere else, here it had to contend with all of them at the same time. Even though your comrades are eager to go and the sailors are about to weigh anchor, do not leave before you see that precious and carefully worked vessel made of solid emerald which Christ, whose love has drawn you so far from your home, is said to have used for a serving dish, a blessed object if it is genuine, but if not, a magnificent piece in its own right because of its beauty.

Proceeding to the left, do not take your eyes from land the whole day, for you will see many things that are much more easy for you to admire than it is for any writer to describe. Wherever you look, you will see exquisite valleys with streams running through them, hills exceptional for their delightful ruggedness and for their marvelous luxuriance, well-fortified towns on cliffs, bustling villages, gilded and marble homes scattered along the shore wherever you turn; and you will be amazed that such a city surrenders to the beauty and charms of its own countryside.

After the passage of twenty miles I think, you will come upon a promontory, which extends into the water and which the sailors call Capomonte, and the harbor of Delphinus (or Portofino as the sailors call it), quite small, but calm and hidden among sunny hills. Next you will come to Rapallo and Sestri Levante and the port famous for the name of Venus, secure from all wind and large enough for all the fleets that are in existence; it is near our Lerici (Sicily also has a place by that name). Lying open to all, the bay welcomes sea-weary ships. The entire shoreline is covered with palms and cedars and is as hostile to Ceres as it is pleasing to Bacchus and Minerva; unquestionably the area takes second place to no land anywhere on earth. So I am all the more amazed that it has been passed over by ancient authors, especially the poets. But I am inclined to think that the cause of the omission is not due to envy or indifference, but because the lushness of the area had not yet been tested and therefore was not yet known. Hence it is that while they often celebrate Meroë and the Falernian district in their famous poems and other lands as well, they have all failed to mention this place, though it is more deserving of praise of this sort than the rest. This has prompted me, junior in talent, style, and age to all those writers, to find a suitable occasion and describe these places somewhere in my *Africa*, in a distinctive and much different style. Unless the brevity of my life, or lack of ready inspiration, or my concern for other writing projects converging at one time, or the barriers of Fortune, to which there is no limit, prevent it, sometime perhaps this work will come to your attention and recall for you the memory of these and many other places which you are about to see. But much of your journey is ahead of us. Let us get on with it.

Not far from here, near the end of Genoa's territory, you will see Corvo, a rock which is famous and which got its name from its color; a little farther along, you will see the mouth of the river Magra, which separates the seafaring Ligurians from the Tuscans; and above the shoreline and the left bank of the river you will see the scattered ruins of Luna, if one can trust rumor. You see, I have nothing else in this part of the world available as a good object lesson for avoiding the passion that often has destroyed the resources and wealth not only of individual men, but also of great cities and rich nations and kings. I grant you that Troy is a better and more ancient example of this lesson.

From this point the mountains give way little by little, and the shoreline is for some distance flat and smooth as there are no rocks; harbors are few; there are some strongholds in the hills, but this stretch of sea is inhospitable. Sarzana, a new and populous town, is a little removed from the shore; after that Avenza, an obscure village. Next a river, cold both in fact and in name, but brilliant with its water and beaches, descends to the sea, past Massa, a most lovely place. Nearby is a city, which they call Pietrasanta, whose founder I hear was a fellow countryman of yours; at that time he was governor of that province and a famous noble at home. And so he applied the name of his family to his foundation.

Beyond that there is nothing worth mentioning except the two citadels of the Pisans, one of which they call Motrone and the other the Viareggio. Not much past here are the mouths of the Serchio and the Arno, the first of which flows past Lucca, the other first flows through the walls of my homeland and then past Pisa. About Lucca I am uncertain, but Florence lies completely out of sight. The pilot will show you Pisa from ship's deck. It is a very old city, but has a modern and beautiful look to it. Although it lies on level ground, it is quite visible with its very imposing structures, whereas most cities have only a few towers. At one time it was a naval power until in the memory of our fathers they were conquered in a great battle with the Genoese and lost not only their maritime strength but also their spirit and determination to sail. A few miles past here there will be the man-made harbor itself (they call it Porto Pisano), and Livorno is very close by, where there is a sturdy tower, on the top of which a flame offers to sailors a sign of safe coastline at night. If you turn from here to the right, Gorgona and Capraia, some small islands that belong to the Pisans, will be at hand, and also a small tower in the middle of the sea, which the common folk call Meliora. It is an unlucky place to that people because there the battle was fought of which I spoke a little before. But if you look sharply, you will also see Corsica, an uncultivated island, but one rich in wild herds. Fifty miles from here or not much more than that, Piombino, a distinguished city, sits off to the left on a fertile hill; its harbor lies below, not big enough for many ships and offering dubious protection. A short distance to the right is Elba, an island rich in "the inexhaustible mines of the Chalybes," as Virgil says. People who have spent prolonged periods of time there maintain that everything needed for a livelihood is produced there in abundance and that after the Pisans lost Sardinia it was their chief source of wealth. Not very far from here there is Populonia, Massa Marittima, Grosseto, and Porto Talamone. Whether it was called this after the father of Ajax or for some other reason, I confess I do not know. From there, again to the right, is the island of Giglio, celebrated for its wine and marble. To the left is the port they call Santo Stefano and soon Port' Ercole, with Monte Argentario in the middle. After that is

Corneto with its towers; it is a noteworthy city, enclosed by a double wall and looking down from a high hill on the sea in the distance. Tarquinii was in the territory of Corneto; it was once a city, but now it is nothing but a mere name and ruins. From it came the Tarquinii who ruled at Rome. After this is located the place which is called Civitavecchia, about ten miles away I think. Next there is the harbor they call the Port of Hadrian; it stands out from all the others, a marvelous piece of work, which lacks nothing except the proper age and Greek boasting to keep it from being numbered among those renowned Seven Wonders of the world.

After you have got past this, there are the outlets of the Tiber off to the left, with Sardinia still off to the right. On the bank of the Tiber is Ostia, a colony of the fourth Roman King, Ancus Marcius. "He placed it on the very edge of the river and the sea, knowing already at that time," as Florus says, "that it was destined that the wealth and provisions of the entire world would be received at the city's warehouse by the sea, so to speak." When you arrive there, know that you are but twelve miles from Rome, the Queen of cities. If I should speak of it in so short a space, I would be intolerably rash. The whole world is too small for its glorious deeds, and all the books and languages are inadequate to do justice to its fame. After the mouth of the Tiber, Capo d' Anzio appears; for that is what sailors call it. There is where the city of Anzio used to be, the capital of the Vulsci, which was at length captured and subjected along with the entire tribe after it had waged many wars with the Romans long ago. Close by is Astura, and next a very high mountain, to which Circe, powerful with her magical spells, is believed to have given her name. For she lived there, they say, and there turned Ulysses's men into wild animals. You know what hidden meaning this transformation refers to. The place is famous both because of the talk of the common folk and the clever devices of writers. Ponza then is off to the right, a narrow island and at one time a prison for famous people.

As you proceed, Terracina, as it is now called but once Anxur, will come into view. Then there will be Gaeta, which preserves the name of Aeneas's nurse. In order that your voyage may be the more prosperous, do not consider it irksome to visit there the sacred tomb of Erasmus, because it is commonly believed that he has been helpful to many in a crisis at sea. Here you will find a bend in the shoreline, a huge bay, woodlands covered with laurels and cedars, and a fragrant and savory grove of evergreen saplings. In this stretch of land are Formia or Formianum and Liternum — I should say "were." The former was made famous by Cicero's shocking murder there and the latter by Scipio's unjust exile and by his ashes, which he denied to his homeland. But these two places you will appreciate more in your imagination than with your eyes, for the one lies in ruins and the other also lies hidden from view, except that at Formia there are two or three large ruins that still catch the eye. But Inarime itself you will be able to see because it lies directly in your way. Called Ischia in modern times, it is an island well known from the acclaim of poets who say that under it the great Typhoeus is rumored to have been buried by order of Jupiter. The rising vapor, as though of someone breathing, gives rise to this story, as well as the fire that usually seethes in the manner of Mt. Etna. Nearby is Procida, a small island, but from it recently came an important man, the well-known John. Unafraid of the formidable imperial power of Charles and mindful of a grave injustice, he considered it revenge to have taken Sicily away from the king, and would have dared to go further if he could have. At the same time, off to the left, you will see Cuma on a low-lying hill, the home of the Sibyl. It is where Tarquin the Proud, driven from the throne and at length deprived of the help of the Tuscans and the Latins, died in exile. This place that is near Milan, on the shore of Lake Larius (Lago di Como) and near the Alps, is Como, not Cuma, a fact I should mention so that you are not misled by a popular misconception. Next the Capo Miseno extends into the sea; it has the name of the Phrygian trumpeter buried there, as Virgil recounts. There are those who think that Misenus was killed there by Aeneas, intending to make sacrifice to the gods of the underworld, which they declare cannot be made without human blood, and that the atrocity of the deed is mitigated by Virgil's eloquence; that of course Virgil had him sacrificed by Aeneas in the same place where earlier Homer had Ulysses perform a sacrifice, the savage character of the rite being equal in the two authors (as some think, for the matter is quite obscure); that the area is moreover suitable for sacrifices of this kind because Avernus and Acheron, names connected with Tartarus, are located there, as is the entrance to Dis's realm, the threshold of no return. From there the descent at Avernus is easy (about which the poet speaks and which he said lies open day and night), but the return is hard and difficult. But because you have read what has been written about this matter, I would be going beyond the limits I have set if I should pursue what I have in addition seen and heard. Here the very large dwelling of the Cumaean Sibyl is seen situated on the rough bank of the Avernus, now half in ruins because of its antiquity. No one lives there, but it is filled with the nests of various birds. In the same bend, hot and warm springs erupt more conspicuously than in any other part of our world, but some belch forth sulfur and hot ash. This is a place where the land without visible fire or water produces of itself healthful vapor and a smoke that has a curative effect on the body. In short you will say that both a remedy for human life and the horror of death have converged in the same area. Under the protection of Capo Miseno one of the Roman fleets always stood at anchor to meet sudden incursions; another was kept at Ravenna. Augustus Caesar very wisely established this practice so that the Upper and Lower Seas, by which a great part of Italy is surrounded like an island, might be safe with this double protection. In the shelter of Capo Miseno is Baia, named after a companion of Ulysses buried there, in a setting of such extraordinary beauty that it seems justly to have been the favorite wintering spot of the Romans. Proof of this are the marble vaults erected over the hot springs and remains of walls which are sufficiently abundant for even a very large city; and written authority supports this. Here people point out the huge initial stage of Nero's pool, for no traces of that other obsession remain that I know of except in literature. He had determined that a canal, from Lake Avernus to Ostia, should be dug over all that distance through so many mountains, not at the expense of the state but by its sacrifice, not by the hard work of people, but by their destruction, so that after nature had been conquered by human endeavor, the journey could be made safely and freely, not in the open sea but in sea water and in ships. This area also has the Lucrine Lake, the "Julian wave," and the "resentful sea," about which the poet spoke when he was writing the *Georgics;* it was work undertaken by Julius and modified by Augustus Caesar; either my memory deceives me or they call it the Mare Morto. Thus have the hands of man subdued the violent onslaught of the sea.

Opposite Miseno and Baia, Pozzuoli can be seen at a distance of three or four miles. Gaius, the fourth Roman emperor, but ranking first after Nero for wickedness, connected this stretch of the sea with an earthen bridge in a silly and expensive display. He himself crossed it dressed first as a charioteer and shortly thereafter in the fashion of one celebrating a triumph, with a great train of princes and with more arrogance than Caesar. Not far from Pozzuoli, the Falernian "Hill" rises, noteworthy for its celebrated grape vines. Between the Falernian "Hill" and the sea, there is a rocky mountain, which has been dug through by human hands, a piece of work which the witless crowd thinks was done by Virgil with magical spells. Such is the reputation of famous men that it is not content with legitimate praise, but often admits mere fictions. Once when Robert, a man famous for his royal bearing, but even more famous for his intelligence and learning, asked me what I thought about this in the hearing of many, I relied on his royal kindness, by which he has won over not only kings, but commoners as well, and jokingly replied that I had not read anywhere that Virgil had worked as a stone-cutter. He approved of this remark with a nod of his most serene head and admitted that at the tunnel there was evidence of iron tools at work, not magic. The tunnel of the excavated mountain is narrow, but very long and black; inside is always a shadowy and frightening night. The public passage up the middle is remarkable and has almost a religious quality about it: the place is inviolate no less in times of war, if what people say is true; and its way stands open, never assailed by brigands. They call it Crypta Neapolitana; and Seneca also makes mention of it in his letters to Lucilius. Towards the end of the dark passage, when one first begins to see the sky, he can see the tomb of Virgil himself on a raised mound. Its workmanship is very old, a circumstance which perhaps accounts for the notion that he had tunneled out the mountain. Nearby there is a small but very sacred shrine just above the exit of the crypt. A little farther on at the base of the mountain on the shore is a church of the Virgin Mother. A great number of people visit there, including those who are constantly arriving in ships. In a valley close by, Naples itself sits among the coastal cities, the product of several mergers. Here is also a man-made harbor, and overlooking it is the royal palace. If you disembark, do not miss going into the royal chapel where my fellow countryman, the finest painter of our time, has left evidence of his skillful worksmanship. I do not have the heart to encourage you to visit the Carthusian monastery which stands on a hill near the city. I know how sailing brings on fatigue and weariness, but do see the famous monastery church of the Virgin Clare, even though it stands at some little distance from the coast; it is a very substantial work of the older Queen. No matter how rushed you feel, no matter how busy you are, do not let that prevent you from seeing two districts of that city — Nido and Capuana, places worth mentioning for their buildings that surpass in size those of an ordinary citizen, for the incredible number of soldiers there before the plague had utterly exhausted the world, and for their beauty. I send you, a soldier, to visit a sea of soldiers, a duty you owe your profession, and not to places known for stories told about them, since you are one eager for the truth. Therefore it will be sufficient to have viewed from a distance the castle known by the name of an egg (Castel dell' Ovo). This is the city where Virgil studied liberal arts, although before that he had studied as a younger man in Milan, your homeland. He very modestly relates that he wrote that work on agriculture here and flourished in obscure leisure. He calls this place sweet Parthenope, for that is another name for the city taken from its foundress. Later, as he lay dying away from home, he remembered Naples with his last breath and chose to be brought here so that having finished with life he might rest in the place he had loved while alive.

When you finally leave, next you will see Mt. Vesuvius with its twin peaks. The popular name for the mountain is Somma, and it is prone to eruptions. When Pliny Secundus, a man of wide scientific learning and great eloquence, came here out of a desire of gaining the experience and knowledge to see this sight on the occasion of one of its eruptions, he was overcome by a wind blowing ash and volcanic dust, a wretched death for such a great man. So these are the varying circumstances which have led to Naples being the guardian of the bones of the citizen of Mantua and of those of the citizen of Verona. The mountain however is remarkable for an abundance of many things, but especially for the richness of its wine, which is described as Greek because that part of Italy was held by the Greeks and used to be called Magna Graecia. Next to the right, you pass the island of Capri, which is surrounded by very rugged cliffs, and was the notorious retreat for the senile pleasures of Tiberius and his workshop for cruelty. In a most beautiful stretch of land to the left stood Pompeii and Herculaneum, once famous cities, but now mere names. We learn from Seneca and others that they were destroyed by earthquakes. Sorrento still remains to be seen, itself also productive of honey-sweet wine. The whole area is Terra di Lavoro today; this name once had referred to a part of Campania; both names denote exceptional fertility. This is the reason people established here a contest between Ceres and Liber, which results in no decisive winner.

After this bay, another soon opens up right after, in which you will see Salerno and the river Sele. I hear that Salerno used to be the fountainhead of medical knowledge, but there is nothing that does not die out with the passage of time. I hope you sail on from here with favorable winds and in so smooth a course as I am carried by my gliding pen to Italy's end. On the left then the Calabrian coast extends in an unbroken line. On the right, however, at a distance are Trinacria and Vulcano and Lipari, and smaller islands which also themselves spew smoke and flames and are so windy that it is a matter either of legend (that, surely) or of history that Aeolus, king of the winds, had his palace there, for I have read it both ways. Hence it is that the islands are called

Aeolian, as is commonly agreed. Where Italy is at its narrowest, there is a town (they call it Scalea). How old it is I do not know, but its name is undoubtedly modern. When you reach the tip of Italy, which bends of course to the west, you will see (with a slight adjustment of your angle of vision and almost at the same time) Reggio, the capital city of Calabria on one side, and on the other Messina, a city of Sicily. Between them is the Strait which people call Messinian. Here are those notorious portents, much feared by sailors — Scylla and Charybdis. Everyone agrees that Scylla is a rock to the left, which is stormy and roars with breakers. Charybdis on the opposite side is a great swirling vortex. And do not worry that Virgil in the third book of his great poem seems to locate them differently: he is following the course of someone coming to Italy, but I the course of someone leaving it. In fact poets and historians do agree on a single cause of so great a whirlpool. For they say that our own Apennines, which enclose us and cut us off, used to extend to Trinacria, until over many ages the two seas, as though they had made a pact, relentlessly beat both sides of the mountain from different directions and forced it to give way to their waves. And so, once the barrier had been removed there, the seas rushed together driven by their own momentum. They say moreover that the most southerly part of the Apennines, thus cut off from the main body of the mountain, also lost its name and took that of the Sicilian mountain Peloro, which is one of the three mountains from which Trinacria got its name. Peloro is near Messina; I do not know for sure what its original name was; but it is well known that the mountain took its current name from Pelorus, Hannibal's navigator. Hannibal, as he was leaving Italy with his entire fleet, as Valerius thinks, or was headed home with only one ship, as others would have it (a more likely situation) and in flight from the victorious Romans, had killed Pelorus, thinking that he had been betrayed when he could see no way out of the strait because it seemed so narrow from a distance. When he at last recognized his mistake, he had Pelorus buried on the land there.

The course for those leaving Scalea as far as Reggio is almost straight south. From there it is again towards the east, as you leave Mt. Etna, the foremost of volcanic mountains, far off to the right. Then, after you have altered your course a bit in a northerly direction and have gingerly sailed past Squillace, infamous for shipwrecks, you will come to Crotone, a city which at one time excelled among the people of Italy in strength of both mind and body, in beauty, wealth, and reputation, but now is scarcely known to the Italians themselves. What does the passage of time not destroy? Here used to be the Temple of Juno Lacinia, of world-wide renown. Next in a remote recess of the sea you will have Taranto pointed out to you, the place where Ennius was born and where Virgil died, although others say Brindisi. The city was the cause of serious warfare for the Romans, when it summoned King Pyrrhus to Italy and much later when it helped Hannibal with arms and fortifications. Roman histories will rank these men as their most dangerous enemies throughout all the centuries.

Now you have come to Italy's end, at which point, when you have made your last stop at Otranto, setting the sheet of your sail athwart the wind, you will cross the Adriatic sea and come upon Corfu, the first island off the opposite shore, and other lesser known islands until you arrive at the first corner of Achaia. There indeed you will wish that the Isthmus had been dug, as some have intended to do, so that your course might be both more direct and shorter for you. There is a mountain separating two seas; and if it were to be removed, Achaia would be an island. On its peak, an impregnable site, is Corinth. This fact provided the pretext for the city's destruction when it was captured by the Romans, "who were keenly aware of its strategic location," as Cicero says, "and were afraid that its very location at some later time would encourage the Corinthians to renew hostilities." But since that water route has been cut off, you have to obey the dictates of nature, pass by Corinth, take the longer route around Cape Malea, and see the Achaian coast with its cities: Modon, Coron, and whatever lands that part of the sea washes, all the way to the last corner of Greece. But while the first corner faces towards Italy, this one faces towards Crete, which is now in the possession of the Venetians, but was once the kingdom of Jupiter and the source and beginning of almost all superstitious beliefs. How changeable are all human endeavors! With Crete on the right and Euboea (which people call Negroponte) on the left, you will make your journey safely, with frequent ports, through the Cyclades, the islands of the Aegean which brighten the sea like stars. Here is Scyros, the site of Achilles's first love and young manhood; torn away from there by Ulysses's cunning, that thunderbolt went to Troy. Here is Cos, the homeland of Hippocrates; Lesbos, home of Theophrastus; and Samos, home of Pythagoras, who left there, came to our land, and won the right to be called an Italian philosopher since by his great enthusiasm and intellectual talent he had adorned the name of philosophy, a term he was the first to coin. But what am I doing? I should not find it much easier to count all the islands of the Cyclades than I would the stars of the sky. Therefore you will sail through these islands and leave at your rear those two glories of Greece, Lacedaemon and Athens, and to your left the entrance to the Hellespont, Sestos and Abydos, well known for their unlucky lovers, and Byzantion and Ilion, the former noted for its rivalry with the Rome's power and the latter for its own misfortune. You will sail straight to Rhodes, once sacred to the Sun, but now to Christ, who is more truly of course the sun, and the headquarters of John's army.

Next Asia Minor now lies off to the left. Once the most peaceful of provinces, it was filled with Greek settlers after the fall of Troy; now it is the fierce region of the Turks, the enemies of the truth. Parts of this region toward the south, Lycia and Cilicia, are near your route. The capital of this region, Isauria, was once the stronghold of all the pirates who were at their full strength at this time and had so infested all the seaways that they actually fought in open engagement with the Roman fleets themselves. They were overcome by the outstanding courage and foresight of Pompey the Great, removed from their acts of piracy at sea, and resettled with people who cultivate the land. To prevent any opportunity from attracting them back to their customary practices, they were taken far from the sight of the sea. Tradition has it that from these pirates Lodi (among other towns) was founded near your homeland and took its name from the praise given Pompey. This colony indeed was situated not only far from the sea, but also far from rivers, until it was recently destroyed. While it was being rebuilt, the settlement was relocated and placed on the bank of a very beautiful river, so that its misfortune might seem to have brought it some benefit. But it is not yet time for you to return home. Let us proceed to what remains. Just opposite Cilicia is Cyprus, a land known for nothing else than laziness and pleasure, which people have rightly said is sacred to Venus. And even today it is also sacred to Venus, more than to Mars or Pallas. Rarely, if ever, has any distinguished man lived there. For in the soft soil of pleasure the tough seeds of virtue do not take root. The heat of the earth and sky are an indication of the passion of the inhabitants. When lands are rather near the sun for most of the time and enjoy a mild climate, this passion burns with unbearable ardor, almost unnaturally so, as though people's temperaments have conformed to the physical environment. Do not stay there long, for it is certainly not a fit place for a soldier and a man of action to live. French arrogance, Syrian luxury, and Greek flattery and deceit all meet on this one island. The best and most precious thing they have is that Hilarion lies buried there, an immigrant with quite different moral standards.

Opposite Cyprus in the farthest corner of the sea lies Armenia Minor. The ship must turn sharply away from here and bear to the right. But now I rejoice that you have come to land, just as if I had shared your danger and weariness. I do not know where you will disembark, for more than one port lies open to your approach. The opinion of the shipmaster, the wishes of your companions, the wind, the day, the place, and opportunity will tell you what you ought to do. For as we are advised by an old proverb, plans are formed as the occasion requires. To proceed, however, from north to south, along that coast there are maritime cities — Tortosa, Tripoli, Beirut, Sur, Caesarea, Jaffa, and Ascalon. In the midst of these, lies Acre, once a noble city, but now overthrown and turned to ashes — the worst and unforgiveable disgrace and most shameful scar for Christian kings, unless the loss of Jerusalem itself is somewhat more shameful. Of course, if you should disembark farther up the coast, you will have the added pleasure of seeing Damascus, the capital of Syria. For it is not just some cosmographer that calls it that but the illustrious prophet Isaiah. Although I am aware that some consider Antioch the first city of Syria and its capital, to which view Hegesippus (following Josephus) subscribes in the third book of his *Histories*, nevertheless, in my opinion, Damascus is somewhat more distinguished and certainly much older. You will see a city worth seeing both for its beauty and age, of which from the time of kings of Israel, many centuries before the foundation of Rome, frequent mention is made in both sacred and secular literature. If you put in farther down the coast, you will save yourself some work, but you will see so much the less: you will be less tired by an overland route because Jerosolyma, and the goal of your proposed journey, is close to where you disembark. Therefore, even though I have pointed out many places for you to seek out and visit along the way, which you might have thoughtlessly passed over, thinking only of the goal of your journey, at this point I do not have any advice for you. Even before you set foot out of your home, you thought out and pondered for a long time everything here ahead of time, since as the philosophers say, the accomplishment of anything ends with its execution, but begins with an intention. You have undertaken all of this toil and trouble just to see with your eyes in that city, sacred because of the death of the Lord, and in nearby places, what you were already seeing in your imagination: the river in which Christ bathed; the temple or the ruins of the temple in which He taught; the place where He suffered bodily pain with the utmost humility so He could free us from our passions; the tomb where His most sacred body rested while He Himself, victorious over death and Hell, was descending to despoil the realm of His enemy and from which He arose, as His guards lay buried in sleep, after He had returned and assumed an immortal body; next Sion and the Mount of Olives; nearby is both the place from which He ascended into Heaven and the place to which it is believed He will return for the Judgment; the place where He commanded the winds and the waves; where He fed a great crowd with a little food; where He turned water into wine, which seemed like a great thing to the guests but was easy for one who had created out of nothing the bread, the wine, the water, and the guests themselves; where finally He selected uneducated and poor fishermen to catch rulers and kings with their hooks and nets; where He caused the blind to see, made lepers clean, the lame to walk, brought the dead to life; and what is greater than all these wonders (except that all things are equally easy for God), He restored to freedom a soul oppressed by demons and buried in sin. There are many things besides which would be too much for me to mention and not at all necessary since you know everything in the Gospels. A pious shudder will enter the devout soul of one intently contemplating these things, as he moves from one place to the next. I remind you about one thing that might have slipped your memory, namely that you are seeing that city which the Romans, the conquerors of nations, considered such a fine piece of work to have conquered that Titus, then in charge of the army and afterwards the empire, upon entering it, marveled at the walls and confessed that his victory was not so much the result of human courage, but of divine grace. And so indeed it was. Christ Himself, whom they thought they had removed from the land of the living, rightly showed favor to those taking vengeance on His enemies; although He was still unknown to them, He would nevertheless be known and worshipped by their successors. And so although it has often happened in other cases, nevertheless it was especially fulfilled in the case of this destruction what is said in His name in the Psalm, "Revive me and I will bring retribution on them," — such was the massacre of men, such the hunger of the wretches and so sad their need. If you want to know about that in detail, read Josephus, who relates not what he has heard, but what he has seen and shared in common with the others.

But what are you thinking now? Or has a longing for us not yet taken hold of you to see your home, your homeland and your friends? I believe so; no, I am certain it could not be otherwise. But there is no motive stronger than virtue. It is that which urges a noble spirit through every difficulty and does not allow it to rest nor to look back; and it forces a man to forget not only his wife's intimacies but also his fine children and loved ones and to choose nothing, to want nothing, and finally to think of nothing other than the beauty of virtue. This motive, which made Ulysses forgetful of Laertes, Penelope, and Telemachus, will I fear now keep you from us longer than we might wish. I see that you have the look of a man who is going farther on. And rightly so. For under what circumstances could you have passed by Bethlehem, the city of David, which the divine seers with prophetic voice had said would be famous for a heavenly birth? There as you look upon the place of the earliest childhood of our King, you will think how humility, which He most clearly sanctified at the birth of His only begotten Son, has always been pleasing to God, and you will think of the unspeakable origin of our Savior, who was begotten before the beginning of time and was born at the end of time, if one pays attention to the number of ages. You will contemplate the Virgin Mother; the Divine Child lying in a manger and crying in his crib; angels singing on high; the amazed and speechless shepherds; kings from foreign lands laden with many gifts, but a native king raging with his sword; the land dripping with the innocent blood of blessed infants and the tears of the grieving mothers and the whole heaven resounding with sad wailing; the holy foster father, in the midst of all this, because of a warning from an angel, trying to go secretly, with the unblemished mother and heavenly foster child, from an ungrateful homeland into Egypt, a safe hiding place for his important charge, the gentiles already then beginning to take hope that once the first-born had been rejected because of his ingratitude, the inheritance of the Supreme Father would pass to the younger son, i.e., to the people of the gentiles.

But now you too, I think, want to follow Joseph, rather Mary, I should say Christ, in flight — a sacred journey and worthy of you. We must follow and seek after Christ on earth so that even so we may learn how to follow Him to heaven and at last find Him, long sought after in the place where He once lived, in the place where He now lives. Now not far from here is the sea which is called the Sea of Sodom; the river Jordan runs into it. Here there are clear traces of destroyed cities and heavenly vengeance. Close by is the solitude of the desert. The journey is hard, I admit, but for one striving for salvation, no journey ought to seem difficult. Our enemy will everywhere put obstacles in your path and make you tired of your companions or your circumstances, in order to hold you back from your undertaking or slow you down; or if he can do neither, at least make you less eager for this sacred pilgrimage. But besides all that, here he will add on the natural roughness of the terrain and the lack of all the ordinary necessities of life. But it will help to recall that everything good is purchased at a great price and apply the passage of Virgil to your own situation, the one where he says, "Devotion overcomes a difficult journey." Also paraphrase Lucan's sentiment, "Hard is the path to righteousness and hard is the way to love for a soul in danger of being lost." Nothing is so hard that fervent virtue and firm commitment may not soften it. Indeed if Marcus Cato is praised for having fled the moderate rule of Caesar over the Libyan Syrtes and the sandy haunts of serpents, will you not flee the harsh and savage yoke of Satan over the same desert where once a whole nation fled the cruelty of the Pharaoh? Will you, a brave young man, not be able to do what old men, boys, and frail women were able to do? God was with them and He will be with you. Moreover you will reflect that in these places Moses was given the law, had a conversation with God and a vision of the bush; that manna fell from heaven, and that there were other divine favors for a dear, but ungrateful people, as well as divine judgments. Perhaps you will feel the desire of seeing the Red Sea, which the poet properly called, not the Red Sea, but the Red Shore; for this name is taken not from its water but from the color of the shore. When you get there, you will not reflect on the Indian perfumes and goods carried from the East into Egypt by this strait and from there into our sea, but rather on a people helped by God and conducted through the middle of the waves with their feet dry. The former is a matter of human greed and lack of resources; the latter is a matter of divine loyalty and power. Here you will look upon the body of the Virgin Catherine in the place where it is said that it was placed by the hands of angels; it is fitting that she, who had fought on behalf of the law of God to the death, should be laid to rest on that very mountain where the law was divinely given. Throughout this area the attacks of the Arabs are dreadful, as are the thirst and hunger and hard work; but there is almost nothing more dangerous than getting lost because there are no signs showing the right way. So be very careful not to let any constraint separate you from your companions.

Finally, by a difficult trail and one exposed on both sides, you arrive in Egypt. There on the Nile you will see the new Babylon, the work of Cambyses, and Egyptian Carrhae, a very populous and large city. They were patterned after the old Babylon across the Euphrates and Assyrian Carrhae. You will see the remarkable boundary between Asia and Africa, opposite the Don. It is a great and awesome river, about which philosophers, poets, and cosmographers have had much to say; Aristotle wrote a whole book on the subject. The river rises miraculously each summer and floods the land with fertile silt; it has countless channels but its source is unknown. The kings of the Egyptians, Persians, and Macedonians, and finally the Roman emperors have all sought certain knowledge of it in vain. To this day the source of the river remains unknown. The opinions and research of scholars and the histories written about this topic are known to many readers. This is the place to mention something famous and noteworthy, which I have heard from distinguished men. They say that there is a clear spring at the place where they hid Christ from the cruelty of Herod, which the Almighty Child brought forth from the dry earth to cool His anxious mother. Christians happily drink from it, they say, but it is more bitter than wormwood to the Saracens, so much so that it is painful for them to taste it ever so slightly with their lips, and they are amazed to see our people drinking from it so eagerly and regard it as some kind of divine portent. Of course, it was not a big thing for the one who created the spring to set down as well the laws He wanted and give a different taste to the water according to the differing faiths of those who drink from it.

Nothing of note now remains which I have not mentioned, except Alexandria, the career of Alexander, the fame of Alexander, and the mausoleum of Alexander. When Julius Caesar came to Alexandria after that day in Thessaly and the death of Pompey, he is said to have visited the mausoleum out of a show of religious piety, after he had been influenced by ominous rumblings of a disturbed crowd. And Augustus Caesar, after his victory at Actium, and after Antony had been defeated and forced to commit suicide, came to the same place and reverently viewed the body of Alexander. And when someone asked him if he also wanted to view the mausoleum of the Ptolemies, he wittily said that he wanted to look upon a king, not dead people. Doubtless he meant that one becomes a king by virtue of one's courage and glorious deeds and not by having a kingdom, a scepter, and a crown. You will apply what Augustus said to this extent, that you want to see saints, not dead people. Nevertheless, because the ancient reputation of famous men does not fire the spirit without certain inducements, you too will be permitted to visit this tomb if it has not crumbled because of its age, and also the urn which is on display as the one containing Pompey's ashes. Greek writers apply the adjective Great to Alexander; Roman writers apply it to Pompey (the French, however, have applied that name to Charles). This one city contains those two men. The one came from the North, Pella, the other from the West, Rome. You will see where Caesar, cut off and surrounded in an unequal battle, performed his scarcely believable exploits. You will see Pharus, from which the common name of "lighthouse" has spread throughout other lands everywhere. You will see the many channels of the Nile, where the Fortune of the Roman people viewed the mutilated and torn body of its own leader, and the weeping victor looked upon the head cut off from the torso, having so divided the world with his son-in-law that the Nile washes the one, and the Tiber washes the other. Oh, the steadfastness of Fortune! Oh, the destiny of human endeavors! As you are certainly quick-witted and a ready student, you will easily learn, with so many great men as your instructors, how much faith you must put in prosperity, and always remember the lesson.

But now you have gone far enough, and I have written enough: let it be this far and no farther that you plow the sea with your oars and cross the land on foot, and that I furrow this paper with a hurried pen. Whether you are tired of travel or not, I am tired of writing, the more so because of the faster pace I have set myself. For the journey you have finished in perhaps scarcely three months, I have finished in the last three days. Here let there be an end to both journeys. You must return home, and I to my research, which I shall do immediately. But for you there is a bit of trouble left to endure, which you will do successfully with the help of Christ. Because of what you have seen and with the help of this guide, you will return, I am sure, more learned and more holy.

COMMENTARY

1 Ad Iohannem de Mandello: the Cremona Manuscript says that Giovanni Mandelli was the recipient of Petrarch's *Itinerarium*, an ascription also found in several other manuscripts (e.g., Lumbroso 1889.24). Petrarch's Giovanni is to be identified with the one described by D. Muoni (*Famiglia Mandelli* in *Famiglie notabili milanesi* [Milan, 1877] tav. VI; quoted by Lumbroso 1889.25) as follows: "capitano generale di Milano nel 1340, pretore di Piacenza nel 1346, governatore di Pavia nel 1351, eletto 2 settembre 1352 capitano generale in Piemonte contro Savoia e Monferrato, 1354 podestà di Bergamo, e 8 dicembre 1359 luogotenente in Milano pel duca Gian Galeazzo Visconti, che onoravolo altresì col titulo di suo cugino germano." Successful both as a soldier and as a civil and judicial administrator, Giovanni, son of Guido and Florimonda, grandson of Matteo Visconti, was a man of action, but he was also well educated and a man of genuine piety. It was primarily these latter qualities that would have formed the basis of their friendship when Petrarch moved to Milan in 1353. Giovanni's most lasting deed as an administrator (governor of Pavia in 1351) was to inaugurate the building of a celebrated bridge over the Ticino, whose dedicatory inscription bore his name (Giulini 1854.5:368–369). It called him a *potens miles* and described him as *egregius* and a noble citizen of Milan. The bridge, which Petrarch thought worthy of high praise (*Sen.* 5.1), collapsed in 1947 as a result of bomb damage (Macadam 1991.207). By a happy coincidence, Rubaconte Mandelli, a kinsman of Giovanni, built an equally celebrated bridge over the Arno while *podestà* of Florence in 1237 (Giovanni Villani, *Cronica,* VII.26; in Porta 1990.1:310). It was named after Rubaconte in Dante's time (*Purgatorio,* 12.102), but was afterwards called Ponte alle Grazie. Like Giovanni's bridge, Rubaconte's was bombed in WWII and like it, has been rebuilt, though not in the original style.

In 1355, after his year of service at Bergamo, Giovanni seems to have made a pilgrimage to Rome by way of Florence. On Christmas day of that year, Petrarch wrote for a Giovannolo a short letter of introduction (*Fam.* 19.6; cf. 19.7.4), which might be presented to Francesco Nelli, Petrarch's good Florentine friend and prior of Santi Apostoli. The letter suggests that Petrarch and this Giovannolo became acquainted at the court (aula) of Archbishop Giovanni Visconti, who had died the previous year (*duce . . . extincto*), though the Archbishop's name is not mentioned. Such is the interpretation of Billanovich (1947.220–221). This view gathers strength from the fact that Giovannolo's desire to make a pilgrimage to Rome is of a piece with Giovanni's desire to go to the Holy Land. The metaphorical language Petrarch uses to describe his and Giovannolo's companionship in service, drawn as it is from military parlance (in eisdem castris militavimus), is quite appropriate if the Giovannolo of the letter is the same as the Giovanni of the *Itinerarium*. Wilkins believes, however, that the Giovannolo of the letter should not be identified with Giovanni Mandelli; he thinks that Giovannolo and Petrarch were in the service together in Avignon at the court of Cardinal Giovanni Colonna, some seven or eight years earlier (Wilkins 1958.112–113). A Giovannolo from Avignon, friend of Petrarch, is otherwise unknown.

Petrarch's high regard for Giovannolo's piety ("a true despiser of the things of this world") is the real point of his letter, a sentiment that is echoed in Nelli's reply to Petrarch (*Ep.* 17 in Cochin 1892). The portrait of Giovanni (Giovannolo) that thus emerges is that of a man with qualities as appealing as they are rare: he is a genuinely spiritual man who is nevertheless energetically involved in the important affairs of his day. This image, which is in harmony with the Giovanni of the *Itinerarium*, may be given sharper focus if the description of a Giovannolo da Ferro written by the contemporary chronicler Pietro Azario may also be referred to the Giovanni of the *Itinerarium*. Azario, close associate of this Giovannolo in the service of the Visconti and a friend of Petrarch, describes Giovannolo as a "legalis homo," a legal expert whom Archbishop Visconti valued above all others as one who was known for the probity and charity with which he lived his life and for his rejection of the vanities of this world: *pompas et tributa odiens et honestissime et cum caritate vivens* (text quoted by Billanovich 1947.221).

At the end of the *Itinerarium* (lines 671–672), Petrarch estimates that it will take Giovanni about three months to complete his journey to the Holy Land, but records have been preserved at Pisa which show that Giovanni was a visitor there about two months after he is supposed to have left Milan. The City Fathers approved on 6 June 1358 an outlay of expenses "in faciendo honorem domino Iohanni Mondelli de Mediolano." As part of Giovanni's reception, the motivation for which is unstated, he was given a special showing of one of the city's most prized possessions, a famous copy of Justinian's *Pandects* (or *Digest*): that would be an appropriate display for a "legalis homo" (document quoted by Billanovich 1947.223). A scant two weeks later (June 17) Giovanni was among the distinguished guests who heard Petrarch deliver an oration at Novara on the occasion of that city's restoration to the Visconti's control (Wilkins 1958.167–169). For a discussion of the time frame for Giovanni's journey, see the Introduction.

The mere fact that the Pisans permitted Mandelli to see their copy of the *Pandects* has in itself a significance that should be noted. The book was regarded almost as a sacred relic, and access to it was limited to a very select few. After the *Digest* was removed to Florence in 1406, the Venetian scholar Francesco Barbaro, who wanted to examine the Greek passages in the text, was denied permission to do so (1416). In 1490, Politian collated the *Pandects* and concluded from his examination of the text that the Emperor Justinian had actually written the preface in his own hand (see di Benedetto 1969.53–112 and Wilson 1992.5–6, 24–25 and 109–111). For the legends concerning Pisa's acquisition of the *Pandects* see Rashdall 1936.1:98–100. That Mandelli was granted access to this famous codex says much about his high status and educational background.

Aside from the *Itinerarium*, only one other letter (*Misc.* 8) from Petrarch to Giovanni has survived. On 6 July 1368, Petrarch wrote a letter to Giovannolo Mandelli from Pavia in which he speaks of an infected leg and uses that as an excuse for taking so long to reply to a letter sent to him by Giovannolo some time before. The tone of the letter is affectionate (amice optime) and forthcoming; this suggests that they probably corresponded on a regular basis.

The letter, in two roughly equal parts, deals first with Petrarch's news. Ever since his horse had fallen with him (23 February 1345; *Fam.* 5.10), his left leg has caused him problems (tibia sinistra, vetus hostis mea). The leg was bothering him in Milan where he had gone to attend a wedding (on 5 June) between Lionel, Duke of Clarence, and Violante, daughter of Galeazzo Visconti. (The young Chaucer, servant in the Duke's entourage, probably was in Milan for the occasion, but if he was, he certainly did not meet "Franceys Petrak, the lauriat poete," whose praises he would later sing in the Clerk's Prologue, 31–33.) On his way back to Pavia (3 July), the leg worsened. Now on 6 July, he was up but very shaky (tremebundus). Soon he hoped he would be heading back to Padua by boat, trying along the way to make contact with Emperor Charles IV (with whom he had been negotiating on behalf of the Visconti). In the second part of the letter, Petrarch turns his attention to Giovanni's situation. It is sad to learn that Giovanni has fallen into disfavor at Milan and has been living in exile, probably for about four years since Milanese documents make no mention of him after 1364 (Novati 1904.53). Giovanni's letter to Petrarch evidently had had much to say about the mutability of human friendships and about the reliability of God's friendship. Petrarch emphatically agrees (illud amicitie prorsus ita est ut dicitis), expanding on what Giovanni had already said on the topic. Petrarch ends the letter by hoping that after their common exile in the prison of the body they may be reunited in their real homeland and in the land of the truly living (relaxati demum nos in patria et in terra viventium videamus!). In his valediction, he addresses Giovanni as *et immerite exul et egregie.* The text of the letter may be found in Wilkins and Billanovich 1978.210–211. The letter was first published by Novati 1904.61–63, with Italian translation and discussion on 48–53 (see 50, note 1 on the form of Giovanni's name in the letter).

There is a certain amount of variation as regards Giovanni's name and place of origin. Petrarch himself calls him both Giovanni and Giovannolo, but in both pieces addressed to him, he is from Mandello (modern Mandello del Lario, about 25 miles east of Como). There is a reference in Petrarch's *Epistolae Variae* (4), written in 1362, to a "Iohannolus de Cumis," Giovannolo da Como, who was to help Petrarch by delivering to him the fair copy of one of his own books he was having prepared. Billanovich (1947.221–222) believes that this is a reference to our Giovanni since the Mandelli family had its origins in Como (see R. Parravicini, "La famiglia dei conti Mandelli di Como," *Giornale araldico di Pisa,* vol. 3, 4 [1875]; cited by Novati 1904.43). This idea deserves a certain amount of attention since in the *Itinerarium* Petrarch takes special pains about the proper form of the name of the city of Como (see note to lines 255–256). Since Giovanni seems to have been constantly on the move, he may have styled himself variously, depending on where he was currently living. The record at Pisa refers to him as Giovanni Mondelli [Mandelli] and says he is from Milan, presumably because Giovanni had so presented himself. And so it may have been when Pietro Azario was writing his description of "Iohannolus de Ferro."

Petrarch had an unusually wide circle of friends, and it may be that the Giovannolo for whom he wrote a letter of recommendation in 1355, the Giovannolo described by Azario as so pious and so highly prized as a legal adviser to the Visconti, and the Giovannolo who will transport books for Petrarch in 1362 are all different people, none of whom, or only some of whom, may be identified with the Giovanni of the *Itinerarium*. On the other hand, perhaps this is the proper place for the application of Ockham's principle of parsimony: *Multi Iohannoli non sunt ponendi sine necessitate.*

3–10 The sentiments on Fortune expressed in the opening few lines may seem no more than rhetorically conventional to the modern reader, but they reflect a serious preoccupation in Petrarch's intellectual life. In the same year he wrote the *Itinerarium,* for example, he would put the final touch on his *Secretum,* large sections of which deal with his personal problems arising from the vagaries of Fortune (see note to lines 56–57). In 1358, he had been working for at least four years on his *De remediis utriusque fortune* (see selections in *Prose,* 606–645), a major work completed finally in 1366 in which he examines the nature of Fortune and the proper response of the individual to both good and bad Fortune. (For a brief discussion on the role of Fortune in both these works, see Trinkhaus 1979.66–69, 121–124.) On 13 January 1361, Petrarch made quite a sensation in Paris with a speech in which he stressed the role of Fortune in the release of John II by the English and his return to France (see Godi 1965 for text and discussion). The king had wanted to quiz Petrarch further on the nature of Fortune, but never got the chance, much to Petrarch's relief since he was lacking his reference library (*Fam.* 22.13 and 14). See also Doren 1922, Patch 1927, and Heitmann 1958 on Fortuna in Petrarch and in general. Both the *Secretum* and the *De remediis* have been recently translated: see Carozza 1989 and Rawski 1991.

Since the "Fortune" that Petrarch says prevents him from sailing with Mandelli is his fear of becoming seasick, he may be playing on the colloquial meaning of "fortuna" in the vernacular as "storm at sea." Says Niccolò da Poggibonsi, "e la notte il mare fece grandissima e pericolosa fortuna, tanto che in questa notte sì perirono nove navili" (Bacchi della Lega 1945.1:4). Cf. the use of "fortuna" at Dante, *Purgatorio* 32.116 in the sense of "storm."

13 peregrinatio: before the establishment of the Latin Kingdom, according to Wilkinson (1988.81), the word *peregrinatio* meant simply "journey," with no additional meaning of a religious nature; by the end of the twelfth century, he says, it had acquired the meaning "pilgrimage." Certainly Urban II's use of the verb *peregrinari* in his proclamation of a holy war at Clermont in 1095 gave new meaning to the word (see the text of the speech as reported in the eyewitness account of Robert the Monk, *Historia Hierosolimitana*, 1.1–3 in *RHC, Occ.* III. 727–730; English translation in Brundage 1962.17–21): Christian warriors were to sanctify themselves by journeying to the Holy Places and by fighting for their recovery. Theirs would be an armed pilgrimage. But the word has a very complex history beginning with St. Augustine (Claussen 1991.33–75 and TeSelle 1996.103–120). By the fifth century, *peregrinatio* commonly meant what we mean by the term "pilgrimage" (Monga 1996.13). During Petrarch's time, *peregrinatio* was the most common term for a crusade (though not the technical one), and crusaders were commonly called *peregrini*. The English word "crusade" did not appear until the eighteenth century, having developed from the seventeenth-century French and Spanish forms (*Oxford English Dictionary*, s.v. crusade).

15–16 victa mors simul et victrix vita sepulta est: cf. 1 Cor. 15:26, 54–55; 2 Tim. 1:10; Heb. 2:14; Rom. 5:12–17, 6:9, and 8:2 (on ending the "reign" of Death). According to Niccolò da Poggibonsi (Bacchi della Lega 1945.1:16), in the church of the Holy Sepulcher of the fourteenth century there was a chapel adorned with six Latin hexametric verses, two of which express paradoxical ideas about Christ's death similar to Petrarch's:

> Vita mori voluit et in hoc tumulo requievit;
> mors quia vita fuit nostram victrix abolevit
>
> (Life chose to die and was laid to rest in this tomb;
> Death, because Life was victorious, put an end
> to our [death])

It is quite possible that Petrarch had heard of these verses and that this passage is echoing their sentiments, or at least their paradoxical qualities.

18–19 Infans . . . pudor loqui prohibet: cf. Horace (*S*.1.6.57): *infans namque pudor prohibebat plura profari.*

23–24 neque enim in loco sed in animo est quod felices facit et miseros: cf. Horace, *Ep*. 1. 11. 25–27,

> nam si ratio et prudentia curas,
> non locus effusi late maris arbiter aufert,
> caelum non animum mutant qui trans mare currunt.

Cf. also Boethius (*De cons. Phil.* 2 pr. 4, 72–73): *Quid igitur, o mortales, extra petitis intra vos positam felicitatem?* The phrase *neque in loco sed in animo* is derived from Horace, and this Petrarch combined with Boethius's sentiment, which he had made use of earlier (1352–53) in the fourth book of his *Invect. contra medicum* (Ricci 1978.85): *Intus in anima est quod felicem et quod miserum facit.*

25–26 Fustra bellum et maria vitamus, frustra . . . parcimus corpusculo: having admitted his fear of the sea and having raised the subject of fear of death, Petrarch reflects on the inevitability of death (lines 24–39). His texts for this brief meditation are not those of Scripture but of Horace, Seneca, and Cicero. His initial statement neatly paraphrases Horace's *C.* 2.14.13–16:

> frusta cruento Marte carebimus
> fractisque rauci fluctibus Hadriae,
> frusta per autumnos nocentem
> corporibus metuemus Austrum:

Note that Petrarch preserves the anaphora of *frustra.* At *Fam.* 3.10.8, a letter of uncertain date, Petrarch quotes these same Horatian verses in the course of a discussion of death. For a series of brief essays on death and dying by Petrarch, see *De remediis* 2.117–132 in Rawski 1991.3:283–338, with commentary 4:460–532, where many of the same themes as those in the *Itinerarium* are discussed (Latin text *Opera* 1554.1:132–254). The whole of book I of the *Secretum* is a meditation on death (*Prose* 28–68).

26–27 in medias voluptuosorum latebras inque ipsos regum thalamos invisa mors penetrat: cf. Seneca, *Ep.* 82.4: *Quae latebra est in quam non intret metus mortis?*; also Lucan (8.405): *in regum thalamis.*

28–29 sepe [mortem] quam forte labor et exercitium distulisset iners luxus anticipat: on the efficacy of exercise and moderate living in staving off death, cf. Cicero, *Sen.* 35–36: *pugnandum tamquam contra morbum sic contra senectutem, habenda ratio valetudinis, utendum exercitationibus modicis, tantum cibi et potionis adhibendum ut reficiantur vires, non opprimantur.*

29–30 hanc mortem ut arcessere vetitum, sic evitare velle dementia est: cf. Cicero, *Sen.* 72: . . . *illud breve vitae reliquum nec avide appetendum senibus nec sine causa deserendum.*

31–32 at equanimiter expectare, tamquam ubique proximam et horis omnibus affuturam: cf. Cicero, *Sen.* 66–76 on the nearness of death for a person of any age and on the reasons why a person should await death's arrival calmly; see especially: *Moriendum enim certe est, et incertum an hoc ipso die. Mortem igitur omnibus horis impendentem timens qui poterit animo consistere?* (74–

75). Petrarch quotes the first part of this passage verbatim at *Fam.* 22.12.12 and 24.1.8.

33 Secundam mortem omni nisu fugere consilium erat: the "second death" is the eternal death of the soul damned to Hell (see Rev. 2:11, 20:6, etc.; Augustine, *De civ. Dei*, 19.28). Petrarch uses the phrase in its religious sense here, but elsewhere he uses it to refer to the time when a man's reputation evaporates with the passage of time, as in *Africa*, 2. 431–432, in *Triumphus temporis (Trionfi, Rime* 553), and in the third book of the *Secretum* (202–204 in *Prose*). Petrarch evidently got the idea for this secular application of the phrase from Boethius, *De cons. Phil.* 2, m 7, 23–26:

> Quodsi putatis longius vitam trahi
> mortalis aura nominis,
> cum sera vobis rapiet hoc etiam dies,
> iam vos secunda mors manet.

39–40 Longam mortem et peiorem mortem, nauseam; non de nichilo quidem, sed expertus metuo: it is not fear of death, says Petrarch, but of seasickness that is the source of his reluctance to sail. Pertinent to an evaluation of this statement is a letter dated 26 November 1343 from Naples. In the letter, Petrarch describes a violent storm and earthquake which struck the area early on the previous morning and lasted well into the day, destroying many ships at anchor in the bay. The loss of life was shocking to Petrarch: he saw torn bodies and parts of bodies washed up on shore. He concludes this letter to Giovanni Colonna as follows:

> te [obsecro] ne me unquam amplius vitam ventis ac fluctibus credere iubeas. Hoc enim est in quo neque tibi neque Romano Pontifici neque patri meo, si ad lucem redeat, parere velim. Aerem volucribus, mare piscibus relinquo; terrenum animal, terrestre iter eligo (*Fam.* 5.5.19).

Scholars believe that Petrarch was true to his word and that he never traveled by sea after this experience in 1343 ("Petrarch resolved never again to venture on the sea — and he never did," Wilkins 1961.42), although he did not hesitiate to travel rivers by boat. The motive behind his decision, to judge from this letter, is clearly fear of the sea, a fear which is akin to the fear many people nowadays have of flying. Petrarch does not mention seasickness as a consideration.

Aside from this passage in the *Itinerarium*, Petrarch never actually claims to suffer from seasickness. On his way to Naples two months earlier in 1343, Petrarch had suffered through some very stormy weather, which caused him to abandon his attempt to reach Naples by sea (*Fam.* 5.3. 1–3). He was held up at Monaco by a storm for a whole day, though the captain made repeated attempts to leave port despite the bad weather (sepe nequicquam retentato abitu). The next day the ship did set out in dangerous weather conditions (ancipiti tempestate) and was tossed about the whole day by high seas (die toto iactati fluctibus). The next day it was decided to continue the trip overland (as far as Lerici at any rate) because of more bad weather. There is no hint of any seasickness. In fact, Petrarch's reaction to this storm was unexpressed irritation that he was being kept from the sea by bad weather (Irasci tacitus). When the decision was finally made to abandon the voyage, Petrarch was furious at the inconvenience (Ibi [at Moritz] indignari altius et ludos maris agnoscere). Not a word about seasickness.

In his description of the voyage (probably his first) that he made with his parents from Pisa to Marseilles in 1312, a boy of nearly eight years, Petrarch only remembers (and that in loving detail) the incredible beauty of the Italian *riviera*, something he would hardly have had much interest in if he had been suffering from seasickness at the time (*Fam.* 14.5.23–26).

The story about seasickness in the *Itinerarium* is not credible. It is certainly understandable, however, why Petrarch would have found it difficult to own up to his fear of the sea to a military man like Mandelli and that he preferred to explain his reluctance to sail by claiming that he suffered from seasickness. But Petrarch might have invented any number of plausible reasons for not going on the pilgrimage (e.g., the press of scholarship, personal commitments, etc.). Why did he resort to this excuse and not another?

The answer may lie in a famous precedent provided by Seneca, an author whose work Petrarch admired despite his criticism of the man in *Fam.* 24.5. In AD 63 or 64 Seneca wrote to Lucilius of a journey by sea that he decided to make from Naples to Puteoli. When the sea turned rough, Seneca began to feel queasy and demanded that the captain put in and let him off the ship. As the ship approached the shore, Seneca could no longer contain his eagerness to be on solid land, plunged into the sea just as he was, and swam to shore. In his letter (*Ep.* 53. 1–4), Seneca jokingly says that the reason why it took Ulysses ten years to sail home was not that he was the victim of Neptune's anger, but that he suffered from seasickness (nausiator erat). If he is obliged to go anywhere by ship in the future, Seneca jokes about himself, it will probably take him twenty years to get there (Et ego quocumque navigare debuero, vicensimo anno perveniam). Seneca intends never to sail again.

It is tempting to see Seneca as Petrarch's model in the matter of seasickness here in the *Itinerarium*: the pose would have appealed to his highly developed sense of communion with the great men of the past (see note to lines 238–241, where Petrarch's desire to duplicate Seneca's trip to Liternum is discussed). It sounds as though Petrarch is alluding to Seneca's little joke about Ulysses when he suggests that nature has imposed the restraint of seasickness on him to put a curb (frenum) on his "animo vago et rerum novarum visione inexplebili oculo," lines 43–44 below. This description could very well serve as a description of Ulysses, whom Petrarch characterized elsewhere as a man "che desiò del mondo veder troppo," *Triumphus fame* 2.18 in *Rime*, 537.

This pose of a man who suffered from seasickness would be comparable then to other literary poses adopted by Petrarch, for example, the one in the fictive *Fam.* 4.1 of a man who has undergone a profound conversion in 1336 (after the manner of Augustine) on the top of Mt. Ventoux: see Billanovich 1947.193–198 and 1966.389–401 where the date of the letter's composition is put around the middle of 1353; for a recent discussion see Ascoli 1991.

5–43, with bibliography. See lines 556–558 below where Ulysses's heroic wanderlust is held up to Mandelli as an example to spur him on to Egypt. For more on Petrarch's fictional letters in the *Seniles* see Wilkins 1951.311–323.

43–44 Hoc forsan animo vago . . . frenum posuit natura: see note to lines 39–40.

45–48 Congressum itaque nunc noti hostis exhorreo . . . stupor ingens sit: Petrarch's final words about his fear betray clearly that it is of the dangerous sea itself rather than of seasickness. Petrarch is thrilled when he looks upon the sea (quam cupide videam) but he cannot bring himself to set foot on a ship (quem vel tangere abhominor). It is the sea that is his enemy, not mal de mer, and his fear of it is the monster (line 41) he has vainly tried to overcome.

51 Ibis ergo sine me: Paolella (1993.119) thinks that this phrase is a probable reference to Tibullus (1.3.1): *Ibitis Aegaeas sine me, Messalla, per undas* (You will go across the waves of the Aegean without me, Messalla). On the face of it, this suggestion is attractive because Petrarch and Tibullus are in somewhat similar situations. Tibullus has set out as a member of Messalla's entourage, headed on an important mission to some eastern province. At Corfu, Tibullus fell ill (seriously, if one can believe him) and wrote his poem declaring his inability to proceed with the trip. The poet calls Corfu by its Homeric name Phaeacia, thus reminding the reader of Ulysses's former visit and establishing himself as a latter-day Ulysses. Just as Homer's hero pined for Penelope on Phaeacia, Tibullus pines for Delia back in Rome, all thought of his mission to the East gone from his mind.

However apt this allusion might be, it does not seem likely that Petrarch knew the verse quoted above. The only Tibullus that Petrarch knew were the some 260 verses contained in the *Florilegium Gallicum*. This collection does contain 16 verses from 1.3, but not the one in question (see Ullman 1928.128–74, esp. 137 and 173–74). If he knew Tibullus from another source, we do not know what it might have been. There is some very slender circumstantial evidence that Coluccio Salutati may have had his complete manuscript of Tibullus (the oldest in existence) copied from one owned and annotated by Petrarch (Reynolds 1986.423), but the fact remains that only three allusions to Tibullus's poetry have been found in Petrarch's work. Of these, as Ullman has shown, one certainly derives from the selections in the *Florilegium* and from no other source. The other two, much less obvious allusions, if they are allusions at all, probably derive from the same source as well.

56–57 Morem enim secutus amantium, cuius presentia cariturus es, imaginem flagitasti: Petrarch compares Mandelli's request for an itinerary to a lover's request for a likeness of his beloved. In this itinerary Mandelli will find the image of Petrarch's soul, not the vain representation of his physical appearance. The comparison, fair enough on one level, seems oddly inappropriate when one considers that it is being suggested to a man of action like Mandelli.

Sometime before leaving for Rome in December of 1336, the great Sienese master Simone Martini (c. 1284–1344; author of the *Maestà*, the *Annunciation,* etc.; see Paccagnini 1958.10:502–508) had made for Petrarch a small (portable) portrait of his beloved Laura, probably more of a sketch than anything else (la ritrasse in carte): Petrarch celebrates the portrait in two sonnets (77, 78) and in the *Secretum*. In Book III of the latter work, which addresses his inappropriate attachment to the married Laura, Petrarch makes Augustine, representative of his better self in the dialogue, rebuke him because he carries the portrait with him wherever he goes and weeps every time he looks at it — in the beginning because of the hopelessness of his love and later because of his sorrow at her death in 1348 (*Prose,* 156). The *Secretum* had been through two major revisions since he began to write it in 1347 (according to some 1342–43). Five years after the last revision (1353), Petrarch read through the *Secretum* once again, made a note to himself at the end of the manuscript recording the year of his inspection (1358), but without noting the exact date.

In his own hand (for the Latin text see de Nolhac 1907.2: 286; for English trans. see Wilkins 1961.77), Petrarch records that he first met and fell in love with Laura on 6 April 1327 (a Good Friday, say *Canz.* 3 and 62, but in 1327 Good Friday fell on 10

April), and that she died on 6 April 1348, Passion Sunday of that year. If one can trust these dates (for a recent discussion see Foster 1984.53–55), Petrarch may have read through the *Secretum* just prior to writing the *Itinerarium*: the subscript of the Cremona manuscript says that he handed it over to Mandelli on 4 April, just six days after Good Friday in the year 1358 (Cheney 1961.104) and two days before the anniversary of Laura's death. If Petrarch reread the *Secretum* in 1358, as we know he did, there could be no more likely time for him to have done that than around the anniversary of their first meeting and of her death. Petrarch had long been struggling to free himself of Laura's spell, but it is easy to believe that he still had her portrait (now lost) and had been recently contemplating the charming likeness that had so often moved him to tears. Mandelli, being a close friend of Petrarch's, may even have seen Laura's portrait and could have appreciated the personal reference. For the complicated problems connected with dating the *Secretum*, see Rico 1974.10–12 and *passim*, and 1984.51–102; Foster 1984.179–185; Baron 1985, especially 72–116 and *passim*. Whatever else, no one doubts that Petrarch reread the *Secretum* sometime in 1358.

Since November of 1356, Petrarch had been working on yet another version of his collection of Italian lyrics (Wilkins 1951. 153–154). By 6 April 1358 (apparently) he had finished a poem for the new collection which dates itself by reference both to his first meeting with Laura and to her death, the last of the "anniversary" poems (on which see Dutschke 1981.83–101). The sonnet (364 in the final form of the *Canzoniere)*, in which Petrarch repents of his long emotional involvement with Laura, distills beautifully this major theme of Book III of the *Secretum (Prose,* 133–188) and catches what one supposes must have been Petrarch's frame of mind when he first agreed to go on pilgrimage with Mandelli.

> Tennemi Amor anni ventuno ardendo
> lieto nel foco e nel duol pien di speme;
> poi che Madonna e 'l mio cor seco inseme
> saliro al ciel, dieci altri anni piangendo;

Omai son stanco e mia vita reprendo
di tanto error, che di vertute il seme
à quasi spento, e le mie parti estreme,
alto Dio, a te devotamente rendo,

pentito et tristo de' miei sì spesi anni:
che spender si deveano in miglior uso,
in cercar pace ed in fuggir affanni.

Signor che 'n questo carcer m' ài rinchiuso
tramene salvo da li eterni danni,
ch'i' conosco 'l mio fallo e non lo scuso.

(Love held me for twenty-one years burning / happily in the fire, and in the pain full of hope; then since my lady and my heart with her / mounted up to heaven, [love held me] weeping for another ten years. / Now I am weary and I reproach my life / for so much error, which all but wasted / the seed of virtue; and what remains of my life, / God on high, I dedicate devoutly to you, / repentant and regretful for my years so spent, / which should have been put to better use / in searching for peace and in fleeing trouble. / Lord, who have enclosed me in this prison, / free me from it safe from eternal damnation: / I recognize my mistake and do not excuse it; cf. trans. in Durling 1976 and in Musa 1996.)

63–64 'mens cuiusque . . . potest': the quotation is verbatim from Cicero's *De republica*, 6.26 (part of the *Somnium Scipionis*). Petrarch quotes the same passage at *De remediis* 1.29 (see Rawski 1991.1:86 and 2:148–149).

71–72 multa que non vidimus scimus, multa que vidimus ignoramus. This appears to be a playful variation on the theme of a short essay (originally a sermon) of St. Augustine's called *On Faith in Things Unseen (De fide rerum quae non videntur*; text in *PL* 40, 171–180). The theme of Petrarch's variation might be entitled *De scientia rerum quae non videntur* (On Knowledge of Things Unseen).

73–79 Parebo equidem . . . magni animi cura est: Petrarch sets forth with admirable clarity the three concerns of his itinerary: he will draw Mandelli's attention to matters of religious, educational, and military interest which are to be seen on the proposed route. This pilgrimage will benefit the whole man. It should be noted that Mandelli has asked Petrarch to address these three specific concerns. The *Itinerarium* is a "customized" piece of writing.

83 Ianuam veniamus: for his knowledge of Genoa, Petrarch relies on his own experience and on local historians. The Genoese chronicles to which he refers in line 92 are those collected in *Annali Genovesi di Caffaro e dei suoi continuatori,* edited by Belgrano and Imperiale di Sant' Angelo and published in 5 volumes in the series entitled *Fonti per la storia d'Italia* by the Instituto storico italiano per il medio evo (Rome, 1890–1929). These works, written by a number of authors, provide a more or less continuous account of the period between Caffaro and Jacopo d'Oria (1099–93). Besides these chronicles, Petrarch is referring to Jacopo da Voragine's (the usual English spelling) *Chronica civitatis ianuensis ab origine urbis usque ad annum MCCXCVII* (Monleone 1941). In this work Voragine (c. 1230–98), author of the famous *Legenda aurea* and eighth archbishop of Genoa, abandons the annalistic method of his predecessors and sets out to write a comprehensive, though certainly not exhaustive, history of the city from remote antiquity to his own day (for a recent discussion see Guidetti 1998.17–36). Voragine is the continuator of Jacopo d'Oria only in a limited sense. Giorgio Stella did not finish his part of the continuation Jacopo da Voragine until 1405 (see reference in note to lines 86–87 below).

Although there is nothing in what Petrarch says to prove that he had actually read any of these chronicles, Jacopo da Voragine's account is likely to have been his source of information here, whether he had read it himself or had heard it from someone who had. Particularly suggestive is the fact that Petrarch takes up in his brief statement on Genoa the following topics in the same order as they are discussed in Jacopo's account: Janus as first king of Italy and founder of the city, the common noun *ianua* as an etymology for the city's name, and finally the ancient spelling of the name.

It may seem excessively cautious to reserve judgment about Petrarch's direct knowledge of the Genoan chronicles, particularly Jacopo da Voragine's, but Petrarch is known on several occasions to have given the distinct impression of firsthand knowledge of a work which he could not have known since it was no longer in existence. Twice he speaks of the lost *De origine et situ urbium*, a work of the Augustan scholar Julius Hyginus (*OCD*, s.v. Hyginus 1), as though he had read it, when in fact he knows of the work only from a reference to it in Servius *A.* 1.277 (see de Nolhac 1907.2:108–109).

86–87 Sua sibi potentia . . . civilium simultatum scatet: the conflicts between the great families of the Doria, Spinola, Adorni, and Fregosi (Ghibellines) on the one side and the Grimaldi, Fieschi, Guarchi and Montaldi (Guelfs) on the other kept Genoa in turmoil for generations. In order to resolve these internal squabbles it became the practice to invite outsiders to serve as chief magistrates: in the fourteenth century there were periods of submission to the Emperor Henry VII (1311–13), Robert of Anjou, King of Naples and leader of the Italian Guelfs (1318–35), and the Visconti of Milan (1353–56). By the end of the century, things became so bad that the Genoese placed their affairs in the hands of Charles VI, the mentally deranged king of France (see Jarry 1896). On the origin of the terms 'Guelf' and 'Ghibelline' and their use in Italy see Waley 1988.145–156, with bibliography on 195.

The factional struggles of the Genoese attracted widespread attention among contemporary observers. Giorgio Stella remarks on them a number of times in his continuation of Jacopo da Voragine, quoting with approval this very passage of the *Itinerarium*. First, he paraphrases Petrarch as follows: *At multa potentia Ianuensium sui civile dissidium sumpsit originem, quare Franciscus Petrarca itinerario sic de Ianua loquens ait . . .* Balbi 1975.45,1–2. The text then quotes Petrarch's line but with an interesting variant after *officit*. Instead of *iugis*, Balbi says he wrote *iurgiis*, the reading of F, the chief witness used by Stella's editor. This reading cannot escape being grossly tautological (*iurgia* and *simultates*), and it blunts Petrarch's point, which is the sheer corrupting nature of power itself. The adjective *iugis* is correct (used again in 113 with *labor*), but it is liable to misinterpretation and corruption because of its hyperbatic position (stressing its predicative and emphatic function) outside the relative clause (unde) to which it belongs. Lo Monaco (1990.43) misinterprets *iugis* as the ablative plural of the noun *iugum*.

Stella quotes or paraphrases the *Itinerarium* on some six occasions, several times at considerable length. Some of these quotes appear in a letter (1405) he had received from Florence's Chancellor, Coluccio Salutati (see Balbi 1975.vi and 7, notes 7 and 9), but he may have had his own copy of it, at least that part of it that had to do with Genoa and the *riviera* to the south. It appears that by the end of the fourteenth century, if not before, the *Itinerarium* was circulating rather widely.

88 Auctorem urbis et nominis: that Janus was the eponymous founder of the city was no doubt the view held by most of the Genoese as line 88 says. But Petrarch, probably in an effort to keep his narrative to the bare essentials, fails to mention that there were three entirely distinct Januses put forward by various authorities as the founder of Genoa: the first Janus who is identified as king of Italy and founder of the city was a king who came to Italy from the East in the time of Moses (or Abraham); the second Janus was a survivor of the fall of Troy and came to Italy at the same time as Aeneas; the third Janus was a king of Epirus who came to Italy after the foundation of Rome and was later deified by the Romans as a result of his heroic deeds on their behalf. This last Janus was the well-known bifrontal god of beginnings (see Voragine's account, *Testo critico commentato*, 2 [85 in the *Fonti* series]: 14–31).

89 an ipse situs urbi nomen dederit: cf. Voragine: *Alii dicunt quod vocata est Janua ex eo quod introitus in Lonbardiam, in Tusciam et in Provinciam* (2: 53).

92–93 apud veteres non Ianue sed Genue nomen in usu est: cf. Voragine: *in omnibus fere libris antiquis civitas nostra non Ianua sed Genua nominatur* (2:56). The medieval form of the name (Janua) apparently came into fashion in place of the ancient form (Genua) at the end of the tenth century. According to Philipp Cluver (1624.70), Liudprand (c. 922–c. 972) was the first to use the spelling *Ianua*, or at least its adjectival form *ianuensis* (*Antapodosis* 4.5), Becker 1915. Cluver's dating for the development of the *Ianua* spelling accords well with Monleone's view expressed in his commentary to Jacopo da Voragine's text (2:59–60): . . . *la denominazione antiqua e classica era "Genua," sulla quale si sovrappose verso il 1000 . . . la forma medioevale "Janua" con le varie interpretazione e le sue leggende* (2:59). G. Stella (Balbi 1975.9, 15–22) also dates the spelling *Ianua* to the late tenth century (987, to be exact).

96–99 sed quantum est intellegere est, prius caput gentis Albingaunum fuerat: in 205 BC Mago, the younger brother of Hannibal, arrived in Liguria with twelve thousand infantry and two thousand cavalry and quickly subdued Genoa (Livy, 28.46; this mention of Genoa marks its first appearance in recorded history). Proceeding west along the coast, Mago made a treaty with the Ingauni, a powerful tribe of Ligurians who held the seaport town of Album Ingaunum or Albingaunum (modern Albenga). Petrarch is inferring from this passage that Albingaunum had been at this time the capital city of the Ligurians since Mago preferred to seek their friendship rather than risk a fight with them even with the large force at his command. Subsequent encounters of the Romans with the Ingauni also suggest that this people held a preeminent position among the Ligurians. In 181 BC the Proconsul Aemilius Paulus fought a very serious battle with Ingauni in which 15,000 of them were killed. As a result of the Roman victory, for which Aemilius was permitted to celebrate a triumph, the whole people of the Ingauni submitted to Rome, and as a consequence all the other Ligurians sent to Rome to sue for peace (Livy, 40.25–28, 34). Cf. Petrarch, *Fam.* 15.7.6: *Maritimi Ligures . . . quorum olim Albingaunum, hodie caput est Ianua.*

97–99 Ipsa . . . Ianua . . . a Romanis ducibus restituta est: Mago destroyed Genoa before he abandoned it. Livy (30.1) records that the praetor Spurius Lucretius was charged with the duty of rebuilding the city in 203 BC. After this, Genoa is mentioned only incidentally by ancient historians.

101–102 in primis classem, quod de Tiria scriptum vides, cuntis terribilem tremendamque litoribus: at the start of the First Punic War, the Carthaginian fleet completely dominated the western Mediterranean. Among the Romans, there were those who lost heart at the very idea of entering Carthaginian waters (Nec defuerant qui ipso Punici maris nomine ac terrore deficerent, Florus, *Epit.* 1.18, 17; Jal 1967). But the writer to whom Petrarch is expressly referring is Valerius Maximus (5.6.ext.4; ed. Briscoe 1998): Ubi sunt superbae Karthaginis alta moenia? Ubi maritima gloria inclyti portus? Ubi *cunctis litoribus terribilis classis*?

102–104 tum molem pelago obiectam . . . nequiquam feriunt procelle: the inner harbor is protected on the south by the Molo Vecchio (540 yards long), begun in 1257. The first mention of a mole in the harbor is in 1134; for more details see Podestà 1913.195–197 and Mazzino 1961.172–184.

108–113 scito te vidisse cotem illam alteram . . . Romanum exercitum haberent: even though he cites Livy as his source (*si quid Livio creditur,* 109), Petrarch is paraphrasing a passage in Florus in which he is talking about two groups of people living in the foothills of the Alps: the Ligurians (Genoese) on the one hand and the Insubrian Gauls (and Illyrians) on the other. Florus says: *Denique utrique cotidiani et quasi domestici hostes tirocinia militum imbuebant, nec aliter utraque gente quam quasi cote quadam populus Romanus ferrum suae virtutis acuebat* (*Epit.* 1.19.3 = 2.3). When Petrarch calls the Genoese "that other whetstone" (*cotem illam alteram*) he has in mind Florus's statement that the Genoese are to be paired with the Gauls as difficult enemies of Rome (*utrique* and *utraque gente*). Without the context provided by Florus, however, the reader is bound to find the word *alteram* quite puzzling since it implies a comparison.

The potential for bafflement regarding this passage is well illustrated in Stella's *Annales Genuenses* (30. 2–18). Here Stella quotes and paraphrases at some length lines 82–112 of the *Itinerarium.* At 30.11, Balbi, Stella's modern editor, offers "cohortem illam alteram" for Petrarch's "cotem illam alteram," because all the manuscripts of Stella's work show this reading except one late and supposedly inferior witness. It would be interesting to know what Stella thought *cohortem* might mean in this context, if that is what he wrote. Petrarch's phrase is puzzling because it is elliptical: *brevis esse laborabat Petrarca; factus est obscurus.* Petrarch, it should be noted, used Florus as a model for his own historical style (de Nolhac 1907.2:34–35), often praising him for his brevity and succinctness.

The manuscripts describe Florus's work as an epitome of Livy, *Epitomae de Tito Livio bellorum omnium annorum DCC libri II.* Many passages are indeed verbatim from Livy or based on Livy, but Florus sometimes contradicts Livy and makes use of sources other than Livy, such as Sallust, Caesar, and perhaps the Elder Seneca. The passage from Florus here paraphrased by Petrarch cannot be traced to any passage in Livy's extant books and may or may not have been taken from or based on Livy. The presumption however is that it came from one of Livy's lost books.

Florus's work, providing as it does an abridgement of 700 years of Rome's history with special reference to her successful wars, was a favorite in the Middle Ages and widely used as a schoolbook through the seventeenth century. It is a book Mandelli would have known very well.

111–114 locorum montana durities . . . otii nichil: Petrarch appears to be expanding the following passage in Florus: *Tuti locis et fuga, durum atque velox genus, ex occasione latrocinia magis quam bella faciebant* (*Epit*. 1.19.4 = 2.3).

117–118 insigne vas solido e smaragdo: the Genoese had a sizeable contingent on hand when the crusaders stormed Caesarea in 1101 (see Gazetteer). Inside the city, the Genoese pursued some of the defenders into a temple built by Herod in honor of Augustus, which had been converted to Christian use. After the battle, the Genoese discovered a green vessel which they believed was made of emerald. This belief led them to accept the dish as their share of the booty, destined to be put on display in their church back in Genoa. This much comes from William of Tyre's *Historia rerum in partibus transmarinis gestarum*, 10.16 (Beugnot 1844).

Voragine confirms the essential points of William's more circumstantial account and adds that many believe that the dish was used by Christ at the Last Supper as a serving platter, while others believe that Nicodemus used it to collect some drops of Jesus's blood when he was helping Joseph of Arimathea take the body down from the cross (John 19:38–42). In time, says Voragine, the vessel was taken to Caesarea where the crusaders later found it (2:309–315).

119 devotum si sic est: Petrarch's skepticism is praiseworthy, but by no means unique. Jacopo da Voragine too had his doubts about the vessel's connection with Christ (2:311): *vulgariter dicitur quod fuit ille chatinus in quo Christus cum suis discipulis in cena comedit. . . . Utrum hoc verum sit ignoramus; sed quoniam Deo nichil est impossibile, ideo nec constanter asserimus nec pertinaciter denegamus.*

William of Tyre (c. 1130–85), who seems not to know the story that connects the dish with Christ, doubts that the dish was made of emerald at all: [*Ianuenses*] *usque hodie transeuntibus per eos magnatibus vas idem pro miraculo solent ostendere, persuadentes quod vere sit id quod color esse indicat smaragdinus* (10.16). The belief that the hexagonal green dish was made of emerald prevailed until it was removed to Paris in 1805, examined, and proved to be the product of the glassmaker's art. When the dish was being returned to Genoa in 1816, it was broken and then repaired as examination showed it to have been a number of times before (Leclercq 1924.6A:900–903). That the glass dish was taken for emerald is not without parallel. The Portland Vase in the British Museum, a virtuoso creation of layered and carved glass, was also once believed to be of precious stone. On the dish as the physical reality which for some time lent substance to the legends of the Holy Grail, at least for some of the Genoese, see Paris 1879 1:353, n. 3 and Jung 1970.17, n. 26.

The dish is still on display in the Treasury of San Lorenzo, as it was when it was first brought to Genoa (Macadam 1991.106). As is natural, the Genoese have always controlled access to their treasure. William of Tyre says that they showed it only to important visitors (magnatibus). In 1764, a young Edward Gibbon, twelve years away from publishing the first volume of his great history, passed through Genoa but was unable to see the dish: *Il y a à S$^{t.}$ Laurent les cendres de S$^{t.}$ Jean Baptiste que je n' etois point curieux de voir et la fameuse Emeraude pour laquelle il faudroit une permission particuliere du Senat* (Bonnard 1961.71). Since Petrarch's old boyhood friend, Guido Sette (*Sen.* 10.2), was about to be elected archbishop of Genoa (2 July 1358), Mandelli need not have worried about the necessary permissions (cf. Stella, *Annales Genuenses*, Balbi 1975. 156,13–16).

121–128 Hinc digressus ad levam . . . delitiisque succumbere: here begins Petrarch's itinerary for the stretch between Genoa and Rome. It was territory that Petrarch knew very well and admired very much. In a letter written to the Doge and Council of Genoa in November of 1352 (*Fam.* 14.5. 23–25) he becomes rhapsodic about the beauty of the city and its *riviera*, as he recalls the first time he saw these places in 1312, a small boy on his way to Avignon from Pisa with his family. This whole section of the *Itinerarium* is reminiscent of the points made by Petrarch in his letter. For example, cf. "*stupebis urbem talem decori suorum rurium delitiisque succumbere*" with "*quis non viator . . . to rpebat, numquam visas in urbibus delitias inter silvarum latebras et remotissima rura conspiciens?*" (*Fam.* 14.5.25).

129–135 Viginti nisi fallor . . . habet enim alterum Sicilia: here begins a long stretch of territory to which, Petrarch tells Mandelli in lines 146–148, he has already given poetic treatment in the *Africa* (6. 856–884). Hannibal's brother Mago, suffering from a serious wound received in Liguria, is called home to Africa for the final stand against the anticipated Roman invasion. Sailing from Genoa, Mago observes the beautiful Italian *riviera* on his way south. As he draws near to Rome, Mago senses that he is dying and makes a speech on the vanity of human endeavors, which brings the book to a close (6.885–918). All of this Petrarch drew out of a brief reference in Livy (30.19.1–5).

Mago's speech became a source of trouble for Petrarch. Called to Naples in 1343 after the death of King Robert, Petrarch allowed Marco Barbato da Sulmona to have a copy of it (the lines may have been inspired by King Robert's death). Without Petrarch's permission, Barbato allowed others to make copies for themselves. Petrarch would have found this annoying enough; but his annoyance turned to wrath twenty years later when some adverse criticism of the passage (and of his *Bucolicum carmen*) got back to him. The critics said among other things, that he was guilty of putting Christian sentiments into the ancient barbarian's mouth. Unburdening his hurt to Boccaccio (in a long letter, *Sen.* 2.1; *Prose,* 1030–1066), Petrarch denies that there is anything particularly Christian in what Mago says and vigorously rebuts the other criticisms as well. By this time (1363), however, Petrarch had probably given up all hope of completing his revisions of the *Africa* (see note to lines 148–151). It was not until 1397 that Pier Paolo Vergerio finally published the first edition of the *Africa* (see Festa 1926.xxxv–lxiv for a history of the text).

The southern extremity of the promontory which Petrarch calls "Caput montis" is still referred to as the Capo (= Punta Chiappa, according to Kretschmer 1909.595). The whole promontory, a square shaped elevation of 2000 ft., is now called Monte di Portofino. Portus Delphini (Portofino) is the name of the town and the harbor, which is small, but well protected by the promontory (*apricis collibus abditum*; cf. *Africa* 6. 845: *luco contectus aprico).* According to the Portolan Parma-Magliabecchi (Kretschmer 1909. 294), Portofino is indeed 20 miles from Genoa; Petrarch gives up trying to record mileage after Rome.

Rapallum (Rapallo) is situated in a sheltered position NE of Portofino at the head of the Gulf of Rapallo. It seems not to have been settled in Roman times. Petrarch does not mention the place in the *Africa.*

Siestrum (*Sestri Levante*) is situated on the mainland coast about eight miles south of Portofino. It is Pliny's Segesta Tigulliorum (*Nat.* 3.48).

By the "port famous for the name Venus," Petrarch means the entire Golfo della Spezia and not Portovenere. Called Lunae Portus in antiquity, it is about eight miles in length and between two and five miles in width, making it one of the largest and safest harbors in the Mediterranean. Petrarch's statement that it could hold all the fleets of the world is not as hyperbolic as it first sounds. According to Froissart (*Chroniques,* XIV.157), the crusaders led by Louis II de Bourbon (1390) put in for the night at "Portovenere" with 120 galleys and more than 300 troop and transport ships (cited by Atiya 1938.410, n.3).

Eryx (Lerici) is a smaller port within the great Golfo della Spezia. Situated on the east shore of the gulf a bit south of Portus Veneris's position on the shore opposite, Eryx was the most important stronghold in the area (cf. *fortissimus Erix, Africa,* 6.858). There was an important city (and mountain) by the same name in Sicily, which Petrarch wants to be distinguished carefully (cf. *Sicule retinens cognomina ripe, Africa,* 6.859). Petrarch had boarded ship at Lerici in 1343 on his way to Naples (see note to lines 39–40), after having been forced to land by rough seas.

136–139 Et hoc quidem litus . . . nulli usquam terrarum cedere certum est: cf. *Africa*, 6.842–844,

> Sensim turgescere colles
> cedriferi — nulli cedens his saltibus ora —
> incipiunt, rareque virent per litora palme.

and *Africa*, 6.849–850,

> Hinc solis vineta oculo lustrata benigno
> et Bacho dilecta nimis . . . .

and *Africa*, 6.860–861,

> Collibus his ipsam perhibent habitare Minervam
> spernentem patrias olei dulcedine Athenas.

The area, says Petrarch, is fit for growing grapes and olives, but not grain. In 1346 Petrarch sent his friend Lello di Pietro Stephano dei Tosetti (Lelius) a bottle of olive oil, the fruit of his own trees, with the following comment: [at Vaucluse] *"posthabitis Athenis, repertricem olee Minervam habitare dicerem, nisi eam iampridem Ianuensi litore ad portum Veneris atque Hericem collocassem in* Africe *mee libris," Fam.* 3.22.11.

139–142 Quo magis id priscis rerum scriptoribus, et presertim vatibus . . . nondum nota fertilitas locorum erat: cf. *Africa,* 6. 854–855:

> Tunc, seu pigra situ, nulli seu nota poete
> illa fuit tellus, iacuit sine carmine sacro . . .

142–145 Hinc est ut cum claris sepe carminibus Meroen Falernumque concelebrent . . . indictam preterierint: cf. *Africa,* 6. 852–853:

> [iuga] quibus haud collesque Falernos
> laudatamque licet Meroen cessisse pudebit.

Meroë and the Falernian "hills" were places fabled in antiquity for their wonderful wine. Although ancient geographers (Pliny, *Nat.* 2.184) described Meroë as an island north of the modern Khartoum, it was not an island, but a large area between the confluence of the Nile and two of its tributaries (the Atbara and the Blue Nile). Wine was not produced at Meroë; rather wines from other places were brought there to mature quickly (Lucan, 10.162–163). On Falernus see note on line 306 and the Gazetteer.

147–150 Id me movit omnium qui scripserunt . . . ut in Africe mee loco quodam . . . genere longe alio: cf. *Africa,* 6. 855–856: *illa fuit tellus . . . / hoc michi nunc cantanda loco.*

148–151 Qui liber nisi vel vite brevitas vel . . . aliorum librorum . . . vetuerint: by 1352 Petrarch had begun to despair of ever finishing the *Africa (Fam.* 12.7, 13.7, 13.12), but this passage in the *Itinerarium* and Book III of the *Secretum (Prose,* 192–198, 202–206, 212–214) indicate that he still had some intention, however faint, of completing the work. On Petrarch's difficulties in completing his work, see Fera 1984.

154–155 Corvum, famosum scopulum et nomen a colore sortitum: Capo Corvo, a well-known landmark from which the entire Golfo della Spezia may be viewed, was of dark color compared with the surrounding limestone cliffs (Punta Bianca) nearby. See *Africa,* 6. 865–866:

> dorsoque nigranti
> arduus assurgit scopulus, cui proxima rupes
> candidior late Phebo feriente refulget.

See also *Fam.* 5.3.4: *Corvum scopulum ingentem a colore nominatum;* and *Fam.* 17.4.5.

156–157 Macre amnis ostia, qui maritimos Ligures ab Etruscis dirimit: cf. *Africa,* 6. 867–868: *Post* [sc. Capo Corvo] *in secessu curvo maris ostia Macre / cernuntur rapidi.* . . . Cf. also Dante, *Paradiso* 9.89–90: *Macra, che per cammin corto / parte lo Genovese dal Toscano.*

158–162 Aliud enim hac in parte . . . exemplum maius et antiquius Troia sit: the reason given by Petrarch for Luna's destruction was sexual misconduct. He had evidently heard the same story as Giovanni Villani (1275–1348) tells in his *Cronica* (II. 13 in Porta 1990.1:78):

> La città di Luni, la quale è oggi disfatta, fu molto antica, e secondo che troviamo nelle storie di Troia, della città di Luni v'ebbe navilio e genti a l'aiuto de' Greci contra gli Troiani: poi fu disfatta per gente oltramontana per cagione d'una donna, moglie d'uno signore, che andando a Roma, in quella città fu corrotta d'avoltero; onde tornando il detto signore con forza la distrusse, e oggi è diserta la contrada e mal sana.

Others tell similar stories, most of them like this one singularly lacking in specific details. A few strive to lend credibility to their narration by adding such information as the name of the wronged husband (e.g., Goro Dati [1362–1435] in his *Istoria di Firenze*). See Sforza 1922. 3–139; Sforza prints Villani and Dati's versions on 17–18. Dante (*Par.* 16.73–81) gives no reason for the downfall of Luna beyond the corruptibility of man and all his works. See note to lines 165–166 below.

165–166 Sarzanum paulo submotum a litore, novum frequensque oppidum: the seat of a bishop since 1204, Sarzanum (Sarzana) was the populous place Petrarch said it was. It was also a new city, whose development came about after the final collapse of Luna in the thirteenth century. The immediate cause of Luna's downfall appears to have been the flooding of the Magra and the resulting plague of malaria (see Ward-Perkins 1978.313–321). Perhaps the malaria was only the final straw: Luna had suffered a number of devastating attacks throughout its long history — at the hands of the Lombards, the Normans, and the Saracens (see

Sforza 1922.27–123 for a number of texts relating to these depredations). Sarzana is mentioned as being a fortress in 963 and as being a town in 1084. The mistaken form of the town's name given by Petrarch may have arisen when he assimilated its gender to that of the noun *oppidum*, which stands in apposition. On the other hand, it may have been an acceptable form of the name, and preferred by Petrarch.

According to Giovanni Villani (IX.42 in Porta 1990.2:70), Sarzana itself may not have been a very safe place to live. Guido Cavalcanti, exiled there in 1300, was recalled because the climate was so unhealthy, but he died soon after his return to Florence. We may note that Villani spells the name Serrezzano.

166 inde Laventia, vicus ignobilis: Petrarch speaks of this town from experience, having seen the place in 1343 on his way to Naples (*Fam.* 5.3.4). It is the modern Avenza.

168–169 fluvius . . . re ac nomine frigidus . . . secus Massam . . . descendit in pelagus: the Frigido or Freddo is a small river which passes Massa about twelve miles from the sea.

169–170 Prope oppidum . . . cuius auctor, ut audio, concivis quidem tuus fuit: Guiscardo da Pietrasanta, son of the distinguished Pagano of Milan, was held prisoner by Frederick II in 1247, but was freed by the Genoese, who later made him *podestà* of their city. In 1254, he was governor at Florence and in the following year he was installed as *podestà* of Lucca. Some contemporary and most modern sources say that this Guiscardo founded Pietrasanta in 1255 while serving at nearby Lucca, but there exists (or existed) an official document issued by Frederick II which is dated "Pietrasanta, 12 January 1242": see Giulini 1855.4:497, with supplementary note. If this is the case, perhaps Guiscardo's father Pagano should be considered the more likely founder of the town. He was a remarkable man judging from his description (vir nobilis et magnificus civis Mediolanensis dominus Paganus de Petrasanta, miles facundus, dives, facieque iucundus) and, like his son years later, *podestà* of Genoa in 1232: on Pagano see Imperiale di Sant' Angelo 1923.3:60, 62, 67; on Guiscardo see 3:175–176 and 1926.4: 9,18. But see also Paolella's note to this passage, where additional conflicting testimony is cited (1993.122).

172–173 duas Pisanorum arces . . . quarum alteram Mutronem, alteram vero Viam Regiam appellant: Motrone and Viareggio, separated by some five or six miles, were established by the Lucchese in twelfth century to insure their ability to load and unload ships in safety. At the time Petrarch was writing, however, Lucca was under Pisa's control along with many of its traditional possessions, including Motrone and Viareggio; see Meek 1980. In 1343 Petrarch had spent a tense night at Motrone, even while the Pisans were defending their new acquisition against the Milanese (*Fam.* 5.3.4); see note to lines 39–40. Petrarch finished his trip to Naples by land from this point, because of high seas.

174–176 Nec multo post Sercli atque Arni . . . tandem Pisas interfluit: the river Petrarch calls the Serclus is the Roman Auser, which flowed past the city of Lucca. Ancient writers say that the Auser joined the Arnus at Pisa (Strabo, 5.2.5; Pliny, *Nat.* 3. 50). The Auser stayed to its ancient path until about the twelfth century, when it broke away from the Arnus and flowed to the sea by a separate course some seven miles north of the Arnus. The name used by Petrarch is derived from a syncopated diminutive form (Au)serc(u)lus. Serclus became the modern Serchio by a familiar formation whereby a Latin (or Greek) "cl" becomes "chi" in Italian (e.g., *chiesa* from (ec)clesia; cf. *Iscla* and the modern *Ischia*, note to lines 243–248). See Gazetteer on Luca, Florentia, and Pisae.

177–181 Pisas . . . civitatem pervetustam sed recenti e decora specie . . . eminentissimis edificiis apparentem: after their defeat at Meloria (below lines 181–183, 189–190), the Pisans threw themselves into large scale building projects in their city; see Herlihy 1958 and Redi 1984.93–127. Petrarch, it will be remembered, lived at Pisa for over a year prior to his family's move to Avignon in 1312. It was here (possibly at Genoa) that Petrarch's father pointed out Dante to him (*Fam.* 21.15.7), the only time Petrarch ever saw the famous man (Foresti 1977.1–7). On Petrarch's negative attitude towards Dante see Bernardo 1955.488–517 and Lerner 1986.204–225.

181–183 [Pisas, civitatem] . . . quondam . . . maris potentissimam . . . magno victi prelio Ianuensium amisere: The Genoese defeated the Pisans in a major sea battle at Meloria on 6 August 1284 (see lines 189–190 below). This defeat was the beginning of the end for the Pisans as a great sea power. Eventually, they were forced to give up Corsica and Sardinia (see lines 198–199). Petrarch also refers to the battle at *Fam.* 14.5.26. See Tangheroni 1984.55–67 and Lemut 1984.75–87.

183–185 Post hec paucis passuum milibus portus . . . Pisanum vocant: ancient sources indicate that the Portus Pisanus was some distance from the city (Rutilius, *De reditu suo,* 1. 532–540, 558–560). Petrarch here confirms that the port was a few miles past the mouth of the Arno and very close to Liburnum in medieval times, probably where it was in antiquity. Although Portus Pisanus suffered damages in the battle of Meloria (1284) and again in 1290, it was still evidently in full operation in Petrarch's day. For a description of Meloria and Porto Pisano see M. Mazzanti 1984.5–53; fig. 1 shows a drawing of Porto Pisano as it was in the thirteenth century. The port remained active as a harbor until the fifteenth century, when Livorno, under the control of the Genoese (1407–21), supplanted it: see Guarnieri 1931.32.

185–187 Liburnum, ubi prevalida turris est . . . signum prebet: Rutilius (*De reditu suo,* 1.527; see Doblhofer 1972.2:229) refers to a place called Triturrita as adjoining the Portus Pisanus; it is called Turrita in the Peutinger Table (c. AD 350). This may be regarded as the prototype of the tower built in 1303 by the Pisans and called Torre del Fanale, here mentioned by Petrarch. For more details on this tower and the port, see Pegna 1967.29–40.

187–188 Gorgon atque Capraria: Gorgon lies about twenty-three miles west of Liburnum; Capraria about thirty-four west of Populonia. Both islands are mountainous. See *Africa,* 6.872–874: *brevissima Gorgon / . . . rigidisque Capraria saxis / insula.*

189–190 Meliora . . . infausta illi populo: a very unlucky place indeed for the Pisans: *Certo, la sconfitta della Meloria pesò molto allora e pesa molto anche oggi e non son pochi i miei amici che vorrebbero cancellare dalla storia e dalle enciclopedie qualsiasi accenno all' isoletta per noi sfortunata,* Burgalassi 1984.72. With the attitude of modern Pisans towards Meloria may be compared the attitude of modern Greeks towards Constantinople. That city fell to the Turks 29 May 1453, a Tuesday. When the Allies suggested that

Papandreou and his exiled government should return to liberated Athens on 17 October 1944, he refused because that day fell on a Tuesday (Bryer 1967.104). On the spelling *Meliora* see notes to text.

193–195 Plumbinum, insigne oppidum . . . securitatis ambigue: Plumbinum is about a mile from the ancient Faleria (Rutilius, *De reditu suo*, 1.371–380; Doblhofer 1972.2:174), situated on the extreme south of the Promontorio di Piombino, opposite the island of Ilva (Elba). The town is located at the entrance of a large, but shallow lagoon. The harbor is often mentioned in the Middle Ages until its use became limited because of sandbars. Lead was mined in the area (on Sardinia), whence is derived the town's medieval and modern name (cf. Leadville, Colorado, U.S.A.). Actually, the mining of lead (plumbum) must be considered in close connection with the production of silver. In antiquity and in the Middle Ages well over 50% of the silver came from lead ore (White 1984.124), which according to one's point of view could just as well be described as silver ore: "[Sardinia] is very rich in silver mines," *in metallis argentariis plurima est*, Solinus, 4.3. When the two metals were separated (Healy 1978.179–181), a high quality lead was produced, much valued by the Romans (French and Greenaway 1986.15–16), which Pliny (*Nat.* 34.98) called *plumbum argentarium*, "silvery lead," from its bright color. Perhaps the lead ore was brought to this area for smelting. Certainly, iron ore from Ilva was brought here to the mainland for processing since at least the first century BC (Strabo 5.6), because of the shortage of fuel on the island. If the furnaces and skilled labor were here for the iron ore, it would make economic sense to bring the lead ore from Sardinia. The town Piombino may have taken its name from the lead ore brought to its port, and Monte Argentario just to the south from the silvery look of the lead product and the silver itself, with an additional reference to the money (argentum) used to buy both these commodities, and the iron from Ilva as well. Petrarch places the town a little to the north of Populonia, but the reverse is the case (see note below).

196–197 Ilva est, 'insula inexhaustis Chalybum generosa metallis': the quotation is verbatim from Virgil (*A.* 10.174). The Chalybes are blacksmiths associated with iron ore. The passage from the *Aeneid* (supplemented by Pliny, *apud* Servius, *A. ad loc.*) led to the belief that the ore grew again in the place where it was taken out of the ground. By coincidence, Rutilius (1.351) also cites Virgil's line in reference to Ilva.

198–199 post Sardiniam amissam: in 1297 Pope Boniface VIII invested James II of Aragon as king of Sardinia and Corsica, but the Aragonese were able to gain possession of Sardinia only after a protracted struggle with the Pisans and the native population. After a great defeat by the Aragonese fleet off Sardinia in June of 1324, Pisa recognized the king of Aragon as King of Sardinia and Corsica. By a treaty of 1326, Pisa finally ceded Sardinia. Pisa's position as a sea power was now lost forever (Roncioni 1844.726–734, Finke 1910.2–:570–640 and 3:497–500, and Tabacco 1989.263 and 318). See Gazetteer s.v. Corsica.

199–200 Haud procul inde Populonia . . . profiteor me nescire: the Port of Telamon is situated on a promontory about half way between the mouth of the Umbro (Ombrone) and the Mons Argentarius. Siena's expensive and futile efforts to make it a great harbor were a favorite joke with Florentines (Dante, *Purgatorio* 13. 151–154, with the various commentators). The port filled up with sand as fast as the Sienese dredged it out. Telamon, a member of the Argonauts, was said to have settled the place (Diodorus, 4.56). See Gazetteer for Massa Maritima and Grossetum. Petrarch has misplaced Populonia; see note to lines 193–195.

Petrarch's mention of Populonia is instructive because it illustrates his keen interest in historical geography. An ancient city of Etruria about five miles north of Piombino, Populonia is represented by Virgil (*A.* 10.172; cf. Servius *ad loc.*) as assisting Aeneas in his war against the Latins. The town was nearly deserted in Strabo's time (he had personally visited the place), but the little harbor was still serviceable (5.2.6). It is described by Rutilius at the beginning of the fifth century (*De reditu suo,* 1. 401–414) as being completely in ruins; so also by Gregory the Great (in a letter cited by Cluver 1624.514) at the close of the sixth century. In the Middle Ages, a fort was erected on the site of the ancient town: it and a few surrounding houses still bear the ancient name. *Portolani* of the fifteenth century do not mention Populonia; nor apparently do any portolan charts. Although Petrarch was not sure of its exact location (he could not find it placed on any map), he includes reference to it because it is mentioned by Virgil and Livy (28.45 and 30.39). Populonia plays a major role in a rather lengthy episode in Petrarch's *Africa* 8.453–546 which is based on Livy.

202–204 Inde rursus ad dexteram Igilium . . . Argentari<us> Mons medius: Igilium (Giglio) lies about ten miles west of Mons Argentarius. Petrarch mentions the island in the *Africa,* also praising its fine marble: *tunc niveo predives marmore retro/ linquitur ad levam Gilium* (6. 875–876). Mons Argentarius is an almost circular mountainous peninsula joined to the mainland by three strips of land forming lagoons. It is well described by Rutilius (*De reditu suo,* 1.315–324) who is the first author to call it by the name it still carries. No evidence of any silver has been found on the peninsula to explain its name, but see note to lines 193–195 above. Cf. *Africa,* 6:876–877: *. . . stant iuga de gemino nomen sortita metallo: / Plumbeus hic vertex, illa est Argentea rupes* (*Plumbeus* refers to Plumbinum). The Portus Herculis (Porto d'Ercole) is a port on the south side of Mons Argentarius; Portus S. Stephani is on the north side. Both ports are still very active. Cf. *Africa,* 6. 878–879: *Nec procul herculei devexo monte recessus / et Thelamonis opus.* On the opposite side of a bay from Cosa, Portus Herculis (name in Strabo, 5.8) was also called Portus Cosanus (Livy, 22.11.7) in antiquity. Indeed, Mons Argentarius was undoubtedly known in antiquity as Promunturium Cosanum (Tacitus, *Ann.* 2.39). The name of Porto S. Stefano in antiquity is not definitely known. According to a suggestion of Lumbroso 1889 (note *ad loc.*), Petrarch's mention of this port is the earliest recorded, but the name appears on the *carte pisane,* the earliest known portolan chart of the late thirteenth century (Almagià 1929.67).

204–208 Post Cornetum . . . Tarquinii prodiere: Tarquinii, located about four miles from the sea, was the capital city of the Etruscan League. According to Livy (1.34), Lucumo emigrated to Rome in the sixth century BC and became its fifth king under the name Lucius Tarquinius Priscus. His grandson was Tarquinius Superbus (see lines 251–253 below). When the Saracens destroyed the city in the ninth century, the survivors established themselves on a well-fortified hill about three miles west of the old settlement, calling their new city Cornetum. In 1922, the citizens renamed the city Tarquinia.

Petrarch is the first to place ancient Tarquinii in the area of Corneto. Domenico di Bandino of Arezzo, member of Coluccio Salutati's circle, may be quoting this passage in his encyclopedia with reference to Tarquinii; see Hankey 1957a.200 and Weiss 1969. 55–56 and 119. The ancient site was not discovered for another three centuries. On Domenico and his massive *Fons memorabilium universi* (c. 1390) see also Hankey 1957.110–130 and 1960.3–48.

208–209 Post hec illa que Civitas Vetus . . . sita est: Trajan was not only responsible for enlarging Claudius's new harbor two miles north of the Tiber (see lines 209–212 below), but he also built a new harbor at Centumcellae (Roman name) about thirty-five miles north of the Tiber (Pliny, *Ep.* 6.31.15–17; Rutilius, *De reditu suo,* 1.237–248). This new harbor followed the Ostian model: it had an inner basin entered from the main harbor, itself protected by moles and an artificially made island. Trajan himself had a villa there, and a town quickly grew up and flourished around the busy port. The Saracens destroyed the city in AD 812. The survivors withdrew into the interior, referring to the ancient city as Civitas Vetus (Civitavecchia). Later the old city was repopulated when harbor service was restored. *Civitas Vetus* was Rome's chief port in Petrarch's time, as it is still today. Petrarch landed here when he came to Rome by ship early in December of 1336.

209–212 Deinde quem Hadriani portum vocant . . . iactantia Graia defuerit: originally Rome's harbor had been at the Tiber's mouth at Ostia, but by the Late Republican period the silt brought down by the Tiber had effectively destroyed Ostia's usefulness as a port (Strabo, 5.3.4). Julius Caesar had plans to build a new port at Ostia (Plutarch, *Caes.* 58), but the project was neglected until necessity motivated Claudius (AD 42) to build an entirely new port some two miles north of Ostia. Part of the harbor was dug out from land, and it was protected by two moles extending out into the sea and enclosing about 160 acres. At the end of the left mole, a lighthouse was built on a concrete-laden merchantman sunk for the purpose (Suetonius, *Cl.* 20), as modern excavation has confirmed. Claudius's new harbor, however, because of its wide expanse of shallow water, could not protect ships against sudden storms (Tacitus, *Ann.* 15.18.3). For this reason Trajan (AD 103) added a new land-locked basin of hexagonal shape (each side measuring about 1180 ft.). This augmented harbor, "the greatest man-made harbor of antiquity" (Casson 1971.368), was connected to the Tiber by an artificial channel called the *Fossa Traiana* (modern, Fiumincio) about a mile and a half above the site of Ostia.

In the ninth century, Ostia came under frequent attack from the Saracens (for a survey of these attacks on Italian cities see Krueger 1969.1:40–53). In these unsettled times the artificial port of Claudius and Trajan also suffered from the same depredations and from neglect. In the reign of Pope Gregory IV (d. 844), a fortified town was built on the Romeward side of the old town of Ostia, which was now completely abandoned. Since the fort was intended in some measure to keep travel and commercial communication open between Rome and the sea, it must be concluded that the artificial port to the north was already choked with sand and was difficult to navigate. Though it could no longer perform its proper function, the harbor of Claudius with its many concrete storehouses and docks, was still very impressive in Petrarch's day. The lighthouse was still standing in the fifteenth century.

In antiquity the name of the harbor built by Claudius and enlarged by Trajan was called *Portus Augusti* or later *Portus Augusti et Traiani* (see Meiggs 1973, especially 51–64 and 149–171). Why Petrarch should call it *Portus Hadriani* is not clear, but a reasonable guess might be that Petrarch had personally observed Hadrian's name on so many of the buildings at Ostia. The evidence of building activity, datable by brick stamps bearing the name of consuls, shows that nearly forty-five percent of the buildings at Ostia were constructed or restored under Hadrian (Mackendrick 1960.253). The Peutinger Table (a map whose original dates to c. AD 350) provides an impressive representation of the harbor (reproduced by Meiggs, 171).

Petrarch's reference to the Seven Wonders of the Ancient World is interesting. By his time, it appears the canon of "wonders" had been fairly well fixed in their modern form: the pyramids of Egypt, the Hanging Gardens of Babylon, the statue of Zeus at Olympia, the temple of Artemis at Ephesus, the tomb of Mausolus, the Colossus of Rhodes, and the Egyptian Pharus. Five of the seven were of Greek construction. Petrarch's list of wonders, however, may have been somewhat different from this modern version: he may have considered Babylon's circuit wall built by the legendary Semiramis as a greater marvel than the Hanging Gardens (descriptions of both in Quintus Curtius, 5.1.25, 32–35); and in place of the Pharus, he may have substituted the Royal Palace at Ecbatana in Media (description in Polybius, 10.27.8). At any rate, such are the variations seen in the *Septem mira,* a list of wonders found in Vatican lat. 4929, at least a partial copy of which is known to have been in Petrarch's possession by 1335 (it is relevant to a general understanding of the *Itinerarium* that this manuscript contained among other things Pomponius Mela's *Chorographia* and Vibius Sequester's gazetteer *De fluminibus, fontibus,* etc.): see Barlow 1938.88 and pl. 14 and Reynolds 1986.290–292; the *Septem mira* has been published as an appendix to Vibius Sequester in Riese 1878.159. The wonders of the *Septem mira* are identical to those found in Hyginus, *Fab.* 223 (*Septem opera mirabilia;* Rose 1934), from which the *Septem mira* clearly derives (Petrarch did not know this Hyginus's work). Antipater of Sidon (fl. c. 120 BC) was the first author known to have put the number of wonders at seven (his short epigram may be found in the *Greek Anthology,* 9.58). Before Antipater, the number of wonders varies from author to author.

In the early Middle Ages, Bede and Gregory of Tours among others had sought to revise this canon, offering Noah's Ark and the Temple of Solomon, for example, as substitutes (Omont 1882). It is surprising that no engineering feat of the Romans was adopted while the canon was still open to revision. See Clayton and Price 1988 for a popular account and bibliography; Brodersen 1992 collects Greek and Latin wonder lists.

There is more than a hint of misohellenism here in the reference to Greek boasting (iactantia) and later on to Greek flattery (blanditie) and deceit (fraudes), line 480. Petrarch stands by no means the last in a long line of Latin authors who admired and imitated the Greeks, but maintained a sense of moral superiority towards them. Authors such as Cicero, Lucan, Pliny, and Juvenal freely accused them of *levitas, perfidia, mendacitas,* and *luxuria.* Christian authors writing in Latin, finding the Greeks anything but orthodox in doctrinal matters, took up the themes of the ancient Roman writers, their inherited dislike now tinged with *odium theologicum.* For a gathering of negative Roman sayings about the Greeks, by no means complete, see Wölfflin 1892.140–146.

213–214 His exactis Tyberine . . . ad dexteram remanente Sardinia: the mouth of the Tiber is some two miles south of Petrarch's Portus Hadriani. Cf. *Africa,* 6. 882–884:

> Iam hinc Sardinia longe
> tabificos aperit colles, hinc aurea Roma
> inque procelloso Tybridis stant litore fauces.

214–218 Supra Tyberis . . . hospitio reciperentur: Petrarch takes this passage nearly verbatim from Florus: *Ancus deinde Marcius . . . Ostiamque in ipso maris fluminisque confinio coloniam posuit, iam tum videlicet praesagiens animo futurum ut totius mundi opes et commeatus illo velut maritimo urbis hospitio reciperentur (Epit.* 1.1.4). There is no comparable passage in what remains of Livy's work. Cf. Petrarch's *Africa* (1.522–523): *Quartus arat muros et Tybridis Ostia fundat, / Presagus quas totus opes huc convehat orbis.*

219–223 scito te a regina urbium Roma . . . libri lingueque omnes non sufficiunt: cf. Petrarch's "Roman" *canzone* (53) and his ringing defense of Rome in his *Invectiva contra eum qui maledixit Italie* (dated in Padua on 1 March 1373) in *Prose,* 770–778. Petrarch seems to have had a greatly exaggerated idea of Rome's size (and grandeur, presumably) in antiquity because of his misreading (*Sen.* 7.1; *Opera* 2:910) of Eusebius's *Chronicle,* where it is said (Schoene 1967.2:147) that a census of Rome in the time of Augustus (AD 14) showed 9,370,000 citizens (adult males). Eusebius's number referred to the total number of citizens throughout the empire, but Petrarch took it to refer to the number of citizens in the city of Rome. The number given by Eusebius/Jerome is itself an interesting distortion of the one given in the *Res Gestae*: 4,937,000 (text in Ehrenberg 1955.8). Modern estimations put the city's total population in the early empire at about a million. Thus fueled by misinformation, Petrarch's imagination may have viewed the ancient city through a lens which magnified it in various ways by at least a factor of ten — this at a time when the Black Death had just reduced fourteenth-century Rome's population by at least a third.

224–226 Civitas ibi Antium . . . subacta est: the Volcii took Antium (Anzio) in the sixth century and made it their principal city for 200 years. At the beginning of the fourth century, the Antiates waged war against Rome almost continuously for thirteen years (386–374 BC) until Rome finally prevailed (Livy, 6.6–33). Again during the Latin War (340–338), they marched against Rome and again were defeated (Livy, 8.1,12–14). From this time on, Antium figured in history only as a colony of Rome.

226–227 inde mons prealtus, cui carminibus potens Circe nomen imposuisse creditur: there is no legendary tradition which explains how Circe gave her name to this mountainous promontory about 30 miles south of Antium and about ten miles north of Terracina. Virgil (*A.* 7.10–24) vaguely places Mons Circeius (Monte Circeo) somewhere between Cumae and the mouth of the Tiber. A Greek tradition (Strabo, 5.3.6) said that there were herbal roots growing in abundance on the promontory, probably a story invented to explain why Circe's name was associated with the place.

226–229 Ibi enim . . . quid misterii vellet nosti: The ancient stories of metamorphosis fascinated and troubled early Christians. St. Augustine (*De civ. Dei*, 18.17–18) refused to believe that people could actually be transformed into bestial form by any power of a demon. He thought it possible, however, that the "phantasm" of a person, embodied in the shape of an animal, might be presented to the senses of others so that a metamorphosis might seem to have taken place. Petrarch is undoubtedly also thinking of Boethius, *De cons. Phil.* 4 pr. 3 (*Ita fit ut qui probitate deserta homo esse desierit, cum in divinam condicionem transire non possit, vertatur in beluam)* and the poem on Circe (4 m.3): her potions could change only the outward appearance; more deadly are those poisons (sin) that affect the soul and transform the inner man.

230–231 Pontie . . . carcer illustrium: Pontiae here refers to a small island about 16 miles west of Circe's Promontory. It is about 5 miles long but very narrow (*brevis insula;* for *brevis* with reference to width see s.v. 1.d, *OLD*), being in some places only a few hundred yards across. The island is also referred to in the singular form (Pontia). Two other very small islands, called Palmaria and Sinonia, lie close on either side of Pontiae; the three islands are referred to collectively as Pontiae Insulae (Isole di Ponza). During the Roman Empire, Pontiae (or one of the other small islands) became a place of exile for political dissidents or other unfortunates who had somehow offended the emperor (Suet. *Ti.* 54.2; *Cal.* 15.1). Pandataria (Ventotene), a small nearby island, which is often considered as belonging to the Pontiae Insulae group, was the place of confinement for Julia, daughter of Augustus, Agrippina, widow of Germanicus, and Octavia, first wife of Nero (Tacitus, *Ann.* 1.53 and 16.63; Suetonius *Ti.* 53). According to Christian tradition, the emperor Domitian exiled his niece Flavia Domitilla to Pontiae for professing Christianity (Jerome, *Ep.* 108. 3; text in Stummer 1935). From Jerome's account, it is evident that pilgrims to the Holy Land, who were setting out from ports in northwest Italy, regularly made a stop at Pontiae to see the place of Flavia's confinement. In 537 Pope Silverius, a victim of political intrigue and theological controversy, was exiled to Palmaria, where he was abused and starved to death. His grave site on the island brought cures and miracles to visitors, and from the eleventh century he was venerated as a martyr for his orthodox faith.

232–234 Progredienti tibi Terracina nunc, olim Anxur aderit, mox Caieta, nutricis Eneie nomen servans: about 65 miles from Rome, Terracina was known to the Romans as Tarracina or Anxur, which was its original Volscian name (Livy, 4.59: *Anxur* *fuit, quae nunc Tarracinae sunt*; Pliny, *Nat.* 3.59). Its position on the Via Appia and its serviceable port made it a flourishing town throughout antiquity and into the Middle Ages.

Caieta lies between Terracina and Formiae. The town is situated on a promontory that forms the north end of a large bay called Sinus Caietanus (Golfo di Gaeta). When Aeneas stopped at the fine natural harbor below the promontory on his way to Latium, his nurse Caieta died (Virgil, *A.* 7.1; Ovid, *Met.* 14.441–444). As the place of her burial (the summit of Monte Orlando), the area adopted her name. After the Saracens destroyed Formiae in the ninth century, Caieta became a considerable town with a fine harbor in the Middle Ages. On 17 June 1394 Niccolò da Martoni, a notary from the nearby town of Carinola, set out from here for Alexandria with a large number of other pilgrims in a ship owned by one Mello Maltaccia. Niccolò's ship formed a small convoy with four others, probably from Genoa (see Legrand 1895.3:578).

234 sacrum Erasmi tumulum: St. Erasmus (Ermo or Elmo, apparently corruptions of Erasmus), is one of the auxiliary saints who are venerated for the efficacy of their help in times of need. Legend makes him a Syrian Bishop who fled Diocletian's persecution, which began in 303, and who eventually became Bishop of Formiae. His relics were venerated there until 842 when the town was destroyed by Saracens. Erasmus's body was then transferred to Gaeta (Caieta). His patronage of sailors seems to have come about from a story that described him preaching through a thunderstorm with lightning striking all around him. St. Elmo's fire, a visible electrical discharge from mastheads observed during storms, was considered a sign of his protection. Castor and Pollux were associated with this phenomenon in antiquity. See entry in Farmer 1987.

238–241 In hoc tractu Formie seu Formianum et Liternum sunt . . . cineribus patrie negatis: Petrarch is misled by Cicero (e.g., *Att.* 1.3 etc.) into thinking that *Formianum* is an alternative name for the town. Formianum is used as a substantive by Cicero to refer to his property at Formiae (cf. also Livy, 120.50; frag. found in Seneca, *Suasoriae* 6.7.7). Cicero stopped at his Formian villa on his flight from Rome after the formation of the Triumvirate in 43 BC. He was able to spend the night, but the next day (7 December) he was overtaken by Antony's soldiers as he tried to continue his flight and was killed.

Liternum, founded in 194 BC on an inauspicious site, was the place that Scipio Africanus Major, disillusioned with public life, chose for his retirement and where he died in a kind of voluntary exile (Livy, 38.52,53,56). A bitter Scipio was said (Valerius Maximus, 5.3.2b; Briscoe 1998) to have caused the following inscription to be carved on his tomb: *Ingrata patria, ne ossa quidem mea habes*. Petrarch opens all the rhetorical stops in describing this epitaph in his biography of Scipio in his *De viris illustribus* (Scipio xii, 45–46; Martellotti 1964a.354). Cf. also *Fam.* 3.10.11.

Seneca (*Ep.* 86) had made a kind of pilgrimage to Liternum to visit the great man's villa and was duly edified by the evident austerity of Scipio's way of living. Petrarch himself had wanted to duplicate Seneca's visit in 1343, but was unable to do so (*Fam.* 5. 4. 9), the reason being the fact that the whole area surrounding Liternum had long since become a "marshy solitude, negotiable at risk only in certain seasons of the year," Frederiksen 1984.20. See also Feo 1974.115–117 on Petrarch's frustrated desire to visit Liternum.

Liternum did not survive much beyond the beginning of the fifth century AD (Maiuri 1963.156–160). Its name does not appear on *portolani* or portolan charts, but three of the earliest charts in existence mention La(go di) Patria, a swampy lagoon near ancient Liternum, just north of Cumae (Almagià 1928.68). The phrase "ungrateful fatherland" (ingrata patria) is generally supposed to have provided somehow the names for the shallow lake and the massive tower at the coast (Torre di Patria). Cumae, famous for its Virgilian associations but infamous in the Middle Ages as a stronghold for brigands and pirates, was utterly destroyed in the thirteenth century (Maiuri 1963.108–109), and does not appear on the charts at all. The name La Patria however does appear on the nautical charts just a little north of where Cumae's name ought to be. This may have been in Petrarch's mind when he refers to Cumae as "Sibyl's fatherland" — *patria Sibille* (see below).

241–243 Sed hec duo loca . . . due seu tres magne supereminent <ruine>. There are still considerable remains to be seen along the coast at Formiae, which Petrarch himself had seen as he had sailed past them in 1341 on his way to Naples. Liternum cannot even be seen from the sea at all, Petrarch says, probably because its ruins were screened from view by sand dunes (see Frederiksen 1984.22–23). Mandelli will get an idea of these two places more by an exercise of his imaginative faculties than from autopsy (extimatione magis animi quam oculis), though he will be able to see two or three large ruins at Formiae, probably the so-called "Villa of Cicero" and the "Tomb of Cicero" (Coarelli 1985. 429–431).

243–248 Ipsa sed in oculis erit . . . Inarime . . . Ethneo more estuare solitum incendium: subject to earthquakes and severe volcanic events, Inarime is located 7 miles SW of Cape Misenum. The usual Roman name for the island was Aenaria (e.g., Mela, 2.7.121 and Livy, 8.22), which was derived from Aeneas's name according to Pliny (*Nat.* 3.82), but because of a mistaken reading of Homer's text (εἰναρίμοις for the correct εἰν Ἀρίμοις, *Il.* 2.783), Latin poets beginning with Virgil called the island Inarime and made it the place of the Typhoeus's confinement (see Pliny, *Nat.* 3.82 and Servius, *A.* 9.712; text in Thilo 1881). Cf. Virgil (*A.* 9.716): *Inarime Iovis imperiis imposta Typhoeo* (also Lucan, 5.99–101 and 6.90–92; and Statius, *Silv.* 2.2.76). Typhoeus was one of the Giants who rebelled against Jupiter. His punishment was to be buried under mountainous Inarime or sometimes under Mt. Etna (Ovid, *Fasti* 4.491 and Silius Italicus, 14.196).

The modern name Ischia is derived from a vulgar name Iscla, most likely a corruption of the Latin *insula* (i.e., as the largest island in the Gulf of Naples, it is *the* island). Conrad von Querfurt, in a letter written about his visit to Italy, Sicily, and the Bay of Naples in 1195, refers to the island by this same vulgar name: *Est ante civitatem eandem [Neapolim] insula, que vulgo Iscla dicitur . . .* , in Arnold of Lübeck's *Cronica Slavorum* (5.19), Lappenberg 1869.196. Petrarch uses the modern form of the name at *Triumphus Cupidinis*, 4.154, but Inarime at *Triumphus Pudicitie*, 113. For more discussion of the sources of Petrarch's knowledge of the name of the island and the myth of Typhoeus see Bisanti 1994.333–341.

248–249 Prochita . . . unde . . . surrexit, Iohannes: John of Procida (Giovanni da Procida) supported the Hohenstaufen cause in Sicily and joined in the conspiracy against Charles of Anjou, who had been offered Sicily by Pope Urban IV. When Manfred was defeated by Charles at Benevento in 1266, John fled to the court of Manfred's son-in-law Peter III of Aragon, where he continued to work against Charles. He secretly visited Sicily and helped prepare for the uprising, which began at Vesper time on Easter Monday, 30 March 1282, a circumstance that provides the name Sicilian Vespers for the rebellion. When the uprising succeeded, John was made chancellor of Sicily under Peter of Aragon, whom the Sicilian rebels chose as their king. See Smith 1968. 2: 65–75.

A considerable legend grew up around John's role in the Sicilian rebellion. He was painted as a master conspirator traveling secretly to various courts in Europe, sometimes disguised as a Franciscan friar; there were stories of Byzantine gold, won by John's persuasion, being passed to Pope Nicholas III to win his support for the enterprise. Trained in medicine at Salerno, where he was born in 1210, John provided his professional services to many important men (he attended Frederick II in his last illness) in his career. Petrarch's admiration for John, grudging to be sure, is matched by other fourteenth-century intellectuals like Villani and Boccaccio; see Runciman 1958.205–213; 288–293. On Petrarch's knowledge of the *Placita philosophorum moralium antiquorum, ex Graeco in Latinum translata a Magistro Joanne Procida,* see de Nolhac 1907.2:140; the Latin text is available in de Renzi 1854. 3: 69–150. The *Placita philosophorum,* possibly a Latin translation of a Spanish version, but certainly not of the Greek original, is no longer believed to be by John: see Billanovich 1948.111–123.

The juxtaposition of John and the hubristic Typhoeus in Petrarch's swift narrative is all he need say about John's political activities. And the fact that John was a physician did not count in his favor in Petrarch's view of things (see note to lines 474–478). Talent John had, and that must command admiration: but admiration is one thing, approval another. As for the *Placita philosophorum antiquorum,* which Petrarch believed was John's work, it provided Petrarch with his first real taste of Plato's *Phaedo* (see de Nolhac 1907.2:140).

249–250 formidatum Caroli dyadema: Charles of Anjou (1227–85), youngest brother of King Louis IX of France and participant in Louis's crusades to Egypt and Tunisia, championed the papal cause in the Kingdom of Naples and Sicily against Manfred, illegitimate son of Frederick II. Having defeated Manfred and established the Angevin dynasty at Naples, Charles allied himself with the deposed Byzantine emperor, Baldwin II, against Michael VIII and fought many campaigns at Corfu and in western Greece. These expeditions were financed by oppressive taxation, especially in Sicily. The resentment thus created led to the revolt that broke out at Palermo in 1282 called the Sicilian Vespers (see note to lines 248–249).

251–253 Simul et ad levam Cumas . . . ubi Tarquinius . . . exul obiit: as Mandelli approaches Inarime (Ischia), he will have a good view of the Cumaean acropolis off to the left, the *patria* of the Sibyl (see note to 238–241 above). *Portolani* and portolan charts mention a Castro Amar in the place where ancient Cumae should be. This fortification no longer exists (Kretschmer 1909.599).

In 510 BC, Tarquinius Superbus was expelled from Rome as a result of his son's rape of Lucretia (Livy, 1.60). Having recruited help from Veii and Tarquinii, he met the Romans in an indecisive battle at Silva Arsia, but his new allies quickly deserted him (Livy, 2.7). Other Latin cities were encouraged to revolt by Rome's example, and Tarquinius was forced into exile at Cumae where he died in 496 (Livy, 2.21 and Pseudo-Pliny, *De viris illustribus* in Sherwin 1973.24). Here it should be noted that the *De viris illustribus,* a series of short biographies covering Roman republican history, is found in the manuscripts of Aurelius Victor's *De Caesaribus* (of the late fourth century). Petrarch believed that these biographies (77 in some mss, 86 in others) were a minor work of Pliny because that is what the manuscripts say (Liber Plinii Veronensis Secundi historici de viris illustribus, etc.). This work, though slight, is important because it was a major inspiration for Petrarch's own *De viris illustribus,* which he worked on intermittently for most of his adult life. There is no so satisfactory modern edition of this work, but Sherwin's is convenient (Reynolds 1986.149–152).

255–256 Comum est, non Cume: the form *Cumum,* printed by Lumbroso as the preferred reading of his manuscripts, poses some interesting problems. There is confirmation that Petrarch spelled the name as *Cumum* in an entry which he made in his own hand at the end of his manuscript that contained the *De agricultura* of Palladius. About a year after the *Itinerarium* was written, on 16 March 1359, the day that Boccaccio arrived for an extended visit, Petrarch planted some laurel trees in the garden of St. Valeria, a little church just east of Sant' Ambrogio. He says in his note that a certain Taddeo had brought him the saplings from *Cumum* (lauros *Cumo* transmissas per Tadeum nostrum . . . seuimus); see de Nolhac 1907.2:267 for entire entry. On 9 December 1362, Petrarch sent a letter *(Epistolae Variae* 4) to Moggio dei Moggi in which he refers to a "Iohannolus de Cumis" (cited in Billanovich 1947.221–222, who thinks that this Giovannolo da Como may be the Giovanni of the *Itinerarium*). If *Cumis* is what Petrarch really wrote, there is an apparent inconsistency. In the *Itinerarium,* Petrarch warns Giovanni against calling Como *Cume* (the classical Cumae), as the common folk would have it, but in the letter to Moggio dated four years after he wrote the *Itinerarium,* we have Petrarch following the fashion of the common folk and using the plural of the name, which makes it identical in form (at least in the ablative) to the Campanian Cumae. There is the further complication that Rossi and Bosco in the National Edition adopt the spelling *Comum* in the two passages where Petrarch refers to the place (*Fam.* 8.5.10 and 17.6.1). Had Petrarch, by the time he had finished revising his collection of letters in 1366, decided to spell the name as *Comum*?

Evidently, there was a common confusion about the names of these two places and perhaps an attempt to fabricate some kind of connection between them. In a letter (*Fam.* 17.6.1), written at the end of 1353, to his good friend Bernardo Anguisolla, governor of Comum, Petrarch says, "Et profecto urbem illam . . . vel semel cupide viderem, Comum, qui campanas totiens Cumas vidi." The *qui* clause is causal: as Petrarch has seen Cumae so often (totiens), he would welcome a chance to see Comum even once. Petrarch seems to imply that Comum and Cumae are companion cities in some sense. Perhaps Petrarch's statement in his letter is best understood as a joking reference to the common confusion of the names to which he here alludes. The joke, incidentally, would have more point if the spelling were *Cumum* (not *Comum*), which may have been what Petrarch wrote in 1358 and later revised.

An ancient source offers a clue about the history of Comum, which may point to a connection with Cumae. According to Strabo (5.1.6), Julius Caesar resettled Comum, originally a Gaulish foundation, with five thousand colonists, among whom five hundred Greeks were the most prominent. The Greeks soon moved on, but not before they gave the new settlement its name, Neo-Comitae (New Town) or Novum Comum in Latin. A local tradition may have grown up to the effect that these Greeks, the bestowers of Comum's name, had come from the ancient Greek colony of Cumae, because of the similarity of the two names. The story was then helped along in the thirteenth century by spelling the name "Comum" as "Cumae" or as Petrarch would have it on occasion "Cumum."

258–263 Sunt qui putent . . . ambigua est valde: this passage touches on matters that had greatly perplexed Petrarch from the time he had first read Servius's note on *Aeneid*, 6.107. Glossing *Acheronte refuso*, Servius says in part (Thilo 1881.3:23–24):

> . . . omnia vicina illic [Acheron] loca calidis et sulphuratis aquis scatent. sine gaudio autem ideo ille dicitur locus, quod necromantia vel sciomantia, ut dicunt, non nisi ibi poterat fieri: quae sine hominis occisione non fiebant; nam et Aeneas illic occiso Miseno sacra ista complevit et Ulixes occiso Elpenore. quamquam fingatur in extrema Oceani parte Ulixes fuisse: quod et ipse Homerus falsum esse ostendit ex qualitate locorum, quae commemorat, et ex tempore navigationis; dicit enim eum a Circe unam noctem navigasse et ad locum venisse, in quo haec sacra

> peregit: quod de Oceano non procedit, de Campania manifestissimum est.

This passage informed Petrarch that the area around Acheron (Servius connects the name with the Greek ἄχαρις [χαίρω], instead of ἄχος; hence the phrase *sine gaudio)* is where the rites of necromancy and sciomancy (Servius explains the difference between the two sorts of divination at *A.* 6.149) must be conducted and that this divination must be preceded by human sacrifice. As examples of what he is talking about Servius says that both Aeneas and Ulysses carried out their rites of divination after killing members of their crews (*occiso Miseno* and *occiso Elpenore*). Petrarch's confusion would have arisen over Servius's statement that Aeneas killed Misenus (*Misenum . . . peremptum ab Enea,* line 258). According to Virgil's account (*A.* 6. 162–174) Misenus aroused the envy of the sea god Triton, who caused him to drown. Misenus had blown his trumpet proudly as a challenge to the god, and for this he was killed. In Virgil's story Aeneas had nothing to do with the killing; in fact he was ignorant of the death until the Sibyl had informed him. Servius must be interpreting Virgil's story (Petrarch thought) as a deliberate softening of the barbarity of human sacrifice (line 260). Still it seemed all very obscure to Petrarch because Misenus had been killed even before Aeneas had expressed to the Sibyl his desire to enter the underworld. As to Homer's account of the death of Elpenor, Petrarch had no inkling in 1358 (see below).

Petrarch's doubts about the Misenus episode are revealed at the very beginning of the sentence (*Sunt qui putent . . .*). When Petrarch arrived at the phrase *pari ritus immanitate,* fresh doubt assailed him and he interrupted the syntax of his sentence with a direct statement: *ut quidam putant; res enim ambigua est valde,* line 263. According to Feo (1974.152–154), this intrusive statement was added by Petrarch in about 1365 after he was able to read Homer's *Odyssey* (at least the eleventh book; see Feo, 136–144) for the first time, not in Greek but in Leontius Pilatus's Latin translation. There he read that Ulysses did not kill Elpenor as a necessary preliminary to his consultation of Tiresias. Far from it. Elpenor's death was the result of a drunken accident (*Od.* 11. 51–83), unrelated to anything Ulysses did or did not do. After reading this, Petrarch could see that neither Aeneas nor Ulysses had killed his companion. The shock of this new knowledge caused him (according to Feo) to insert the statement quoted above, confessing to still more confusion about the Misenus episode.

Petrarch's confusion about the Misenus episode had been with him from the start. He had in 1358, however, no cause to fret about the last part of Servius's note. According to Servius, Homer speaks of Ulysses's entrance into the underworld as taking place far across the Ocean (in extrema Oceani parte); but this, says Servius, is only a thinly disguised fiction: the geography in Homer's description of the underworld and its environs really corresponds to the area in Campania surrounding the Bay of Baia. This part of Servius's note is reflected in the correlative adverbs *illic . . . ubi* of lines 262–263; Virgil said that Aeneas sacrificed Misenus in the place where Homer said Ulysses sacrificed Elpenor.

According to Feo (see above), Petrarch's intrusive statement of lines 263–264 (*ut quidam putant*, etc.) was also inspired by reading in Pilatus's translation (of *Od.* 11.13–19) that the scene of Ulysses's entrance into the underworld was set not in sunny Campania, as Petrarch expected to read, but in the land of the Cimmerians, a place of perpetual darkness: *ubi Cymmeriorum virorum populusque civitasque / caligine et nube velati; nunquam ipsos / sol lucens aspicit . . .* (quoted by Feo, 141). (Here it should be noted that the presence of Ulysses in Campania is fully attested in ancient Greek sources: see, e.g., Phillips 1953.53–67.) It does not seem likely, however, that Petrarch's intrusive statement of line 263 was inserted, as the result of his reading the eleventh book of the *Odyssey* in 1365 or after. The statement is not nearly strong enough to reflect Petrarch's newfound knowledge. Feo himself (118–119, 151) has drawn attention to a revision in *Fam.* 5.4, which Petrarch made as a result of reading the *Odyssey* in 1365. In this letter, written in 1343 and prepared for Petrarch's edition of his *Familiares* in 1352–1353, Petrarch describes his tour of the scenes described by Virgil in *Aeneid 6* as follows (quoted from Feo, 118):

> Baias ego, clarissimis viris Iohanne Barrili et Barbato meo comitantibus, vidi . . . Vidi loca a Virgilio *et, quod maxime mireris, ab*

> *Homero multum ante* descripta. *Vir graius antiquissimus atque doctissimus et nulli secundus ingenio, insignem et qualem res exigebat locum, nusquam inveniens, ab Italia mutuatus est.* Vidi Averni et Lucrini lacus, Acherontis quoque stagnantes aquas . . . (*Fam.* 5.4.4–5).

In his revision of this letter completed in 1366, after he had read Pilatus's translation of the *Odyssey*, Petrarch deleted the italicized words. He was no longer able to let stand his former statement (inspired by Servius, *A.* 6.107) that Homer had borrowed his geography for the underworld from Italy. If, as Feo has shown, Petrarch felt compelled to delete such a statement in *Fam* 5.4, it does not seem very likely that he would allow the same statement to stand in the *Itinerarium*, assuming that he had set his hand to revise it in 1366 or after.

The intrusive addition of line 263 (*ut quidam putant,* etc.) probably belongs, then, to a time when Petrarch still felt secure in the knowledge that Virgil and Homer had both sent their heroes into the underworld in Campania (i.e., sometime before 1366). But he grew more perplexed as time progressed about the Misenus episode, a fact to which the "*ut quidam putant,* etc." clause bears testimony.

For a more detailed treatment of Pilato's relationship with Petrarch and Boccaccio and for a discussion of the translations he produced of the *Iliad* and the *Odyssey* see Pertusi 1964 and Wilkins 1959.59–63, 81–82, 87–93, and 146–150. Crude as Pilato's translations are (for extended specimens see Pertusi), Petrarch eagerly read them and carefully annotated the copy of both poems made for him in 1369 by Giovanni Malpaghini (Par. lat. 7880): see especially de Nolhac 1907.2:165–188. Petrarch had studied Greek briefly with the Basilian monk Barlaam in the summer and early fall of 1342 at Avignon, but his knowledge never progressed beyond the elementary level (Wilkins 1961.33–34). Sadly he was never able to read the Greek *Iliad* which he had acquired (now identified as Ambr. I 98 inf.; Pertusi 1964.8). See also Berschin 1988.267–270.

263–267 esse autem huiuscemodi sacris apta loca . . . operosi reditus: the conclusion of the long sentence begun in line

258 consists mainly of allusions to *Aeneid,* 6.126–129 and offers no special difficulties.

The Acheron was one of the rivers of the underworld (*A.* 6. 295), which was thought to feed Lake Avernus (*A.* 6.107); Tartarus in Virgil was a place where the worst sinners were punished (*A.* 6. 548–627). Virgil calls the entrance to the underworld *ianua Ditis* (*A.* 6.127); Petrarch refers to it as *Ditis ostia* and says its threshold is one across which there is no return (limen irremeabile). The adjective *irremeabile* is a Virgilian word (*A.* 5.591, 6.453; perhaps a coinage), but Petrarch found the whole phrase in Statius (*Theb.* 1. 96). Virgil says that the entry to the underworld is easy at Avernus (*A.* 6.126). *Averno* is read in many manuscripts and is defended by many modern editors (e.g., R. Mynors in the Oxford edition of 1969); Petrarch's *Averni* has many able defenders (E. Norden's 1957 edition and commentary on the sixth book). Virgil says that the door to the underworld stands open throughout every night and day: *noctes atque dies patet atri ianua Ditis, A.* 6.127; Petrarch says: *quem patentem diebus dixit ac noctibus.* His paraphrase is mildly curious. Since no one knew Virgil's famous line better than Petrarch, why did he change the accusatives (*noctes* and *dies*) to ablatives? Grammatical correctness is not really an issue since the ablative is sometimes used even in Classical Latin to express duration of time just like the accusative. He probably made the change to achieve the *cursus tardus* or *medius* with the clausula "díxit ac nóctibus" (see Appendix). Virgil says that although the descent to the underworld is easy, the way back is hard: *sed revocare gradum superasque evadere ad auras / hoc opus, hic labor est;* cf. Petrarch's *laborosi atque operosi reditus* (genitive of description).

267–269 de qua re quia quod scriptum est legisti . . . extra propositi metas eam: what Petrarch had read and heard regarding the entrance into the Land of the Dead was considerable: see Feo's entire article (1974.115–183) for more information and extended discussion. It is sufficient to say here that Avernus was far from being considered the only entrance to the underworld even in the limited area of the Bay of Naples. See following note.

269–276 Hic Sibille Cumane domus maxima super horrentem Averni ripam cernitur . . . volucrum nidis frequens: Petrarch was under the impression that the large Roman bath on the southeast shore of Lake Avernus, in a semidilapidated state in his day, was the place where the Sibyl had made her residence. The main part of the domed brick and concrete structure, dating to the Neronian period, is octagonal in form with a circular interior 120 ft. in diameter; other smaller buildings are attached. The whole complex would have made a *domus maxima* indeed. Petrarch observed that the *domus* was abandoned except for a large number of birds that made their nests there. This reference to birds was prompted by Virgil's *A.* 6.236–242, a passage that explains that poisonous vapors arise from a yawning cave near Lake Avernus so that birds cannot safely fly in this area. On the "lucus a non lucendo" principle, Isidore (*Etym.* 13.19.8) derives the name Avernus from *aves* as follows: *Avernus autem lacus vocatus quod aves ibi supervolare non possent* (Lindsay 1911). Avernus was derived from the Greek *Aornos* (= birdless).

Since Petrarch speaks of the "domus" of the Sibyl as situated "above the rugged bank" of Avernus, it is clear that he could not have considered the long tunnel (1100 yards) linking Cumae and Avernus through Monte Grillo on the west bank as the home of the Sibyl, nor likewise the shorter tunnel on the south end of the lake linking Avernus with Lake Lucrinus (both tunnels the work of Lucius Cocceius). These two tunnels were both variously identified in later times as the home of the Sibyl and the entrance to the underworld. For a general survey of the area see McKay 1972.1:7–30 and for the confused testimony regarding the "grottos" of the Sibyl see Clark 1977.482–495 and 1996.217–243; and especially Monti 1991.39–59 and 1994.19–34. Petrarch speaks here as though he thought that one of the tunnels (a "cave" he calls it) was the entrance to the underworld (cf. *Fam.* 5.4.5) or at least an entrance; but the discussions of Feo (1974. esp. 120–122) and Clark (1996a.261–272) must be pondered in this connection. Following Servius *A.* 6.237 (qua ad inferos descendebatur, non ubi fuerat Sibylla vaticanata), he would have carefully distinguished the Sibyl's oracular cave from the entrance to the underworld (the catabatic cave), and he evidently thought her dwelling was separate from the catabatic cave. At *Fam.* 5.4.5 he says, "I have seen the native land and home of the Sibyl, and that horrible cave from which fools do not return and which the wise do not enter" (vidi Sibille patriam ac domum, et horrificum illud specus, stultis iremeabile, doctoribus inaccessum). Since Virgil at *A.* 6.53 and 81 refers to the Sibyl's oracular cave as her "domus," this was probably Petrarch's view of the matter. If Sibyl's "domus" was at Lake Avernus, there also was her oracular cave. They were the same as far as Petrarch was concerned. That Petrarch also considered the Sibyl's *domus* and oracle to be Apollo's temple (Virgil, *A.* 6.14–41) will emerge from the following discussion.

First we should record an interesting passage in a letter written in 1195 by Conrad von Querfurt, vicegerent of Emperor Henry VI in Naples and Sicily. Writing home to Arnold of Lübeck of his travels in Campania and Sicily, Conrad says, "In the same place there is the palace of the Sibyl, a structure with elaborate rooms, in which there is a bath, which is called nowadays the bath of the Sibyl" (*Ibidem est palatium Sybille, operosis constructum edificiis, in quo est balneum, quod hodiernis diebus balneum Sybille nuncupatur*; text in Lappenberg 1869.195). This bath of the Sibyl Conrad seems to locate at Baia, but his narrative shifts from one geographical area to another with amazing disregard of logical progression. The most likely view is that he is talking about Nero's bath at Lake Avernus. Petrarch's "domus Sibille" and Conrad's "palatium Sybille" look like a match. Conrad does not otherwise mention Lake Avernus in his letter.

Next may be noted the description of a bath called De Ferris by Peter of Eboli in his *De balneis Terre Lavoris* (c.1200), a collection of epigrams, each consisting of six elegaic couplets. Peter purports to describe in verse thirty bathing establishments between Naples and Baia, famous for their medicinal properties. The only modern edition of the poem is that of D'Amato 1975.425–426, but see now also the Latin text with a late fourteenth-century French translation in Hanly 1996.225–255. D'Amato's text, thrice altered and slightly repunctuated, is as follows:

Balneum quod de Ferris dicitur

Ante domum vatis lacus est qui [D'Amato:ubi] dictus Averni.
Grande ruinose preminet [D'Amato: preminit] artis opus.

> Hic [D'Amato:hoc] lavacrum ferri, quod habet ferruginis instar,
> Dicitur umbrosa sed caret unda domo.

> (Before the house of the prophetess is a lake which is named Avernus. Though in ruins the large work of art [the domus] is quite impressive. Here is a bath said to be of iron, because it [the water in the bath] has the appearance of rust, but there is no water in the shady house.)

Perhaps the house is called shady because it is associated with the underworld, the place where the shades (umbrae) reside.

If this is the correct way to understand the verses, Peter seems to represent the De Ferris bath as part of the Sibyl's *domus*, yet distinct from it since he makes a point of saying that (bath) water is lacking in the house itself. This interpretation can be seen as consistent with Conrad's description of the Sibyl's "palatium," written not very long before Peter wrote his verses. Perhaps by Petrarch's time (about 150 years later) the process called bradyseism or a more dramatic seismic event had dried up the thermal spring which had fed the bath referred to by Conrad and Peter, a far from remote possibility. For instance, the popular baths at Tripergula just to the east of Lake Avernus were completely wiped out by the volcanic eruption that created Monte Nuovo in September of 1538 (see D'Amato 1975.353–356). Petrarch does not say anything about a bath in connection with the Sibyl's *domus* probably because it was no longer in use. It should be noted that the bath in question here is different from the one associated with the large tunnel at the south end of Lake Avernus known as the "Grotta della Sibilla" (see Maiuri 1963.152–153 and Amalfitano 1990.175–176). In a later tradition, which Virgil gives no sign of knowing, the Sibyl ritually purified herself before prophesying (first recorded in the third century by Pseudo-Justin the Martyr). According to Peter of Eboli's epigram the bath at the Sibyl's *domus* was valued for its medicinal uses (for ailments of the eyes, ears, and head) and is not said to have any connection with the Sibyl's preparations for prophesying. Conrad, Peter, and Petrarch are probably all talking about the same place: the large thermal bath established by Nero, impressive in its ruined state but entirely dysfunctional as a bath in Petrarch's day. The bath at the "Grotta della Sibilla" is probably to be identified with the one called "Palumbaria" by Peter of Eboli (Amalfitano 1990.176), the only other bath in the immediate area of Lake Avernus and called a "Cripta."

Benvenuto da Imola, who wrote his massive commentary to Dante's *Divine Comedy* over a period of some ten or fifteen years (1365–80), paraphrases (without credit) this passage of the *Itinerarium* in his remarks on the third canto of the *Inferno* as follows (Lacaita 1887.1:123):

> Ibi fuit maximum templum sibillae Cumanae, in ripa lacus qui dictus est Avernus, cuius parietes adhuc hodie apparent alti sed nimia vetustate semiruti, nec habitat aliquis ibi nisi quod variae aves faciunt nidum suum; et incolae illorum locorum adhuc ostendunt speluncam ipsius Sibillae intra domum.
>
> (There [at Cumae] was the very large temple of the Cumaean Sibyl, on the bank of the lake called Avernus whose high walls can still be seen today, but they are in a semidilapidated state because of their excessive old age; no one lives there apart from various birds that have built their nests in it. The locals still point out the cave of the Sibyl herself inside her home.)

The first and last sentences are particularly important because Petrarch's *domus maxima* is replaced by *maximum templum,* which is then described as the Sibyl's *domus,* her home. The last sentence of Benvenuto da Imola's account makes explicit what can only be inferred from Petrarch's text with help from Virgil and Servius's commentary. Benvenuto says that the Sibyl's *domus* is also her oracular (certainly not catabatic) cave or rather some presumably large subterranean area within her home (actually Nero's bath), which Virgil variously calls a "huge cave" (*antrum immane, A.* 6.10) or "inner sanctuary" (*adytum, A.* 6.98). Benvenuto says that this is what the local guides tell tourists, a detail which has an authentic ring to it and which must have come from Boccaccio, as we shall see. Since Benvenuto calls the Sibyl's *domus* a "very large temple," he probably thought that her *domus* was also

Apollo's temple, which actually lay in utter and unimpressive ruins on the Cumaean acropolis, as did her oracular cave (and *domus*): see Maiuri 1963.115–140. Indeed it would be remarkable if the structure were not identified as a temple since its great dome (or what remained of it) was only a little less impressive than that of the Pantheon in Rome, which almost everyone at this time believed to be the temple of Cybele.

Benvenuto da Imola, who never traveled to the Bay of Naples, must have gotten some of his information from Boccaccio, when he traveled from Bologna to Florence in 1373 to hear Boccaccio lecture on Dante's *Divine Comedy.* Boccaccio, who lived at Naples from about 1327 to 1341, and had plenty of opportunity to tour the area, has left in various works relevant testimony about Lake Avernus. In the *Filocolo* (4.73.4), written between 1336 and 1338, Boccaccio draws on his own experience to portray his hero passing some pleasant time sightseeing at Avernus. There Filocolo visits "the Temple of Apollino and the oratory of the Sibyl" (il tempio d'Apollino, e l'oratorio della Sibilla; text Quaglio 1964. 455). In a note, Quaglio correctly identifies the Temple of Apollo with the structure on the east shore of Avernus, now recognized by modern scholars as a thermal bath dating to the Neronian period (note *ad loc.* 886). He also cites the following passage from Boccaccio's *De montibus,* s. v. *Baiarum fontes* (Stocchi 1998.7–8: 1884):

> nam ibi videre est Apollinis oraculum ingens opificum artificio non deitate numinis venerabile Sibyllae insuper Averno supereminens lacui vetustissimam atque ingentem aedem.
>
> (For there [at Avernus] it is possible to see the huge oracle of Apollo, which commands our respect because of the skill of human laborers, not because of the divinity of the Sibyl's power, as it juts out over Lake Avernus, a very ancient and large temple.)

This passage makes clear that Boccaccio considered Apollo's Temple and the Sibyl's oracle to be the same, and since his sources (Virgil) insist that the Sibyl's oracle was also her *domus*, that must have been Boccaccio's view of the matter as well.

In his short essay on the Cumaean Sibyl in his *De mulieribus claris*, 26 (text by Zaccaria 1967), Boccaccio says,

> Huic insuper in baiano litore secus Averni Lacum dicunt insigne fuisse oraculum quod quidem et ego vidi audivique quod servet ab ea cognomen usque in hodiernum; quod etsi corrosum sit vetustate plurima et incuria semirutum etiam sit, in ruinis maiestatem servat veterem et admirationem prestat, adhuc intuenti, magnitudinis sue.
>
> (They say moreover that she [the Sibyl] had a famous oracle on the shore of Baia, along Lake Avernus. I myself have seen it and I have heard that it keeps her name to this day. Although it is crumbling because of extreme old age and is in a semidilapidated condition because of lack of maintenance, it preserves its ancient majesty amid the ruins and still provides to visitors cause for admiring its great size.)

In his note, Zaccaria also cites a passage from Boccaccio's *De montibus*, s.v. *Avernus* (in *de lacubus*) as follows:

> huius [Averni] in margine semesi vetustate parietes adhuc sibyllini oraculi testantur, opus magnificum [. . .]. Vidi ego ex hoc lacu, Roberto [. . .] rege vivente (Stocchi 1998.7–8:1897–98).
>
> (On the edge of this [Lake Avernus] there still stand as witnesses the walls of the Sibylline oracle, though half eaten away by age, a magnificent work still . . . I myself have seen [them] from this lake, while King Robert . . . was still alive.)

In his comment on this passage from the *De montibus* (503), Zaccaria agrees with P. G. Ricci that the reference is to the "Grotta della Sibilla" on the southwestern shore of Lake Avernus. Naturally, the same identification is intended to apply to the passage in the *De mulieribus*, which could be understood as Zaccaria and

Ricci would have it, but the passage from the *De montibus* makes such an interpretation impossible. Boccaccio explicitly says that his view of the ruins was "from this lake"; that is, he was sitting in a boat on Lake Avernus. But the "Grotta della Sibilla," being subterranean, would not be visible from this vantage point. To quote Maiuri (1963.152), "about 300 meters beyond the red house of the custodian, a path through a clump of chestnut trees leads to the low, half-interred entrance to the so-called Grotto of the Sibyl." Boccaccio would have been lucky even to spot the entrance while sitting on the lake in a boat.

The evidence from Boccaccio all fits nicely with that provided by Benvenuto da Imola. Both considered the Neronian both to be Apollo's temple and the Sibyl's oracle and home. It seems clear that Benvenuto, as he paraphrased Petrarch's *Itinerarium*, believed that Petrarch shared his and Boccaccio's views on the matter. It should be noted that none of the three mention anything at all about a bath. In this connection recall Peter of Eboli's verse cited above: "there is no water in the shady house."

Benvenuto da Imola may have obtained his copy of the *Itinerarium* on his visit to Florence to hear Boccaccio lecture, but he may also have obtained it directly from Petrarch at an earlier date. Although we have only one of Petrarch's letters to Benvenuto (*Sen.* 15.11; dated 9 February 1373) and only a fragment of Benvenuto's reply (text in Lacaita 1887.1:xxviii–xxix), it is clear that they corresponded regularly. Benvenuto earned his living at Bologna by giving lectures not only on classical authors like Virgil, Lucan, and Valerius Maximus, but also on Dante's *Divine Comedy* and Petrarch's twelve eclogues, called collectively the *Bucolicum carmen*, producing commentaries on both works. The value of his commentary on Petrarch's eclogues (published by Avena 1906) may be judged from the frequent references to it in Bergin's notes to his translation (1974.217–250).

In his reply to Petrarch's letter of February 1373 (if it is genuine), Benvenuto says that he finished his commentary on Dante the year before and will be sending Petrarch a copy as soon as he can find somebody trustworthy enough to deliver it. We know however that Benvenuto extensively revised and expanded his commentary after his move to Ferrara after 1375 so that material from the *Itinerarium* might have been added at this time, i.e., after his visit to Florence in 1373–1374. On Benvenuto, see Paoletti 1966.8:691–694 and Mazzoni 1970.1:593–596.

272–277 In eodem flexu fontes calidi . . . mortis horrorem: there are two large volcanic zones in the Naples area — the Mt. Vesuvius complex and the Campi Flegrei complex. Naples sits roughly on the boundary between the two. The whole area, called "la Solftara," is full of hot springs and fumaroles. The hot water and steam were considered beneficial to the health, but here also were thought to be various entrances to the underworld, whence the hot water and steam sprang. In this area, thoughts of renewed life and inevitable death were inextricably bound together.

Benvenuto da Imola also paraphrases this section of the *Itinerarium* rather closely, but gives Petrarch credit (not quite full credit) and even mentions the title (Lacaita 1887. 1:125):

> Nec miror quod in eadem parte circa praedictum lacum erumpunt fontes tepentes notabilius quam in aliqua parte Italiae, quorum aliqui emittunt cinerem sulphureum ac ferventem. Est etiam aliquis locus ibi ubi terra sine igne visibili, sine aquis, producit salutarem vaporem et fumum medicinalem corporibus infirmorum. Ideo bene novissimus poeta Petrarca in quadam Epistola sua, quam *Itinerarium* vocat, dicit: sic dicere potes quod in eisdem locis convenerint remedium vitae et horror mortis.

The paraphrasing continues rather closely to line 287 of our text.

277–282 Et sub Miseno . . . Romanarum una classium . . . presidio tuta essent: Augustus was the first to maintain a fleet at Misenum for the defense of the Tyrrhenian or Lower Sea and to establish Ravenna as a permanent station of a fleet for the defense of the Adriatic or Upper Sea (Suetonius, *Aug.* 49, Tacitus, *Ann.* 4.5, Vegetius 4.31, and Livy, 5.33.8, whose words Petrarch echoes here). Billanovich 1960.53 notes that Petrarch cross-referenced the passages in Suetonius and Vegetius in his personal copies of these authors. On the Roman Imperial Navy, see Starr 1960. Porto Miseno was not in use in the fourteenth century. See note to line 290.

282–283 Baie . . . ab illic sepulto Baio quodam socio Ulixis appellate: cf. Servius (*A.* 6.107): . . . *a Baio socio [Ulixis] illic mortuo Baias constat esse nominatas.* Varro is Servius's authority for this information (Serv. *A.* 9. 707); cf. Lycophron, *Alex.* 694.

283–287 situ longe amenissimo . . . astipulatur fides: Baiae is situated on the SW side of the bay between Misenum and Puteoli. Of the beauty of this bay, Horace says: *nullus in orbe sinus Bais praelucet amoenis* (*Ep.* 1.1.83), a statement Petrarch echoes with *situ longe amenissimo.* Baiae came into fashion as a resort before the time of Cicero: Lucullus and Marius had villas there, as did Pompey and Caesar later on (Seneca, *Ep.* 51.12). These early visitors to the area built on the hill overlooking the bay, but later ones preferred the shoreline, even extending great piers into the bay upon which to build luxurious palaces (Horace, *C.* 2.18.20; Virgil, *A.* 9. 710–714). Baiae quickly became a place that Cicero (*Pro Caelio,* 15. 35) and Seneca (*Ep.* 51.3) could enthusiastically condemn as a "resort for vice" (diversorium vitiorum). Following a long tradition, Boccaccio condemned the place with venomous curses for corrupting his chaste love in Sonnet LXXII (Marti 1969.1:100–101).

Besides the natural beauty of the place, the bounteous thermal springs acted as a magnet for those in ill health. Pliny (*Nat.* 31.2–3) speaks of these waters as surpassing all others in number and variety and says that their different properties (sulphureous, aluminous, bituminous, etc.) made them sought after for all sorts of diseases. There were three great thermae at Baiae, the oldest (the "Temple of Mercury") dating to the Augustan period and the other two (the "Temple of Venus" and the "Temple of Diana") to Nero's time. Petrarch may be alluding to these baths when he speaks of *marmoree testudines calidis fontibus superiecte.* The word *testudines* might refer to the great vaulted ceilings of these establishments, which were made of cement, but stuccoed to have the appearance of marble.

More likely, however, Petrarch is referring specifically to the great bath near Baiae called the Sudatorium Trituli (see Mailler 1979.141–153 and 1988.79–98, and Amalfitano 1990.180–181), which he describes at length in *Fam.* 5.4.6:

> vidi rupes undique liquorem saluberrimum stillantes et cuntis olim morborum generibus omniparentis nature munere adhibita, post medicorum invidia — ut memorant — confusa balnea, ad que tamen nunc etiam e finitimis urbibus ingens omnis sexus etatisque concursus est; vidi non cryptam modo, que Neapolitana dicitur, . . . sed passim perforatos montes atque suspensos testudinibus marmoreis eximio candore fulgentibus, et insculptas imagines, quis latex cui corporis parti faveat, manu apposita designantes.

Feo (1974.161–168) is certainly right to connect Petrarch's description of this bath with others circulating from the twelfth to the fourteenth centuries in the works of Conrad von Querfurt, Gervasius of Tilbury, Peter of Eboli, and the anonymous author of *Cronica di Partenope*. A synoptic version of the story of the baths, based on these authors, might say that the baths (with their medicinal virtues) were the gift of Virgil to the poor so they could be cured of all their ills without having to pay exorbitant fees to greedy doctors. These baths Virgil provided with plaster (so specified by Conrad) statues or perhaps stucco reliefs adorned with inscriptions informing the patrons which waters were beneficial for which diseases. But three greedy members of the medical profession (from Salerno) went secretly to the baths and switched the inscriptions around (Petrarch's *confusa balnea*?) so the patrons would not know what bath to use. Nevertheless, the poor still came in droves. The wicked doctors were punished for their deed when they suffered shipwreck on their way home. It may be that in the passage from the *Familiares* just quoted Petrarch is referring to two separate baths: one in which the medicinal waters are identified by inscriptions that could be easily switched around, and another in which the waters are identified by statues whose hands are placed on the parts of the body to be cured, thus eliminating the need for signs.

Feo has shown that the details of Petrarch's description of the Baths of Puteoli bear some striking similarities to the accounts of the authors mentioned above. To be especially noted here is that all of them (except Peter of Eboli) give the credit for creating the baths to Virgil. This detail Petrarch pointedly ignores in his letter since he objects strongly to all the stories circulating at that time about Virgil the wonderworker and magician (see below on lines 307–309 and 340–343). Soon he will actively discourage Mandelli from visiting the Castel dell' Ovo for this very reason (lines 340–343 below). For additional information on the baths see Comparetti 1941.2: 25, 28, 39–40 and the relevant excerpts from the primary sources in the convenient "Testi di leggendi virgiliane," e.g., 173, 177, and 184; also see Kauffmann 1959, especially 1–7 and 57–65, and bibliography; D'Amato 1975.97–103 and 468–471, and Petrucci 1979.99–129.

Petrarch's description of his visit to the baths is rather academic in tone and singularly lacking in specifics. One is inclined to think that he did not join the locals in enjoying the pleasures of the baths. Poggio, by way of contrast, gives a vivid description of his visit to the baths at Baden, Switzerland in May of 1416 in a letter to Niccolò Niccoli (Fubini 1964.3:1.1.1–10; translation in Gordan 1974.24–31). The seminude mixed bathing quite charmed Poggio; but embarrassed by his poor German (he says), he did not actually join in the frolicking group. He contented himself with the role of spectator, occasionally tossing coins to the prettiest of the women bathers, who recovered them in a most delightful display. On bathing and hygiene at this period, see Thorndike 1928. 192–203. For a general account of the history and archeological remains of Baiae in the Roman period, see McKay 1972.2: 31–75 with bibliography.

287–288 Hic Neroniane piscine . . . exordia: Suetonius says (*Ner.* 31.3) that Nero put men to work on a covered pool, surrounded by colonnades and stretching from Misenum to Lake Avervus. The pool was to be fed by all the hot springs of Baiae district. No other ancient author mentions such an enormous project (the pool would have been several miles long). Although there are no remains today, schematic drawings of the Baian shoreline etched on several glass flasks of the third century AD show Nero's pool (called *Stagnum Neronis*) still very much in existence at that time. See McKay 1972.1:64, 69–71 and Ostrow 1979. 77–140.

It was perhaps inevitable that the *piscina* mentioned here by Suetonius would be associated with the so-called *piscina mirabilis*, a great subterranean structure measuring 260 by 100 Roman feet, located on the side of the highest hill east of Mare Morto and probably the terminus of the Serino aqueduct. This reservoir belonging to the Augustan period was designed primarily to supply the needs of Augustus's new naval base at Misenum (McKay 1972.1:88–91 and Amalfitano 1990.250–252). Popular tradition however associated the *piscina* with Nero and linked it to the *Stagnum*. Indeed Petrarch himself links the *piscina mirabilis* to Nero by calling it "the pool of Augusta [Agrippina], unfortunate because of the cruelty of her son [Nero]" (*piscinam infelicis nati saevitia Auguste, Fam.* 5.4.5). It is clear from this passage of the *Itinerarium* that he thought it represented the initial stage (exordia) of the pool mentioned by Suetonius, the *Stagnum Neronis*.

288–294 nam furoris alterius . . . vestigia remanserunt: Suetonius (*Ner.* 31.3) also describes another project of Nero's: to connect Lake Avernus with Ostia by means of a canal large enough for two merchant ships to pass. Nero imported captives and convicted criminals from all over the empire to begin excavation on a canal, which would be about 125 miles long (Suetonius says 160 miles). The project, begun in 64, was abandoned at Nero's death in 68, after a considerable amount of work had been done (Tacitus, *Ann.* 15.42; Pliny, *Nat.* 14.61). Although the views of Tacitus and Suetonius on this canal are very negative (impendiorum furor), modern scholars take it more seriously; see Meiggs 1973.57–58. No sign of Nero's canal can be seen today.

294–295 Hic angulus et Lucrinum habet et undam illam Iuliam atque equor indignans . . . immutatum: the passage in the *Georgics* (2.161–163) to which Petrarch refers runs as follows:

> An memorem portus Lucrinoque addita claustra
> atque *indignatum* magnis stridoribus *aequor*,

Julia qua ponto longe sonat *unda* refuso
Tyrrhenusque fretis immittitur aestus Avernis?

Lake Lucrinus is a shallow land-locked lagoon, situated in the inner part of the deep bay between Baiae and Puteoli and separated from the outer bay by a sandbar (natural in origin, but attributed by Roman poets to the work of Hercules). Farther inland to the north is Lake Avernus, separated from Lake Lucrinus by a narrow strip of land; it is a deep fresh water lake formed in the crater of an extinct volcano. According to Servius *(G.* 2.161), Julius Caesar fortified the sandbar to protect valuable oyster beds in Lake Lucrinus, which were famous for their excellent produce (e.g., Hor. *Epod.* 2.49, *S.* 2.4.32, and Juv. 4.141).

In 37 BC Agrippa, under orders from Octavian (later Augustus, line 299), undertook massive construction in the area during the hard campaign against Sextus Pompey. First, he united Lake Lucrinus with Lake Avernus by opening a canal; then with masonry construction (Lucrinoque addita claustra), he strengthened the sandbar between Lake Lucrinus and the sea for more protection against storms (indignatum . . . aequor); and finally, he opened a passage in the now fortified sandbar to allow the entrance of ships, dredging a channel through the shallow Lucrinus to the deep waters of Avernus for the larger ships. The harbor thus formed was known as the Portus Julius (Iulia unda).

This description of Agrippa's work on Lake Lucrinus accords best with the surviving literary accounts (e.g., Florus's brief but lucid treatment, *Epit.* 2.18). The construction was apparently the engineering marvel of the time, but it did not last long, in large part because the channel dredged between the two lakes could not be kept clear for large ships (Strabo 5.4.6). It seems, however, that in Cassiodorus's time (*Var.* 9.6, Fridh 1973) the canal between Avernus and Lucrinus was still open, as well as the entrance to Lucrinus. Today the two lakes are separated by a substantial expanse of land, the result of a volcanic eruption which formed Monte Nuovo in 1538 and filled up a large part of Lake Lucrinus, closing the entrance to the sea (if it was not already closed) and leaving Lucrinus much smaller than it was in Petrarch's time. See Frederiksen 1984. Plate XIV for an aerial photograph of the Portus Julius area, with the superimposed outline of the ancient shoreline and the construction work done by Agrippa; see also Paget 1968.159–169 and 1969.25–32.

297 Mare Mortuum: Petrarch seems to think Lake Lucrinus was also known in his day as Mare Morto or the Dead Sea. Mare Morto however was the name properly applied to Lacus Misenus, a large basin of water formed in the crater of an extinct volcano and separated from Portus Misenus by a quite narrow strip of land. After the battle of Actium (31 BC) Augustus ordered his engineers to connect Mare Morto with the outer harbor by a navigable canal. Dockyards, warehouses, and barracks were constructed around the inner basin (Mare Morto) and exercise grounds were established on its southern boundary at the beach called today Miliscola (= militum schola): see Paget 1971.22–38 and McKay 1972.1:1–39.

Why should Petrarch have fallen into confusion as to the identification of Mare Morto? First of all, the name Mare Morto does not occur on any of the seven fourteenth-century portolan charts collated by Almagià (1929.68), and out of the over twenty-three *portolani* and portolan charts used by Kretschmer in his commentary (1909.599), only one *portolano* dated to the middle of the fifteenth century mentions Marmorto, and another somewhat later in date mentions a Cape Mare Morto (Chauo di marimorto), evidently referring to Cape Miseno. None of the *portolani* and portolan charts used by Kretschmer mentions Porto Miseno; only one of the fourteenth-century portolan charts collated by Almagià mentions Cape Miseno (cauo di Misene). In the sixteenth century, Benedetto di Falco (Morisani 1972.70) thinks that Mare Morto refers to the Gulf of Pozzuoli as a whole. The bay is called Mare Morto because the waters lie "quietamente e sensa onde."

It seems safe to conclude that the *portolano* and portolan chart(s), which Petrarch is thought to have owned, showed no reference to either Mare Morto or Porto Miseno. Presumably, Porto Miseno, always plagued by silting and bradyseism, was simply not in operation during the fourteenth century and probably well into the sixteenth. He must have heard the name Mare Morto from the locals on one of his two trips to the Bay of Naples but had been misinformed as to its whereabouts. The *De civitate*, an anonymous antiquarian tract of the fourteenth century later incorporated into Francesco Griffolini's popular *Libellus de mirabilibus civitatis Putheolorum . . .* (Naples 1475), illustrates one way Petrarch's confusion about Mare Morto may have come about. The manuscript of this text (Vat. Lat. 3436), which is being prepared for its first publication by J. D'Amato, says:

> Iuxta hunc montem [Misenum] portus olim fuit quem veteres portum Julii vocaverunt. Nunc aut<em> vulgo portus maris mortui nuncupatur. Hunc portum Julius Caesar effodi fecit . . . (text courtesy of J. D'Amato)
>
> (Near this mountain [Miseno] there was once a port which the ancients called Portus Julius. But now it is commonly called the Port of the Dead Sea. This port Julius Caesar caused to be dug out . . .)

This passage shows that the name Portus Julius had been mistakenly transferred from Lake Lucrinus to Lake Misenus or Mare Morto sometime in the thirteenth or fourteenth centuries, or earlier. One can see how this might have come about. Augustus Caesar undertook major engineering projects of a very similar nature at both places, first at Lake Lucrinus and then at Lake Misenus. When Petrarch's local informants told him that Portus Julius was also called Mare Morto, he assumed that they must have been referring to Lake Lucrinus, because he knew from the ancient sources that Lake Lucrinus was Portus Julius. Incidentally the text of the *De civitate* makes it clear that Porto Miseno was not in operation in the fourteenth century (olim fuit, "there once was"). The name Mare Morto may have come about through a corruption of a form of the name Mirteo mare, reported by Boccaccio at *Filocolo*, 4.73.3: . . . si dilettava di videre l' antichità di Baia, e *il Mirteo mare* [The Myrtle Sea], el monte Mesano. . . . This name Boccaccio explains at 5.5.2 as follows: *'l mare, le cui rive, abondevoli di verdi mortelle* [myrtle] *Mirteo il fanno chiamare* (cited from Quaglio 1964). For further discussion of Portus Iulius and Mare Morto in the medieval tradition see Jacono 1937.37–59 and

D'Amato 1996.215–264: esp. 239–247. D'Amato believes that Paolino Veneto (in his *Chronologia magna*) is principally to blame for the conflation of written sources regarding Portus Julius and Lake Misenus and for the resulting confusion described above.

301–306 Hoc maris intervallum Gaius . . . permeavit: Petrarch is referring to Suetonius's account (*Cal.* 19) of what the ancients considered one of Caligula's most extravagant displays. Two years after he became emperor (AD 39) Caligula decided to span the northern part of the bay of Naples from Puteoli to Baiae with a bridge of ships, a matter of about 2.2 miles by modern calculations. He anchored a double line of merchant ships and constructed a road over them on the model of the Appian Way. On two successive days, Caligula crossed back and forth on the bridge in the manner of a Roman general celebrating a triumph. On the first day, he rode on horseback; on the second, he dressed up like a charioteer and rode across driving a team of two famous horses with the son of the Parthian king beside him in the chariot. Caligula's critics said he undertook the project to rival Xerxes's famous bridge across the Hellespont.

In July of 1347, Petrarch gave poetic treatment to this episode as follows (*Metr.* 3.4.39–43, *Rime*, 776):

> sic quoque Baiano temerarius equore Gaius
> tertia construxit tumidi spectacula fastus,
> que nunc sparsa vident naute numerantque sub alto.
> Hic Hellespontus, Baie michi Brundusiumque,
> hic ferro fodiendus Athos.

A classical source for the above passage more important than Suetonius is a passage in Lucan (2.610–756), where the Roman poet describes the engineering feat of Julius Caesar at Brindisi to prevent Pompey's flight from Italy during the Civil War. This same passage in Lucan is certainly in Petrarch's mind as he wrote the *Itinerarium*. The note in *Rime* to 3.39–40 cited above mistakenly takes them to refer to a theater, left unfinished by Augustus and Tiberius and completed by Caligula (Suetonius, *Cal.* 21). The signs of construction which Petrarch says sailors report seeing beneath the surface of the water in 3.4.41 are not those of a theater nor those of Caligula's bridge, which by the nature of its construction was only a temporary arrangement, but of the huge mole or pier (1130 ft. long and 49 ft. wide) constructed by Augustus (Strabo, 5.4.6). It should be noted that modern scholars tend to take Caligula's bridge, or at least the idea that motivated it, more seriously than the ancient sources: see Balsdon 1934.51–54 and Barrett 1990.211–212. As for his wickedness, Seneca says (*Cons. Helv.* 10.4) that Nature produced Caligula to show what a supremely vicious man can accomplish when he has every opportunity to indulge his vices.

300 Non longe a Puteolis, Falernus collis attollitur: the Falernian district (not a hill) was in the northern part of Campania on the north side of the Volturno. At about 25 miles' distance, it was not so close to Puteoli as Petrarch suggests; but the wine was, as he says, one of the most celebrated vintages in antiquity (e.g., Horace, *C.* 1.20.10, 2.3.8, 2.11.19 etc.; Virgil, *G.* 2.96, Propertius, 4. 6.73). Petrarch himself was not a wine drinker (see *Sen.* 12.1). See Porena 1952.75–81 and the Gazetteer on Petrarch's Falernian "Hill."

307–309 mons est saxeus, hominum manibus perfossus, quod vulgus . . . magicis cantaminibus factum putat: the rocky promontory Petrarch refers to is called Posillipo, named after a Roman villa once located on the summit and having the name Pausilypon (Greek for 'Trouble's End'). The tunnel was the work of Lucius Cocceius, the engineer who served Octavian and Agrippa in their efforts to expedite the movement of men and supplies during the conflict against Sextus Pompey following Caesar's death (see note to lines 294-295): it connected Naples with Puteoli and the west side of the bay by a shorter route than the coast road and an easier one than the one that passed over the ridge of Posillipo. Much altered in the course of time, it was originally 21 ft. wide, 70 ft. high in places, and a half-mile long. The old tunnel, now closed, was replaced by a new one in 1895 (Grotta nuova di Posillipo.)

Virgil's reputation as a great poet and man of learning grew rather than declined as Rome's empire disintegrated. This was true generally, but especially at Naples, where Virgil lived for many years and where he was buried. A legend developed of a Virgil endowed with wonderful, even magical powers, who showed his love for his adopted city by certain benefactions in the form of protective talismans (e.g., a bronze fly which would drive away flies from the city) and by amazing feats of engineering. Notice of the marvels wrought by Virgil was first put into print by visitors to Naples like Gervasius of Tilbury, Conrad von Querfurt, and John of Salisbury. Soon the stories were circulating all around Europe, and Virgil's deeds became more marvelous with each retelling.

In this passage, Petrarch refers to one of Virgil's most celebrated deeds, the making of Posillipo's tunnel with magic spells. Among the many who testify to the fame of this deed is Christopher Marlowe (*Doctor Faustus,* Act III, sc. 1):

> There saw we learned *Maroes* golden tombe:
> The way he cut, an English mile in length,
> Thorough a rocke of stone in one nights space:

For the spread of the legends of the tunnel, see Comparetti 1941, especially 2: 129–131; Comparetti quotes the passage from Marlowe's *Doctor Faustus;* see also Spargo 1934.292–295, with notes and bibliography on 444–446.

310–316 De quo . . . ferri vestigia esse confessus est: after Petrarch returned to Naples from an excursion to Posillipo in March of 1341, King Robert put Petrarch to a little informal test by asking him what he thought about the story that Virgil had constructed the tunnel by magic. The wit of Petrarch's reply is obliterated by the reading "magicarium," which is printed by many early editions of the *Itinerarium* (1501, 1503, and 1554) and is accepted by some modern scholars ("Petrarch replied that he had never read of Virgil's being a magician," Wilkins 1961.26), for of course Petrarch had read many works that asserted Virgil was a magician. To Petrarch, the most obvious fact about the tunnel's construction was that it had been made by laborious excavation: if Virgil really made the tunnel, he must have a stonecutter (marmorarium); but Petrarch had never read that *that* was the case.

This incident is best viewed as part of King Robert's examination of Petrarch to prove his worthiness to receive the laurel crown, the ultimate recognition of poetic accomplishment and scholarship. The formal testing took place over a period of three successive days sometime in late March, during which Robert quizzed Petrarch from noon to evening. The crown was bestowed in Rome on 8 April. See *Posteritati* (in *Prose,* 14–15) on the formal examination and Petrarch's sketch of King Robert in *Rerum memorandarum libri,* 1.37 (*Prose* 276–282). In *Fam.* 4.7.10–12 Petrarch compares Robert's patronage of the arts to that of Augustus Caesar (Suetonius, *Aug.* 89.3).

318–320 publicum iter . . . belli quoque temporibus inviolatum, si vera populi vox est, et nullis unquam latrociniis attentatum patet: the idea that the Crypta Neapolitana was inviolate and protected from all sorts of crime arose, says Petrarch, from the proximity of Virgil's tomb to its eastern entrance. Gervasius of Tilbury (c. 1152–c. 1220) is the first author to record (in his *Otia Imperialia*) that Virgil brought it about that no robbery or crime could ever take place in the tunnel, although the darkness provides a perfect place for ambush. See Comparetti 1941.2:29, 48–49, 126–129; Camparetti quotes Gervasius's Latin text on 177. This superstitious awe that prevented crimes is also probably related to the legend which brings St. Paul on a visit to Virgil's tomb (justified by Acts 28:13–14), where the Apostle regrets (in six lines of verse) that Virgil did not live to be converted to Christianity (Peebles 1964.2:169–190 and Trapp 1984.3–4 and 8):

> Ad Maronis Mausoleum
> Ductus, fudit super eum
> Piae rorem lacrimae;
> Quem te, inquit, reddidissem
> Si te vivum invenissem,
> Poetarum maxime.

Famously translated by John Addington Symonds (Symonds 1912.46, n.1) as,

When to Maro's tomb they brought him
Tender grief and pity wrought him
To bedew the stone with tears;
What a saint might I have crowned thee,
Had I only living found thee,
Poet first and without peers.

This fragment from a sequence of a Mass is in the "Stabat mater" form: eight-syllabled (verses 1, 2, 4, 5) and seven-syllabled trochees; the rime scheme is aabccb. It was part of a hymn sung at the Mass celebrating St. Paul's conversion (25 January). Petrarch, the earliest witness to the text of these verses, quotes them on the flyleaf of his Virgil now in Milan. He also refers to the legend at *Fam.* 21.10.13.

320–322 Cryptam Neapolitanam . . . Seneca mentionem facit: Seneca, *Ep.* 57.1–2. Seneca once used the tunnel to shorten his trip from Baiae to Naples and regretted it. He complains of the darkness, dust, and lack of ventilation.

322–324 Sub finem fusci tramitis . . . perforati montis opinio: the traditional site of Virgil's tomb is near the eastern entrance to the tunnel of Posillipo (Crypta Neapolitana). The tomb, "of very old workmanship" as Petrarch says, is datable to the Augustan period. In the shape of a cylinder on a square podium, the tomb is a columbarium with ten niches for cinerary urns. Ancient testimony (Donatus, *Vita* 36), however, places Virgil's tomb near the sea along the Via Puteolana less than two miles from the city. If that is so, the actual tomb of Virgil has disappeared without a trace. For a convenient review of all the evidence for the location of Virgil's tomb see Trapp 1984.1–31; see also Trapp 1986.1–17 and Capasso 1983, which contains a useful collection of *testimonia* (ancient, medieval, and early Renaissance) on Virgil's tomb. Unless the *Cronaca di Partenope* can be dated earlier (see note to line 325 below), Petrarch may be the first to set down in writing that this columbarium at the entrance to the Crypta Neapolitana is Virgil's tomb; but he is merely recording what appears to be a very old tradition.

325 Iuxta breve sed devotissimum sacellum: even before one exits the Crypt at the east end, he can see the tomb of Virgil off to the right (south) at an elevation of some fifty or sixty feet. Off to the left of the exit, there is a stairway cut into the slope of the mountain leading to a path, which turns back (to the west) over the top of the exit of the Crypt and carries to another stairway down to the level of the tomb of Virgil.

Return now to the stairway to the north. Once one has climbed the stairs and is proceeding along the path over the Crypt, one comes upon another path which branches off and leads to a small area carved out of the side of the mountain at an elevation of some twenty feet above the floor of the crypt, positioned close (iuxta) above the exit of the Crypt (supra ipsum Crypte exitum), and facing at an angle the tomb of Virgil opposite. The area is open to the elements on one side, with a domed ceiling decorated with a very faded fresco. This is Petrarch's *sacellum,* a term he has selected with care: a *sacellum* is defined as a small, uncovered place consecrated to a divinity (Festus's definition: *OLD* s.v: *sacella dicuntur loca diis sacrata sine tecto).*

Originally the area was constructed as a place where water was collected: a spur from the Aqua Serino, the great Augustan aqueduct which ran parallel to the Crypt, leads directly into the place (see McKay 1972.2:172–173 and n.14 on 248). The water would be collected in a settling tank and then offered to thirsty and dusty travelers in water jars (hydriae) at the end of their journey. That the latter was the practice is suggested by the name this *sacellum* was called after it had been converted to Christian use. The *Cronaca de Partenope* (Altamura 1974.78) agrees with Petrarch in locating Virgil's tomb in close proximity to the sacellum and supplies it with a name: *[Virgilio] fo sepellito in quello luogo dove ogie se chiama Sancta Maria dell' Itria, in una sepoltura ad un piccholo templo quadrato* (quoted by Trapp 1984.10). In 1535 Benedetto di Falco in his *Descrittione dei luoghi antiqui di Napoli e del suo amenissimo distretto* (Morisani 1972.12–15), paraphrasing Petrarch's *Itinerarium,* puts both the tomb and the chapel, which is called Santa Maria dell' Hydrie, at the eastern end of the tunnel. Still later the *Descrittione del regno di Napoli,* by E. Bacco, C. d' Engenio Caraccioli et al. (published in 1616 and reissued many times in the seventeenth century) also puts Virgil's tomb near "the ancient chapel with the name S. Maria dell' Hidriae," Gardiner 1991.18–19. Bacco and collaborators clearly have Petrarch's *Itinerarium* open before them. They cite it on the previous page.

The name of the "ancient chapel" attracts interest. It appears to mean "Holy Mary of the Water Pot(s)," referring presumably to the original function of the *sacellum*, namely the collection and distribution of water in hydriae (see Canzanella 1999.35–36 for other possible interpretations of the name). The fresco, very old and faded, high on the wall of the *sacellum*, appears to be that of Christ the Pantocrator. The name for the shrine is evidently justified in part by another fresco on the opposite side of the passageway of the Crypt, which adorns a recessed rectangular panel not far from the tomb of Virgil: it is the faded image of a Madonna with Child, datable to the fourteenth century. Possibly the name S. Maria dell' Idria, aside from the reference to water, was also felt to refer to the urn supposed to contain Virgil's ashes buried in the columbarium close at hand, since the hydria was commonly used as a cinerary urn (*OLD*, s.v.). For testimony on the existence of Virgil's burial urn see Trapp 1984.11,13–15 and *passim.*

For a short discussion (with bibliography) of the *sacellum* and of the aqueduct, see Amalfitano 1990.38–42; there are color photographs of the two frescoes (38–39) and an excellent diagram of the area confirming the accuracy of Petrarch's description.

326–327 Et mox ad radicem montis in litore Virginis Matris templum, quo magnus . . . fit concursus: after exiting the Crypt, one follows a winding path down to the foot of the mountain (ad radicem montis) and there finds the S. Maria di Piedigrotta, not exactly on the shore, as Petrarch says, but very close to it. The church that Petrarch saw when he visited Naples had been there at least since 1207, but that old church was replaced entirely in 1353, and a large monastery was attached, run by the Canons Regular of the Lateran (with sixty members in the community in the seventeenth century, according to Gardiner 1991.15 and 52). It was a popular church, since every traveler to the area would want to see the Crypt and the tomb of Virgil; and the church lay exactly on the way, if one set out from Naples. For more details on the church, see Porcaro 1958.

328–329 Neapolis . . . una quidem ex paucis: the original settlement in this part of the bay was a colony sent from Cumae; its name was Parthenope (Strabo, 5.4.6–7 and 1.2.18; see note to lines 345–348 below). In time, more colonists appeared and established a separate settlement nearby named Neapolis (New Town). The original settlement was then designated Palaeopolis (Old Town; Livy, 8.22), but eventually the two places merged their identities in the name Neapolis. When Petrarch says that Neapolis was the product of several settlements (a small number, but more than two), he is thinking of the late arrival of the Angevin French (1265); see *Metr.* 2.16.11–13 (with note to line 11 in *Rime,* 765):

> meniaque ampla tenens quibus est a virgine nomen
> urbibus atque ubi iam fuerat gens una duabus,
> nunc gentes una urbe due populusque biformis.
>
> ([Naples] with its great walls, which took the name of a virgin [Parthenope], and where there had been one people from two cities [Palaeopolis and Neapolis], now there is one city with two different peoples [original population and Angevin French].)

Petrarch may also be referring to a number of *casali* (hamlets) that surrounded Naples, but were really part of the city. In the early seventeenth century, a guidebook counts 37 hamlets and says that they form one body with the city (Gardiner 1991.32).

330–332 capellam Regis . . . in qua conterraneus . . . reliquit manus et ingenii monimenta: Petrarch is referring to the chapel in Castel Nuovo, built for Charles I of Anjou between 1279–1282; Giotto is the *conterraneus* mentioned. In Naples between 1328/29 and 1332/33, he is said to have executed a number of works, nearly all of which have been lost. The fourteenth-century chapel is now being restored. See Leone de Castris 1987.

Petrarch himself acquired sometime between 1365 and 1370 a Madonna by Giotto of which he was very proud. In his will he left the panel, which is thought to be no longer in existence, to Francesco da Carrara, a work "cuius pulchritudinem ignorantes non intelligunt, magistri autem stupent," (Mommsen 1957.78–81 and the editor's comments on 22–25). Petrarch had met Giotto perhaps as early as the 1320s (cf. *Fam.* 5.17.6; Wilkins 1978a.301). For Petrarch's extended discussion of his love of painting and sculpture, see his *De remediis* 1.40 and 41 (Latin text in *Opera* 1.50–52). For translation and commentary, see Rawski 1991.1:125–134. For discussion of these important dialogues, see Baxandall 1971. 51–66 and 140–143. See Contini 1980.120–121 (with pl. 1) for a reproduction of the so-called "Madonna del Petrarca" at Padua and discussion.

332–333 Non audeo te hortari ut . . . Cartusie domum adeas: the monastery referred to is San Martino, situated on the summit of Sant' Elmo about a mile from the harbor; work began on it in 1325 and the church was consecrated in 1368 (details in Strozzullo 1968.179–200). "Cartusie domum" literally means "a house of [Grande] Chartreuse," the place where St. Bruno established his contemplative order in 1084. Petrarch's brother Gherardo, three years his junior, entered into that order in April of 1343 (at the monastery in Montrieux), an event that had a profound effect on Petrarch's outlook on life and on his writings. Early in 1347, Petrarch traveled to Montrieux to visit Gherardo, whom he had not seen for four years. His brief visit inspired him to write during the Lenten season of the same year a treatise in praise of the wonderful freedom from earthly concerns which Gherardo and his fellow monks enjoyed (*De otio religioso*). This hortatory work is addressed to all the monks at Montrieux, but Petrarch admits that he had really written the work for his own benefit. See also *Fam.* 10.3 (dated 25 September 1349), in which Petrarch lavishes praise on his brother's new life, urging him to perseverance. Petrarch, immensely proud of Gherardo, saw his way of life as a constant reproach to his own.

334–336 At Clare virginis preclarum domicilium . . . regine senioris amplissimum opus: Petrarch is referring to the great Franciscan church and convent of Santa Chiara, built in 1310–1328 for Queen Sancha, second wife of Robert; the church was consecrated in 1340. In 1343, the notorious Giovanna succeeded her grandfather Robert to the throne, with dowager Queen Sancha serving as regent for a time. Giovanna's reign was beset by many problems (cf. Petrarch, *Fam.* 5.3.9–15). For the history of this period, see De Frede 1969.2:9–354.

Clare (1194–1253), after whom the church was named, was the foundress of the Poor Clares. Inspired by the teaching of St. Francis and aided by him, she established a community of women at Assisi according to the rule and spirit of St. Francis. This order of nuns lived a life of extreme poverty and austerity, but new foundations quickly spread all over Europe. Clare herself never left Assisi; she was canonized two years after her death. For Sancha's connection with the Poor Clares, see Musto 1985.179–214. Sancha, widow of Robert, died at Santa Chiara as a nun; both are buried there, facts about which Petrarch was well informed (*Rerum mem.* 3.96.10).

336–338 Illud nulla festinatio . . . impediat quin illius duos urbis vicos . . . videas: the *seggi* (district councils) of (Porta) Capuana and Nido represented the ancient nobility of Naples, both having as their coat of arms the horse, the insignia of Naples before foreign domination; see De Frede 1969.2:200–204 and Gardiner 1991.2–3 and 132–133. Benedetto di Falco cites this passage and dwells on it at some length (Morisani 1972.59–60), calling these districts "il loco delli principali gentil' uomini."

338–339 antequam pestis orbem terre funditus exhausisset: by 1346 reports of a terrible plague, which had arisen in China and had spread through Central Asia, India, Mesopotamia, Asia Minor, Syria, and Egypt, had reached Europe. In October of 1347 Genoese trading ships from the port of Caffa (Feodosiya) in the Crimea put in at Messina in Sicily with dead and dying men aboard. Soon the Black Death had reached Naples, a city with a population of an estimated 100,000 at this time (Miskimin 1978. 73). By the end of the fourteenth century, Naples had lost nearly two thirds of its citizens according to a contemporary observer (see Zeigler 1969.52). It was widely believed that the cause of the plague was the conjunction of Saturn, Jupiter, and Mars in the nineteenth degree of Aquarius at 1:00 P.M. on 24 March 1345 (Grant 1974.773–774), but Petrarch scoffed at this astrological explanation (*De remediis* 2.114; Rawski 1991.3:274 and 4:447–448). See also Campbell 1931.40, Williman 1982, and Gottfried 1983.

The mortality rate for Naples was high: modern demographers estimate that overall — for the area extending from the far north to India — a third of the world's population perished. Europe's population did not return to its pre-plague levels until the early sixteenth century (see Russell 1958.5–152 and Postan 1963. 37).

The plague naturally had a profound effect on Petrarch's life, as it did on everyone who lived in those times. His kinsman Franceschino degli Albizzi, an aspiring poet who had lived with Petrarch at Vaucluse the better part of two years, and his beloved Laura died in the first onslaught, as well as many others. His son Giovanni, not yet twenty-four years old and many friends, including his old friend "Socrates" (Ludwig van Kempen), succumbed in a reoccurrence of the plague in 1361. For some of the sad reflection of the plague in Petrarch's literary productions, see Wilkins 1961.76–81 and Rawski 1991.4:355–358 on *De remediis* 2.92. On the positive side, Petrarch was filled with joy and pride upon learning of his brother Gheraldo's heroic stance against the plague at Montrieux: he was the only member of his community to survive (*Fam.* 16.2).

340–343 Militem ad militie pelagus . . . non . . . ad fabulas, et idcirco Castrum Ovi . . . eminus aspexisse satis fuerit: Petrarch sends Mandelli to the districts of Capuana and Nido where he will associate with many noble military men like himself and will hear the right sort of talk, but he steers him away from the Castel dell'Ovo, where he would hear a lot of silly stories about Virgil. Initially the story about Virgil and the Castel dell'Ovo was that he had presented the city with a palladium, a small model of the city enclosed in a narrow-necked bottle that was supposed to protect the city from its enemies. The city, however, did fall to foreigners, and as the story evolved the model became an egg in a glass bottle. This talisman was kept in a castle formerly called Castello marino or di mare; but in consequence of possessing the magical egg the castle was now called Castel dell'Ovo. This last name was apparently a product of the fourteenth century. In the rules of the Order of the Holy Spirit (1352), the castle is called the *Castellum ovi incantati*, the Castle of the enchanted egg. Now the castle does not contain the egg, but it is built on it. In fact, some said that the whole city was balanced on the egg and would tremble if the egg shifted position (Naples's enemies were now earthquakes instead of invading foreigners) or sink into the sea if the egg was broken. Virgil was said not only to have given the city the palladium but also to have built the Castel dell'Ovo itself — magically just as he built the *Crypta Neapolitana.*

Petrarch reacted negatively to these stories because he himself had been accused of being a necromancer and magician, the alleged proof being primarily his devotion to Virgil's poetry (*Fam.* 9.5.15–17 [nigromanticus ac magus appareo . . . quia Virgilii libros lego], *Fam.* 13.6.28–29, *Sen.* 1.2, *Sen* 1.4 [at considerable length], and *Misc.* 2, the only letter in Italian accepted as genuinely Petrarchan). The slanderous story had been in fact fabricated in an effort to discredit Cardinal Giovanni Colonna through Petrarch. This was not a story that Petrarch could ignore or shake off with a laugh since it was believed by many powerful men at the papal court, including Etienne Aubert who continued to believe the story even after he had become Pope as Innocent VI (1352). For more details, see Segrè 1903.99–124 and Feo 1988.61–63. Whether the story actually harmed Petrarch's ecclesiastical career is difficult to say because he never aimed at success in it as his contemporaries usually defined the term. He sought only those positions that would provide him with a comfortable living while leaving him ample leisure to pursue his artistic and scholarly interests. Various chaplaincies, canonries, rectorships, and archdeaconships served his purpose quite well. The canonry in Padua (received in 1349), for example, was a particularly happy arrangement, providing him with an annual 250 gold ducats until the end of his life. Nor is there any evidence that Petrarch actually suffered in other ways because of this story about his magical powers, but he certainly worried that it might damage his reputation and prevent his getting a desired benefice (on Petrarch's clerical career see Wilkins 1955.3–32 and 63–80). According to Bishop (1963.228 and 384), who is quoting Carrara, the peasants of Reggio nell' Emilia still speak of Petrarch as a magician who could conjure up a rainstorm to suit his purpose. For an overview of magic in the Middle Ages see Kieckhefer 1990 and Flint 1991.

For a systematic account of all Virgilian legends connected with the Castel dell' Ovo, see Spargo 1934.87–99, with extensive notes 354–358, and Dattilo 1963; see also a collection of relevant texts in Comparetti 1941.2:173 ff. On 60–68, Spargo has a useful table of authors who relate Virgilian legends of whatever sort; see also the various references to Petrarch listed in Spargo's index. For an interpretation of the phrase *militem ad militie pelagus* see Feo (1974.182)

345–348 Hic se carmen illud georgicum scripsisse . . . civitati nomen: Virgil composed his *Georgics* while living in Naples (Parthenope), as he himself testifies: (*G.* 4.559–566). Naples got its ancient name Parthenope from one of the Sirens who was said to be buried there (Servius, *G.* 4.563 and *A.* 5.864).

351–352 Hinc tandem . . . flammas eructare solitus: from literary and pictorial evidence it is all but certain that Vesuvius was a single coned volcano in antiquity. Probably a result of the eruption of 79 (early afternoon of 24 August), the present cone of Vesuvius was formed within the original coned structure of which the peak now called Monte Somma is a remnant, being the partly preserved caldera rim on the northern and western sides of the mountain. Yet it is not entirely clear when Vesuvius became twin-peaked. Was it in 79 or the occasion of one of its many subsequent eruptions? Frederiksen (1984.8) says, "By about AD 1500, we can be sure that Mt. Vesuvius had its modern double form, as is attested by an accurate drawing of Campania made by Ambrogio Leone." In describing Vesuvius as *biceps* (two-headed; cf. *bifidum Vesevum, Metr.* 2.16.9), Petrarch is providing eyewitness testimony for the mountain's double form, which predates Leone's by over 150 years. See Fredericksen's entire discussion on 6–12 with bibliography and following notes.

352–356 Ad quod olim spectaculum visendum . . . tanti viri exitus: Pliny the Elder (AD 23–79) was a man of exceptional accomplishments, whom Petrarch admired very much. He began his career as a cavalry officer, and continued it as a lawyer, administrator, and prolific author. At the time of the eruption of Mt.

Vesuvius, he was serving at Misenum as an admiral of the Imperial Fleet. Eager to see what was happening and to bring aid to those in need, Pliny immediately set sail for the area and established his headquarters at Stabiae just a few miles south of Pompeii. Within a short time he was overcome by volcanic ash and died.

A full account of Pliny's final hours was later recorded for the benefit of the historian Tacitus by his nephew, Pliny the younger, a boy of seventeen at the time of the disaster and living with his uncle at Misenum (*Ep.* 6.16 and 20). Although Petrarch did not know the *Epistolae* of the younger Pliny (de Nolhac 1907. 1:129, n.1), he had certainly read the account of the elder Pliny's death in Suetonius's now fragmentary *De viris illustribus* (Reifferscheid 1860.92). Compare Suetonius's phrase "vi pulueris ac favillae oppressus" with Petrarch's "vento cinerem ac favillam excitante compressus est." See also Petrarch's sketch of Pliny at *Rerum memorandarum libri,* 1.19 (*Prose,* 270–272). On 6 July 1350 in Mantua, Petrarch acquired his copy of Pliny's *Natural History,* now in the Bibliothèque Nationale; it was one of his prized possessions.

356–357 Sic Neapolis . . . ossa custodit: the ancient lives of Virgil are unanimous that the poet was born at a village near Mantua and was buried at Naples (e.g., Donatus, *Vita* 2 and 36). Petrarch thought that Verona was Pliny's native city because he calls the poet Catullus, a native of Verona, his *conterraneus (Nat. praef.* 1). Petrarch however did not understand that Pliny was using the word *conterraneus* jocularly, in a slang meaning given it by soldiers (castrense verbum). Catullus was Pliny's "opposite number" because Catullus wrote a very small book of poems, while Pliny has written a very large book of prose. Pliny was a native of Novum Comum (Como), located south of Lacus Larius (Lago Como) not far from Verona, and therefore Catullus was also Pliny's *conterraneus* in the sense that they both hailed from the same general area. The manuscripts of Pseudo-Pliny's *De viris illustribus* also describe Pliny as being from Verona (Veronensis), confirming Petrarch in his mistake (see note to 251–253). The combined weight of this testimony overbalanced that of Suetonius (Reifferscheid 1860.92), who says that Pliny was from Como (Novocomensis), and that of St. Jerome, who is following Suetonius. There is no ancient tradition about the place of his burial.

Most editors do not print Rackham's *concerraneus* (1938. 1:3) for *conterraneus* in the preface to the *Natural History*. That rare word means something like "mess mate."

357–359 Mons est . . . Magna Grecia dicebatur: although in modern times Vesuvius is well known as an active volcano (last eruption in March of 1944), in the time of Virgil it had been in a relatively quiescent state for so long (well over a millenium is considered plausible by volcanologists) that it was known primarily for the great fertility of the land surrounding its base and extending up its sides (see Sigurdsson 1982.39–51). In his *Georgics* (2.217–225), Virgil lavishes praise on the mountain's bounty, calling it Vesaevus (Vesevus), a metrically acceptable spelling that Petrarch follows. A famous wall-painting recovered from the House of the Centenary at Pompeii shows a single-peaked Vesuvius covered with terraced vineyards; on the left stands Bacchus wearing a robe made of grapes (see reproduction in Feder 1978.15). Vesuvius's vineyards produced a celebrated wine, ancestor of the modern Lacrima Christi (Pliny, *Nat.* 14.34–35; Martial, 4.44).

After the devastating eruption in 79, Vesuvius was quiet until 202 (Cassius Dio, 77.2; not an eyewitness to the event, as Frederiksen says 1984.7). Thereafter it erupted in a major way on the average once every century until the tenth century records three eruptions and the eleventh records four. The last recorded activity before Petrarch's time was in 1139. So when Petrarch visited the area, Vesuvius probably had been quiet for over two hundred years. The lines that Petrarch had read in the *Georgics* must have seemed as appropriate in his time as they were when Virgil wrote them, even if Vesuvius remained a threat.

Magna Graecia was the term used in antiquity for the Greek colonies on the southern Italian peninsula (Pliny, *Nat.* 3.95 et al.) and it was still in common use in the Middle Ages. Since the Fourth Crusade (1204) the Eastern Empire was known as Romania, a term which included Greece and the Greek islands (Wolff 1948.1–34).

359–362 Hinc ad dexteram Capree insula . . . officina sevitie: cf. Suetonius, *Tib.* 40–41, 60–62; see also Petrarch, *De vita solitaria,* 1.7 (376 in *Prose*).

362–364 Pulcherrimus terrarum tractus . . . Seneca inter alios teste didicimus: Petrarch, relying on Seneca's authority (*Nat.* 6.1–2; cf. Tacitus, *Ann.* 15.22 and *Hist.* 1.2), seems to think that Pompeii and Herculaneum were irrevocably destroyed by the earthquake which occurred in the area on 5 February AD 62 (or possibly 63). He seems not to know that the cities, although heavily damaged at this time, had been largely rebuilt and were once again thriving when Vesuvius erupted and destroyed them in 79.

Since by all accounts Petrarch had no knowledge of Tacitus's works when he was writing in 1358 (or at any later time), it is difficult to know what other authors besides Seneca (inter alios) he had in mind; see Reynolds 1986.407–408. Although Petrarch had heard of Tacitus from a few Christian authors he had read (e.g., Orosius), he himself never mentions the historian's name (de Nolhac 1907.2:43–44). Suetonius *(Titus,* 8.3) is clearly referring to the eruption of 79, but he does not refer to Pompeii or Herculaneum by name.

If Petrarch had somehow acquired an old Roman *itinerarium pictum* (see Introduction), it might have shown him the exact location of Herculaneum and Pompeii. The Peutinger map, dated to the middle of the fourth century, shows these places correctly long after their destruction, evidently drawing on a much earlier source (see Dilke 1987a.1:238).

365 Surrentum . . . mellifluo palmite generosum: situated on the southern side of the Bay of Naples about seven miles from the Minervae Promontorium, Surrentum is rarely mentioned in ancient literature except as a place famous for its wine. Here Petrarch is thinking of Ovid, *Met.* 15.710: *et Surrentino generosos palmite colles;* see also Martial, 13.110 and Statius, *Silv.* 3.5.102. Pliny (*Nat.* 14.64) is less enthusiastic in his praise. Quoting some quite negative comments about the wine from the emperors Tiberius and Caligula, he suggests it is to be valued primarily for its medicinal qualities.

366–367 Tota regio Terra Laboris . . . ubertatis appellatio: according to Pliny (*Nat.* 3.60, 18.109–111) Campania comprises that stretch of western Italian coastline from Mons Massicus (Monte Massico) in the north to the Sorrentine promontory on the south end of the Bay of Naples and all the land within those northern and southern boundaries that extends from the Tyrrhenian Sea to the Apennines. The great plain to the north and west of Naples as far as Mons Massicus, a particularly fertile area, was called Campus or (Ager) Campanus and within that area between the Volurno and the Campi Flegrei there was a still more fertile area called the Campi Leborini. This last area is Petrarch's *Terra Laboris* (Terra di Lavoro), geographically speaking.

When Petrarch says that the whole region is known as *Terra Laboris* in his day (hodie), but that formerly it had been part of Campania, he is making a political statement rather than a geographical one. Playing upon a possible literal meaning of the phrase (Land of Difficulty), he is referring particularly to the chaotic state of affairs that developed at Naples after the death of Robert in 1343. This *jeu de mots* pleased Petrarch, and he often used *Terra Laboris* in his correspondence (*Fam.* 7.1.4, 12.2.13, 15.7. 9, 19.9.9.) to refer to Campania as a whole or, rather, to the political entity known as the Kingdom of Naples or, it may be, the province of *Terra Lavoris*, one of eight into which Robert's kingdom was divided (see *Fam.* 4.2.11, with Dotti's note *ad loc.*). See Gribaudi 1907.193–210 for more on the history of the name.

Since the phrase *Terra Laboris* may also be understood in a more positive way, namely as the Land of Hard Work (sc. for the farmers who plant and harvest its bounteous crops) Petrarch adds that *Terra Laboris* and Campania (from *campus*, a flat plain suitable for crops) are names synonymous with fertility.

367–368 Quo pretextu . . . statuere: cf. Florus: *Omnium non modo Italiae, sed toto orbe terrarum pulcherrima Campaniae plaga est. Nihil mollius caelo: denique bis floribus vernat. Nihil uberius solo: ideo Liberi Cererisque certamen dicitur* (*Epit.* 1.11.3); Pliny (*Nat.* 3.60): *summum Liberi Patris cum Cerere certamen.* The idea that Liber (Bacchus), the god of wine, and Ceres, the goddess of grain, were engaged in a competition to see which one could bestow the greater gifts on Campania was already a commonplace when Pliny wrote (*ut veteres dixere*). The idea had its roots in the Greek myth about the competition between Athena (Minerva) and Poseidon (Neptune) for the right to bestow gifts on Athens (Ovid, *Met.* 6.70–82). Petrarch also mentions the contest between Liber and Ceres at *Fam.*11.5.8.

370–371 Fuisse hic medicine fontem . . . nichilo quod non senio exarcescat: toward the end of the eleventh century Salerno emerged as the most important center of medical learning in Europe. Sometime before 1065, Constantine the African had arrived there and had translated into Latin Arabic versions of several works of Galen and Hippocrates made in the ninth century. He also translated some original Arabic works on diet, fever, and urine. This infusion of Greek and Arabic knowledge, with its strong theoretical foundations, stimulated new approaches to the practice of medicine, which became the trademarks of the Salernitan School.

Constantine's work led to a new collection of translations in the twelfth century which further enhanced Salerno's position of leadership. A leader in theory, Salerno did not neglect practice and made contributions to the study of anatomy that were revolutionary for the time. Following Salerno's lead, scholars elsewhere (Pisa and Cremona) added new translations of both Greek and Arabic medical works.

Early in the thirteenth century, Montpellier and Paris pioneered new procedures and techniques in surgery that put them ahead of Salerno. By Petrarch's time in the fourteenth century, Bologna and Padua had established themselves as the most progressive in Europe by introducing into their curricula new works from the Galenic corpus, in Latin translations made directly from the Greek. See Kristeller 1945.138–194 (the classic study of Salerno's contribution to medicine) and the articles on the "History of Medicine" and "Schools of Medicine" by McVaugh and Demartre (respectively) 1987.8:247–254 and 254–261; see also Riddle 1974. 157–170, Saffron 1975.12:80–83, and Siraisi 1990.5–13.

The topic of senescence (everything grows old) was a popular one with Roman authors (e.g., Sallust *Iug.* 2.3: *Omniaque orta occidunt et aucta senescunt;* Pliny, *Nat.* 2.118, and Aulus Gellius 3.10.11), and it very much appealed to Petrarch, who quotes or paraphrases Sallust on five or six occasions (*Fam.* 6.3.11, 9.13.3 etc.). Not only do individuals grow old, but also institutions, great empires (for this popular topos see Curtius 1953.27–28), and the world itself (see commentary below). See also Rawski's commentary on *De remediis* 1.16 (1991.2:100–103).

374–377 Dextera autem . . . lectum est: Petrarch is here thinking primarily of Virgil's account of Juno's visit to King Aeolus, together with Servius's note to the passage. Virgil (*A.* 1.52–54) says that Juno

> Aeoliam uenit. hic uasto rex Aeolus antro
> luctantis uentos tempestatesque sonoras
> imperio premit ac uinclis et carcere frenat.

Servius's note informed Petrarch that although poets say that Aeolus was king of the winds, the learned Varro says that he was an actual king. Because he was able to predict how the winds would blow by observing the clouds and smoke produced by the islands, he seemed to the ignorant to be able to control the winds. Servius goes on to report that Agamemnon sent Aeolus to the islands, which later bore his name, to forestall an attack on the Peloponnesus. At that time, Liparus was king of the islands. Aeolus married the king's daughter Cyana and took up residence on one of the seven islands, eventually succeeding his father-in-law as king.

In Petrarch's view, the story of Aeolus did indeed have a basis in historical fact, as suggested to him by Servius's note primarily, but also by Pliny, *Nat.* 3.92 and Mela, 2.69. But when the poets (Virgil, *A.* 1.52–63; Ovid, *Met.*14.223–227) applied their creative talents, the story was transformed into a most elegant fiction (elegantissimum figmentum). So Petrarch calls the story in a letter to his young friend Federico of Arezzo (*Sen.* 4.5, written sometime between 1365–1367), and then proceeds to provide, as a demonstration of critical exegesis, a moralizing interpretation of it that his friend Pierre Bersuire (of *Ovide moralisé* fame) would have been proud of: Aeolus represents Reason controlling the lower appetites (the winds = anger). The story pleased Petrarch: he had given it similar treatment in his *Secretum (Prose,* 124): *de animo atque ira animum turbante dici omnia const[at].* Whether Petrarch knew Homer's version of the Aeolus story (*Ody.* 10. 1–79; in Leontius's Latin version) when he wrote his letter to Federico is an issue too complex to review here: see Ross 1927.341–355 and Feo 1974, especially 130–136 and 157–159.

378–380 Ubi angustissima Italia est, Scaleam vocant . . . nomen hauddubie modernum: the town Scalea is situated on the "instep" of Italy's boot, some fifty or sixty miles north of where the peninsula is the most narrow, namely in Calabria in the "toe" of Italy between the gulf of S. Eufemia and the Gulf of Squillace. Pliny appears to be Petrarch's authority here. At *Nat.* 3.95 he names a place called Castra Hannibalis as marking the narrowest part of Italy (nusquam angustiore Italia) and says that Dionysius of Syracuse wanted to cut a canal across the peninsula at this place. Petrarch is merely guessing that Scalea, not mentioned by Pliny or any other ancient source, is close to the place mentioned by Pliny. In fact Castra Hannibalis lay on the eastern coast in the Gulf of Squillace.

Thought to be close to the ancient Greek settlement of Laos (sixth century) whose name the nearby river Lao retains, Scalea had its name regularly written in red ink on portolan charts indicating its importance to the medieval mariner. Settled by the Argonese in 1283, Scalea was an easily recognized landmark (limestone cliffs rise to over 100 feet high around the town) by which passing ships could measure their progress even when visibility was poor. Its importance may have been derived from this fact rather than that it was a regular port of call. Croton (usually spelled Cotrone on the charts) was also so marked in red, although in other respects it was insignificant, as Petrarch attests: see Campbell 1987.1:378–379; 379 has a map showing names of places habitually picked out in red ink on portolan charts of the fourteenth and fifteenth centuries.

383 In medio Pharus est qui Messanensis dicitur: in this context *pharus* means "strait" and not "lighthouse" as it usually does (on the meaning "lighthouse" see below on lines 660–661).

The mainland part of the greater medieval kingdom of Sicily, founded by the Norman French, with the capital at Palermo, extended as far as the territory of Naples, which was referred to as the Kingdom of Sicily *citra Pharon* (the land on the far side of the Strait of Messina). After Charles of Anjou came to power in 1266, he made Naples his capital instead of Palermo. Sicily then became that part of the Kingdom of Sicily *ultra Pharon* (beyond the Strait). This way of referring to the Strait of Messina (as the *Pharus*) must have originated with Norman French and remained a peculiarly French mode of expression. For example, the fourteenth century Insular French Version of *Mandeville's Travels* explicitly says that the narrow arm of the sea between Sicily and Italy is called "le far de Messine." The anonymous author of the English version of this same work, called the "Cotton Version," composed about 1400, translates the whole passage as follows: *And betwene Cycile and Itaylle there is not but a lytille arm of the see that men clepen the Farde of Mescyne* (Seymour 1967.40 and 261). The English translator, not being familiar with the French expression for the Strait of Messina, corrupts *far de* by writing it as one word and then attempts to save the situation by inserting the preposition "of."

The word *far* then developed the general meaning of "strait" in Old French, which it kept at least through the sixteenth century, as in the following passage of Rabelais: . . . *mon tonneau Diogenic, qui seul m'est reste du naufrage faict par le passe au far de mal'encontre* (*Prol.* Book III). The French language to this day may refer to the Strait of Messina as *le Phare de Messine* (Hatzfeld and Darmesteter 1964.2, s.v. *phare*). See also Gervasius of Tilbury (c. 1152–c.1220): *Sicilia ab Italia modico freto distinguitur, in quo Scylla et Charybdis, marinae voragines, quibus navigia absorbentur aut collidun-tur, quem locum Pharum nominant*, in Liebrecht 1856.11. The scholarly Gervase had traveled extensively in Italy. The Portolano Parma-Magliabecchi (datable to the first part of the fifteenth century) has the following helpful advice: "Lo farro di messina a gran corrente e bissogna auere piloto che intende la corrente," Kretschmer 1909.308.

It cannot be argued that Petrarch is here using the word *pharus* to refer to the promontory on the NE extremity of Sicily that extends into the Strait. If *pharus* is taken to refer to the promontory (or the lighthouse thereon that existed at least in Servius's time; see *A.* 3.411), Petrarch's statement that *pharus* is the place where Scylla and Charybdis are located (*pharus . . . in quo sunt . . . illa portenta,* line 383–384) would place both monsters at the promontory on the south and not on either side of the strait — an arrangement that would make nonsense out of the universal understanding of the myth. Petrarch himself says that Scylla is to the left (on the north) and that Charybdis is opposite to it (on the south), lines 386–389.

389–394 Causa vero tante vertiginis . . . undis succumbere coegerunt: the notion that Sicily and Italy were once joined, but were separated by the force of opposing seas was a commonplace in antiquity: see, for example, Virgil, *A.* 3. 414–419 and Servius *ad loc;* Mela, 2.115, Pliny, *Nat.* 2.204 and 3.86; Ovid, *Met.* 15. 290–293; Lucan, 2.435–438; and Claudian, *De raptu Proserp.* 1(33).142–146. Petrarch makes the same comment on the Apennines at *Sen.*12.1 (*Opera* 2.993).

396–398 montis Siculi Pelori . . . unde Trinacrie appellatio sumpta est: in ancient times Sicily was called Trinacria because of the three promontories which marked the corners of its triangular shape (τρεῖς ἄκροι, three peaks): Cape Pelorus on the NE, Cape Pachynus of the SE, and Cape Lilybaeum on the west. Although the name was used mainly by Roman poets to lend an antique flavor to their work, Petrarch often used it even in his prose writing. After the war of the Sicilian Vespers, by the treaty of Caltabellotta in 1302, Frederick III agreed to style himself the "King of Trinacria," and so Petrarch's use of the term here may reflect recent history (see Smith 1968.2:78 and 83).

399–405 Hoc enim a Peloro gubernatore Hanibalis . . . notissimum: Cape Pelorus (Punta del Faro) formed the NE extremity of the island of Sicily. It is that point of Sicily that projects closest to the opposite coast of Italy. Roman authors derived the name of the cape from the name of Hannibal's pilot, though the Greeks knew that name (Thucydides, 4.25.3) several centuries before the time of Hannibal. Strabo (1.1.17) says Pelorus was a Libyan pilot, in a context that may date him to the time of the Persian Wars, but the name Pelorus probably derives from the Greek πέλωρος (monstrous), with reference to the monsters Scylla and Charybdis (cf. Pomponius Mela, 2.116). According to Valerius Maximus (9.8. ext. 1) and Servius (*A.* 3.411) the Pelorus incident took place when Hannibal, defeated in Italy, was retreating to Africa prior to the battle of Zama; according to Pomponius Mela (2.116) it happened when Hannibal was headed to King Antiochus's court seven years after his final defeat at Zama (202 BC).

Even though the story of Pelorus is unhistorical, it can best be fitted into an historical context if it is assigned to the time of Hannibal's flight from Italy to Africa as Valerius says. Setting sail from Petilia just north of Croton on the east coast of Italy, Hannibal might naturally decide to sail through the Strait of Messina and down the west coast of Sicily on his way to Carthage (Valerius says he was forced to do that by pursuing Romans.) But if one adopts Mela's account and assigns the story of Pelorus to the time of Hannibal's flight to the East, there is no logical or historical reason why Hannibal would sail north through the Strait of Messina. Yet it is Mela's chronology that Petrarch adopted in his *Africa* (8.299–329): in the margin of his Servius he wrote, "Pomponius aliter, quem in *Africa* mea sequor" (de Nolhac 1907.1:154). By the time he came to write this account in the *Itinerarium,* Petrarch had evidently rethought the story's logical (if not historical) place in Hannibal's career and switched his allegiance from Mela to Valerius and Servius's authority.

In criticizing Valerius for saying that Hannibal escaped Italy with his entire fleet (*tota cum classe Italiam linquens, ut Valerio placet,* lines 400–401), Petrarch looks to be indulging in a feeble bit of academic nit picking. It should be noted that Valerius does not say that Hannibal left Italy with his *entire* fleet; he merely says, "classe Africam repetens." There is no sign of a *tota* in the manuscripts reported by modern editors of Valerius, though it is certainly possible that Petrarch saw or thought he remembered seeing the word in his copy. Petrarch's authority, if any were to be assumed, for saying that Hannibal took flight with one ship only (patriam suam puppe unica repetens, 401) would seem to be Livy (33.48). But Livy is describing Hannibal's flight to the court of

Antiochus after the battle of Zama; he has nothing to say about Pelorus. Petrarch also refers to the story of Pelorus at *Fam.* 9.5.48.

In the scene in the *Africa* in which Hannibal flees Italy for Africa, we find an interesting anachronism. Making his escape under cover of darkness, Hannibal relies on his navigator's skill in reading the stars and in his expert use of the compass (*Africa,* 6. 565–570):

> Tum dux concussa quieti
> Membra dedit dubie; certamque obversus ad Arthon
> Classis agens curas et sidera nota magister,
> Solicitat nautas quibus est custodia puppis
> Magnetis ferrique vias spectare sequacis
> Et simul insomnem studio traducere noctem.
>
> (Then the leader [Hannibal] surrendered his weary limbs to restless composure, and the captain of the fleet, keeping a watch on the North and its familiar stars, roused the sailors whose job it was to take the helm: to observe the directions of the magnetic and compliant iron and to pass the night in wakeful concern.)

The merchants of Amalfi claimed to have invented the compass at the beginning of the twelfth century, and Jacques de Vitry, bishop of Acre, wrote in 1218 that the compass was a navigational necessity (Taylor 1956.92–95). By Petrarch's time, the use of the compass at sea had been common for only about 150 years.

408–410 Inde . . . Scyllaceum naufragiis infame transiliens: cf. Virgil's *navifragum Scylaceum (A.* 3.553).

410–413 Crotonem . . . vix ipsis Italicis bene notam: cf. Cicero, *Inv.* 2.1–3; Justin, 20.2–4 (Seel 1972); Ovid, *Met.* 15.1–59. Cicero describes the physical beauty of Croton's women and the athletic ability of its men; Justin describes its early military ventures; and Ovid describes its reputation as a place of great learning after the arrival of Pythagoras from Samos. Croton, however, is scarcely mentioned in later antiquity except as a place that had fallen from its former greatness, as in Livy 23.30 and Petronius, *Satyrica* (116.2–9), a work unknown to Petrarch it should be noted. In his *Africa,* (6.451–483) Petrarch provides a lengthy description, which includes Hannibal's massacre of the Crotoniates and the desecration of Juno's temple (suggested by Livy, 30.20).

The polysyndeton of the phrase *et animorum robore et corporum et forma* should be carefully observed. The third *et* joins the nouns *robore* and *forma,* which are to be taken closely together, but which do not constitute an hendiadys. The first two *ets* (= both . . . and) link the genitives *animorum* and *corporum,* which are subjoined to the *robore* and *forma.* Foster (1984.119) notes Petrarch's fondness for polysyndeton in his *Canzoniere.* There is a reminiscence of Horace's "ver proterit aetas" (*C.* 4.7.9) in Petrarch's "Quid non proterit longa dies?"

413 Hic Iunonis Lacinie . . . percelebre: cf. Virgil: *attollit se diva Lacina contra,* (*A.* 3.552). This temple, on the promontory of Lacinium about six miles distant from Croton, was very famous in antiquity (Livy 24.3). According to Cicero, (*Inv.* 2.1–3) the interior of the temple was adorned by paintings executed by the celebrated Zeuxis. Hannibal was tempted by the temple's treasures, but refrained from touching them for fear of being struck blind (Cicero, *Div.* 1.24). The temple, however, was plundered by Sextus Pompey in 36 BC during the civil war (Appian, *BC* 5. 133) and quickly declined. Little remains of the temple today.

414–416 Tarentum . . . Ennio natalis, Virgilio fatalis locus, quamvis alii Brundusium dicant: a fragment of Suetonius's *De viris illustribus* (preserved by Jerome in his translation and continuation of Eusebius's *Chronicle;* text of Schoene 1967.2:123; also found in Refferscheid 1860.24) gives Tarentum as Ennius's place of birth. Sounder ancient traditions give Rudiae, a town of Calabria about 20 miles from Brundusium, as the poet's native city. On Petrarch and Eusebius (Jerome) see de Nolhac 1907.2: 156,160,206,242.

Ennius (239–169 BC) had a rank of importance in Petrarch's mind all out of proportion to what Petrarch actually knew of his poetry: only about 600 lines of Ennius's epic the *Annales* have survived in quotations in Cicero, Aulus Gellius, Macrobius, and others. But Petrarch saw Ennius as his precursor (he calls himself a "second Ennius" at *Africa,* 2.443) in the telling of the glorious deeds of Scipio Africanus, Petrarch's ideal Roman (but see note to lines 658–660). At the end of the *Africa*, Petrarch introduces Ennius as a character in his narrative and uses him to enunciate his own theory of poetics: the substance of Ennius's speech resembles ideas expressed in his coronation speech in Rome, as noted by Corradini 1874.469. Endowed with prophetic powers, Ennius is able to foresee that Petrarch will one day celebrate Scipio's deeds in verse and produce the *De viris illustribus*, the *Rerum memorandarum libri*, and other works as well (9.216–283). On Ennius's prominent role in the *Africa*, see Bernardo 1962.43-45, 47–50, 160–162 and *passim*. For a translation of Petrarch's coronation speech, see Wilkins 1955.300–313.

Some manuscripts of Servius say that Virgil died of sunstroke at Tarentum: *periit autem Tarenti in Apuliae civitate* (Rand et al. 1946.2:3). Hardie (1957.19) rightly rejects the passage (*Vita Servii*, note to line 42). Modern scholarship agrees with Donatus (*Vita*, 35) that Virgil died at Brundusium. On Petrarch's knowledge of the sources for Virgil's life, see Stuart 1917.364–404, with criticisms of R. Sabbadini's earlier work on this subject, and Feo 1988.61. For the lives of Virgil in antiquity, see Suerbaum 1981. 1156–1262, and in the Middle Ages, Upson 1943.103–111. See also Lo Monaco's note to this passage (1990.110–111).

416–417 Pyrro rege in Italian accersito: Pyrrhus (319–272 BC), King of Epirus in western Greece, was invited in 281 by the Tarentines to protect them from the Romans. In 280 he defeated the Romans in a major battle at Heraclea and then threatened Rome itself. He won another major victory at Asculum in 279, but lost so many troops that he is reported to have said, "Another victory like that over the Romans and we are done for," (Plutarch, *Pyrrh.* 21). In 275 Pyrrhus withdrew from Italy, undefeated but having lost two-thirds of his expeditionary force and destined to give his name to a victory won at too great a price. Since Livy's account of these events, contained in the second decade of his history, is lacking, Petrarch had to rely on Justin's epitome of Pompeius Trogus's *Historiae Philippicae* (18.1–2; 25.3–5), Florus (1.13 [18]), Orosius (4.1), and Eutropius (*Breviarium*, 2.11–14; text in Santini 1979). Plutarch's *Life of Pyrrhus*, the most important extant literary source, was unavailable to Petrarch.

417–418 adiutoque . . . Hanibale: Hannibal recognized the strategic importance of Tarentum early in the Second Punic war, but did not gain control of it until 212 BC when the city's pro-Carthaginian party betrayed the city into his hands (Livy, 25.8–10). Fabius retook the city in 209 (Livy, 27. 12,15–16).

418–419 quos hostilium ducum primos . . . numerabunt: Petrarch's ranking of Pyrrhus and Hannibal as Rome's two most dangerous enemies was inspired by Hannibal's ranking of great generals in Livy (35.14.5–12). Speaking at Ephesus with Scipio, who had defeated him at the battle of Zama, Hannibal ranks Alexander first, then Pyrrhus, then himself. When Scipio bursts out laughing and asks where Hannibal would rank himself if he had won at Zama, Hannibal replies that he would have claimed first place before Alexander. It then occurs to Scipio that Hannibal is setting him apart from the others as one whose excellence is beyond compare.

Petrarch elaborates on this story in the *Africa* (8.102–231), and there is reference to it in *De viris illustribus* 21, Scipio, 1.2–3 (text in Martellotti 1954) and *Invective contra medicum* (3.120–131). For more on the rating of great generals of the past see note on lines 641–642.

421–423 Hydruntem attigeris . . . Corcyram . . . invenies: Hydrus (modern Otranto), a port of considerable importance throughout antiquity and the Middle Ages, marks the place of shortest passage from Italy to Western Greece (about 47 miles). It was the usual point of departure for those passing from Italy to the southern part of Greece and beyond. The phrase *pedem habens obvium* has caused unnecessary consternation among editors: Lumbroso (1889.40) feels compelled to emend; Feo (1974.182), following the authority of the Cremona Manuscript and repunctuating, restores the correct reading, but says he is plagued by doubts; Lo Monaco (1990.66–67) repunctuates Feo's text and mistranslates. The problem seems to arise from lack of attention to the technical meaning of *pes*: a rope attached to the bottom (foot) of a sail for the purpose of setting it to the wind. The square-rigger in which Mandelli no doubt sailed would have to tack (pedem facere) to sail southeast to Corfu. The word *pes* is amply doc-

documented in this sense in ancient literature, oddly enough primarily in the works of poets like Virgil and Lucan, but apparently is not found in this sense in the Latin of the Middle Ages. At any rate, Du Cange and Jal (1848, s.v. *pes*) refer only to ancient sources for this meaning. The phrase, therefore, would have a pronounced antique and even epic quality about it, quite in keeping with Petrarch's narrative strategy.

Corcyra is a large island off the coast of Greece (modern Albania), identified in antiquity with Homer's Scheria or Phaeacia (Pliny, *Nat.* 4.52). Its modern name Corfu is an Italian corruption of the Greek κορυφαί, "crests," from the mountain peaks at the northern end of the island. The Angevins of Naples controlled Corcyra at the time Petrarch was writing his *Itinerarium,* just as they did Otranto. A short time later (1386), the island became a Venetian protectorate, which gave way to sovereign control in 1401.

424–425 Illic quidem optabis . . . brevior cursus sit: the narrow breadth of the Isthmus (about 4 miles in places) frequently inspired thoughts in antiquity of digging a canal through it. Among the Romans, according to Suetonius, Julius Caesar (*Jul.* 44), Caligula (*Cal.* 21), and Nero (*Ner.* 19) all made plans for a canal, but Nero was the only one who actually began work (in AD 67). According to Josephus (*B.I.* 3. 540, Thackeray 1926), six thousand Jewish captives were sent by Nero's general Vespasian for this work. On Petrarch's knowledge of Josephus, see note to lines 493–494.

426 Mons est duo maria . . . insula esset Achaia: the same idea appears in the *Africa,* 8.333–334:

> Leva brevem dabat inde viam, si fluctibus Isthmos
> Cederet ac gemini limes maris alta Chorintus.

Petrarch is using Lucan (1.100–104) as his model:

> Qualiter undas
> Qui secat et geminum gracilis mare separat Isthmos
> Nec patitur conferre fretum, si terra recedat,
> Ionium Aegaeo frangat mare . . .

When Petrarch's itinerary leaves Italy, and Virgil and Livy fail him as sources, he turns immediately to Lucan's *De bello civili,* whose influence prevails throughout the rest of the *Itinerarium.*

427–430 Id sibi . . . locus ipse adhortari: cf. Cicero, *Off.* 1.11.35. Petrarch quotes part of Cicero's sentence verbatim.

When Rome defeated Macedonia (196 BC), Corinth became the chief city of the Achaean League, a group of free city-states under Rome's protection. When Rome wanted to curtail the League's freedom, Corinth rebelled and suffered complete destruction in 146 at the hands of Lucius Mummius, who sent all the city's treasure to Italy. It was a cynical action to eliminate a potential rival, which later Romans shamelessly pretended was just revenge for the sack of Troy by the Greeks (Purcell 1995.133–148; esp.138). Florus (*Epit.* 1.32 = 2.16) provided Petrarch with the fullest account of this episode.

433 urbes in litore, Mothona, Corona: in 1209, by a treaty with Geoffrey of Villehardouin, prince of Achaea, Venice secured its authority over Modon and Coron and maintained it over these Morean seaports for nearly 300 years. Both harbors marketed the agricultural products of southern Greece (grain, wax, and silk) and provisioned Venetian fleets sailing between the Adriatic and the Aegean. Both places were regular ports for pilgrims to the Holy Land. Pietro Casola, a visitor to Modon in the late fifteenth century, found little that pleased him about the place: things must have been much the same in the fourteenth century (see Newett 1907.191–194). The Venetians allowed the Genoese into the harbor, but strictly controlled their movements ashore in Petrarch's time.

435 Cretam respicit, nunc possessionem Venetorum: after Constantinople fell to the Crusaders in 1204, Boniface of Montferrat took Crete as his share of the spoils, but soon sold it to the Venetians, who established peace, brought in colonists, and promoted commerce. Their administration was so repressive that fourteen rebellions are recorded between the years 1207–1365, the most dangerous revolt being led by Venetian colonists themselves. See Petrarch's letters to his friend Luchino dal Verme, who successfully dealt with one of these rebellions for the Venetians in

1364–*Sen.* 4.1, which is often entitled *De officio et virtutibus imperatoris,* and *Sen.* 4.2. In *Sen.* 4.3 Petrarch describes the joy in Venice when a messenger ship arrived to announce the quelling of the Cretan rebels.

436 olim Iovis regnum: Crete was Jupiter's kingdom because he was born and raised there. Petrarch is thinking of Virgil's line in the *Aeneid* (Creta Iovis magni medio iacet insula ponto, 3.104) together with Servius's commentary on it. Lucan says that the Cretans falsely claim that Jupiter was buried on their island (8.869–872), but Cristoforo Buondelmonti was greatly impressed by the "tomb," when it was pointed out to him on Mt. Juktas early in the fifteenth century (Weiss 1969.136): an area of the isolated peak near Knossos can be seen as a reclining bearded god. There are impressive Minoan structures nearby, which would lend a certain authenticity to the legend. The idea that Jupiter had died and consequently had need of a tomb can be traced to Euhemerus (fl. c. 300 BC), who in his *Hiera Anagraphe* (preserved in fragments) argued that the gods were originally heroes elevated to the rank of gods by their grateful followers and were only mortals after all. Christian writers, especially Lactantius, liked this idea and used it as evidence of the fraudulent nature of pagan deities. See Müller 1993.276–300 on Euhemerus.

The story about Jupiter's tomb on Mt. Juktas, largely the product of a local oral tradition, may be a source for Dante's Old Man of Crete (*Inferno,* 14.103), even though he places the Old Man on Mt. Ida. Mt. Juktas is not otherwise famous in myth or history and its name probably was unknown to Dante. Many ancient sources speak of the Tomb of Jupiter on Crete, but do not say exactly where it is located. A few put it vaguely "near" Knossos and a few place it in a cave on Mt. Ida (see Rohde 1966.1:96–97, with notes on 109). Rohde does not seem to be aware of the tradition, still alive, which puts the tomb on Mt. Juktas (see Cook 1914.1: 157–163 and Cameron 1988.209).

436–437 superstitionum fere omnium fontem atque principium: cf. Sallust *apud* Servius, *A.* 3.104: *primos Cretenses constat invenisse religionem.* At *Africa* 2.211 Petrarch calls Crete "superstitionum ingens domus atque magistra"; cf. *Fam.* 15.7.14.

438 Eubeam, quam Nigropontum vocant: a large island 90 miles long NE of Attica and Boeotia, Euboea is separated from the mainland by a narrow and shallow strait, easily bridged even in antiquity. In 1204, Venetians claimed the island from a disintegrating Byzantine empire but did not control it entirely until 1390. They gave the island the name Negroponte (Black Bridge), which is a twofold corruption of Euripus, the name of the narrowest part of the channel along the west coast of the island. Euripus became Egripo, which was further corrupted by the Venetians to Negroponte, apparently with reference to one of the two bridges that spanned the Euripus. The name was applied to the whole island as well as to the principal city of the island (the ancient Chalcis). See Robbert 1985.5:418–428. Niccolò da Martoni (1395), who gives a lengthy description of Negroponte (Legrand 1895.3:653–655), says that armed guards protected the two bridges at all times.

439–440 Cyclades . . . que siderum . . . illustrant: cf. Petrarch's *Africa,* 2.213–214: *celo velut astra sereno / Cyclades effuse medio*; cf. *Africa,* 10. 196–197.

440–441 Scyros Achillei amoris . . . sedes: Scyros, one of the northern Sporades, lies east of Euboea, a long distance from Mandelli's recommended course north of Crete. According to legend Achilles's mother (Thetis) foreseeing her son's death at Troy, tried to save him by hiding him as a boy on the island. There he later married Deidamia, by whom he became the father of Neoptolemus (Pyrrhus). When Ulysses came to recruit Achilles for the war, Achilles attempted to disguise himself in women's clothes; but Ulysses unmasked him by a trick and led him off to fight.

This myth was one of the most popular throughout the medieval period, most widely known from Statius's version in his unfinished epic *Achilleid,* which was one of six Latin texts collected in the *Liber Catonianus,* a medieval schoolbook (Clogan 1968). The myth was also well known in Ovid's succint narrative (*Met.* 13.162–170). Scyros is the site of Achilles's first love; at Troy, he fell in love with Briseis. *Prima* logically qualifies *amoris* (Achilles's first love), but by a common figure of speech (hypallage or transferred epithet) is made to modify *sedes.*

Paolella (1992.82) appears to think that Scyros, the Hellespont, Troy and the other places mentioned in this section are being represented as an actual part of Mandelli's itinerary, but Lo Monaco recognizes that their mention has "una funzione eminentemente esemplare" (1990.112).

442 fulmen illud: Petrarch probably derived his description of Achilles as a thunderbolt from Virgil's description of the two Scipios in the *Aeneid* (geminos, duo fulmina belli, Scipiadas, 6.842–3). The metaphor certainly caught Petrarch's attention: he quotes Virgil's line at *De vita solitaria,* 2.13 (550 in *Prose*); cf. *Triumphus fame,* 1.26 (*Rime,* 565). At *De bello civ.* 1.151 Lucan likens Caesar to a *fulmen*.

442–443 Hic Cous Ypocratis, Lesbos Theofrasti, Samos Pithagore: Hippocrates was a contemporary of Socrates (d. 399), but little reliable biographical information has survived. The so-called Hippocratic books, dealing with all aspects of medicine, are probably the remnants of the medical literature circulating in the fifth and fourth centuries, none being certainly from Hippocrates's own hand. Hippocrates however became in the Middle Ages, as he was in antiquity, the type of an ideal physician (see also notes to lines 474–478 and Temkin 1991). Niccolò da Martoni visited Lango (Cos) in 1395 and viewed with great curiosity the ancient ruins on the island, which he correctly associated with Hippocrates (Legrand 1895.3:643–645).

Theophrastus (c. 370–c. 288 BC) was the pupil, collaborator, and successor of Aristotle. Petrarch knew of Theophrastus's work mainly from quotations and references to him in the works of Cicero, Seneca, and Pliny the Elder. The *Liber de nuptiis,* ascribed to Theophrastus and preserved in Latin translation in St. Jerome's *Against Jovinian* (1.47; colls 289–291 in *PL* 23, 215–291), was also well known throughout the Middle Ages both to scholars like Abelard and John of Salisbury and to authors of popular literature like Jean de Meun (*Romance of the Rose*) and Chaucer. Petrarch often refers to this short tract with approval (e.g., *De vita solitaria,* 2.5 in *Prose* 442). The work, which argues that a wise man will not marry, was often mistakenly entitled *Aureolus* or the *Little Golden* [*Book*], an error which has persisted to modern times.

Theophrastus's *Characters, De historia plantarum,* and *De causis plantarum,* which would have interested Petrarch greatly, were not known in the West until much later. On the sources of medieval knowledge of Theophrastus and of the *De nuptiis,* see Schmitt 1971.257–270.

Pythagoras emigrated from Samos to Croton in c. 531 BC. Though he probably wrote nothing, various works were later attributed to him. By Aristotle's day, his life and work were already obscured by legend. What Petrarch knew of his teachings he had gleaned from his translations of Aristotle, Cicero, Seneca, Ovid, Aulus Gellius, Justin, and Macrobius primarily. He was chiefly known for his ascetic way of life and for his belief in the transmigration of souls. His reputation for deep wisdom derived from his accomplishments with numbers such as his discovery of the mathematical basis of musical intervals and for the theorem that is known by his name (see Burkert 1972; also notes to lines 410–413). See Petrarch's sketch of Pythagoras at *Rerum memorandarum libri,* 1.24 (*Prose,* 272–276).

444–445 philosophie nomen, quod primus invenerat: cf. Cicero, *Tusc.* 5.3.7–9; Valerius Maximus 8.7. ext. 2: Augustine, *De civ. Dei.* 8.2; and Isidore, *Etym.* 8.6.2–3.

448 illa duo Grecie lumina, Lacedemonem et Athenas: related to each other by antithesis, Sparta (to use its more familiar name) and Athens were assigned by the Greeks themselves a unique position in their country's intellectual topography. These two city-states, as defined by Thucydides, Plato, Aristotle, Xenophon, and Plutarch (*Parallel Lives* and *Moralia*) primarily, provided contrasting models of law, politics, education, morality, and warfare. Athens was democratic and liberal; Sparta was diarchic and conservative. Italian thinkers of the fifteenth and sixteenth centuries such as Leonardo Bruni and Donato Gianotti, armed now with a knowledge of the Greek sources and possessed of a thirst for things Greek, turned to the history of Sparta and Athens in an effort to articulate and define their views on constitutional law and politics. Florence saw itself as the new Athens; Venice compared its constitution to Sparta's and so on.

In Petrarch's time, with its limited knowledge of the Greeks, the light projected from ancient Sparta and Athens was very dim, but he did know Aristotle's *Politics* in Latin translation (see note to lines 623–624). And he knew Vegetius, a military writer of the late fourth century, who had contrasted the two cities: Sparta was to be admired for its skill in warfare; Athens for its cultivation of the arts *(Epitoma rei militaris,* iii, *praef.*). Justinian derived all civil law from these two great societies (*Institutes* 1.2. 10; text in Birks and McLeod 1987), a text Petrarch undoubtedly knew from his law studies at Montpellier or at Bologna. This is the same text that Dante refers to at *Purg.* 6.138–139, when he speaks of "*Atene e Lacedemone, che fenno / l'antiche leggi e furon sì civili . . .* " By 1358, he also knew Cicero's eulogistic characterization of the two city-states in the *Pro L. Flacco* (see Sabbadini 1905.2:172 and Billanovich 1946.101–102):

> Adsunt Atheniensis, unde humanitas, doctrina, religio, fruges, iura, leges ortae atque in omnis terras distributae putantur. . . . Adsunt Lacedaemonii cuius civitatis spectata ac nobilitata virtus non solum natura corroborata verum etiam disciplina putatur; qui soli toto orbe terrarum septigentos iam annos amplius unis moribus et numquam mutatis legibus vivunt *(Flac,* 62–63).

Petrarch also knew Cicero's views on the two city-states from his philosophical works, and he knew the scattered statements of the two Senecas and Valerius Maximus. Petrarch was especially impressed by the gallant Spartan stand against the Persians at Thermopylae (see, e.g., Seneca, *Ep.* 82.20–21). When a crusade against the infidels, proposed by Philip VI of France (see Housley 1986.23–29), seemed at last about to get underway in 1333, Petrarch wrote an exhortatory poem addressed to Giacomo Colonna in which he recalled (*Canz.* 28, 100–101):

> le mortali strette [Thermopylae]
> che difese il Leon [Leonidas] con poca gente . . .

For Petrarch, Sparta embodied the kind of fighting spirit which he thought should motivate the crusaders. At *Fam.* 11.8.32, Petrarch, hoping to restrain Venice's behavior towards Genoa, invokes Sparta's honorable treatment of defeated Athens at the end of the Peloponnesian War as an example:

> illud scio quod in emulatione olim pari sed conditione longe impari, dum evertendi infestissimam Athenarum urbem Lacedemoniis oblata esset occasio, . . . e duobus Grecie luminibus eruturos se alterum negaverunt.

On the whole subject of Sparta (especially) and Athens as *topoi* for philosophical and protreptic discourse in the Middle Ages and Italian Renaissance, see Rawson 1969.116–157. Petrarch found the phrase *duo Grecie oculi* in Justin (*Epit.*, 5.8), who was the source for the passage in the *Familiares* just quoted. The phrase *duo lumina* (with *lumina* = glories, as in Petrarch) is found in Livy, 34.32.5. Cf. also Cicero (*Manil.* 11): *Corinthum . . . lumen Graeciae extinctum esse . . .*

449 Sextonque et Abydon: Sestos, a city on the west coast of the Hellespont, and Abydos, a city opposite on the east coast, were the homes of two famous lovers, Hero and Leander. Hero was a priestess of Aphrodite (Venus) at Sestos. Leander (of Abydos) saw Hero at a festival and fell in love with her. Afterwards he would swim the Hellespont nightly (a matter of three or four miles) to see his love until one night he tried the crossing in a storm. The wind extinguished the light by which Hero usually guided him to shore, and Leander was drowned. Hero committed suicide by throwing herself into the sea after her lover. The myth is of late origin, a product of sentimental Alexandrian invention. Petrarch knew the story from Virgil (*G.* 3.257–263) and from Ovid (*Ep.* 18 and 19), but he is also thinking of Lucan 9.954–955, who alludes to the story as he describes Julius Caesar's crossing of the Hellespont after the battle of Pharsalus. Cf. Lucan's *amore notatum aequor* [the Hellespont] with Petrarch's *Sestonque et Abydon . . . amoribus notas.* Abydos (Aueo, Auedo, Eueo in the *portolani* and portolan charts) survived as the toll station of the Hellespont until late Byzantine times; Sestos (Sexto) survived in *portolani* and portolan charts because a promontory near the ruins of the ancient city had acquired its name (Kretschmer 1901.639 and 652).

450–451 illud emulatione Romani imperii, hoc propriis famosum malis: Petrarch is referring to the political and religious rivalry which developed between the eastern and western parts of the Roman empire especially after Constantine moved his court to Byzantium and changed the city's name to Constantinople in AD 330.

Lo Monaco (1990.112) draws attention to a passage in *Sen.* 3.6 in which Petrarch takes issue with Sozomen, a Greek ecclesiastical writer of the fifth century, for saying that Constantinople is richer and more powerful than ancient Rome was. Beyond the passage's relevance to this context, it shows that Petrarch had read with some care the *Historia Tripartita,* which includes Sozomen along with the works of two other Greek ecclesiastical historians, Socrates and Theodoret, in the sixth-century Latin version of Epiphanius Scholasticus. Petrarch no doubt had read the work at Avignon, in the manuscript still there today. See Laistner's informative account of this work in the Middle Ages in 1948.51–67, esp. 64. Sozomen's Greek text may be conveniently compared with the Latin translation at *PG* 67, 843–1630. The Latin version in the *Historia Tripartita* has greatly abbreviated and rearranged the order of Sozomen's Greek text. The passage Petrarch alludes to in the *Seniles* is at 2.18.16–18 (p. 116 in Jacob's edition of 1952).

451–452 Rhodon petes, olim Soli, nunc Cristo (verius scilicet soli) sacram: Petrarch calls Christ the true sun because the light of his knowledge penetrates everywhere. The reference is to Boethius's *De cons. Phil.* 5. 2 m., where the power of the sun (Phoebus) is shown to be limited since its light cannot pierce the density of matter, but the Founder of the world (magni conditor orbis) can see into everything and everywhere at a glance. One ought to call Him the true sun (Sol) since He alone (solus) sees all (*quem, quia respicit omnia solus, / verum possis dicere solem,* 13–14). Boethius incorporates into these concluding lines the etymology that derived *sol* from *solus* (not so say modern authorities: Ernout 1959.632 and 634). This etymological connection can be traced to Varro's *De lingua latina* (5.68): *sol vel quod ita Sabini, vel <quod>*

solus ita lucet ut ex eo deo dies sit. Petrarch did not read these words until 1355 when he received from Boccaccio a partial copy (books 5 and 6 complete) of Varro's work (Billanovich 1947.203–207). Most likely he first became aware of the etymology from reading his copy of Isidore's *Etymologies* (3.71): *sol appellatus eo quod solus appareat, obscuratis fulgere suo cunctis sideribus.* Isidore is here indebted to Cicero's statement of the matter in *De nat. deorum,* 2.68:

> . . . *sol dictus sit vel quia solus ex omnibus sideribus est tantus vel quia cum est exortus obscuratis omnibus solus apparet.*

Petrarch also used the etymology at *Africa* 8.224–225: *[Sol] imo stat per se solus, et inde nomen habet.* For more on other authors who make use of the etymology see Pease 1958.2:727–728.

The very earliest Christian writings, both Greek and Latin, equate Christ with Helios or Sol in a large variety of texts (Rahner 1963.89–154). Boethius's phrase "true sun" (sol verus) reappears in the ninth century in Sedulius Scottus's Easter poem: *Surrexit Christus sol verus vespere noctis (Carm.* 3:2.17 in Traube 1896.3.151–240). But the phrase "sol verus" is not Boethius's invention, and both may be remembering another earlier source such as St. Ambrose's hymn "Splendor paternae gloriae," where in the second stanza we find: *verusque sol illabere / micans nitore perpeti* (referring to Christ); text in Lietzmann 1910.10.

Petrarch is also alluding to Lucan's *claramque relinquit / Sole Rhodon* (8.247–248). Rhodes is famous because the Rhodians erected a colossal statue in honor of Helios between 294–282 BC. Petrarch does not mention that wonder because he knows it had long ceased to exist (Pliny, *Nat.* 34.41). An earthquake broke it off at the knees in about 226 BC, and the Arabs hauled off the remaining bronze fragments when they plundered Rhodes in AD 654 (see Clayton 1988.124–137).

453 militie domicilium Iohannis: the John to whom Petrarch refers is John the Baptist, who gave his name to the religious order founded in Jerusalem in the eleventh century, the Order of the Hospital of St. John of Jerusalem. The order had its origin in a hospice that Italian merchants of Amalfi established in about 1070 near the church of St. John the Baptist to care for sick pilgrims and merchants. The church gave its name to the order's first establishment and subsequently to the order itself. It is possible that Petrarch knew the account that made St. John the Almsgiver (d. c. 620) the original patron of the order.

After the crusaders captured Jerusalem in 1099, the order was able to enlarge its activities: crusader knights, who had been nursed back to health in the hospital, generously endowed the order, and some were even moved to embrace its religious ideals. In this way the order became wealthy, and soon it was led by its powerful new members to consider fighting the Muslims as part of its mission. When the Muslims retook Jerusalem in 1187, the Hospitallers moved their headquarters to Acre. After the fall of Acre in 1291, the order with support from the Pope and the Genoese moved successfully against Rhodes, which they ruled as an independent state for more than 200 years. The Order of the Knights of Rhodes, as it was called while it ruled the island (1310–1522), joined with its members on Cyprus and elsewhere to harass the Muslims in any way possible. The ultimate goal was to regain Jerusalem.

Although the order had not lost sight of its original purpose and continued to provide care for the sick and wounded, its military character predominated, accounting for Petrarch's use of the term *militia*. The order, founded for the sake of action, generally lacked learned men among its members, but late in his life Petrarch himself was to do intellectual combat with Jean de Hesdin, the only member of the order to achieve fame as an intellectual. For a detailed account of the incident, see Wilkins 1959.233–240; for more information on Jean de Hesdin, and the Hospitallers, see Smalley 1981.345–392; Luttrell 1975.3:278–313. Niccolò da Martoni (1395) gives a glowing description of the hospital at Rhodes and of the charitable works done there (Legrand 1895.3:584–585).

454–456 Iam hinc Asia Minor . . . nunc Turcorum veri hostium ferox regio: prior to the end of the eleventh century a large number of European pilgrims traveled to the Holy Land partly by sea and partly by land. First, they sailed from an Italian port (Genoa or Venice, most commonly) to Constantinople to visit the renowned collection of relics there. Naturally, they wanted to see the very pillar at which Christ had been scourged and fragments of the *lignum crucis,* said to have been brought there by St. Helena. Of even more interest perhaps were the remains of the many saints and martyrs: every pilgrim wanted to bring back a relic, and for the right price such relics could be had at Constantinople. The pilgrim then proceeded to travel the excellent Byzantine (Roman) roads through Asia Minor and Syria. By 1080 however, the land route from Constantinople had been effectively cut off to the ordinary pilgrim by the invading Seljuk Turks. These were not always hostile to pilgrims, but sometimes they were, and they were always very greedy tax collectors. Besides, they had allowed the roads and bridges to fall into serious disrepair: see Runciman 1969.1:68–78.

Pilgrims of the twelfth century and later were obliged to make their journeys entirely by sea, but pirates were now the problem (see Burns 1980.165–178). In Petrarch's day, there had been a marked escalation in Turkish piracy and raiding throughout the Aegean (see Housley 1986.25–39). The Emirates of Aydin and Menteshe (on the coast of Asia Minor north of Rhodes, extending as far as Smyrna [Izmir]) were the chief offenders. In 1325, Venice, which was suffering the heaviest losses, tried to organize a coordinated effort against these pirates. Ten years later, the league had managed to scrape together a small expeditionary force of some 40 ships and 800 men, but the alliance collapsed. By 1342, the Venetians were afraid that they might actually lose Crete, their most profitable colony. Finally, in 1344 a feeble force of twenty-four galleys was launched from Negroponte, and rather by luck it managed to take the port of Smyrna. This success inspired the hope that the league could use Smyrna as a bridgehead for expansion into other parts of Asia Minor and launch a full-scale crusade, but this never happened (Housley 1986.303–309). Europe was now enmeshed in the Hundred Years War (for a recent survey see Allmand 1988). In 1356, the Battle of Poitiers took place; and in the late 1350s mercenary bands began to exploit the civil disorder in France and Italy. All of these sad events are reflected in Petrarch's work (e.g., *Fam.* 9.8, 14.5 and 6, 15.7, 17.3,

22.1, 22.14, and *Eclogue* 12). For Latin text and translation (with commentary) of *Eclogue* 12 see Bergin 1974.196–213 and 250–252.

A persistent theme in Petrarch's anguished pleas for reform is the sharp contrast he draws between the corrupt and feckless modern leaders and the great Romans of the past. In a passage of the *De vita solitaria,* 2.9 *(Prose,* 494–496; translation in Zeitlin 1924), Petrarch imagines what would be the result if Julius Caesar were to return from the dead and, possessed of his former courage and power, were to become a Christian (Cristi nomen agnosceret). Would he allow the Egyptian brigands (egiptius latro) to hold Jerusalem? Likewise, the two Scipios and Pompey the Great. If they were to return and become Christian (Cristiane fidei sacris inititi), would they not also destroy the enemies of Christ? These great Romans Petrarch contrasts with the leaders of his own day — braver than lions they are in their bedrooms, but in the field more timid than deer (in thalamo leonibus fortiores, in campo cervis timidiores). They look like men, but they are really women (ora virilia muliebribus animis dehonestant). *Fam.* 22.14 plays on this same theme.

For a military man such as Mandelli, Petrarch need not dwell on the inability of the Western leaders to deal with the Turkish problem. The bungling of the situation with the pirates had gone on for at least a generation, only one example amid infinite ineptitudes. With admirable restraint, Petrarch simply proceeds to sketch Pompey's brilliant efficiency against the very troublesome pirates of long ago (see notes to lines 458–460 and 453–454 below). On the fourteenth-century pilgrims' fear of pirates, see Hyde 1993b.89, 91, and 102–104. Giacomo da Verona (1335) says that he arrived at Cyprus in great fear because a pirate by the name of "Bartholomeus Malopolus" (crudelis spoliator maris) had been spotted nearby (Röhricht 1895.3:176). Some pirates were Christian, and by no means were all victims of Christian pirates non-Christian (Braudel 1972.2:873).

458–460 Isauria, arx olim omnium pyratarum . . . decertarent: the threat to Rome from pirates grew very serious after the death of Sulla (78 BC). These brigands were scattered throughout the Mediterranean, but were especially entrenched in Cilicia. The favorite scene of their depredations was the coast of Italy from Brundisium on the east to Ostia on the west: they intercepted corn supplies from Egypt and carried off wealthy Romans for ransom. In a passage Petrarch seems to have in mind here, Cicero records (*Man.* 33) that in 68 the pirates attacked and destroyed a Roman fleet under consular command just off the coast at Ostia: he then recounts Pompey's incredible efficiency in running the offending brigands to ground (34–35). See *Fam.* 22.14 for Petrarch's knowledge of this speech of Cicero's, known variously as the *De lege Manilia* or the *De imperio Gn. Pompei.* But Petrarch's chief source for this whole section is Florus, *Epit.* 2.41 (= 3.6). On piracy in the ancient world, see Ormerod 1924.

460–463 Summa tamen Pompeii Magni virtute . . . abstracti sunt: in 67 Pompey was given an extraordinary command to deal with the pirates. In a systematic amphibious operation, Pompey swept the Mediterranean and Black Seas with a fleet of 270 warships and pressed his advantage ashore with 100,000 legionaries. In the space of three months (Florus says forty days), Pompey had taken care of the last threat from the pirates by capturing their strongholds in Cilicia. He then reorganized the territory by populating many of the areas with the more cooperative remnants of the pirates. It was claimed that he resettled some captives in Greece and southern Italy (Calabria). The old man described by Virgil (*G.* 4.125–148) as living an idyllic life near Tarentum tending his gardens and his bees was thought in antiquity to be one of those rehabilitated pirates (see Servius's commentary on the passage). It seems likely that Petrarch had this Virgilian passage in mind here, together with Servius's notes.

464–465 Laudensem Coloniam . . . traditur: Pompey's defeat and relocation of the pirates in 67 BC had nothing to do with the place Petrarch is referring to. According to Pliny (*Nat.* 3.124), the town, located about 16 miles SE of Milan, had been founded by a tribe of Gauls. Pompeius Strabo, Pompey the Great's father, championed Latin rights for the towns of Gallia Transpadana during his consulship in 89 BC (Asconius, *In Pison.* 3 in Clark 1907.3). The town probably assumed the name *Laus Pompeia* at that time as a compliment to the elder Pompey, although there is no ancient testimony to that effect. Petrarch had no doubt heard a more romantic tale, inspired by local patriotism, which connected the town's name with the younger, more famous Pompey, such as the one told by Galvano Fiamma in his *Manipulus florum* (passage cited by Lo Monaco 1990.113). Laudatory descriptions of cities constituted a minor, but flourishing genre in the medieval and renaissance period. Two such descriptions of Lodi in Latin verse have survived from the thirteenth century (see Hyde 1993a. 1–33; esp. 17). Cf. Lorenzo Vitelli's elegy of 1453, in which he makes the absurd claim that Corneto was founded by Electra, daughter of Atlas and mother of Dardanus, and her husband Corythus, who gave his name, slightly adjusted, to the town (Martini 1972.347–354). Through Dardanus, then, Corneto is the mother city of Troy and ultimately of Rome:

> Quae nunc Cornetum est, Italorum ante omnia regna
> Urbs erat haec olim regia metropolis.
>
> (This city, which is now Corneto, was once, before all
> the Italian kingdoms, a royal metropolis.)

465–468 Que quidem . . . obtinuit: in the Middle Ages *Laudensis Colonia*, now called by its modern name Lodi, grew into an important place and was an independent republic until it was destroyed in 1111 by the Milanese. In 1158, Frederick Barbarossa restored the city, but transferred it to its present location on the right bank of the Adda. The ancient site is still the location of a village called Lodi Vecchio about four miles west of the modern city. See the account in Giulini 1854.3: 23–25, 470–478 and Carretta 1958.93–109. Petrarch also refers to Frederick's treatment of Lodi at *De remediis* 2.69: *at Mediolano proxima laudum* [variant: *laudem*] *Pompeii ultima, ut aiunt, mutavit locum eisdem barbaricis manibus* (But the one [town of Lodi] near Milan, the least of Pompey's praises as the expression goes [for the phrase *laudum ultima* see Livy 30.30.4], changed its location, under duress from the same barbarian [pun on Barbarossa = "red beard"]. Cf. the translation in Rawski 1991.3.160. For a contemporary account of Frederick's attempts to impose his rule on the emerging republics of Northern

Italy, see the unfinished verse epic by an anonymous Bergamask (translation and notes by Carson 1994) where the description of Frederick's siege of Milan in 1162 is given rhetorical treatment in the classical mode of Lucan.

470–471 Cyprus, quam . . . Veneri sacram dixere: Venus's close connection with Cyprus, where she emerged from the sea, is amply attested to among Roman poets, who often refer to the goddess simply as the Cyprian (e.g., Horace, *Carm.* 1.3.1, Tibullus, 3.3.34, etc.); see also Lucan, 8.456–459 and Isidore (*Etym.* 14.6.14): *Ipsa [Cyprus] est et Paphos Veneri consecrata.* Petrarch knew from Justin (18.5.4) of the institutionalized prostitution practiced by Cyprian women in antiquity, and probably believed from things he had heard that this activity remained a speciality of the island even to his own day. Ludolph von Suchem has an extended essay on Cyprus in his pilgrim book (1350), in which he says, "in Cyprus men are lustful by nature beyond those in other lands" and in Famagusta "dwell numberless exceeding rich courtesans, some of them possessing more than a hundred thousand florins, about whose riches I dare say no more" (Stewart 1895.39 and 42).

474–478 Libidinem incolarum terre celique fervor indicat . . . complexio ad elementa transierit: Petrarch's statement that the warm climate of Cyprus is responsible for the Cyprians' inclination to softness and sexual indulgence and that it predisposes them to a lack of courage (*Veneri magis quam Marti seu Palladi sacra est,* lines 471–472) is likely to have its immediate source in Lucan 8.363–390; but he may well have read the Hippocratic essay *Airs, Waters, Places (Peri aeron hydaton topon),* one of the most interesting tracts in the Hippocratic corpus. It was circulating in a Latin translation as early as the fifth or early sixth century, and was translated again in the twelfth century by Marcus of Toledo, probably from an Arabic version (one version of the Latin title: *De aeribus aquis locis*). See Kibre 1975.123–126.

This Hippocratic essay describes the effects of geography and climate not only on man's health, but also on his physical and moral constitution. In the warm climate of Asia (= Asia Minor and Middle East) all of nature is prolific: the crops of the field, the animals, and man himself all thrive much better than in the cold of the north; but the people are prone to luxuriousness and are lacking in a warlike spirit (*Aer.* 12 and 16). The essay however merely sets forth in a sober and scholarly fashion what folk wisdom had long ago framed in a proverbial expression (Herodotus, 9.122): "Soft men usually come from soft countries."

Whether Petrarch had actually read this tract is impossible to say. It is well known that he was actively hostile towards the medical profession (but not, he insists, towards the art of medicine itself or good doctors, *Invective contra medicum,* 1.423–426 [Ricci 1978]). For this very reason, it is hard to believe that he did not take the trouble to acquaint himself with some of the less technical (at least) writings of the medical profession, even though he is admittedly defiant in owning up to the fact that he had not read Galen's *De Terapentica* (De Therapeutica) and never intended to (*Inventive contra medicum,* 3.39–45: *Prose,* 650). But if he did not read *Airs, Waters, Places,* he certainly had read Vitruvius's treatise on climate in *De Architectura* (de Nolhac 1907.2:105 and Ciapponi 1960.80–81), which was derived from the Hippocratic tract (1.1.13, 6.1.3–12). Although the great architect refrains from a discussion of the sexual behavior of those in southern climates, he does say that they are lacking in courage because their fighting spirit is drained away by the heat of the sun *(. . . habent exuctas ab sole animorum virtutes,* 6.1.10). For a survey of Petrarch's views on medicine, see Henschel 1846, Martinelli in Ricci 1978.205–249, and Bergdolt 1992.

479–480 fastus Gallicus . . . convenere: for a similar characterization of the French, Syrians, and Greeks, although in an entirely different context, see Petrarch's *Africa,* 2.290–292:

> Non semper Romanus aget; quin Syria mollis
> Porriget ipsa manum, mox Gallia dura, loquaxque
> Grecia . . .

481–482 illic . . . veniens iacet Hilarion: According to St. Jerome, Hilarion (c. 291–371), a native of Palestine, converted to Christianity in Alexandria. He came under the influence of St. Anthony and lived for a time as a hermit in the Egyptian desert. Returning to Palestine, he established a way of life famous for its rigorous asceticism. To escape crowds of pious visitors, Hilarion left for Egypt again, then for Sicily and western Greece, and finally for Cyprus where he died. He was buried near Paphos, but his remains were later transferred to Maiumas of Gaza (where they were visited by the Piacenza Pilgrim in c. 570; Wilkinson 1977.85 and 164b). Jerome adds however that the Cypriots refuse to admit that Hilarion's body had been removed to Palestine. Petrarch seems to have sided with the Cypriots' claim to Hilarion's relics since Jerome leaves the question unresolved.

Hilarion is counted as the founder of the anchoritic life in Palestine by Jerome, the chief authority for Hilarion's life (Migne, *PL* 23, 29–54; for translation Ewald 1952). Petrarch is known to have thought very highly of Jerome's biography (*Sen.* 8.6; cf. *De vita solitaria*, 2.1, 416 and 418 in *Prose*).

483 in extremo maris angulo Minor latet Armenia: at the beginning of the fourteenth century Armenia controlled a considerable tract of Cilician coastal territory, which was called Cilician Armenia or Lesser Armenia. By Petrarch's time the Seljuk sultanate of Konya had regained a substantial amount of their territory, so that Lesser Armenia was constricted in the way he described (see Riley-Smith 1991.115 and 143). On the history of Cilician Armenia during this period see Der Nersessian 1969. 2: 630–659 and the various essays in Boase 1978. Petrarch cannot have been unaware of the strategic importance of Armenia in fourteenth-century plans to retake the Holy Land. For an interesting contemporary account of Armenia and the early crusades, see Dostourian 1993.

487–488 Magistri sententia, comitum consensus, ventus . . . te agere oporteat dicent: for the phraseology, cf. Ovid, *Am.* 1. 4.54: *consilium nobis resque locusque dabunt* (also Ovid, *Trist.* 1.1.92).

The *magister* of Mandelli's ship was the representative of the ship's owner, the shipmaster; sometimes he might be the owner himself, though in the fourteenth century at Genoa a ship was likely to be owned by a group of wealthy businessmen, who bought shares called *loca* (Byrne 1930.12–21). The authority of the *magister,* who may be the captain, was decisive in any emergency; but if a ship were leased, the provisions of a written contract detailing the rights and responsibilities of both owner and passengers would be strictly enforced. According to Ludolph von Suchem, usually considered a reliable contemporary witness, pilgrims in 1350 had to disembark at Beirut because the Sultan had blocked the port at Jaffa out of fear of French attack (Stewart 1895. 49; Latin text in Deycks 1851.1–104). Jaffa's harbor, like those of Acre, Sur, and Damietta in Egypt, was already blocked when Giacamo da Verona arrived in Syria on pilgrimage in 1335 (noted by Atiya 1938.167).

Wherever the pilgrims came to anchor, they would have to stay on board until given permission to land. A waiting period of up to ten days was not uncommon: before disembarkation, the names of the pilgrims had to be registered with Muslim authorities, taxes and fees collected, important papers (e.g., the all-important safe-conduct guarantee) had to be signed in Jerusalem (four days travel round trip), an official Muslim interpreter engaged, and suitable transportation arranged for the group. Once these matters were settled and the pilgrims were on the move towards Jerusalem, they soon faced more bureaucratic delays at Ramla (ar-Ramlah), three hours' ride inland. All pilgrims were required to pay a visit to the *Custos Terrae Sanctae*, a Franciscan friar whose office it was to check credentials (all were required to show written papal permission to visit the Holy Land), assign guides to the group, and deliver a lecture (spoken in Latin, which always needed to be translated into various vernaculars) about proper Christian behavior in a country ruled by far from friendly Muslims. Any modern visitor to a predominately Muslim land will know the kind of thing the pilgrims heard: for a list of "do's" and "don'ts" see Savage 1977.4:52–53. It appears for example that as a general rule (established in 1304 in Cairo) Christians were required to use only asses or mules for transportation (Tritton 1930. 121). The practical advantage of this rule for the Muslims, in the event of a conflict with Christians, is too obvious to need further comment; but since it was also forbidden to Christians to carry weapons of any sort (though of course some did), one supposes that the rule was intended as much for an insult as for any other reason. Any aristocratic pilgrim (such as Mandelli), used to riding his horse, would doubtless have chaffed at riding the lowly ass. In 1413, Niccolò d' Este and his group were supplied with asses at Ramla, as was the practice. Luchino dal Campo, Niccolò's scribe, comments: *è noto che niuno cristiano non osa cavalcare cavallo in quel paese* (Ghinassi 1861.118).

Hostile emotions must have been very close to the surface, vituperative speech on both sides being more or less unrestrained. When Petrarch, far removed from the scene, rages against the "Egyptian dog" who controls the Holy Land *(De vita solitaria,* 2.9; *Prose,* 482: *terram . . . nobis ereptam . . . nunc egiptiacus canis tenet),* the word *canis* is not just a general term of abuse against the Egyptian Mamluks who held Palestine at this time; he is thinking of the Egyptian jackel god Anubis, whose canine likeness is immediately identifiable with Egypt. Petrarch's phrase echoes and partakes of the contempt found in Virgil, *A.* 8.698 and Juvenal's *illic / oppida tota canem* [Anubim] *venerantur* (15.7–8). He is also probably making reference to the common notion that at least some of the Saracens (Ethiopians) were to be identified with a marginally human race of monsters called Cynocephali (Dog-headed People), who were known from ancient sources, depicted on many *mappaemundi,* and mentioned by all the medieval encyclopedists (see Wittkower 1942.159–197 and Friedman 1981.59–86). See Ziada 1975.3:486–512 and Irwin 1986 on the Mamluks.

The Muslim, for his part, thought it quite fitting that the Arabic words for "Venetians" (banadqa) and "bastards" (banadiq) sounded very much alike (Barthelémy 1935.63–64). Nor was this hostility confined to words. In 1353, some Frankish merchants were arrested and punished by Muslim authorities at Acre for engaging in a religious ceremony, even though they had secured local permission for their activities. A Muslim commentator on the case later wrote (1370) that it was lawful to slay any merchant from an enemy land who comes to Muslim territory without safe-conduct: see Kedar 1976.29 and notes 21 and 24. For more on Western attitudes towards Muslims, see also D'Ancona 1889. 199–281, Southern 1956, Daniel 1975, and Setton 1992.

Both Christians and Muslims were guilty of brutalities and injustice in their dealings with one another. A recent study concludes, "The Muslim experience under Christian rule was not really so different from that of minority Christians under Muslim rule," Powell 1990.207. In general, the Christian pilgrim could feel reasonably secure of his person as long as he was careful not to give the slightest offense and stayed with his group. The Mamluks considered it highly desirable that the pilgrims with their gold ducats should continue to come to visit their holy shrines. This in fact was the reason why pilgrims had to have papal permission to go to the Holy Land. The Popes wanted to control the amount of gold flowing into the infidel hands, with nothing but shriven souls to show for it (on this point see Bagatti 1948.8). For a recent discussion of the considerable expense of a pilgrimage, see Pinto 1982.257–286.

489–490 Nam ut antiquo proverbio monemur, consilia capiuntur pro tempore: cf. Cicero, *De off.* 2.33: *consilium ex tempore capere posse;* Livy, 33.98: *ex tempore capto consilio;* also esp. Caesar, *Gal.* 5.8.1: *consiliumque pro tempore et pro re caperet.*

491–492 Tortosa, Tripolis, Baruth, Sur, Cesarea, Jaffa, Ascalon: Petrarch enumerates in their correct order (from north to south) the towns on the Syrio-Palestinian coast which were considered the most important in the Middle Ages. Acre, south of Sur and north of Caesarea, is "in the middle" (horum in medio . . . Acon), as Petrarch says. There can be little doubt that Petrarch is here using as his guide a portolan chart very similar to that made by Angelino Dalorto, who shows exactly these same eight names in red, as compared to some 25 names in dark ink (Hinks 1929. sheet 4). The majority of portolan charts of this period (1300–1500) omit Caesarea and Ascalon from this list of rubricated names (see the reference to Campbell cited in note to lines 378–380). It should also be observed that Petrarch uses the spellings Sur and Baruth, found in portolan charts, rather than their classical forms (Tyrus and Berytus), which he would have seen in Pomponius Mela and Pliny. Tortosa is a purely medieval appellation (the ancient Antaradus, not mentioned by either Mela or Pliny; the modern Tartús). Ancient Joppe (Joppa, Jope) had become Jaffa (modern Tel Aviv) at least by the time Anna Comnena (AD 1083–1153) wrote her *Alexiad* (11.7), the history of the reign of her father, Byzantine

Emperor Alexius I, which provides an interesting perspective on the first crusade. For a fuller account of these places see Gazetteer.

493–495 Acon, summum dedecus . . . ipsa Ierusalem: on 28 May 1291 Acon (Acre), fatally weakened by rival merchant factions, fell to the Mamluks of Egypt (Ricoldo da Montecroce in Röhricht 1884.258–296, Atiya 1938.29–33 and Irwin 1986.77–78). Jerusalem had fallen to Egyptian mercenaries already on 23 August 1244 (Irwin 1986.19). This began 650 years of uninterrupted Muslim control of the Holy City. With the *turpissima cicatrix* (483), Petrarch is alluding to Publilius Syrus (433 in Duff 1935): Non *turpis* est *cicatrix* quam virtus parit (the scar which bravery begets is not ugly). It is clear what Petrarch thought of the courage of those who were supposed to defend Acre and Jerusalem. Petrarch knew the *sententiae* of Publilius Syrus, a mime writer of c. 40 BC, as the work of Publius (e.g., *Fam.* 5.521 and 6.1.1).

496 caput Syrie Damascum. Sic enim vocat . . . Ysaias: Isa. 7:8.

498–499 Antiochiam Syrie primam ac metropolim haberi . . . Hegesippus: Petrarch is referring to a Latin version of Josephus's *Bellum Iudaicum (B.I.)*, produced around 370 and traditionally attributed to Hegesippus. The work is not so much a translation as it is a free reworking of Josephus's materials. Hegesippus compresses into five books what was originally seven; omits many passages in the original and expands others; adds many sources not used by Josephus: Latin prose authors such as Sallust, Ammianus, Tacitus, Suetonius, and Livy; Latin poets such as Horace, Virgil, Lucan, Terence, and Ovid; Christian writers like Ambrose and Eusebius, and the New Testament. Above all Hegesippus wrote as a militant Christian: his intent was to base his version on Josephus's Greek text but to give the facts a true interpretation according to Christian beliefs. Josephus, he said, lamented the destruction of Jerusalem in AD 70 and the fate of the Jews, but he did not understand the true cause of this suffering, sc., the Jews' crucifixion of Christ (*prol.* 2).

The name Hegesippus is probably the Hellenizing form of the Hebrew name Josephus (Yosippos), altered under the influence of the name of the second-century Hegesippus who served as a source for Eusebius's *Historia ecclesiastica*. The identity of the "translator" has been much debated: Ambrose, a Pseudo-Ambrose, the unknown author of a commentary on Paul's *Epistles*, and Isaac of Judea have been nominated as possibilities. The Latin text has been edited by Ussani 1932.

Pertinent here is the fact that there was another Latin version of the *B.I.* produced after the Hegesippus version and before Cassiodorus wrote his *Institutiones* around 550. Cassiodorus was not sure who did the translation (perhaps Jerome, Ambrose, or Rufinus) but he considered it a first-rate job (*Inst.* 1.17.1, Mynors 1937). This version is in seven books, just as Josephus's is, and is a fairly close translation of the Greek. Later in the Middle Ages, manuscripts usually ascribed this version to Rufinus (345–410), a well-known translator of a number of Greek works, but the actual translator is unknown. This Latin version of the *B.I.* is nowadays referred to as that of Pseudo-Rufinus or simply the Latin Josephus, a designation that extends and is properly applied to the Latin translation of Josephus's *Jewish Antiquities* and the *Contra Apionem*, which was made under Cassiodorus's direction as he says in the same passage mentioned above. To add to the confusion, Rufinus's name, already attached to the Latin version of the *B.I.*, also became associated with Cassiodorus's translations in fifteenth-century manuscripts

The Latin Josephus, comprising the Pseudo-Rufinus version of the *B.I.* and the Cassiodoran translation of the *Antiquities* and the *Contra Apionem*, has not, until rather recently, received any critical attention since Froben published his edition at Basel in 1524. In 1898, Boysen published a critical edition of the *Contra Apionem;* and in 1958 Blatt began to publish his critical edition of the *Antiquities;* the Latin version of the *B.I.* still awaits a modern edition, being available only in rare editions such as Froben's.

Petrarch's high regard for Josephus has been extensively documented by de Nolhac (1907.2:152–156), Sabbadini 1905.1:28 and 2:264, and Ussani (1943–44.447–467). Petrarch, for example, owned a manuscript containing the first eleven books of the *Antiquities* and the two books of the *Contra Apionem* (now in Paris at the Bibliothèque Nationale, Lat. 5054, one of the 171 manuscripts considered by Blatt for his edition). The numerous marginal notes in this manuscript in Petrarch's own hand show how carefully he had read the text.

In assessing Petrarch's knowledge of the *B.I.*, de Nolhac simply cites several passages in Petrarch's work and declares that they are derived from Hegesippus's version. Ussani, however, in a much more analytic study, is able to adduce a passage from Petrarch's *Rerum memorandarum libri* which is undoubtedly based on the Pseudo-Rufinus version. This passage will be discussed below in the note to lines 537–540, which refer to the same passage in the *B.I.* as the one in the *Rerum memorandarum* discussed by Ussani. Having proved Petrarch's knowledge of the Pseudo-Rufinus version from this passage and one other that de Nolhac believed was derived from the Hegesippus version, Ussani too quickly concludes that Petrarch knew only the Pseudo-Rufinus version. Here it is sufficient to note that Ussani (and de Nolhac) has overlooked this passage in the *Itinerarium*. In view of the fact that Petrarch here expressly identifies Hegesippus as his source, it is impossible to avoid the conclusion that Petrarch knew both Latin versions of the *B.I.* The testimony of Petrarch's revised version of his *Triumphus Fame* (III), first published in 1950 (for text and brief discussion see *Rime*, 577), points unambiguously to the same conclusion:

> e in ciò sembiante il veritiero ebreo
> Iosefo ed Egesippo, in cinque libri
> che poi l' istoria sua più breve feo (103–105).

The statement for which Petrarch here names Hegesippus as an authority further confirms Petrarch's firsthand knowledge of Hegesippus: *Antiochiam Syrie primam ac metropolim haberi*. The corresponding phrasing in Hegesippus is: *urbs ea* [sc. Antiochia] *Syriae sine retractione prima ideoque metropolis habetur* (3.5.2 = 3.29 of Josephus's Greek). Both statements are brief and simple, but it should be noted that the selection of syntax (if Petrarch's statement is transposed into direct discourse), vocabulary, and word order is almost identical. Josephus's (and therefore Pseudo-Rufinus's) original statement is somewhat different: it says that Antioch is the metropolis of Syria and without doubt deserves its ranking as third greatest city in the world (sc., after Rome and Alexandria). Petrarch is saying that Damascus is the foremost city of Syria; Hegesippus provides him with a simple contradictory statement to be rejected. But see fuller discussion in Gazetteer s.v. Syria.

500 Iosephum secutus: this phrase indicates that Petrarch considered Hegesippus's version so different from Josephus's account as he knew it in the Pseudo-Rufinus translation that Hegesippus deserved to be counted almost as an independent authority, however reliant on Josephus. In this regard, Petrarch does not differ from a number of other medieval writers who considered Josephus and Hegesippus as separate authorities, e.g., Otto von Freising (d. 1158) and Radulfus de Diceto (d. 1202); see Schreckenberg 1972.145 and 154 for brief discussions. In his *Speculum historiale,* Vincent of Beauvais (d. 1264) names Hegesippus, not Josephus, as his source for the capture of Jerusalem (Stanford 1935.136). Comparing Hegesippus's reliance on Josephus to Livy's relationship to Polybius, a recent dissertation argues that Hegesippus deserves to be considered an historian in his own right (Bell 1977). See also Feldman 1984.40–43.

501 Videbis civitatem et forma spectabilem et etate: seventy miles from its port at Beirut and bordered on three sides by desert and on the west by the mountains of Lebanon, Damascus nevertheless flourished owing to the river Abana, which flows from the heights of the Anti-Lebanon onto the plain, making the whole area a teeming oasis (al-Ghuta), and from there into the city (population about 100,000 at this time). Christians (some at any rate) believed that Abraham's servant founded the city and gave his own name to it; the city is near the place where Cain killed Abel (Gen. 4:8) and near the place where Paul was converted (Acts 9:1–5). As the Mamluk capital in Asia (controlled by the Sultan in Cairo), Damascus received loving attention from Saif al-Din Tankiz, viceroy from 1313–1340, who tried to beautify it in every way possible. Jerusalem, by contrast, with a population of about 10,000, had little commercial or administrative importance (Ziadeh 1953.97). Niccolò da Poggibonsi, who visited Damascus in 1348, gives an enthusiastic description of the city's wealth and beauty (Bacchi della Lega 1945.1:90–91). He is particularly impressed by the fact that one could buy good food in the streets any time it was desired.

504 Si infra magis applicueris: if Mandelli decides not to visit Damascus, he would disembark at Jaffa (Tel Aviv), the principal port of Palestine at this time, even though the harbor may have been largely blocked up. The trip from Jaffa to Jerusalem is forty miles, about a two days' journey.

506 Ierosolima: the Septuagint form of the city's name, followed by Jerome in his Latin Version, is the indeclinable *Ierusalem*. In the later extra-canonical books such as 1 Esdras and 1–4 Maccabees, and in the New Testament, the strange *Hierosolyma* or *Ierosolyma* is introduced: it is sometimes a declinable neuter plural and sometimes a declinable feminine singular (see Rahlfs 1935, notes on 1 Esd. 1:47 and 1 Macc. 1:20). It is quite possible that the form of the Hellenistic *Ierosolyma* had its origin in the phrase *(h)ieron Solomonos*, the assumed Greek etymology of the city's name, meaning the "Temple of Solomon"; see Eupolemus, a Palestinian Jew writing c. 160 BC (Jacoby 1958.III. C.2, 723.F.2.11):

> προσαγορευθῆναι δὲ τὸ ἀνάκτορον πρῶτον μὲν ἱερὸν Σολομῶνος, ὕστερον δὲ παρεφθαρμένως τὴν πόλιν ἀπὸ τοῦ ἱεροῦ Ἱερουσαλὴμ ὀνομασθῆναι, ὑπὸ δὲ τῶν Ἑλλήνων φερωνύμως Ἱεροσόλυμα λέγεσθαι.

> The shrine (they say) was first called the "Temple of Solomon"; later, by way of corruption, the city [Salem] was named "Hierusalem" from the Temple [hieron], but is eponymously [pheronumos] called "Hierosolyma" by the Greeks [i.e., the Greeks have assimilated Salem to Solomon's name].

Lactantius (*Div. Instit.* 4.13, Brandt 1890) also connects the city's name with Solomon's; Josephus (*Ant.* 7.3.2; *B.I.* 6.10.3; and *Apion* 1.22) connects the first part of the name with *hieron* (temple), although he is doubtful about the last part. Tacitus (*Hist.* 5.2) connects the last part of the name with a people called Solymi (from Lycia), who he says founded the city, as do other ancient authors. The normal Septuagint form *Ierusalem* and the late Hellenistic *Ierosolyma* frequently stand side by side in the New Testament as in Luke 2:41–43 (Vulgate). Petrarch's practice follows what he observed in the Vulgate; he uses the two forms of the city's name side by side with apparent indifference, *Ierosolima* always as a declinable feminine singular. Petrarch also considered the indeclinable form *Ierusalem* as a feminine singular (*ipsa Ierusalem,* line 495 above; cf. *De vita solitaria,* 2.9, 492 and 498 in *Prose).*

511–513 finis rerum . . . in intentione primus est: cf. Thomas Aquinas, *Quaestiones quodlibetales* (Parma, 1859), *quodl.* 8, *quaest.* 1, *art.* 2, *ad* 1 (ed. crit. 575a): *Ad primum ergo dicendum quod id quod est primum in intentione, est ultimum in executione.* On the importance of the doctrine of intention in medieval ethical theory, see Gilson 1936.343–363. Much ethical controversy lay behind Isabella's plea on behalf of the wicked Angelo in Shakespeare's *Measure for Measure* (Act 5, sc. 1, 450–454):

For Angelo,
His act did not o'ertake his bad intent,
And must be buried but as an intent
That perish'd by the way. Thoughts are no subjects,
Intents but merely thoughts.

503–520: Petrarch quickly and in no particular order lists some places in and around Jerusalem that Mandelli will be sure to visit. The style of this swift summary seems to be modeled after Augustine, *De civ. Dei,* 10.8. For an idea of what the Christian pilgrim of the fourteenth century saw there, or thought he saw, see the widely available accounts written by Burchard of Mt. Sion (AD 1280), Marino Sanudo (1321), and Ludolph von Suchem (1350), all translated by Stewart 1895–96. For a modern account of the monuments at the various sites mentioned by Petrarch, see Wilkinson 1977, Taylor 1993, and Murphy-O'Connor 1998. Wilkinson's Gazetteer summarizes and evaluates all the Byzantine reports of the various sites.

Petrarch betrays no knowledge of what he thinks is actually to be seen at the various places he mentions, basing his remarks almost entirely on the Scriptures or tradition. Whatever else a pilgrim had on his list of things to see, the most important of all was unquestionably the Tomb of Christ (*que iustior peregrinatio quam ad sepulcrum* . . . line 13 above), enclosing which was the church of the Holy Sepulcher, completed by the crusaders in c. 1168 (see Boase 1977.4:74–84).

Usually the pilgrim made two visits to the church, once for an all night vigil, during which a Franciscan friar of Mt. Sion efficiently organized his activities. As to the other sites, there was a regular circuit of places to be visited, each place clearly marked by a "T" or a "P" to indicate that a visit to the site provided a temporal or plenary indulgence to those "vere penitentibus et confessis" (for a handy summary of indulgences associated with various sites see Bacchi della Lega 1945.1:xliv–l). Side trips to Bethlehem and to the River Jordan (and the Dead Sea) were common. The trip to Bethlehem was a three-day excursion, but the trip to the Jordan (about fifty-five miles round trip) was rather a more serious matter, usually requiring a military escort, since the route lay through an area infested with robbers. The pace there and back was fast (best to keep moving), and the whole trip was completed in only two or three days. If Mandelli's group traveled to the Sinai and Egypt, it certainly would have hired an armed escort.

In general, the guides hurried the pilgrims right along (even as they do today), so that the pilgrim saw what he came to see in a short time. Giacomo da Verona, on a pilgrimage made in 1335, followed pretty much the itinerary recommended by Petrarch for Mandelli (including a trip through Galilee and a visit to Damascus), yet he completed his tour in the Holy Land in a little over two months (a quick trip indeed: such a land tour might take up to three months). For bibliography and discussion of Giacomo's trip see Savage 1977.4:58, n. 61 and 59–60; see also 54–57; see also Prawer 1972.192–213. The places mentioned by Petrarch are:

1. *amnem quo lotus est Cristus:* The traditional site for Christ's baptism is Bethany-beyond-Jordan, about 25 miles east of the city.

2. *templum seu ruinas in quo docuit*: Luke 2:40–52. Josephus (*B.I.* 6.249–267) describes the destruction of the temple by the Romans in AD 70.
3. *locum ubi . . . passus est corpore:* Jesus was crucified at a place resembling a skull (John 19:17); the traditional site of Golgotha is a short distance away from Jesus's place of burial.
4. *sepulchrum ubi . . . corpus . . . ad regna hostis spolianda descenderet . . . unde resurrexit:* Golgotha is the place of the Crucifixion and the Resurrection (John 19:41–42). Early and medieval Christians were heavily influenced by non-Christian views of the underworld or the land of departed dead in their interpretation of Christ's Descent into Hell. See Patch 1950, Clark 1969. 300–307, Campbell 1982.107–158, and Morgan 1990; for the influence of these pagan views on Petrarch see especially Feo 1974.159–171; on this passage in the *Itinerarium* see 164 n.2. Petrarch's ideas about Hell were no doubt colored by the vivid portrayals of Judgment and Hell, which he had seen on the vault of the Florence Cathedral's baptistery and on Giotto's entry wall to the Scrovegni family's "Arena Chapel" in Padua (Rothschild 1928.31–35). There were similar scenes in the cathedral at Torcello (near Venice) and in Sant' Anastasia in Verona which he had probably seen as well.
5. *Syon:* According to 2 Sam. 5:7 Sion (Zion of the Old Testament) was the stronghold David took for his city. Much confusion about Sion has prevailed through the centuries because there are two strongholds close together, divided by a rift called the Valley of Tyropoeon. Modern excavation shows that the smaller, less elevated eastern hill was David's citadel but Christian tradition has always considered it to be the larger and higher western hill. Sion was believed to be the place where the Last Supper took place; where Jesus was scourged at Caiaphas's house; where the Holy Spirit

came upon the Apostles (Pentecost); the place where Mary lived with John after Jesus's death until she "fell asleep"; the place where James was beheaded by Herod, and where Stephen was stoned to death. There is little or no scriptural evidence for locating any of these events on Sion, but long before Petrarch's time all these traditions were well established.

6. *Oliveti Montem; ad hec . . . reversus creditur:* The Mount of Olives, about a half mile east of the city, was where it was believed that Christ taught His Apostles the Lord's Prayer; where He suffered the agony in the Garden of Gethsemane; and where Mary was buried. Above all, it was on or very near to the Mount of Olives where Christ ascended into heaven (Luke 24:50–52 and Acts 1:9–12) and the place or some place very near to it where the Last Judgment would take place (Joel 3:2,12; Zech. 14), with Christ as Judge (Acts 1:11). The Judgment is generally associated with the Valley of Jehoshaphat, now known as Kidron Valley, because "Jehoshaphat" means "Yahweh has judged." Cf. Thomas Aquinas (*Summa theol*, III *Suppl.* q.88, art. 4): *probabiliter potest colligi ex Scripturis, quod circa locum montis Oliveti descendet, sicut et inde ascendit ut idem esse ostendatur qui descendit et qui ascendit.*
7. *ubi ventis et fluctibus imperavit*: The Sea of Galilee, about 65 miles north of Jerusalem: Matt. 8:23–27, Mark 4:35–41, and Luke 8:22–25.
8. *ubi cibo exiguo maximam turbam pavit:* The feeding of the five thousand took place on the NE shore of the Sea of Galilee: Matt. 14:13–21, Mark 6:31–44, and Luke 9:10–17, and John 6:1–5. Matt. 15:29–39, Mark 8:1–9 tell of a second feeding of the multitudes.
9. *ubi aquam vertit in vinum:* Cana was about 12 miles west of the Sea of Galilee and about 8 north of Nazareth (John 2:1–11).

10. *ubi denique elegit indoctos:* Jesus called the Twelve Apostles to service near Capharnaum on the NW shore of the Sea of Galilee (Matt. 10:1–4).
11. *ubi cecos illuminavit:* Matt. 9:27–31; Mark 8:22–26; Luke 18:35–43; John 9:1–7.
12. *leprosos mundavit:* Matt. 8:1–4, Mark 1:40–44; Luke 5: 12–14.
13. *paraliticos erexit*: Matt. 9:1–8, Mark 2:1–12, Luke 5:17–26.
14. *mortuos suscitavit*: Matt. 9:20–26; Mark 5:21–43; Luke 8: 40–56; John 11:1–43 (Lazarus).
15. *demonibus ac peccatis oppressam sepultamque animam restituit libertati:* Matt. 9:32–33; Mark 9:17–29; Luke 11:14.

537–540 Titus . . . fateretur: this passage is an abbreviated paraphrase of a passage in Pseudo-Rufinus's version (= 6.409–411 of Josephus's Greek), which runs as follows: Intro autem Titus *ingressus* et alia et civitatis munitiones ac turrium causas *miratus est* quas tyranni per dementiam deseruerunt. Conspecta quidem earum solida altitudine itemque magnitudine subtilique lapidum *compagine* singulorum quantumque paterent uel quantum erigerentur: *deo inquit plane adiuuante pugnauimus*: et deus erat qui *detraxit ab istis munimentis* iudaeos. *Nam quae hominum manus* aut quae machinae *ad istas ualerent?* (quoted from Ussani 1943 cited above, who is using Peter Maufer's edition of the Latin Josephus published at Verona in 1480). Certain phrases have been italicized for ease of comparison with the passage quoted below.

Ussani has demonstrated (1943.462) from a passage in book three of Petrarch's *Rerum memorandarum libri*, which shows many verbal and structural resemblances to this Pseudo-Rufinus text, that Petrarch knew Josephus in this version. For the sake of convenient comparison, this Petrarchan text will be quoted from Ussani's article, which cites the *Rerum memorandarum* from page 491 of the 1554 Basel edition of Petrarch's works: Ierosolimam victor *ingrediens*, et murorum *compaginem* turresque et propugnacula urbis *admirans, vere, inquit, deo iuuante pugnavimus. Deus ipse ab his menibus* hostes nostros *depulit. quid enim aduersus hec manus mortalium ualuisset? (Rerum mem.* 3.37.1; Billanovich 1943.127–128).

There can be no doubt that Petrarch had Pseudo-Rufinus's text ready to hand when he wrote this passage because there is no such passage corresponding to Josephus's Greek in Hegesippus's eclectic version. Ussani justly concludes, "non credo impossibile spigolare nella vasta opera del Petrarca qualche altro passo che porti così evidente l'impronta della dipendenza della versione semiletterale [i.e., the Pseudo-Rufinus version] del *Bellum,*" 1943. 462.

Ussani was not aware of the abbreviated and paraphrased version in the *Itinerarium,* but it too is clearly dependent on Pseudo-Rufinus's version.

540–542 Cristus . . . adversus suos hostes suis merito favebat ultoribus: the notion that Christ exacted punishment from the Jews through the agency of Vespasian and Titus was a commonplace of Christian historiography and apologetics. For sentiments similar to those here expressed by Petrarch, see the examples in Schreckenberg 1972.68–171 and Schreckenberg 1977.27–53. In both these works Schreckenberg, proceeding author by author from antiquity through the sixteenth century, lists citations and borrowings from Josephus, as well as ideas inspired by Josephus's text. Petrarch's statement, which Schreckenberg does not mention, has striking parallels in authors as widely separated in time and place as Paulus Orosius (fl. 420), the African mythographer Fulgentius (d. ca. 532), Frechulph of Lisieux (d. 852), Peter of Blois (d. 1212), and Sicard of Cremona (d. 1215). To cite several brief examples, Fulgentius says, "Nam Vespasianus . . . quem suae Christus iniuriae elegerat vindicem . . . " cited in 1977. 31; Sicard of Cremona says, "post XL annum Dominus Vespasianum et Titum Hierusalem adduxit, qui ipsam civitatem funditus destruxerunt," cited in 1972.156. The idea that Vespasian and Titus destroyed Jerusalem as agents of God's will is naturally a Christian inference from Josephus's report of Titus's statement in lines 539–540 that the city was taken by the grace of God, not the courage of his troops. Petrarch had planned for some time to conclude his *De viris illustribus* with a *Life of Titus (Secretum,* 192 in

Prose). Cf. Dante, *Purg.* 21.82–85 and *Par.* 6.92–93 and 7.19–51. Dante is following Orosius 7.3.8 and 7.9.9, the first to record the idea of Titus as Christ's agent of revenge.

542 licet adhuc illis incognitus: Petrarch rather pointedly adds that Vespasian and Titus were unwitting agents of retribution against the Jews. He may have been aiming this comment at two versions, widely circulated and likely to have been known to him, which make the two Romans (Christian contrary to historical fact) set out purposely to destroy the enemies of Jesus. In the first, Titus is cured of a disfiguring cancer of the face through faith in Jesus. He then summons Vespasian to help him destroy the Jews for their iniquitous treatment of the Savior. In the second version, Vespasian is relieved of a bizarre affliction (from his childhood wasps [vespae] have been nesting in Vespasian's nose) again through faith in Jesus and then leads Titus to destroy Jerusalem. The first story, perhaps dating to the seventh or eighth century, is called the *Vindicta Salvatoris* (the Avenging of the Savior); the Latin text may be found in von Tischendorf (1876.471–486). The second version constitutes chapter 67 of Jacopo da Voragine's *Golden Legend* (Graesse 1890.297–303). A detailed summary of both versions, considerably more complicated than the brief descriptions above indicate, is available in James 1924.159–161. See also Schreckenberg's discussion of both versions in 1977.53–68, with additional material on the theme of the *Vindicta Salvatoris* in Latin as well as the vernacular languages. Often the theme received poetic treatment on an epic scale, as in *La Venjance Nostre Seigneur*, a work of over 3,400 lines in its longest form; see Gryting 1952.

Petrarch stresses the fact that Titus is Christ's unwitting avenger also in his *Invectiva contra eum qui maledixit Italie* (written in 1373): *nec tantum apostolorum et martirum, sed sui proprii sanguinis, quamvis ignarum rei, romanum tamen ultorem sibi Cristus elegit* (778 in *Prose*). At *Africa*, 2.271–273, Petrarch alludes to Vespasian and Titus as destroyers of Jerusalem and punishers of the Jews. Nothing is said about their intentions.

543–547 Itaque . . . Iosephum lege: as Lumbroso has noted in his edition of the *Itinerarium*, Petrarch had already expressed himself in a similar vein in the first book of his *De otio religioso,* written in 1347 (Rotondi 1958.23). Both Petrarchan passages are based on Josephus 6.193 ff. (present in both Latin versions), a passage that culminates in the famous story of Mary, daughter of Eleazar, who was driven by hunger to eat her own child (6.201–213). The story was so famous that Dante needed only to allude to it at *Purgatorio,* 23.30. The quotation from the *Psalms* is at 41:11 (40:11 of the Vulgate; Gryson 1994).

547–548 non audita sed visa . . . referentem: Josephus, in command of the Jewish forces of Galilee early in the Jewish revolt, was captured in 67 when the Romans took Jotapata (*B.I.* 3.141 ff.; present in both Latin versions). He saved his life by prophesying that Vespasian would become emperor (3.400–401; a famous passage in the Middle Ages, which Hegesippus omits). When the prediction came true in 69, Josephus was given his freedom (4. 623–629; a passage also omitted by Hegesippus). Josephus then stayed with Titus until the fall of Jerusalem, a witness to all the events about which he wrote.

549 Quid vero nunc cogitas?: here begins an extended passage (to line 558) which uses Ulysses as an *exemplum* of *virtus* to urge Mandelli to continue his journey into the Sinai and Egypt. Feo (1977.383–388) sees in Petrarch's Ulysses an affinity to Dante's character in *Inf.* 26. This is fair enough, but Petrarch goes on to use several more *exempla* in his exhortation, drawn from Virgil, Lucan and above all from the Bible (see Introduction). The quest for new knowledge was part of the pilgrimage from the very beginning (que ad notitiam rerum et ingenii ornamentum . . . pertinere videbuntur explicem, lines 74–76), but only a part. For the other parts the Holy Family, Aeneas, Cato, Moses, and even Lot's wife are offered as appropriate exemplars.

554–555 non voluptatum modo sed honestorum pignorum atque affectuum: in view of the references to Penelope, Telemachus, and Laertes below, it is best to take the abstract nouns *voluptates, pignora,* and *affectus* in the concrete sense they often carry in the plural. In line 573 Petrarch uses *pignus* to refer to the Christ child. See Feo (1977.384–385) on this passage.

559–561 Bethleem civitatem David, quam celesti ortu claram fore divini vates . . . cecinerant: Micah 5:2, paraphrased in Matt. 2:5–6; also Isa. 7:14, 9:6–7, and 11:1–8. Petrarch is also thinking of the apocryphal prophecies of the Erythraean Sibyl, contained in the *Liber Erithree Sibille,* which he owned (de Nolhac 1907.1:205). For his use of this book in a similar context, see *De otio religioso* (Rotondi 1958.27–29). The manuscript owned by Petrarch (Par. lat. 8500) only contained a rather brief selection of the oracles, but it included the all-important description of Christ's birth at Bethlehem (*SibOr* 8.456–479); see Petrarch's own description of the contents in *Rerum mem.* 4.30.7 (Billanovich 1943.211). Cf. Augustine, *De civ. Dei,* 18.30 on Micah's prophecy and 18.23 on the preeminence of the Erythraean Sibyl's prophecies concerning Christ; see also Virgil, *Ecl.* 4.4–9 and *A.* 6.792–800 on the birth of the Divine Child, texts commonly interpreted as referring to the birth of Christ. On the Sibyls in general (ten of them), see Lactantius, *Div. Instit.* 1.6.8–12, a text (based on Varro) Petrarch had read carefully, Rzach 1923, and Parke 1988. For an account of some of the anonymous Latin verse translations and prose paraphrases of the Sibylline oracles circulating during the Middle Ages, see Bischoff 1966.150–171. For their great influence on the religious and social life of the period, see Reeves 1969 and McGinn 1973. The original Greek should be consulted in Geffcken 1902.

Bethlehem, the place of David's birth (1 Sam. 16), is about five miles south of Jerusalem. Luke (2:17) says that Mary laid the child in a manger because there was no room in the inn. From very early times, there was the tradition that the place of Jesus's birth was in a cave or grotto (Finegan 1992.22–43, with photographs). It was over this grotto that the emperor Constantine built the Church of the Nativity (dedicated by his mother St. Helena in 339). At the eastern end of the basilica, an elevated octagonal structure was built over the grotto, through the roof of which an opening (oculus) was made to allow pilgrims to look upon the very place where Jesus was born. After 529, Justinian replaced the basilica of the fourth century with a structure larger than but after the plan of the earlier one, though pilgrims could no longer look down into the cave from above. This building, though battered, remains in use to this day. The Holy Innocents were believed to have been buried in a nearby grotto. In yet another nearby grotto, St. Jerome took up residence in 384 to work on his new translation of the Old and New Testaments (the Vulgate).

564–566 ante principium genitus, in fine temporum, si ad etatum numerum attenditur, natus est: when Petrarch refers to the number of ages, he alludes to the commonplace notion of the Six Ages of the World as a reflection of the six days of creation, a doctrine prescribed for the Middle Ages by Augustine (in *De civ. Dei* 22.30 and elsewhere). The notion was taken up by Isidore (*Etym.* 5.38.1–6) and Bede who refer to the doctrine frequently (as in *De temporum ratione, De temporibus,* and *Epistola ad Pleguinam de aetatibus saeculi*). The first age extends from Adam to Noah, the second from Noah to Abraham, the third from Abraham to David, the fourth from David to the Babylonian Captivity, the fifth from Babylon to the birth of Christ. The sixth age is the Christian era, which consists of no set period but will be wiped out with the death of the secular world. So it is that Christ can be said to have been born at the end of time (in fine temporum), an expression that has its origin in the New Testament (2 Petr. 3:3, 1 Tim. 4:1, etc.; cf. Boethius, *De fide cath.* 193 in Stewart and Rand 1918: *in ultimis temporibus . . . unigenitum suum deus per virginem nasci constituit*). Such periodization of history was also a characteristic of the pagan Sibyls, as in the *ultima aetas* of Virgil's Cumaean Sibyl (*Ecl.* 4.4), or in the ὑστατίοις . . . χρόνοις of the Sibylline oracles (*SibOr* 8.456), which is the exact Greek equivalent of Boethius's *in ultimis temporibus*.

These Six Ages of the World are often made to correspond to the biological progress of the individual person from birth to old age. By this reckoning, the sixth age corresponds to the individual's senility and impending death. Under the influence of Claudius Ptolemy (*Tetrabiblos*, 4.10. 204–207; text in Robbins 1940), the idea that there were seven ages of man had prevailed by the fourth century, as may be seen in Prudentius's *praefatio* to his poems (Cunningham 1966.1–2). Naturally, there was a tendency to harmonize the ages of the world and of man, whatever their number. See for example Fulgentius's *De etatibus mundi et hominis*

(Helm 1898.129–179), a strange lipogrammatic effort, where the number of ages, both of the world and of man, is extended beyond the number seven to twelve, to correspond to the twelve books of the *Aeneid*.

565–571 Virginem matrem . . . mestis resonans celum omne gemitibus: Petrarch summarizes the story of the nativity (Matt. 2:1–12 and Luke 2:1–20) and the Killing of the Innocents (Matt. 2:16–18). As Lo Monaco points out (1990.116), this long sentence is closely modeled on a section from St. Jerome's letter to Eustochium (*Ep.* 108.10.2; text and Latin commentary in Stummer 1935.27–49).

571–574 inter hec, monitu angelico . . . ad populum gentium esse venturam: the story of the Flight into Egypt is told by Matt. (2:13–15). For the idea that the Gentiles succeeded the Jews as the heirs to God's kingdom, see Gal. 3:27–29; Eph. 3:1–11; Rom. 11:11–12, etc.

581–582 non longe hinc mare quod Sodomorum dicitur: the earliest biblical designation for this body of water is the Salt Sea (Gen. 14:3; Vulgate: *Mare Salis)*. Its common name among classical authors is *Asphaltitis Lacus* (Asphalt Lake). The name best known in medieval times and adopted on the authority of Justin (36.3.6) is *Mortuum Mare* or the Dead Sea. The name Petrarch gives the body of water (Sea of Sodom) is difficult to find in literary texts, but the sea is so named on some portolan charts of this period such as that of Angelino Dalorto (Hinks 1929. sheet 4). He calls it so again at *Fam.* 10.4.29: *Iordanis . . . qui quidem in mare Sodomorum fertur descendere.* Its Arabic name today is Bahret Lut, "Sea of Lot."

The reference to Sodom would inevitably recall to Mandelli the story of Lot's wife and the pillar of salt. He would then doubtless remember the moral so commonly drawn from her example in the Middle Ages: do not look back as you travel the road to salvation (e.g., Augustine, *De civ. Dei*, 10.8.10–16). Petrarch has just been urging him not to think about returning home (looking back) before he has made the difficult journey to Egypt. For a discussion of the story of Lot's wife in the Middle Ages, with special reference to Dante, see Spillenger 1991.241–168. The *exemplum* of

Lot's wife is unspoken, but a pious pilgrim such as Mandelli would hear it loud and clear. As often in Petrarch, silence is more eloquent than the spoken word. Though Petrarch leaves the moral unspoken here, he draws it out at considerable length for the benefit of Pope Urban V. In a letter written in 1367–68, he praises the Pope for bringing the Curia back to Rome and urges him not to look back to Avignon (*Sen*. 9.1; *Opera* 2:941). The *exempla* are Lot's wife and Orpheus, who lost Eurydice by looking back.

Many pilgrims of the fourteenth century, such as Ludolph von Suchem and Burchard of Mount Sion (Stewart 1885.117–118 and 1896.59), report seeing the pillar of salt, which they believe had been Lot's wife. They were encouraged to believe that a pillar of salt could have survived several thousand years because the historian Josephus (*Antiq*. 1.11.4) reported having seen it himself. If the pillar of salt could have survived from the time of Abraham to the time of Christ, they had no doubt that it could survive to their own time. For more pilgrim reports from the earlier period, see Wilkinson 1977.164

582–583 ubi consumptarum urbium vindicteque celestis vestigia apparent: the cities of Sodom, Gomorrah, Admah, and Zeboim were destroyed by burning sulfur (Gen. 19:23–26). The remains of these cities were probably pointed out to visitors in the time of the Apostles (2 Petr. 2:6 and Josephus *B.I.* 4.483–485), as they certainly were to Christian pilgrims in later times; see, for example, the testimony of Ludolf von Suchem (Stewart 1895.116–118). The "remains" of the cities were probably stones blackened by desert varnish and common in the area.

591–592 Vicit iter durum pietas: these are among Anchises's first words of greeting to his son Aeneas in the underworld (*A*. 6.687–688). Petrarch often quotes them in his letters.

592–593 Durum iter ad leges animeque ruentis amorem: this is a paraphrase of Lucan, 9.385: *Durum iter ad leges patriaeque ruentis amorem*. The line comes from a speech of Cato's in which he exhorts his followers to make the difficult march across the desert of North Africa. Petrarch casts himself in Cato's role and urges Mandelli to make the journey to Egypt. The paraphrase was apparently intended to mean that the sinful (ruentis) soul (Petrarch substitutes *anima* for *patria*) must win God's love by undertaking arduous tasks. But Petrarch's adoption of Lucan's brevity of expression leaves precise interpretation open to doubt.

594–598 Equidem si per Syrtes Lybicas . . . sevitiam Pharaonis: Petrarch's argument is *a fortiori*. If Cato and his men could endure such hardships (the Syrtes and Libya's serpents: Lucan, 9.294–937) in their struggle against Julius Caesar, who might easily let them off with slight penalties for resisting his control, how much more determined should be Mandelli's struggle to avoid the power of Satan, who would never show any mercy. To avoid the cruelty of the Pharaoh (Exod. 1), the Israelites (with all their weak and infirm) were strong enough to make (in reverse) the same journey that Petrarch is urging upon Mandelli. But Satan is crueler than any Pharaoh.

Syrtes is the name given to two bays on the north coast of Africa, one between modern Tripoli and Benghazi, the other between Tripoli and Tunis. They were proverbial in antiquity for being almost unnavigable (Mela, 1.7; Pliny, *Nat.* 5.26; Lucan, 9. 294–347.) Today, the larger bay (Syrtis Maior) is called the Gulf of Sidra, and the smaller the Gulf of Gabès.

600–603 His autem locis . . . tecum volves: Petrarch quickly and somewhat haphazardly summarizes some major events in the Book of Exodus: *legem datam* (20:1–7); *colloquium cum deo habitum* (20–31); *visionem rubi* (3:1–4); *delapsum celo manna* (16); *ceteras . . . blanditias* (e.g., the waters of Meribah, 17:1–7); *divina iudicia* (presumably for worshipping the Golden Calf, 32). This section is closely modeled on Augustine *De civ. Dei* 10.8 in style and content (cf. above note to 515–532).

603–604 quod proprie a poeta non Mare sed Litus Rubrum dictum est: cf. Virgil (*A.* 8. 685–688):

> hinc ope barbarica uariisque Antonius armis,
> uictor ab Aurorae populis et *litore rubro*,
> Aegyptum uirisque Orientis et ultima secum
> Bactra uehit, sequiturque (nefas) Aegyptia coniunx.

Among the Romans, the term Red Sea (Rubrum Mare) need not refer to the gulf now known to us by that name. Pliny, for example, sometimes used the term to refer to the Persian Gulf (*Nat.* 6.137; so also Quintus Curtius, 5.1.10), using the term *Sinus Arabicus* to designate our Red Sea (Pliny, 6.164). At other times, however, Pliny inconsistently used the term to refer to the Red Sea (6.197). Other authors extended the term to mean the Indian Ocean, including the Persian and Arabian Gulfs, as in the Virgilian passage to which Petrarch alludes (cf. also Horace *C.* 1.35.32). Petrarch's use of the term is unambiguous: it refers to the extension of the *Sinus Arabicus,* now known as the Gulf of Suez, where the Jews are supposed to have crossed over to the Sinai peninsula. *Mappaemundi* and portolan charts of Petrarch's time, if they were at all colored, habitually portrayed the area of the Red Sea in the appropriate color (see Harvey 1987.1:326, 393). To this Petrarch objects. Possibly too he is invoking Virgil's *litus rubrum* in silent criticism of Lucan's *mare discolor unda* (8.293), which description however clearly refers to the Indian Ocean and the Persian Gulf, not the Arabian Gulf. Undoubtedly Petrarch is aiming some criticism at Isidore (*Etym.* 13.17.2):

> Rubrum autem mare vocatum eo quod sit roseis undis infectum; non tamen talem naturam habet qualem videtur ostendere, sed vicinis litoribus vitiatur gurges atque inficitur; quia omnis terra, quae circumstat pelago, rubra est et sanguineo colori proxima.

Isidore, Petrarch would concede, got it at least partly right when he said that the sandy shores of the Red sea are red (the color of blood), but the water itself is not dyed red.

Pliny (*Nat.* 6.107), without committing himself, gives a nice round summary of ancient speculation on the origin of the Red Sea's name:

> Mare . . . quod Rubrum dixere nostri, Graeci Erythrum a rege Erythra, aut, ut alii, solis repercussu talem reddi existimantes colorem, alii ab harena terraque, alii tali aquae ipsius natura.

Modern scholars favor the name's derivation from the effect produced by a form of algae (Trichodesmium erythraeum), which on occasion gives a red color to the surface water (Weikert 1987.97). Henry Salt, one of the great freebooters of nineteenth-century Egyptology, provides a vivid description of the phenomenon (1814.195–196).

In the Sinai in late October of 1384 Lionardo Frescobaldi stood on a mountain top from which he could view the Red Sea about 15 miles away. The water looks blood-red, he reported, not because the water is not white and clear, but because the surrounding sand is bright red: *il Mare rosso . . . pare sangue a vedere; e non è perciò che l'acqua non sia blanca e chiara, ma è perchè l'arena è rossa come cinabro* (Angelini 1944.114). But at a distance of 15 miles how could Frescobaldi know the water was white and clear despite its appearance of redness? The obvious answer, that a local guide so informed him, may not be the correct one. Local guides founded their careers on telling Christian pilgrims tall tales about all kinds of things. Frescobaldi's description of the apparent color of the water as blood-red suggests that he was remembering his Isidore (sanguineo colori proxima), for Frescobaldi was a fairly well-educated man (*Lionardo s' è rivelato pian piano homo di lettere*, Angelini 1944.131 n.1), but he may be using some other literary authority to correct Isidore, possibly this passage from Petrarch's *Itinerarium* in the copy presumed to be in Guido del Pagalio's possession and hence available to him (see commentary on lines 630–637 below).

605–608 Quo cum perveneris . . . sicco pede, transvectum meditabere: Petrarch seems to be recalling Lucan's description (10.111–171) of the lavish banquet to which Cleopatra invited Caesar. Mandelli is not to think of such luxuries brought to Egypt by way of the Red Sea, but of the miracle wrought by God to bring his people to the Promised Land (Exod. 14).

610 Katherine Virginis corpus cernes: Catherine of Alexandria, a young woman of exceptional beauty and learning, was martyred according to legend for protesting Maxentius's persecution of Christians early in the fourth century. Before her death, she disputed so successfully with fifty philosophers who had been called to persuade her of the errors of Christianity, that they were executed for their poor showing. In the ninth century, her body is reported as being at the great monastery on Mt. Sinai, where it had been transported by angels.

Catherine enjoyed extraordinary popularity in the Middle Ages, being considered the patroness especially of scholars, although other details in her picturesque legend than the ones mentioned above made her also the patroness of young girls, nurses, and certain craftsmen. For many pilgrims a visit to Mt. Sinai and Catherine's monastery ranked in importance just below a visit to the Holy Sepulcher itself. In Alexandria, pilgrims were taken to see the prison where she was confined before her execution. Guides pointed out a small opening in a wall, through which they said angels brought her food (Niccolò da Martoni, Legrand 1895. 3:589). For information on the growth and scope of her cult, see da Ottone 1940. For more on the monastery, which was built by Justinian between 548 and 565 and dedicated originally to the Holy Virgin, see Forsyth and Weitzmann 1973.

There is evidence that Petrarch had a special devotion to St. Catherine. On the first guard leaf of his Virgil manuscript Petrarch recorded the death of his friend Giacobino de' Bossi. The entry notes that Petrarch learned of the death as he was leaving Sant' Ambrogio on a Saturday, 25 November 1357, after attending a mass in honor of St. Catherine (for text see de Nolhac 1907.2: 284). As he attended the service on this day Petrarch might well have been contemplating the possibility of a visit to Mt. Sinai as a member of Mandelli's party. The Collect of the Mass in honor of St. Catherine reads as follows (*MR* 1949.756):

> Deus, qui dedisti legem Moysi in summitate montis Sinai, et in eodem loco per sanctos Angelos tuos corpus beatae Catharinae Virginis et Martyris tuae mirabiliter collocasti: praesta, quaesumus; ut, ejus meritis et intercessione, ad montem, qui Christus est, pervenire valeamus.

This prayer was clearly in Petrarch's mind as he wrote this passage in the *Itinerarium.* The Holy See suppressed her Feast (25 November) in 1969.

613–614 Per hec loca formidabiles esse solent Arabum incursus: this is the only place where Petrarch expressly cautions Mandelli about danger — attacks from Arabs, thirst, hunger, etc. Nothing is more dangerous, he says, than getting separated from the group and losing one's way in the desert. It was just here in the Sinai that a member of Niccolò da Poggibonsi's group became separated and was never found despite the efforts of a party sent out to search for him (Bacchi della Lega 1945.1:122). The dangers to pilgrims were in fact many and great at every stage of their journey. Of the seven friars whom Niccolò counted as companions, all but one died along the way (Bacchi 1945.1:157).

Arabs, who are clearly distinguished from Saracens in most pilgrim texts, are Bedouins, nomadic folk of North Africa, Arabia, and Syria who live in the desert (see Lewis 1993.1–14 on etymology and meaning of the name). They were considered wild and very dangerous by pilgrims. Saracens were identified with the Ishmaelites of the Bible, descendants of Ishmael, the son of Abraham and the Egyptian Hagar, whom Sarah drove away after the birth of Isaac (Gen. 16:8). For this act Sarah's name forms part of the word "Saracen." As for the rest of the word, St. John of Damascus (*De haeresibus compendium* 101, *PG* 94, 764) says that Saracens are the descendants of Hagar, whom Sarah sent away empty, as if the word were Σάρρας κένοι (Bereft ones of Sarah = ones sent away empty-handed by Sarah). This Greek tradition was not unknown in the West, but Isidore only knew enough of it to connect the name with Sarah (*Etym.* 9.2.6). He apparently thought that the Saracens were falsely claiming to be the legitimate sons of Abraham. The name "Saracen" is often said to be derived from the Arabic Sharqiyin, "Easterner," but see O'Conner 1986.2:603–632, who reviews the evidence and concludes that it means something like "confederate" or "associate." For Islam as a heresy see Sahas 1972.

The Arabs against whom Petrarch warns Mandelli here are poor relations to the "learned" Arabs whom he himself fears in another way. He says he hates the lot of them (odi genus universum) because contemporary Italians have accorded their scientific and medical works excessive praise and respect. He goes so far as to say that he does not believe anything good could ever come from Arabia (*Sen*. 12.2; *Opera* 2:1009).

618 videbis Babilonem novam, Cambissis opus: the Babylon to which Petrarch refers was a fortress at the apex of the Delta, probably built by the Persian Cambyses in 525 BC. Petrarch's source of information was the Latin translation of Josephus's *Antiquities* (2.315) which he owned (see note to lines 498–499). In the margin next to this passage, Petrarch wrote a note to himself: *Babilon egyptia a Cambisse condita* (de Nolhac 1907.2:155; cf. Ussani's supplementary remarks 1943.451–452).

During Augustus's reign, one of the three Roman legions in Egypt was stationed at Babylon; and Trajan had the whole complex rebuilt. After the Arab Conquest of Egypt in the seventh century, the fortress lost its defensive utility and was taken over by Coptic Christians, who built several churches and cloisters within its precincts. Some parts of the Roman gates and towers still survive.

619 Carras Egiptias, frequentissimam urbem: Carrhae (*Carras assyrias* in line 620) was a town in the NW part of Mesopotamia. It was famous in Roman history as the place where the Parthians inflicted a disastrous defeat on Crassus in 53 BC (Florus, *Epit*, 1.46 = 3.11; Pliny, *Nat*. 5.85; Lucan, 1.103–106). By "Egyptian Carrhae" Petrarch means Cairo, which was founded in AD 969 by the Fatamids; the city's name is from the Arabic Al Qahirah, which means "the victorious." The mistaken association of Cairo's name with the Carrhae of Mesopotamia is based partly on the accidental similarity of the two names, and partly on Lucan's use of the phrase *Assyrias . . . Carrhas* (1.105), which can be interpreted as implying the existence of a Carrhae elsewhere. Many medieval writers call Cairo "Babylon" without any qualms (cf. Du Cange 1883, s.v. Babilonia).

When Petrarch calls Cairo a "frequentissimam urbem," he is touching on a theme found in most European accounts of the city in the fourteenth century (see Dopp 1950.117–149). Several scholars put the pre-plague population of Cairo between 600,000 and 500,000, though conservative estimates put it at about half that size. Even at the conservative number, Cairo was seven or eight times larger than London during this same period: see Raymond 1975.201–215. The primary reason for Cairo's large population was its favored position on the Red Sea/Nile spice route; it also became a place of refuge for thousands who were fleeing the advance of the Mongols in the late thirteenth century. The Black Death may have reduced the city's pre-plague population of perhaps a half million by 200,000 (Dols 1977.69).

621 Spectabis insignem Asie atque Africe limitem, adversum Tanai: the Nile fixes the boundary between Asia and Africa in the south; to the north the Tanais (the Don), opposite the Nile (cf. Lucan 9.413–414), fixes the boundary between Asia and Europe. Although his portolan chart showed him a much different view of the world, Petrarch here refers to the outline of the world as represented in a T-O map, in which the O represents the surrounding Ocean and the T represents the division among the three continents of the ancient geographers. Cf. Mela (1.1.8): *Hoc mari* [the Mediterranean] *et duobus inclutis amnibus, Tanai et Nilo, in tres partes universa dividitur,* and Pliny (*Nat.*3.3): *Terrarum orbis universus in tres dividitur partes, Europam Asiam Africam . . . termini amnes Tanais et Nilus.* See in the Budé series Pomponius Mela, Silberman 1988.100–102; Dilke 1985.173–174, 178–181; and for more detail Woodward 1987.1:286–370.

623–624 Aristotiles vero libro integro disseruit: Petrarch is here referring to a work whose existence is well attested in antiquity: the Alexandrian lexicographer Hesychius (fifth century AD) mentions it as a separate item in his catalogue of Aristotle's works and gives the title as Περὶ τῆς τοῦ Νείλου ἀναβάσεως, and a handful of later Greek authors, such as Strabo, paraphrase the book or make reference to it. Part of a collection of short essays called *Problemata,* this little work is considered pseudepigraphical by its first modern editor and datable to some time before Eratosthenes (d. 194 BC). Accepted as genuine during the Middle Ages, it was translated into Latin in the thirteenth century (title: *Liber Aristotelis de inundacione Nili)*: for the Latin text (the

Greek has been lost) see Rose 1886. frg. 248, 191–197 and Bonneau 1971.3–7; the work, though short, is complete; it is called a fragment because it forms a part of a much larger work, the *Problemata,* parts of which may be genuinely Aristotelian.

Some modern scholars maintain (e.g., Wilcken 1967.130) on the basis of the ancient *testimonia* (see frgs. 246 and 247 in Rose's edition) and the *Liber Aristotelis de inundacione Nili* (which is assumed to be genuine) that Alexander the Great, after his arrival in Egypt in November of 332 BC, was directed by his mentor Aristotle to settle by means of a scientific expedition how it is that the Nile's flooding always begins in the heat and dryness of midsummer rather than much earlier in the year after the winter's precipitation. Accordingly, Alexander dispatched to the Sudan an expedition of scholars led by Callisthenes (Aristotle's nephew and Alexander's "press secretary") to study the cause of the Nile's inundation. These scholars returned with the answer that the rise in the Nile's water is produced by moisture-laden clouds in Ethiopia. When the clouds drop on the Ethiopian mountains, the result is a great downpour of rain that is carried into Egypt. The *Liber Aristotelis de inundacione Nili* is taken as Aristotle's written response to the findings of this expedition. Completely satisfied with the report (since it agreed with his *a priori* reasoning), Aristotle wrote about the cause of the inundation, "This is no longer a problem" (τοῦτο οὐκέτι πρόβλημά ἐστιν, frg. 246 = the Latin *iam non problema videtur esse, 197*). But see Tarn, who rejects this story as apocryphal, 1933.6:378–379, with bibliography on the *Liber Aristotelis de inundacione Nili* at 596, D.2.b; Pearson does not deny that such an expedition took place, saying only that Callisthenes could not have been involved with it (1960.30–31). On the confusion which has arisen about the authenticity of the *Fragmenta* first edited by Rose in modern times and considered by him to be pseudepigraphical, see Wilpert 1960.257–264. For a fresh discussion of the authenticity of the *Liber de inundacione Nili* and an updated bibliography see de Nardis 1992. He believes that Aristotle, drawing on earlier Ionian research, wrote the *Liber de inundacione Nili* even before Alexander's expeditions of conquest

(1992.107). De Nardis joins many others who now count the work as genuinely Aristotelian.

Eighty-three manuscripts of the little work have survived, which shows that it was widely circulated; but there is nothing in what Petrarch says to show that he had read Aristotle's work, though he certainly makes it sound as though he had. For what little he has to say about the Nile, Petrarch seems to be relying on Lucan's account (10.190–331), though there seem to be a few verbal echoes from Pliny's (*Nat.* 5.51–60). As it happens, Lucan's account has a distant connection with Aristotle. Lucan, Seneca's nephew and close associate at Nero's court, is commonly supposed to have had the benefit of his uncle's thinking on the Nile and may even have read Seneca's account of the Nile in his *Naturales Quaestiones* (a work Petrarch also knew). There Seneca informs his readers (4.2.16) that Theophrastus was one of his authorities on the Nile. Seneca does not mention Aristotle (in connection with the Nile), but Theophrastus was the collaborator and successor of Aristotle. His work on the Nile, now lost except for a few fragments, certainly contained the core of Aristotle's research on the Nile. In his extant, certainly genuine work, Aristotle discusses the Nile in the first and second books of his *Meteorologica*, where the characteristics of rivers in general are the subject of inquiry.

Petrarch's attitude towards Aristotle and Aristotelianism should be briefly noted. If one were to judge from this single passage from the *Itinerarium*, he would certainly suppose that Petrarch was a great admirer of Aristotle. This surmise would be true only in a limited sense. Petrarch freely expresses himself on this topic in *obiter dicta* throughout his work, but nowhere more forcefully than in his *De sui ipsius et multorum ignorantia*, a work he completed in 1370 (on Aristotle see especially 716–726, 740–746, and 748–756 in *Prose*). Petrarch's views on Aristotle were based on much more than a casual acquaintance with the philosopher's work. Petrarch claimed to have read all of Aristotle's books on ethics and even to have attended lectures on some of them (*omnes morales, nisi fallor, Aristotilis libros legi, quosdam etiam audivi* . . . 744 in *Prose*). In fact he owned Latin translations of the

Nicomachean Ethics and the *Politics* (de Nolhac 1907.2:241 and 293). In addition, he was familiar with (whether in Latin translations or through commentators is often difficult to say) the *Physics,* the *Metaphysics,* the *Rhetoric,* the *Economica,* the *Parva Naturalia (De somno* and *De divinatione per somnum,* cf. *Fam.* 5.7.3), various logical works from the *Organon,* and finally (to bring this sketch to an arbitrary end), the *Problemata,* of which the *De inundacione Nili* is but a small part. Perhaps Petrarch had read much more of the *Problemata* than has been hitherto suspected since he alludes to it in a way that suggests more than a nodding acquaintance with the work in the *Invectiva contra eum qui maledixit Italie* (800 in *Prose*). Thus Petrarch was quite familiar with a considerable number of Aristotle's works, much more so in fact than with those of Plato (he knew only the *Timaeus,* the *Phaedo,* and the *Meno*); but as the history of Platonism in Western thought shows, it is not necessary to have read much Plato to qualify one as a Platonist.

Petrarch's attitude towards Aristotle is somewhat analogous to his attitude towards Hippocrates: he admired the man and acknowledged the greatness of his work, but detested the excesses of his followers, who accepted Aristotle's authority slavishly and (Petrarch would maintain) without a true understanding of the master's work, especially of its limitations, or at least of its limits. Petrarch felt that in the hands of such followers Aristotle was positively dangerous: *maxime vitandus Aristotiles non quod plus errorum, sed quod plus autoritatis habet ac sequacium (De sui ipsius et multorum ignorantia,* 740 in *Prose;* note the pejorative sense of *sequax,* "addict").

For more on Petrarch's attitude towards Aristotle, see Kristeller and Randall 1948.5–7 and 9–16; this volume also contains a translation of the *De sui ipsius et multorum ignorantia* by Nachod, 47–133; see also Kristeller, "The Aristotelian Tradition" and "Renaissance Platonism," 1961.24–47 and 48–69, with references to Petrarch *passim,* Foster 1984.149–155, and the first three chapters of Cophenhaver and Schmitt 1992. Petrarch, inspired by Cicero, Apuleius, Macrobius, St. Augustine, and Boethius, was instrumental in fostering Platonism in the later Renaissance. On Petrarch's knowledge of Plato's dialogues, see Minio-Paluello 1972. 107–113.

625–628 fontis incogniti, cuius certitudinem . . . omnes quesiere. Fons hactenus ignoratus manet: this is a paraphrase of Lucan, 10.268–271:

> Quae tibi noscendi Nilum, Romane, cupido est,
> et Phariis Persisque fuit Macetumque tyrannis,
> nullaque non aetas voluit conferre futuris
> notitiam; sed vincit adhuc natura latendi.

Knowledge of the Nile's source eluded discovery until the explorations of Sir Richard Burton, John Speke, Samuel Baker, and Henry Stanley in the 1860s and '70s. For a rousing popular account, see Moorehead 1971 and Hibbert 1982.

630–636 Clarum quiddam et relatu dignum . . . ceu monstrum aliquod admirentur: there were a number of stories circulating in the Middle Ages about the miraculous activities of the Infant Jesus in Egypt. One version of them in particular, contained in a large number of manuscripts, had wide influence: the Gospel of Pseudo-Matthew (for Latin text see von Tischendorf 1876.85–93; for English translation [excerpt] see James 1924.74–76). This story (von Tischendorf, 87–88) mentions a miraculous spring drawn by Jesus from the roots of a palm (or sycamore) tree to refresh his mother on the way to Egypt. The Arabic Infancy Gospel (von Tischendorf, 181–209), also well known in Petrarch's day, said (193) that the Virgin drew water from this spring (at a place called Matarea, identified as the ancient Heliopolis by Montet 1957.1:155–162 and Ball 1942.17 and *passim*) to wash the Infant's clothes, and when she threw the water away, balsam-bearing shrubs (with leaves resembling basil, say the Italians) grew up where the water had fallen. This balsam, an aromatic oleoresin, was supposed to have great curative powers and was highly prized therefore by Christian pilgrims: see Ludolph von Suchem's wonderful account of the Balsam Garden near Cairo in his *Description of the Holy Land* (Stewart 1895.68–70 and that of Burchard of Mount Sion [AD 1280], translation in Stewart 1896.62–63 [Latin text in Laurent 1873.1–100]).

The rather simple story outlined above appears in a large number of variations throughout the medieval period. Sometimes the Child is said to create (with a finger, a foot, or an act of the will) the spring to quench his mother's thirst, but sometimes His own. The Virgin herself is sometimes said to create it (by prayer) to quench the Child's thirst. In other versions, the spring already exists when the Holy Family arrives at Matarea, i.e., the Child does not create it. The water of this spring becomes charged with divine power only when Mary washes the Child's clothes (or bathes the Child) in it: when Mary discards the water, the balsam shrubs spring into existence or assume miraculous powers. Most versions somehow bring the story of the spring's creation together with the creation or at least the maintenance of the balsam garden.

The story that Petrarch tells makes no explicit connection with the balsam garden, nor is the spring specifically located at Matarea; but his version is undoubtedly to be placed within the capacious literary (and oral) tradition just sketched. Petrarch's account of the spring's creation is quite the usual thing, but the part about the bitter/sweet nature of the water is quite a rare bit indeed. The only other certain example of this part of the story is that found in Simone Sigoli's account of his visit to Egypt. Before discussing it, some background information will be necessary.

In August of 1384 thirteen Tuscans (six in the capacity of servants) set out together for the Holy Land from Venice, beginning their grand tour in Egypt. Some time after their return the following May, three of them — Lionardo Frescobaldi, Giorgio Gucci (more correctly di Guccio), and Simone Sigoli — more or less independently wrote descriptions of their adventures to circulate among their families and friends. Sigoli's account has always been valued above the others primarily for the purity of its prose style and as a result it has been favored with numerous editions (most of them in the nineteenth century), but the texts of the other two have fared less well. Nevertheless G. Gargiolli has brought all three texts under one cover (*Viaggi in Terra Santa di Lionardo Frescobaldi e d'altri del secolo XIV* [Florence, 1862]); this is the only edition of Gucci's account, in many ways the most valuable of all. The texts of Frescobaldi and Sigoli have been joined in Angelini's *Viaggi in Terra Santa* (1944), hereafter cited as *Viaggi.* All three texts have been translated into English under the title *Visit to the Holy Places of Egypt, Sinai, Palestine, and Syria in 1384,* Bagatti 1948, hereafter cited as *Visit.* For a recent study of the manuscript tradition of these three pilgrim texts and a rating of available published editions, see Delfiol 1982.139–176.

In his preface Bagatti persuasively argues (*Visit,* 22–24) that the order of composition was Frescobaldi, Gucci, and Sigoli: Gucci seems deliberately to fill in details omitted by Fresobaldi, and there are clear signs that Sigoli, who dated the completion of his manuscript 4 October 1390, tried to fill in gaps he saw in the accounts of the other two. Over all Sigoli's account is shorter by a third than the other two, as though he were left short of material by their preemptive compositions. This order of composition, accepted by both Delfiol 1982 and Cardini 1986.193, has a bearing on the story of the spring that Sigoli tells.

Both Frescobaldi and Gucci (*Visit,* 53–55 and 106–108) have lengthy and lively descriptions of their visit to Matarea. They tell pretty much the same story about the spring. When the Holy Family arrived there, Mary was very thirsty and told the Child of her thirst. He thereupon struck the ground with His foot, and water sprang up. After she was refreshed, Mary washed Jesus's clothes in the newly created spring and spread them out to dry on some nearby bushes, which afterwards produced the precious balsam. Frescobaldi says that the spring is large, and its waters copious and very good; Gucci adds that the large spring has been divided by the enclosure wall of the balsam garden, so that one might speak of two fountains.

Frescobaldi and Gucci are both fascinated by the balsam plants (this is the only place in the whole world that the plants grow, they both say). Frescobaldi tells us that he and some others in the group bribed their way into the balsam garden, kept under guard by the Sultan, because they were bent on acquiring some of the balsam. Gucci, a member of this group, tells us that a "very small phial" of the stuff costs two gold ducats, an outrageous price. The two of them describe in detail how the plants were harvested. It is a lengthy process, says Frescobaldi; Gucci is more specific: it took two hours to fill up one small ampule the size of about one quarter of a small glass. During the whole time, Frescobaldi and Gucci were watching the gathering process like hawks, because Gucci had heard that the Saracens cheated the tourists by spitting into the small bottles to fill up the amount. Frescobaldi says the group spent the whole day in the balsam garden.

Before the group left Matarea Frescobaldi says they stocked up on water from the spring, supposing that that would be their only supply until they reached St. Catherine's monastery, a ten-day trek. Traveling with the Tuscans were perhaps a half dozen Saracens in various capacities (one named Ali was their interpreter; *Visit* 152). Neither Frescobaldi nor Gucci mentions a word about the water being bitter to the lips of Saracens, no doubt for the best of reasons: they saw Saracens drinking the water very happily both at Matarea and on the journey through the Sinai.

If one accepts the order proposed by Bagatti, he might expect to find that Sigoli's account of the visit to Matarea varies somewhat from the other two but he is not prepared to find the story of the bitter / sweet water (first in the Italian: *Viaggi,* 260) as follows:

> In questo luogo della Matarea vi capitò una volta la vergine Maria col suo figliuolo Gesù Cristo; di che il nostro Signore affaticato chiese da bere, e non gli volle essere dato, cioè dell'acqua, di che Cristo percosse i piedi in terra, e fecevisi incontanente una fonte d'acqua chiara e bella della buona del mondo, la quale è per ogni verso circa a un braccio e mezzo. E quando niuno Saracino volesse bere della detta acqua, gli pare tanto amara, quanto è il veleno: e per questa cagione niun Sarcino non ne può bere, perchè non pare sia piacere di Dio. E quando uno Cristiano ne beesse, si è molta buona.

And now in the fairly literal translation of Bellorini and Hoade (*Visit,* 197):

> In this place of Matarea chanced once the Virgin Mary with her son Jesus Christ; so our Lord being tired asked

> to drink, and it was not given to him, that is of the water, so Christ struck his feet in the ground and caused at once a fountain of water, clear and beautiful, of the best in the world, which is each way a braccio and a half. And when any Saracen wishes to drink of the said water it seems to him as bitter as is poison: and for this reason no Saracen can drink of it, because it does not seem to please God. And when a Christian drinks of it, it is very good.

Sigoli's account matches Petrarch's in every essential particular, linking it thereby to Matarea, the place of the famous balsam garden. One phrase in Sigoli's account gives pause: the Child, tired and thirsty, has asked (of no one by name) for a drink, but "non gli volle essere dato, cioè dell' acqua." Without delaying to discuss this unusual expression ("it refused to be given to him, that is the water"), one may confidently say that no human agent is said to have denied the Child a drink: water is simply not available. The Child, in a gesture typical of any frustrated child, stamps his foot, a vivid touch by Sigoli. Petrarch uses a much more generic word (eduxerit), which suggests that he was thinking of the act of the spring's creation as an act of the will alone. In both Petrarch's and Sigoli's account, it does not appear that the Saracens are being punished for any specific wrongdoing. This water is sacred, and the profane are prevented from drinking it by the relatively harmless expedient of making the water unpalatable to them. It is not even suggested that the Saracens will go thirsty; they may get water elsewhere easily.

Sigoli has some more surprises in store for his readers. He goes on to say that there are two separate springs at Matarea: one, whose water tastes bitter only to Saracens; the other, whose water produces the balsam. These two springs are about a hundred yards apart. The spring which produces the balsam already existed when the Holy Family arrived at Matarea. It was in this spring (mistakenly said by Sigoli's friends to have been created by the Child) that Mary washed the Child's clothes, and the balsam plants come from the water of this spring. Two different springs, two different miracles.

Sigoli's description of the balsam garden is short and perfunctory; there is no sign in it of any personal experience except of the most general sort. It is not likely that Sigoli was among those who bribed their way into the balsam garden. Frescobaldi and Gucci were the ringleaders in this enterprise, and Sigoli did not belong to their social group (Cardini 1986.193 and 195–196). While Frescobaldi, Gucci, and one or two others spent the whole day in the balsam garden, Sigoli must have had time on his hands. As he wandered about Matarea, he came upon a second spring some distance from the one next to the balsam garden. Sigoli may not have a bottle of spittle-free balsam to show around among his friends, but he could correct Frescobaldi and Gucci's mistaken accounts of the spring's creation.

Did Sigoli hear the story of the bitter / sweet water from a local guide, as Bagatti says (*Visit,* note on 198)? This seems unlikely for two reasons. The first has to do with the improbable nature of the story itself. It does not seem to be the sort that a guide would concoct to tell visitors. It could all too easily be disproved by anyone who happened to see a Saracen drinking the water to no ill effect. It might be possible for a clever guide to gull a group of Christians on a given occasion, but such a ruse could not be maintained except by total and almost perpetual cooperation of every Saracen in Matarea, for pilgrims were passing there at all times of the year. To suppose that everyone would abstain from perfectly good water in a land as hot and dry as Egypt to maintain such a silly story is not to be believed. In any case, what possible motive could there have been for such an improbable trick? To sell the water at a higher price than they might otherwise? Why would Christians buy it if they could buy good water elsewhere, for example, at the equally miraculous spring next to the balsam garden, as Frescobaldi says they did?

The second thing that argues against Sigoli's having heard the story from a local guide is the fact that no other parallel for the story (except Petrarch's) has yet come to light. If guides in Egypt were telling this story, one would expect it to be repeated, if only to be scoffed at, but such is not the case. Bagatti (*Visit,* note on 198) cites as a parallel a story told by a Franciscan named Antonio de' Reboldi, a pilgrim to the Sinai in 1330; Bagatti calls it the "same story," referring the reader to Golubovich 1919.3:336. Turning to this text, one reads:

> Item non potest crescere balsamum, nisi irrigatur non de omni aqua, set de aqua fontis beatae Virginis, quem fecit isto modo. Nam cum fugisset persecutionem Herodis et Egyptum venisset, et in uno casali aquam petisset et illi negassent, processit ulterius, et facta oratione fecit ipsum fontem, dicens: «De isto fonte possint omnes bibere, exceptis hiis qui nascentur in isto casali!» Et factum est in futurum, quod vineae Egadi quae faciunt balsamum, fuerunt translatae de terra sancta in Egiptum, et juxta istum fontem plantatae fuerunt, et quantum potest se extendere aqua istius fontis, tantum dilatant se ipsae sacrae vineae, seu arbusculae, et faciunt balsamum. Et sub coelo non nascitur nisi ibidem.

Pace Bagatti, however, this is not the same story as Sigoli's (or Petrarch's). In Reboldi's account, when Mary is refused water by members of a single household (in uno casali; possibly *casale* means "village") she prays for a spring to be created. That accomplished, she immediately prays (this part smacks of the *lex talionis,* Exod. 21:23–25 or perhaps of Dante's *contrapasso*) that everyone might be able to drink of the water except those (and their descendants) who denied her water. In Sigoli's account, all Saracens, for no particular offense, will be excluded from the water's use. Reboldi connects the spring with the balsam garden, but the garden does not come into existence because of the newly created spring: at a later time balsam plants were brought to Egypt from the Ein Gedi, an oasis west of the Dead Sea (this variation, known in other accounts, is too complex to comment on here).

In Reboldi's account the taste of the water is not mentioned, and it cannot be assumed that the members of the accursed household or village would be prevented from drinking it by its bitter taste. It might just as easily be understood that they would be prevented from approaching the water by some invisible power, much in the same way that pilgrims with mortal sins on their souls are physically restrained from entering the church of St. Mary of Egypt (St. Pelagia) on the Mount of Olives until they have their sins forgiven, according to Frescobaldi (*Viaggi,* 132; *Visit,* 72).

While Bagatti may consider Reboldi's story as a parallel to Sigoli's, Golubovich himself does not cite Sigoli's as a parallel to Reboldi's, though Golubovich knows Sigoli perfectly well, citing him in another connection on the very same page as that on which Reboldi's story appears. To Reboldi's version Golubovich is able to cite no parallel whatsoever. This fact gains considerable weight when one reflects that in his five-volume work Golubovich gathers and edits over 500 documents (itineraries, letters, etc.) produced by Franciscan missionaries and pilgrims about their experiences in Egypt and the Holy Land over a period of several hundred years. In introducing and commenting on each of these documents, Golubovich ranges impressively through all kinds of related literature of the period, but when it came to Reboldi's story, no parallel suggested itself to Golubovich.

A number of other fourteenth-century pilgrims (Marino Sanudo, Giacamo da Verona, Niccolò da Poggibonsi, Burchard of Mt. Sion, and Niccolò di Martoni) report visits to Matarea, but do not say anything about the bitter / sweet water. All of those just mentioned do report the absurd story of the pious oxen that refuse to draw water to irrigate the balsam garden on the Lord's Day (see Stewart 1896.62 on Burchard; Bacchi della Lega 1945.1: 109–110 on Niccolò da Poggibonsi; and for the others see Legrand's note on Niccolò di Martoni in 1895.3:603). This seems to be the Arab guides' favorite story to tell Christian pilgrims at Matarea. The anonymous pilgrim of c. 1350 (Colker 1964.2.93–143) does not mention either the bitter / sweet water or the pious oxen, saying only that both Christians and Saracens bathe in the spring created by the Infant Jesus (134). The water was said to prevent or cure leprosy and eye disease.

If Sigoli did not hear the story of the bitter / sweet water from a local guide in Egypt and if there seems to be no parallel to his version except Petrarch's, one is bound to ask whether there might be some connection between the two stories. As it happens, there is a strong probability that the source for Sigoli's story is none other than Petrarch's *Itinerarium*. Sigoli might have read it for himself (he knew some Latin), but it is more likely that he got it through an intermediary in the way now to be described.

Frescobaldi informs his readers (*Viaggi*, 40–42; *Visit*, 31–32) that the whole idea for the pilgrimage had originated with Guido di Tomasso del Neri (also called Guido del Palagio), but that Guido had withdrawn at the last moment (much as Petrarch himself had done) because of the press of diplomatic and family duties. In fact, Guido, a very wealthy merchant and man of affairs, had suggested the pilgrimage to Frescobaldi when they were both in Arezzo in 1381 on an important diplomatic mission. Now this Guido traveled regularly for diplomatic and business reasons to Venice where he had a number of important connections. Of relevance here is the fact that Guido was a great admirer of Petrarch and had planned to meet him on one of his trips to Venice, but was prevented from doing so by Petrarch's death 18 July 1374. This we learn from several letters written to him by the Augustinian humanist Luigi Marsili, himself a great admirer of Petrarch and his good friend. We learn from Marsili (texts cited by Billanovich 1947.373–376) that Guido had hopes of getting Petrarch's permission to make copies of some of his writings. These hopes, frustrated by Petrarch's death, were soon revived when Guido became friends with Francescuolo da Brossano, Petrarch's son-in-law and inheritor of the bulk of Petrarch's estate, including his library (see Mommsen 1957.40–50 for a succinct account of Francescuolo and the questions surrounding the disposition of Petrarch's books).

Guido may have acquired the *Itinerarium* at this time (1375 or 1376) or he may have become acquainted with it much earlier. Boccaccio almost certainly brought back to Florence a copy of the *Itinerarium*, one of the fruits of his extended visit to Petrarch in March–April of 1359 (Billanovich 1947.224–225; so also Wilkins 1958.183). Sometime before 1348 Boccaccio assumed leadership of a group of Florentine intellectuals bound together by their love of the Latin Classics and by their admiration for Petrarch (see Billanovich 1947.93–96). The group included Bruno Casini, Francesco Nelli, Zanobi da Strada, and (by 1359 or 1361) Coluccio Salutati,

Florence's future Chancellor (1375). Guido del Palagio was a junior member of this group. We have already seen (note to lines 86–87) that Salutati was able to quote the *Itinerarium* to Giorgio Stella; he probably had his copy of it shortly after he joined Boccaccio's group. Given Guido del Palagio's status in Florentine society, one might assume that he was well acquainted with Salutati. We know in fact that they were very close friends (Guasti 1880.1:8), their admiration for Petrarch being one of the things that cemented their friendship.

The conclusion that Guido had a copy of Petrarch's *Itinerarium* or at the very least had read it is difficult to resist. Much of Petrarch's *Itinerarium* would not have been of any practical value as Guido began to plan his own pilgrimage in 1381, because Guido and his friends would leave from Venice (not Genoa). But Guido may have been guided by Petrarch's recommendations to Mandelli that he visit Egypt, St. Catherine's, and Damascus. The inclusion of these places added considerable expense and danger, and many pilgrims omitted them. On their departure from Venice, Frescobaldi comments that all the other pilgrims he knew of did not intend to go to Egypt and St. Catherine's but only to the Holy Sepulcher in Jerusalem (*Viaggi,* 44). Petrarch's description of the Holy Land and Egypt is very sparse. The one really striking thing he has to say about Egypt is the story of the bitter / sweet water of Matarea. In urging his friends to visit Egypt, Guido would have undoubtedly mentioned the story. It stuck in Sigoli's mind. With so great an authority as Petrarch behind him, Sigoli does not hesitate to correct the accounts of his two friends, defective mainly by omission. Frescobaldi and Gucci were after all too busy with their balsam to notice the second spring (the one of which Petrarch had spoken).

If there is good reason to suppose that Sigoli got the story from Petrarch through Guido del Palagio, from where did Petrarch get it? It should be noted that Petrarch emphasizes that he had heard the story: he uses the verb *accipere,* which commonly means to learn by listening (*OLD,* s.v. *accipio* 18). Since Petrarch was always on the move and had a very wide circle of friends and acquaintances, he could have heard it almost anywhere he traveled or at any time. The story has a folktale quality about it, but no parallel is forthcoming from that direction. Tales about magical fountains, rivers, and lakes abound in the Middle Ages (Wright 1925.203–205), but none matches Petrarch's story of the water that is at once both sweet and bitter. There is a good sample of such marvelous waters in Boccaccio's *De montibus* (Stocchi 1998.1881–1995), which may also be consulted in Liburnio's Italian translation (1978.61–172). The fabulous fountains Petrarch speaks of in *Canz.* 135.46–97 are derived from classical sources (Pliny and Pomponius Mela) and bear no resemblance to the one in Egypt. Such is Petrarch's child-like enthusiasm for the story that one could almost be persuaded that it was a story that he had heard as a boy, dreaming of far away places, and had never thought to challenge as a man, yet that would be a mistaken attitude. In St. Augustine (*De civ. Dei*, 21.5 and 7), he had read of a spring in Epirus, which like other springs extinguishes lighted torches, but also relights extinguished ones, contrary to the usual nature of springs. Augustine has no problem in believing in this marvelous spring: the Almighty Creator had willed this spring to behave so. Petrarch takes his cue from the admired Augustine regarding the Egyptian spring of the bitter / sweet water. Where he got the story remains to be discovered.

Although recently published guidebooks usually are not very informative on the matter of the miraculous spring, older ones do the story some justice; see Budge 1911.466: ". . . a stop should be made at the village of Matariyah, where are the Tree and Well which tradition connects with the Virgin Mary." For new translations and further bibliography and discussion of the apocryphal Infancy Gospels, see Hennecke 1963.1:363–417 and Elliott 1993.

641–642 Alexandriam, Alexandri opus, Alexandri nomen, Alexandri bustum: founded by Alexander in 331 BC, Alexandria became the administrative capital of the Ptolemies and the site of the greatest library in the ancient world. Its population in Roman times, according to Josephus (*B.I.* 2.385), who claims that he is basing his statement on tax records, was half a million. Although Alexandria suffered some decline after the foundation of Cairo in the tenth century, it was still magnificent in the fourteenth century, with two harbors divided by the Pharus Island — the eastern reserved for Christian ships and the western for Muslim. Alexandria was not located on the Nile, but was linked to it by a channel built (or rather reconstructed) in the early fourteenth century, which ran eastward to the Rosetta Branch at the town of Fuwa. European goods could be taken through the canal and upstream to Cairo, about 140 miles south at the apex of the Delta, a journey of about six days, and from there to the Red Sea.

Alexander died in Babylon (in Mesopotamia) in 323 BC; but his body was taken to Egypt, where he wanted to be buried near the temple of Zeus Ammon in the western desert. There are various versions as to how the body came to rest at Alexandria. Quintus Curtius (10.10.20) simply says that Ptolemy Soter first took the body to Memphis and then several years later transferred it to Alexandria. Popular tradition erroneously places the tomb (called the Sema or Soma) beneath the present site of the Mosque of Nebi Daniel, at the main crossroads of the ancient city. Excavations beneath the mosque have uncovered only a Muslim cemetery of the tenth–twelfth centuries. Herodian's account (4.8.9) of Caracalla's visit to Alexandria in AD 215 is the last time any writer mentions the Tomb of Alexander as being in existence. For a more detailed discussion, see Fraser 1972.1:15–17 and notes 2: 79–92. See note to lines 647–648.

At the beginning of Book 8 of the *Africa*, Petrarch disparages Alexander's military achievements and ends by proclaiming Hannibal's superiority over Alexander (*Africa*, 8.227–231). In so doing Petrarch's aim is to exalt Scipio all the more (see note to lines 418–419). On Petrarch's negative attitude towards Alexander, see Bernardo 1962.192–194. See also the related Petrarchan text discovered by Ullman at the University of Pennsylvania (Cod. Lat. 7). The full title of the manuscript is given as *Collatio inter Scipionem Romanum, Alexandrum Macedonem, Hanibalem Penum, et Pyrrum Epyrotarum regem, quis eorum prestantior fuerit. Collatio* here means "a comparison," sc. [to find out] who was the most outstanding general. The intention of the piece is the same as in the Africa, to demonstrate Scipio's undoubted superiority over the rest. The final ranking is Scipio, Hannibal, Alexander, with Pyrrhus a poor fourth. The text is introduced and edited by Martellotti 1964.2:145–168. For a survey of Petrarch's quite negative attitude towards Alexander, see Cary 1950.43–55.

Petrarch's negative views on Alexander (expressed especially in the *Africa* and in his *Life of Alexander* in *De viris illustribus,* Martellotti 1964a) were largely derived from Quintus Curtius's *Historiae Alexandri Magni* (c. AD 50), which portrays Alexander at first as gifted and noble, but finally as corrupted by constant good fortune and oriental luxury (quem arma Persarum non fregerant, vitia vicerunt, 6.2.1; Müller 1954). He also knew and used Justin's account (*Epitome,* books 11 and 12 and *passim;* see de Nolhac 1907. 2:94–98). Justin's account was in turn the basis for Paulus Orosius's relentlessly hostile assessment of Alexander in the third book of his *Historiarum adversum paganos libri septem* (Zangemeister 1889). Petrarch knew Orosius (see de Nolhac 1907.2:30,39, and 80), but preferred Curtius's characterization of Alexander because it offered more opportunity for drawing moral lessons with particular reference to the whims of *fortuna* (see analysis in Baynham 1998).

These historical accounts, all essentially negative in their evaluation of Alexander, were more than counterbalanced in the popular imagination by the various fictional accounts (called Romances) of Alexander's career, which were circulating in the Latin West from the fourth century in Julius Valerius's translation. These accounts, derived from the Greek original (which also circulated in the East in various versions), generally idealized Alexander as clever and daring, and preternaturally equipped to cope with any situation no matter how fantastic. On one occasion, for example, Alexander harnesses two griffins and is carried on their wings high above the earth. Some later vernacular accounts based on the Latin versions viewed Alexander as the ideal courtly prince. This fictional view of Alexander was usually far from Petrarch's artistic and moral purposes. Yet some of the fictional material, less fantastic than Alexander's Celestial Journey and told with a serious moral intent, did claim Petrarch's interest. For example, the fictional exchange of letters between Alexander and

Dindimus (or Dandamus), the Brahman king, called the *Collatio Alexandri cum Dindimo per litteras facta* (in several versions; see, e.g., Pfister 1911.10–20, and Cary's note 1954.124–129), prompts a serious discussion of the moral and cultural values of the East and the West (*De vita solitaria*, 2.11; 518 in *Prose*). This text of course is very critical of Alexander and the West (for commentary see Le Goff 1980.189–200 and 345–346). So also, in the same chapter of the *De vita solitaria*, Petrarch discusses the *De moribus Brachmanorum* (Scheiwiller 1956), whose authorship he thinks should be attributed to Palladius rather than Ambrose, among whose works it is found: *Qui [liber] non plene michi redoleat Ambrosii stilum, inter Ambrosii tamen libros medius est . . . non Ambrosii, sed Palladii liber est* (514 in *Prose*). This work, in fact a Latin version of part of a work in Greek by Palladius (d. c. AD 430; ed. by Berghoff 1967), records a letter written by an Indian ascetic (gymnosophist) named Calanus to Alexander the Great and reports an extended conversation between the two men about the life of the Brahmans. Calanus had joined Alexander's entourage and had followed him back to Persia. For this, he was despised by his fellow Brahmans who felt that he had been corrupted by the Western way of living and by Alexander's promises of wealth. Calanus, however, rejected Alexander's offers of gold, silver, fine clothes, and rich food, but he did accept a gift of oil so as not to seem completely disdainful of Alexander's generosity. Soon Calanus fell gravely ill and insisted on being burned to death on a funeral pyre. As he calmly prepared for his death, he predicted Alexander's own imminent death (cf. Cicero, *Div.* 1.47 and Petrarch, *Rerum mem.* 4.38). The story of Calanus, a famous example of the type known as the *exitus clarorum virorum* (deaths of noble men), is told by a large number of authors in antiquity. It appealed to Petrarch because of Calanus's disdain for riches and his contempt for death and because of the implied criticism of Alexander — no nonsense here about Alexander being a god. There may be some grain of truth in the Calanus story; but since it shows so many parallels with a number of stories circulating in later antiquity about the noble deaths of virtuous men standing up to or disdainful of the power of the tyrant, it should be considered largely fictional, the product of Stoic and Cynic moralizing: see Wilcken 1967.180–181, Hadas 1959.178–180 with notes, and Stoneman 1995. It is clear that Petrarch did not regard the stories of Dindimus and Calanus as unhistorical in any way. For the Gymnosophists as a symbol of natural goodness in the West, see Hahn 1978.213–234.

For more evidence of Petrarch's knowledge of the Alexander Romance, see de Nolhac 1907.2:231–232. Besides the early Latin versions, he knew the *Alexandreis* of Walter of Châtillon (fl.1170), a popular ten-book Latin epic of some 5,500 verses, based in part on Julius Valerius's fourth-century version. Carrara 1932 thinks that Petrarch wrote his *Africa* to offset Walter's glorification of Alexander (text in Colker 1978).

For more background on the fictional Alexander, see Hägg 1983.125–143. An English translation of the various Latin versions (principally the tenth-century version of Leo of Naples) of the Alexander fictions is now available in Kratz 1991. On the enormous popularity in the Middle Ages of Alexander, both the historical one and the fictional one, see Cary 1956, Aerts 1978, Ross 1988, and Stoneman 1994. As Chaucer says in his *Canterbury Tales* (Monk's Tale, 7.2631–33):

> The storie of Alisaundre is so commune
> That every wight that hath discrecioun
> Hath herd somwhat or al of his fortune.

642–644 Ad quod Iulius Cesar . . . descendisse legitur: Caesar, sensing that the Egyptian population was in a dangerous anti-Roman mood, made a show of visiting various national shrines, including Alexander's tomb, as a sign of his respect (cf. Caesar, *Civ.* 3.106 and Lucan, 10.9–24). Caesar had arrived in pursuit of Pompey, whom he had defeated at the battle of Pharsalus in Thessaly (6 June 48 BC). Pompey escaped, but was assassinated in Egypt (28 September); see note to lines 662–663. The phrase *Thesalicum diem* is at Lucan, 7.202. This borrowing inspires a similar turn of phrase a few lines below: *victoriam Actiacam*, line 645, borrowed this time from Suetonius (*Aug.* 18); or perhaps the phrase stuck in his mind from his reading of *Vita Donati,* 27 (post Actiacam victoriam).

647–648 Cumque ex eo . . . non mortuos: the anecdote is from Suetonius (*Aug.* 18, slightly paraphrased); cf. Lucan, 8.692–699. Petrarch refers to the story in *De viris illustribus (Prohem.,* 222 in *Prose*), perhaps written sometime between 1351 and 1353. Cassius Dio, an author Petrarch did not know, tells the same story (51.16.5) as Suetonius, but adds that Augustus accidentally broke off a piece of the nose of Alexander's mummy.

According to Zenobius (*Epit.*3.94, in Leutsch 1839.1:81), Ptolemy Philopater (c. 244–205) built a single mausoleum for Alexander and his three predecessors (Ptholomeum, line 647), who had previously been buried separately, in an area near the sea called the "Palaces" (Zenobius and Strabo, 17.1.8). Ammianus Marcellinus (22.16.15) records that this whole area suffered great destruction in the reign of Aurelian around AD 273. The Sema probably did not survive this incident. If there are any remains of the Sema still to be found, they are probably buried under many feet of silt and water.

Petrarch, having read Lucan's description of the combined mausoleum (8.692–699), is clearly hoping it is still in existence, but has his doubts (*poteris et hoc bustum, si nondum senio cesserit, spectare,* lines 638).

654–655 nec minus urnam que Pompeii cinerum ostenditur: see note on lines 662–663 below.

656–657 Galli . . . transtulere: Petrarch thought the French were presumptuous to give the name *magnus* to Charlemagne: . . . *Carolum regem, quem Magni cognomine equare Pompeio et Alexandro audent* . . . (*Fam.*1.4.7).

658–660 Videbis ubi . . . vix credibilia gessit Cesar: Lucan, 10.434–546; Suetonius, *Jul.* 35 and 64. Petrarch did not become acquainted with Caesar's *Commentaries* until 1366 or so. They then became the basis for his *Life of Caesar (De gestis Cesaris)*, perhaps intended to be published as an independent work or, as some believe, as part of his *De viris illustribus* despite its great length (70,000 words). Petrarch did not live to see the work in its fair form: that task was taken in hand by his friend Lombardo della Seta who published it early in 1379 (Wilkins 1959.283–302). Incidentally, Petrarch knew Caesar's *Commentaries* as the work of

Julius Celsus, a common attribution in the Middle Ages (Brown 1981.321–324). See Petrarch's revision (1371) of his *Triumphus fame*, 3.106–107: *E Iulio Celso* [referring to the author of the *Commentaries*] *ch' io non so qual vibri / meglio o 'l ferro o la penna (Rime,* 577). Petrarch's own *Life of Caesar* was ascribed to this same Julius Celsus until the last century (de Nolhac 1907.2:38–39). Caesar treats of his own exploits in Egypt at *Civ.* 3.102–112; cf. also *B. Alex.* 1–33 (written by Caesar's continuator Aulus Hirtius). Petrarch's admiration for Julius Caesar grew over the years and to a considerable extent supplanted his earlier devotion to Scipio; see Martellotti 1949.51–80 and Baron 1962.24–34.

660–661 Videbis Pharon unde hoc phari nomen . . . diffusum est: the Pharus, the great Alexandrian lighthouse, took its name from the island in the harbor of Alexandria on which it was built. Construction began probably in the reign of Ptolemy Soter around 297 BC and was completed some fifteen years later, the last to be admitted eventually into the canon of the Seven Wonders of the Ancient World. The appearance of the Pharus in antiquity is best attested on Roman coins dating from the time of Domitian and later. These show that the lighthouse was a three-tiered structure, polygonal in shape in its lower two tiers and tapering to an estimated height of about 330 ft. Near the top upon which stood a statue of Zeus Soter, a fire was kept burning that projected light for thirty or more miles out to sea; polished bronze mirrors could direct the light.

Later Islamic descriptions tell of changes in the Pharus, most notably the conversion of the third tier (originally a round structure) into a mosque. The last reasonably authentic representation of the Pharus before it was badly damaged in 1303 by an earthquake is a mosaic set in the ceiling of the chapel of Zeno in St. Mark's Cathedral in Venice, dating to about 1200 (see photograph in Clayton 1988.156). It shows a ship with St. Mark in the stern sailing into Alexandria's harbor, past the Pharus, whose top is adorned with the mosque mentioned above. It seems likely that Petrarch had seen this mosaic; it is also possible that Petrarch, who was an enthusiastic collector (*Fam.* 19.3.14–15), may have seen a likeness on a Roman coin (see Weiss 1964.2:207–208).

The Pharus suffered further damage from an earthquake in 1323, so that if Mandelli had reached Alexandria in 1358 he would have seen the lighthouse largely in ruins. In 1384, thirteen Tuscan pilgrims sailed into the port of Alexandria and did not so much as mention the Pharus (see references in note to lines 630–636). Today the site is occupied by the Islamic fort of Kait Bey, built in the fifteenth century from the remains of the foundations and lower level of the lighthouse.

The Pharus lives on in another way: its name provides the common noun for lighthouse in Italian and Spanish *(faro)*; in modern French the word is *phare*. For more detailed information on the Pharus, see Fraser 1972.1:17–20; vol. 2, notes 94–128; Clayton and Price 1988.138–157.

662–663 fortuna populi Romani truncum . . . caput flens victor aspexit: after his defeat at Pharsalus, Pompey fled to Egypt with no clear plan in mind. He was stabbed to death as he disembarked from his ship by order of the young Ptolemy XII in September of 48. According to Lucan (9.1014–1108), the head was severed from the body and later presented to Julius Caesar, Pompey's former father-in-law (Caesar and Pompey were identified simply as *socer generque* as early as Catullus 29.24). In Lucan (9.1037–1039) Caesar's grief was feigned:

> Utque fidem vidit sceleris tutumque putavit
> Iam bonus esse socer, lacrimas non sponte cadentes
> Effudit gemitusque expressit pectore laeto . . .

With Lucan's verses compare the first stanza of Petrarch's sonnet (*Canz.* 102. 1–4):

> Cesare, poi che 'l traditor d'Egitto
> li fece il don de l'onorata testa,
> celando l'allegrezza manifesta,
> pianse per gli occhi fuor, sì come è scritto;

Other sources known to Petrarch (Pseudo-Pliny, *De viris illust.*, Sherwin 1973.180) represent Caesar's grief as genuine. The *sì come è scritto* probably shows Petrarch's reluctance to believe such hypocrisy of Caesar. On *Canz.* 102, see Hainsworth 1988.24–29.

According to Lucan's long account of Pompey's betrayal and death (8.472–870), Pompey's headless body was hastily cremated and buried by a certain Cordus (or Codrus, as Petrarch spelled the name; *Fam.* 2.2.17) along the bank of the Nile. In a graveside eulogy, Cordus hopes that Pompey's wife Cornelia will be able one day to transfer the remains to an urn (8.770) and give them proper reverence. It is this urn to which Petrarch is probably referring in line 654. Petrarch makes it sound as though he has heard of an urn on display in Alexandria, said to contain the ashes of Pompey. On Fortune's role in Pompey's death, see especially Lucan, 8.701–742.

664 partitus orbem ut illum Nilus, Tybris hunc abluat: Pompey had been literally washed by the Nile, into whose waters his headless body had been thrown (*truncusque vadosis / huc illuc iactatur aquis,* Lucan, 8.698–699). Caesar's body received no such treatment, although Suetonius mentions (*Jul.* 82) that the conspirators had wanted to throw his body into the Tiber, disgraceful usage reserved for only the most despised (Suetonius, *Vit.* 17.1; *SHA, Commod.* 17.4). The literal meaning of *abluat* inspires such reflections, but perhaps Petrarch does not mean the verb to be understood in quite such a literal sense, intending to say only that both Caesar and Pompey were killed and buried near the rivers named.

Petrarch has adapted this line from Lucan, 6.810–811. The witch Erichtho calls forth from the underworld a corpse of one of Pompey's soldiers, killed at Pharsalus, who predicts the deaths of Pompey and Caesar:

> quem tumulum Nili, quem Thybridis alluat unda
> quaeritur, et ducibus tantum de funere pugna est.

Alluat (or *adluat)* is the superior reading in Lucan's line (meaning "flows past"), although *abluat* is the reading in several good manuscripts (see Shackleton Bailey 1988 note to line 6.810). Petrarch's copy of Lucan undoubtedly read *abluat,* which Housman 1926 (note *ad. loc.*) considers an error, not merely an inferior reading.

664–665 O fortune fides: Petrarch returns to the themes with which he began the *Itinerarium,* Fortune and death, but in reverse order. Thoughts on the particular deaths of Alexander, Pompey, and Caesar replace the theme of the universality of death found in the beginning and introduce Petrarch's final lesson for Mandelli: Fortune rules the destiny of all, great and small. He claims (*Fam.* 22.13.7 and especially *Sen.* 8.3; *Opera* 2:923–926) that Fortune is only an empty word corresponding to nothing in reality, but he is far too preoccupied with this "nothing" to be quite believable; cf. *Fam.* 18.16.7, where Petrarch (quoting Virgil, *A.* 8. 334) admits that Fortune is omnipotent and inescapable (ineluctabile fatum).

668–670 hactenus . . . sulcaverim: the *sulcaverim* is a jussive subjunctive, with an implied negative in the *hactenus* — thus far (and no farther). For a similar use cf. Virgil, *A.* 6.62, a passage Petrarch might well have had in mind here: both Mandelli and Petrarch, like Aeneas, have finished a difficult journey.

The metaphor of sailing / writing as plowing was very common throughout antiquity and the Middle Ages: for the metaphor as applied to sailing, it will suffice to refer to the examples cited in *OLD,* s.v. *sulco,* 1.b and as applied to writing, *OLD* s.v. the synonymous (and more common) *aro,* 1.d and 3.b; for more on the metaphor as applied to writing see Curtius 1953.313–314. Here Petrarch extends the metaphor in a quite unexpected way to walking as plowing. This novel application of the metaphor is brought out when Petrarch makes explicit all the terms of the comparison by enumerating what it is that is being "plowed" (maria, terram, papirum) and the means by which the acts of "plowing" are accomplished (remis, pedibus, calamo). How can it be said that Mandelli has "plowed" the earth with his feet? Petrarch is undoubtedly referring to the journey across the desert to Egypt: Mandelli and his companions will have made furrow-like trails in the sand with their feet. This plowing of the Egyptian sands then resonates with *papirum,* since papyrus was a writing material primarily associated with Egypt, which had always enjoyed a monopoly in its production and manufacture.

The metaphor of plowing, verging on the baroque in its elaboration, seems intended to be taken in all seriousness. By "plowing" over that great distance and through so many dangers, Mandelli will have prepared the way for the seeds not only of renewed piety but also of new knowledge, thanks in part to Petrarch, who had labored so hard in "plowing" his papyrus with his reed pen. It is the fruitfulness of this "plowing," even though it may be of the sand, that Petrarch wants to emphasize, perhaps in contrast with the proverbial expression *litus arare* (to plow the sand = expend great effort to no purpose), which may be in the back of his mind (for the proverb, see Ovid: *Quid arenae semina mandas? Non profecturis litora bubus aras!, Ep.* 5.115–116).

Petrarch's use of the terms *papirus* (papyrus) and *calamus* (reed) is of course anachronistic. These writing materials had long ago given way to parchment and paper and to the quill pen, but authors often continued to use the old terms, after the fashion of the older writers (see Bischoff 1990.7–19). It is quite possible that in using the terms in this Egyptian context Petrarch is alluding to Apuleius's line "*papyrum* Aegyptiam argutia Nilotici *calami* inscriptam non spreueris inspicere" (*Met.* 1.1), from a passage he knew well, having made a copy of it and quoted it elsewhere (*Fam.* 1.1.12; cf. *Fam.* 22.2.11).

672 hoc ego triduo consummavi: this statement need not be taken quite literally. In the Preface of his *De remediis utriusque fortune*, Petrarch says that his work was planned and executed within a very few days (*[opus] paucissimis diebus ceptum perfectumque)*: this is a work that Petrarch finally completed after some twelve years of work (see Wilkins 1958.71). An author's assertion that he has hurriedly put his work together is a falsely modest way of disclaiming much merit for his effort. This belongs to the well-worn *topos* of affected modesty, most commonly seen at the beginning of a work. Just above Petrarch (lines 670–671) resorted to a *topos* often seen in the conclusion of a work: he is bringing his work to an end because he is exhausted (see Curtius 1953.83 and 90). The coincidence of the number three in this sentence (*tribus* *mensibus . . . triduo*) is also more than a trifle suspicious. As Petrarch says in the *Secretum: Ego vero numerum ipsum ternarium tota mente complector, non tam quia tres eo Gratie continentur, quam quia divinitati amicissimum esse constat* (128 in *Prose*); on number symbolism see Curtius, 502–514.

Though it may not be literally true that Petrarch wrote the *Itinerarium* in three days, it does seem likely that he did write it in an uncomfortably short period of time.

673 domum . . . redeundum: surely a reminiscence of *De remediis fortuitorum: peregrinatio est vita: cum multum ambulaveris, domum redeundum est*, attributed to Seneca in Haase, 1886.3:447.

676 doctior nobis ac sanctior: possibly an ablative of comparison (Howard 1980.33), but if so Petrarch is in danger of sounding intolerably smug and condescending: Mandelli will return from his journey more learned and holier than Petrarch (is)! Better to take *nobis* as a dative of the person judging (in my view, in my opinion).

GAZETTEER

The Gazetteer is intended primarily as a supplement to the commentary, though inevitably there will be some overlapping of information. A number of places not mentioned or discussed in the commentary at all will find their place here (see, e.g., Milan, Massa Marittima, Malea, Syria, etc.). Sometimes Petrarch does not name a place but rather describes it in a poetic fashion, lending an epic patina to the narrative. Instead of Portovenere, he says "a port famous for the name of Venus" (cf. *Africa,* 6.857: "a port pleasing to Venus"); the Frigido is a "river cold in fact and in name." The names of such places are boldface italicized. Occasionally, he discusses a topographical feature of a place he does not name. He places a miraculous spring in Egypt, but he does not say where in Egypt (Matarea). These names are also italicized. Only some of the notable places he mentions in connection with Naples and Jerusalem (and environs) have separate entries. The disproportionately large number of toponyms for the coastal and inland areas of Liguria and Tuscany reflect Mandelli's status within the Visconti family, which had expansionist aspirations in these parts: by 1401 Gian Galeazzo had control of Perugia, Siena, and Pisa and in 1402 he died laying siege to Florence. The numbers in parentheses refer to the numbered lines of the Latin text.

Abydos (449): ancient town on the Hellespont (Dardanelles). It functioned as a toll station until late Byzantine times. Nearly opposite Sestos on the European shore, it was well known as the scene for the story of Hero and Leander. See Sestos.

Achaia (423): here intended by Petrarch to refer to the whole peninsula forming the south part of Greece (Peloponnese), though elsewhere he restricts its use to one of the seven traditional divisions of the peninsula, following Mela and Pliny (see de Nolhac 1907.2.77 for a marginal note in Petrarch's Pliny). It was only after the Peloponnese became a Roman province (146 BC) that Achaia acquired its wider meaning. In the Middle Ages (after the early thirteenth century), the peninsula was often called Morea, owing to its resemblance on a map to the leaf of the mulberry tree (morum), an idea found in Mela, 2.38.

Acheron (264): one of the rivers in the underworld. In Virgil (*A.* 6.295), it is the river that separates the living (or the unburied) from those in the underworld.

Acon (493): known as Acco in the Old Testament, it is regularly called Ptolemais in the New Testament and in many early Christian writings until about the seventh century. Acon, along with Jaffa, became especially important after Caesarea's artificial harbor silted up following its capture by Arabs. Baldwin took the city in 1104 and made it the main link between the Latin kingdom and Europe. In the late twelfth century, it became headquarters for the Knights of St. John (Hospitallers) and in consequence was called St.-Jean-d'Acre. Weakened by quarreling factions of merchants, especially the Venetians and the Genoese, the city fell in 1291 to the Mamluks, the Turkish-speaking warrior caste, which ruled Egypt and Syria as an united kingdom since 1260. It lay in ruins for the next 450 years.

Adriatic Sea (421, Adriaticum equor): arm of the Mediterranean Sea between Italy and the Balkan Peninsula, about 500 miles long. The Romans commonly referred to it as Mare Superum or Upper Sea, as at line 274. Navigation on the Adriatic was proverbially dangerous because of frequent and sudden storms.

Aegean Sea (439, Egei Maris): arm of the Mediterranean Sea between Greece and Turkey, about 400 miles long by 200 wide.

Aeolian Islands (376, Aeoliae [Insulae]): a group of small volcanic islands in the southeast Tyrrhenian Sea off the north coast of Sicily; correctly numbered seven by ancient geographers, the chief of them being Lipara (mod. Lipari) and Vulcanus (Vulcano). These islands resonate strongly with Virgil's epic. Not only do winds from the Aeolian Islands shipwreck Aeneas in book one of the *Aeneid*, but also, in a more positive vein, the craftsman god Vulcan fashions armor for the hero's protection on the island named after him (*A*. 8. 416–453).

Albenga (97, Albingaunum): a port city on the coast of Liguria, about 50 miles southwest of Genoa; in ancient times capital city of the Ingauni. Petrarch inferred from his ancient sources that Albenga's dominance in Liguria preceded Genoa's.

Alexandria (641): founded by Alexander the Great in 331 BC, the city became a center of Hellenic culture and the site of the greatest library in the ancient world. Most of the ancient landmarks and monuments, such as Alexander's tomb, were long gone in Petrarch's day. The famous lighthouse called the Pharus had only recently collapsed because of an earthquake. The quest for Alexander's tomb has become almost an intramural sport for professional and amateur Egyptologists.

Antioch (498, mod. Antakya): founded in 300 BC by Seleucus, an officer of Alexander, the city is located where the south coast of Asia Minor (Turkey) meets the north coast of Syria about 20 miles inland on the Orontes river. It quickly became the most important city in northern Syria and retained its prominence after it became a Roman province in 64 BC. About 100 years later it became an important center of the early Christian religion: it was here that the followers of Christ were first dubbed "Christians" (Acts 11:26). By the fourth century, it ranked after Rome and Alexandria as the third Patriarchal see. The rise of Constantinople and later Jerusalem to the Patriarchate status reduced its importance. It fell to the Mamluks in 1268, and its decline was rapid thereafter. As early as the sixth century the Placenza pilgrim reports nothing more of interest to see in the city than the tombs of several little-known saints (Wilkinson 1997. 89). It is only rarely mentioned by pilgrims.

Anzio (223, Antii Caput): called *cauo danza* on the portolan charts. It was a pirate stronghold of the Volscians, but came under control of Rome (33 miles distant) in the fourth century BC. Hometown to two of Rome's nastier emperors, Caligula and Nero, the place fared well until the Saracens destroyed the harbor. It was an insignificant place in Petrarch's day.

Apennines (391): mountain range in central Italy, extending the full length of the peninsula in a bow-shape from near Savona in the northwest to Reggio di Calabria in the south, about 840 miles in length and 25 to 80 miles wide. It is the source of most of Italy's rivers and streams. Geologically speaking, Sicily is a continuation on the north and east of the chain of the Apennines, as Petrarch claims.

Argentario, Mt. (204, Argentarius Mons): mountain promontory, 7 miles in length and 4 miles wide; 2,100 feet in height and joined to the mainland by three narrow strips of land (described by Rutilius, *De reditu suo*, 1. 315–324, and given its modern name). Porto S. Stefano is at its north end and Port' Ercole at its southern extremity.

Armenia Minor (484): first country to adopt Christianity as its national religion (AD 303). Armenia Minor (Lesser) or Cilician Armenia was that part of Armenia that extended along the south coast of Turkey (anc. Cilicia), in its most prosperous days (twelfth and thirteenth centuries) almost as far west as the west end of Cyprus to its immediate south. By Petrarch's time, Armenia Minor had given up most of this coastal territory and was confined to the *extremus maris angulus* on the north end of the Syrian coast, as Petrarch says. It remained, however, an essential part of crusader strategy to recover the Holy Land, since the Armenians were able to hold out against the Turks to the northeast and the Mamluks to the south until 1375.

Arno (174): flows west from the Apennines 150 miles through Florence and Pisa into the Tyrrhenian Sea.

Ascalon (492, mod. Ashquelon): 41 miles west-southwest of Jerusalem, Ascalon was a city by 2000 BC. The city enjoyed Herod the Great's favor, and its loyalty to Rome during the Jewish revolt of AD 66–70 won it many privileges. It was able to maintain its position into the early Arab Period (640–1099), but its fortunes varied greatly during the crusades. The city was destroyed by the Mamluks in 1270 and never recovered.

Asia Minor (454): forms the west extremity of Asia, between the Black Sea on the north and the Mediterranean Sea on the south and bordering on the Aegean Sea on the west; forms the greater part of modern Turkey.

Astura (226): a small island off the coast between Anzio and Monte Circeo, a favorite retreat for Cicero and others of the Roman wealthy. It was an island in antiquity, but at some later time it was connected to the mainland by a causeway. The name appears on the earliest portolan charts.

Athens (448, Athene): with a population of c. 8,000–10,000 and in the possession of Catalan mercenaries, Athens' assets in the fourteenth century were little more than the intact Parthenon, now converted to a church dedicated to the Virgin Mary, and the distorted memory of its glorious history. For Petrarch, the city's name represented a complex of political and intellectual values, especially when set in contrast with Sparta.

Avenza (166, Laventia): a fortified castle about 2-1/2 miles southwest of Carrara, which Petrarch passed on his trip to Naples in 1343. It was a dangerous place at that time because Luchino Visconti, motivated by pride and greed (*Fam.* 5.3.4), was waging war with Pisa in the area. Arrangements for peace were concluded in May of 1345 at Pietrasanta. It is interesting to note that Petrarch does not refer to Luchino by name; he is simply the tyrant.

Avernus (264): volcanic lake 8 miles west of Naples, about 2 miles in circumference and 110 ft. deep. Surrounded by a dense forest until Agrippa cut it down and united Avernus with the sea by a canal via the Lucrine Lake and with Cuma by means of a tunnel on the northwest shore of the lake. Another long gallery and chamber cut into the rock on the south shore, also the work of

Agrippa, has been identified as the entrance to the underworld (Grotta della Sibilla). The Sibyl's *domus*, mentioned by Petrarch, was really the Neronian bath on the east side of the lake. See Cuma.

Babylon (618, Babilon): founded in 525 BC by the Persian Cambyses as a fort at the apex of the Nile delta and named after the Babylon of Mesopotamia. In Roman times this was headquarters for one of the three legions stationed in Egypt. In AD 641, invading Arabs took it over and founded al-Fustat (Entrenchment) or "Old Cairo" nearby. Babylon's name is often misused for Cairo in the Middle Ages.

Bacoli (287, anc. Bauli): located on the west coast of the Bay of Naples between Baia and Capo Miseno. This place is not named by Petrarch, but here is located the *piscina mirabilis* to which he refers. It was the reservoir that supplied the naval base at Porto Miseno with water, though Petrarch thought it was part of Nero's Pool (Piscina or Stagnum Neronis), which extended from Baia to Lake Avernus.

Baia (286, Baiae): a dependency of Cuma in antiquity, it never became a city in the Roman sense of the term (municipium), but flourished as a fashionable spa from the first century BC until the third century AD, when earthquakes and malaria sent it into decline. Medieval interest in the medicinal properties of its hot springs gave it resurgent popularity.

Beirut (491, Baruth; anc. Berytus): rarely, if ever, mentioned in the Old Testament, this port city became a thriving cultural center famous for its law school in the Graeco-Roman period. In the mid-sixth century, it suffered a devastating earthquake and fell into steep decline after falling to the Arabs in the seventh century. It rose again as an important crusader port, until it fell into Muslim hands again in 1187. Retaken and rebuilt by Christians in the thirteenth century, it surrendered in 1291 to the Mamluks who made it once more an important port. In 1350, Ludolph von Suchem has high praise for the harbor facilities and mentions an area nearby as the place where St. George slew the dragon (Stewart 1895.135).

Bethlehem (559): located 5 miles south-southwest of Jerusalem, this town was the place where King David was born (1 Sam. 16). Though an insignificant village in the time of Jesus, it was always associated with Messianic hope. According to early Christian tradition, Jesus was born here in a cave, and Constantine built a church over it in AD 339. After 529 Justinian pulled down the old church and rebuilt it on a larger scale. The church, which provides access to the cave, survives today. Now, as then, pilgrims are shown, without historical justification, adjoining caves said to be where the Holy Innocents were buried and where St. Jerome lived and translated the Bible into Latin (Vulgate).

Brindisi (415, Brundusium): seaport on the Strait of Otranto about 30 miles north of Taranto. The Romans took control first in 244 BC and extended the Via Appia to it about this time. Thereafter, it was the principal route from Italy to Greece. In 49 BC Julius Caesar attempted to cut off Pompey's retreat from Italy by blocking the entrance to the harbor, an engineering feat that intrigued Petrarch because of the overblown description of the operation in Lucan's *De bello civili* (2.610–756 etc.; cf. Petrarch's *Metr.* 3.4.31–46 in *Rime*, 774–776). Petrarch planned a visit to Brindisi in 1343, but he never made the trip.

Byzantion (450, Bizantion): ancient port city founded c. 660 BC on the west side of the Bosporus. Its name was changed in AD 330 to Constantinople, "city of Constantine," when that Roman Emperor chose it as the site for the capital of the Roman East. The elevation of the city to the seat of empire initiated the rivalry with Rome which led to the latter's long decline. The name Istanbul was officially adopted in 1930.

Caesarea (492): situated 22 miles south of modern Haifa, the city was built by Herod the Great (37–4 BC) on the site of an ancient anchorage called Strato's Tower and named after Caesar Augustus. In his *Jewish War* and *Antiquities*, Josephus gives lyrical descriptions of the place, which modern archaeologists are proving to be largely accurate. After the Romans assumed direct control over Palestine in AD 6, Caesarea became their capital. Pontius Pilate, Prefect of Judea, had his residence there (AD 26–37); and Cornelius, a centurion of the Roman garrison in Caesarea, was the first gentile converted to Christianity (Acts 10). The city fell in 640 to the Arabs, who allowed the harbor to silt up. When the crusaders took the city in 1101, the Genoese found during the looting the "emerald" dish that they thought was the Holy Grail. The Mamluk sultan leveled the city in 1265, and it lay abandoned until the late nineteenth century, when there was a vain attempt to repopulate the site. On the excavations at Caesarea, see Raban 1996, valuable for its attention to the medieval period.

Calabria (381): Petrarch means the region of Italy on the "instep" of Italy's boot. Here the term corresponds with the Bruttium of the ancient geographers. In antiquity, the term Calabria was vague and fluctuating, but usually referred to the "heel" of Italy's boot.

Campania (366): the exact boundaries of this region varied at different periods. Petrarch uses the term with reference to the particularly fertile area northwest of Naples, though it generally had much more extensive application.

Capo Corvo (155): well-known landmark just north of the Magra river. The black promontory set amid white limestone cliffs caught the attention of navigators. The name appears on the earliest portolan charts.

Capo Miseno (256, Misenus Collis): promontory that marks the northwest boundary of the Bay of Naples. Its resemblance to a burial tumulus gave rise to the legend that it was the burial place of Misenus, the trumpeter of Aeneas.

Capomonte (130, Caput montis): southern extremity of a promontory called today Monte di Portofino. Petrarch's *portolano* told him Capomonte was 15 miles from Genoa.

Capraia (188, Capraria): volcanic islet north of Elba about 30 miles from Populonia, the nearest point on the mainland. The name is derived from the number of wild goats that originally inhabited the island, according to Varro.

Capri (360, Capree): island off the southwest tip of the Bay of Naples, about 4 miles long and 2 miles at the widest point. Acquired by Augustus Caesar, who built aqueducts and roads, the island became the permanent residence of Tiberius in AD 27. Stories of his profligacy and cruelty told by Suetonius and Tacitus made the island famous. One of the emperor's luxurious villas was excavated in the 1930s.

Carrhae (619, Carre): Petrarch mistakenly thought that the ancient city of Carrhae in Mesopotamia gave its name to Cairo in Egypt because of the similarity of names. Cairo was founded about 9 miles south of the apex of the Delta in AD 969 by the invading Fatimid dynasty. It is said that the city is called "Victorious" because its construction began when the planet Mars (al-Qahir) had been in the ascendant. The city reached its greatest prosperity in the Middle Ages as the capital of the Mamluk sultans in the thirteenth and fourteenth centuries.

Carthage (98): traditionally founded by colonists from the Phoenician kingdom of Tyre in 814 BC, but represented anachronistically by Virgil's *Aeneid* as founded immediately after the fall of Troy (c. 1200 BC). Dominant in the western Mediterranean by the fourth century, the city came in conflict with Rome in the third and second centuries. The Second Punic War (218–201 BC) constituted Rome's greatest danger in her early history. Scipio Africanus, however, defeated Hannibal at the battle of Zama, a victory that led to Rome's complete dominance in the western Mediterranean and soon in the East. The city was utterly destroyed by the Romans in 146 BC, but later flourished in the early empire and became an important center of Christian learning until taken by the Arabs in AD 697. Scipio's defeat of Hannibal is the subject of Petrarch's ambitious epic *Africa*, a project never finished and left unpublished at his death. The epic themes of this work, along with those from Virgil's *Aeneid* and Livy's prose epic, *Ab urbe condita*, enliven the first half of the *Itinerarium* and imbue it with an exemplary value that constitutes it as a most unusual specimen of "recovery literature."

Castel dell' Ovo (342): located on the rocky islet called Megaris in Roman times, in the Bay of Naples. It was later connected to the mainland by a mole, forming a small harbor now called Porto di Santa Lucia. Constructed by Frederick II of Hohenstaufen as a stronghold for his treasures, the castle later became associated with the poet Virgil through fanciful stories told about his magical powers. So negatively does Petrarch react to these stories that he warns Mandelli not to go near the Castel dell' Ovo.

Cilicia (457): name of an ancient country and region in southeast Asia Minor, extending along the Mediterranean coast south of the Taurus Mts. In Roman times, it became a stronghold for pirates until subdued by Pompey the Great and made a Roman province. In the late eleventh century, the eastern part of coastal Cilicia became an independent Armenian principality (Armenia Minor, q.v.).

Civitavecchia (208, Civitas Vetus; anc. Centum Cellae or Traiani Portus): seaport 39 miles west-northwest of Rome. This port was the work of Trajan, following the general plan of Claudius's harbor at Ostia (see Hadrian's Port). Pliny the Younger (*Ep.*, 6.31, 15–17) provides the earliest description of it (c. AD 107), which accords reasonably well with Rutilius Namantianus's poetical account of AD 417 (*De reditu suo*, 1.239–245). After suffering much damage from marauding Saracens in 812, the city and port, now called Civitavecchia, were later restored and have served as Rome's harbor to the present.

Como (255, Comum): situated on the southern end of Lacus Larius (mod. Lago di Como). Gauls originally founded the town. After Rome took control of Cisapine Gaul in the second century BC, Como's population was augmented several times by Roman colonists and the city was renamed Novum Comum. The town flourished to the end of the Roman imperial period and even maintained its prosperity into the Middle Ages when the city's name is often written Cume (anc. Cumae) or Cumum for reasons far from clear. It is the ancestral home of the Mandelli family.

Corfu (422, Corcyra): large island off the coast of southwest Albania. For those sailing from Otranto around southern Greece, Corfu would be the first significant landfall. At *Africa* 8.331, Petrarch mistakenly gives Cephalonia (Cefalu) as the first island to be encountered (see Fera 1984.374–375). Petrarch identified the island with Scheria, land of Homer's Phaeacians, following Pliny.

Corinth (427, Chorintus): ancient city with a long history. It is interesting to Petrarch because of Rome's cynical destruction of the city in 146 BC and because of its location near the isthmus, where so many had tried to dig a canal. *Portolani* and portolan charts of this period mention the "streto di Coranto" but do not refer to the city itself. Like Athens and Sparta, Corinth had fallen into obscurity.

Corneto (204, Cornetum): called Tarquinii in antiquity. The population was transferred about a mile and one-half to the present site after the ancient city was devastated by incursions of Lombards and Saracens (sixth-eighth centuries). In 1922, Corneto assumed a form of its ancient name, Tarquinia. Petrarch appears to have been the first to connect the modern town with the ancient city, founded according to legend by Tarchon, ally of Aeneas and the Trojans (Servius, *A*. 10.179 and 198).

Coron (433, Corona): controlled by the Venetians from the early thirteenth century, this port of call lies 20 miles southeast of Modon on the Messenian Gulf.

Corsica (191): island west of north Italy. It became a Roman province in the third and second centuries BC. With the collapse of the Roman Empire, the island was invaded, occupied, or claimed by Vandals, Byzantines, Lombards, Franks, and Arabs. Through a donation of Charlemagne, the Pope had become titular ruler of Corsica, but delegated its administration only after the ejection of the Arabs. In 1077, Gregory VII entrusted the administration to Pisa, but Pisa's control gave way to Genoa after the battle of Meloria in 1284. Confusion and hostility ensued when Boniface VIII invested James II of Aragon with control of the island in 1297. The Genoese and the Aragonese struggled for control throughout the fourteenth century.

Cos (442): island off southwest Turkey; site of the famous temple of Asculapius; birthplace of Hippocrates c. 460 BC.

Crete (435): island about 60 miles south-southeast of Cape Malea in south Greece. It is the fifth largest island in the Mediterranean, 160 miles long and from 5 to 35 miles wide. It was the center of the Minoan-Mycenaean civilization (3000–c. 1100 BC), some of whose remains could still be seen in the Middle Ages.

Part of the Byzantine empire in later times, Crete passed to the Venetians as a result of the Fourth Crusade (1204). Petrarch mentions the place primarily as the place where pagan religion (superstition) had its origin.

Crotone (410, Croton): celebrated Achaean colony of the eighth century BC, on the "sole" of Italy's boot. It produced famous Olympic athletes and distinguished physicians, and it became the home of the philosopher Pythagoras (c. 540). At a distance of six miles from the city was the great temple of Lacinian Juno. Only one of an original 48 temple columns stands today. It gives the modern name to the promontory on which the temple stood, Capo Colonna. It had fallen far from its former glory by the end of the Roman Republic, as had the city, which however remained rubicated on portolan charts.

Crypta neapolitana (320): a tunnel made in 38 BC through a rocky ridge called Mons Pausilypus by the engineer L. Cocceius, to connect Naples with the new harbor installations at Pozzuoli and the Lucrine Lake (Portus Julius). The original dimensions of the tunnel (now closed) are estimated at 21 feet wide, with a maximum height of 70 feet along a passage of some 2,700 feet. On the Neapolitan end of the tunnel are located the shrine of S. Maria delle Hydrie and the Roman columbarium identified by Petrarch as the "Tomb" of Virgil. A short distance away is S. Maria di Piedigrotta.

Cuma (252, Cume): 10 miles northwest of Naples on the Campanian coast, this was the first Greek settlement on the Italian mainland (c. 740 BC). It dominated the area for about 250 years, in turn founding Naples, Pozzuoli, and other places, and promoting Hellenic culture with its Italian neighbors, the most important being Rome. Loyal to Rome during the Punic Wars, Cuma adopted Latin as its official language in 180 BC. The harbor and acropolis were rebuilt under Augustus Caesar: the Temple of Apollo and the Sibyl were important to Augustan ideology. During the third-fourth centuries, Cuma declined but remained important until the eighth century, when the acropolis became a stronghold for pirates and other malefactors. Naples led an attack on the acropolis in the early thirteenth century, pulled down the temple, and buried the Sibyl's cave. Thereafter, nothing was to be seen on the site, and in time, the locals in their imaginations transferred Apollo's Temple and the Sibyl's cave to Lake Avernus and identified them with monuments there. Modern philologists and archeologists such as Amedeo Maiuri have largely dispelled the confusion and restored these monuments to their proper places on Cuma's acropolis (see Caputo 1996 and McKay 1997. 78–88).

Cyclades (434): a group of islands in the south Aegean Sea, so called because they lie in a circle (*kuklos*) around the sacred island of Delos. The ancient sources known to Petrarch (Mela and Pliny) put their number at 12. Evidently, Petrarch is extending this meaning of the term, since he says to name them all would be like counting the stars. Nowadays, the term is used to refer to a group of about 220 islets and islands in the south Aegean Sea between the Peloponnese and the Dodecanese.

Cyprus (470): third largest island in the Mediterranean, 60 miles west of the coast of Syria and 40 miles south of the coast of Asia Minor (Turkey). To offset the tradition of Cyprus's decadent reputation, Petrarch mentions the ascetic Hilarion, who he mistakenly thinks is buried on the island. Richard the Lionheart took the place during the Third Crusade (1101) and bestowed lordship of it on Guy of Lusignan, beginning a dynasty that ruled 1192–1474. After the fall of Acre in 1291, Cyprus, along with Rhodes and Armenia, remained the focus of crusader strategy to recover the Holy Land.

Damascus (496): situated about 70 miles east of Beirut, this ancient city is mentioned as early as the sixteenth century BC in Egyptian texts. Thus, the city is some 1,200 years older than Antioch. It was overshadowed in the Graeco-Roman period by Antioch, but became very important under the Mamluks. The most important artery in this vital kingdom was the road from Cairo to Damascus, since Damascus had become a kind of second capital, the Mamluks' bulwark against Mongolian encroachment in the fourteenth century. Renowned for its artisans and scholars, the city is described by many European visitors in the fourteenth century such as Ludolph von Suchem and Niccolò da Poggibonsi in rhapsodic terms.

Don (622, Tanais): a river in southwest Russia; 1,225 miles long, it empties into the Sea of Azov. This river is a major feature of the *mappaemundi*: it divides Europe from Asia in the north, according to ancient geographers, just as the Nile separates Africa from Asia in the south. Although the Don appears on the later portolan charts, such as Petrarch was using, the river is not a dominant feature in them. The prominence given the Don in this passage of the *Itinerarium* is a vestigial element derived from Petrarch's *mappamundi*.

Egypt (573): a highly organized political entity from about 3000 BC, Egypt's dynastic history ended with Alexander's conquest in 332 BC. Greek dominance gave way to Roman in 30 BC, and Roman and Byzantine to Muslim in AD 640. The invading Fatamid caliphs, who ruled from 969–1171, built Cairo, quarrying building materials from the ancient capital Memphis. From the middle of the thirteenth century to 1517, Mamluks ruled Egypt and Syria (in the medieval sense of the term) from Cairo, with Damascus as a second capital. Henceforth, crusader strategy to retake the Holy Land concentrated on Egypt.

What people of medieval Europe knew about ancient Egypt before the Greeks and Romans was derived from the Bible and various Bible commentaries and from Josephus' *Antiquities* primarily. The accuracy of this information was not good. In San Marco's in Venice, for example, Petrarch would have seen a mosaic representing the pyramids as the granaries (Horrea) of Joseph, a bit of misinformation derived from the *Cosmographia* of Julius Honorius (fifth century AD) and often repeated in pilgrim texts (see edition of Riese 1878.51). True Egyptomania did not seize Europe until the arrival in Florence of Horapollo's *Hieroglyphica* in about 1422. This work, with its incomplete and misleading conception of Egyptian hieroglyphic writing, became the unchallenged authority for centuries and inspired numerous scholars and artists. In Petrarch's day, however, the Egyptians were "dogs" who barred fervent Christians from the Holy Land.

Elba (196, Ilva): about 6 miles from Piombino on the mainland, the island is about 17 miles long and 12 wide at the most. Celebrated throughout its history for its iron ore, the island came into the Pisan's possession in the eleventh century and remained in their control until 1399, when the island was sold to the Visconti of Milan. The island also produces in the eastern and central areas good grapes, olives, and fruit.

Etna (408, Ethna): active volcano in northeast Sicily, near the coast, about 11,000 feet in height. There was a severe eruption in 1329.

Euboea (438, Eubea): large island to the east of central Greece, 90 miles long and 4 to 30 miles wide. In the central part of its west coast, the narrow Euripus Strait separates it from the mainland. The Venetians claimed the island in 1204, but did not fully control it until 1366. The Venetian name for the island (Negroponte) evolved through several stages of corruption from the term Euripus.

Falernian Hill (306, Falernus Collis): at *Africa*, 6.852 Petrarch refers to this place in the plural (Falerni Colles), no doubt for metrical reasons. At *Fam*. 5.4.7, Petrarch refers to Falnerus as a mountain (mons), whereas almost all ancient sources speak of Falernus as open country (ager). Of the ancient sources, only Florus's *Epitome* (1.11.5 = 1.16) speaks of Falernus as a *mons*, and Petrarch is evidently following his authority. In fact, Falernus refers to a fertile tract of land in northern Campania, at the foot of Mons Massicus. This "mountain," in reality a series of low-lying and connected hills, was, like the Falernus ager, celebrated for its wine (e.g., Virgil *A*. 7.725–726 and Horace, *C*. 1.1.19). In the letter cited above, Petrarch says he saw the Falernian Mountain. What he must have seen was Monte Massico, covered with grape vines and misidentified by his guides.

In the *De montibus*, Boccaccio also calls Falernus "mons," clearly referring to the same wine district as Petrarch (Stocchi 1998.1849, with note on 2049). He may have been led into this error by reading the *Itinerarium* in 1359, since he did not use Florus as a source in the *De montibus* and may not have had access to the text.

Florence (176, Florentia): about 50 miles east of Pisa on the Arno, 145 miles north-northwest of Rome, Florence was established as a colony for Julius Caesar's veterans in 59 BC. The fact that his father had been a Florentine citizen made Petrarch one also. At times he and others referred to Florence as his *patria*, as in line 172, but he never lived there and had only visited there briefly on two occasions, both times in October of 1350 on his way to and from Rome. Although Boccaccio and others, whom Petrarch met for the first time on these visits, tried unsuccessfully to bring Petrarch permanently to Florence on numerous occasions, he never found the enticements offered sufficient motivation.

Formia (238, Formiae or Formianum): a favorite residence of Cicero, who often referred to his place as the "Formian" (Formianum). It remained a flourishing place until Saracens destroyed it in 856. Formia is represented on the portolan charts as Mola or Molla (di Gaeta), indicating dependency on the neighboring town. A famous legend (e.g., Horace, *C.* 3.17) made Formia the site of the story of the Laestrygonians in the *Odyssey* and the Roman clan of Lamiae descendants of Lamus, king of those legendary people.

Frigido (166–167, Fluvius Frigidus): small river or stream that runs past Massa.

Gaeta (233, Caieta): located in central Italy between Terracina and Formiae, it derived its name from Caieta, nurse variously of Aeneas, Ascanius and Creusa, whom Virgil represents as being buried here. Gaeta was an important port throughout the Middle Ages, especially after the destruction of Formiae in the ninth century.

Genoa (83, Ianua): came to history's notice during the Second Punic War. Taken by Mago in 205 BC and destroyed by him before his departure two years later, Genoa afterwards became a Roman *municipium* and the chief emporium of the Ligurians, but never attained the importance it had in the Middle Ages, though its full potential was constantly undercut by civil discord. The medieval form of the name (Ianua) is first found in Liudprand, a Lombard writer of the tenth century; the classical form is Genua, first found in Livy. Petrarch had visited in Genoa on three occasions (1311, 1347 and 1353). On the last occasion of his visit to Genoa, Petrarch was representing the Visconti, who controlled Genoa from 1353–1356.

Gorgona (187, Gorgon): volcanic islet north of Elba, about 20 miles from the mainland on a line with Livorno.

Grosseto (200): set about 7 miles inland and 43 miles southwest of Siena, this town lies on a plain through which flows the Ombrone; identified on the *carte pisane* as "foce d. Grosito," i.e., "mouth (of the Ombrone) of Grosseto." It did not begin to develop until the ninth century when the Saracens sacked Rusellae, an ancient Etruscan and Roman stronghold about 5 miles northeast of Grosseto. By the twelfth century, it had its own bishop, but fell under Siena's control in 1224. Petrarch probably mentions Grosseto because he knows that Visconti ambitions extend this far south. In 1399, Siena made Gian Galeazzo Visconti *signore* of the city.

Hadrian's Port (211, Hadriani Portus): following up on a plan of Julius Caesar's, Claudius undertook in AD 42 to build an enclosed harbor two miles north of Ostia. A deep basin was excavated and protected by two moles with a lighthouse that rivaled that of Alexandria. Some 60 years later, Trajan undertook major improvements that made the harbor usable throughout antiquity until the ninth century. In antiquity, it was known as Portus Augusti or simply as Portus. Why Petrarch connects it with Hadrian is not known.

Hellespont (449): mod. Dardanelles; narrow strait between Europe and Turkey, 38 miles long and 3/4 to 4 miles wide; connects the Sea of Marmora with the Aegean Sea.

Herculaneum (363): small town built on a spur projecting from the lower northwest slopes of Vesuvius, about 5 miles southeast of Naples. The eruption of AD 79 overwhelmed the wealthy resort with a mudflow, rather than volcanic ash. Like Pompeii (q.v.), Herculaneum had been badly damaged by an earthquake in 62 or 63, but was not entirely destroyed at that time, as Petrarch believed. Its location was never forgotten, but excavations did not begin until the middle of the eighteenth century.

Isauria (458): ancient district in Asia Minor on the north slope of the Taurus Mts. By the first century BC its boundaries included the west end of Cilicia. Known in antiquity as a wild race of people, the Isaurians confined their marauding ways to land, after Pompey had broken them of their piratical habits.

Ischia (245, Iscla or Inarime): this large island, about six miles off the mainland in the Tyrrhenian Sea, marks the northern boundary of the Bay of Naples. Burial place of the legendary Typhoeus (Virgil, *A.* 9.715–716).

Jaffa (492, anc. Joppa; mod. Tel Aviv): located 35 miles northwest of Jerusalem, Jaffa was central Palestine's most important port for pilgrims in the Middle Ages. The Mamluks blocked up the harbor in 1335 to discourage crusaders, but it remained the port where most pilgrims landed despite the difficulties. Christians especially revered the city as the place where Peter saw in a vision that gentiles should be admitted into the church (Acts 9:36–10:23).

Jerusalem (495, Ierusalem and Ierosolyma): the city had its origin in a fortress located in the smaller and eastern of two hills, 35 miles from the Mediterranean and 13 miles west of the north end of the Dead Sea. David captured the acropolis c. 1000 BC, and his son Solomon built walls and the first temple in the tenth century. Petrarch singles out for mention the city's destruction by the Roman Titus in AD 70. Another Jewish rebellion (132–135) brought on Hadrian's wrath, causing him to level the city again and rebuild it as Aelia Capitolina, a name that is still found in Christian texts of the seventh century. With the rise of Christianity, there was a sharp rise in pilgrimages. The zeal to locate precisely holy places in the city and in Palestine led to the building of numerous churches and monasteries in the fourth and following centuries. When the city fell under Muslim control in 638, Christian pilgrims continued to come, unimpeded and unmolested for the most part, until the Seljuk Turks captured the city in 1071. Their ill treatment of pilgrims led in a straight line to the first crusade and the recapture of Jerusalem in 1099. After the city fell to Saladin in 1187, recovery of the city was the goal of several crusades in the years that followed. Christian efforts were temporarily successful, but the city was lost to the Muslims in 1244, along with the rest of the crusader holdings in the Palestine by the end of the century. Controlled now by the Mamluks of Egypt who took little notice of the city, Jerusalem became in the fourteenth century a political limbo to which out-of-favor emirs were banished, of interest only to pilgrims and scholars. The places especially recommended by Petrarch: ruins of the temple, the Holy Sepulcher and Golgotha, Mt. Sion, Mt. of Olives and various places outside the city, unnamed but easily identified by famous deeds of Jesus done in them, as reported by Scripture.

Jordan River (582): arises in Syria and flows c. 200 miles through the Sea of Galilee to empty into the north end of the Dead Sea. Pilgrims visited it at a place about 5 miles north of the Dead Sea to see the place where St. John baptized Jesus (Matt. 3:13–17). This same place was thought to be the spot where Joshua crossed over into Israel and where Elijah was taken up into heaven (2 Kings 2:11).

Lacedaemon (448): the ancient city, better known as Sparta, occupied a large triangular area on the right bank of the Eurotas river in south central Peloponnese (anc. Laconia). After a long and distinguished history, the city was badly damaged by Alaric in the late fourth century, and in the ninth century, its citizens abandoned the site when the Slavs invaded. The Byzantines tried to revive the city, but by the middle of the thirteenth century, it faded from history. Like Athens, Sparta retained its iconic status. It stood for a whole range of political, intellectual and social values in the Middle Ages.

Lerici (135, Herix): seaport on the north shore of the Gulf of La Spezia; visited by Petrarch on his way to Naples in 1343. The place was connected in Petrarch's imagination with Eryx, name of an ancient city and mountain in west Sicily, places that were associated with the hero Aeneas and the Trojans. At *Africa*, 6. 858–859, he called Lerici "Ausonian [Italian] Eryx, keeping the name of the Sicilian coast."

Lesbos (442): island in east Aegean Sea off the northwest coast of Turkey, in possession of a Genoese adventurer when Petrarch wrote his *Itinerarium*. He notices the place as the birthplace of Theophrastus, associate and successor of Aristotle. Theophrastus was best known in the Middle Ages for an antimarriage tract preserved by St. Jerome (*The Golden Book of Theophrastus on Mar-*

riage). The work was well known in the Middle Ages in various vernacular versions. Chaucer quotes it approvingly in the Merchant's Tale.

Libya (595, Lybia): ancient Greek name for that part of North Africa immediately west of Egypt. Marcus Cato's march around the larger of the two Syrtes (q.v.) through a hostile desert region became famous as a feat of endurance and serves Petrarch as an *exemplum* for Mandelli.

Liternum (239): 5 miles north of Cuma, settled as a Roman colony in 194 BC, Literno's site was badly chosen: the whole area was marshy and unhealthful and the nearby shoreline of the coast inhospitable. The place never rose to any importance except as the place Scipio Africanus chose for his retirement, really a self-imposed exile. Petrarch had wanted to visit the place while at Naples, as Seneca had once done (*Ep.* 86), but could not find a proper guide. There would have been little or nothing of the ancient town for him to see, though modern archeologists have uncovered a few things of interest.

Livorno (185, Liburnum): this port city began its rise as the major port in Tuscany when Porto Pisano fell into serious decline in the early fifteenth century. There was an impressive lighthouse in operation here in Petrarch's day.

Lodi (464, Laudensis Colonia): called Laus Pompeia by Pliny, the town became a Roman colony in 89 BC in the consulship of Pompey Strabo, father of Pompey the Great, and probably took its name from that event. Little is heard of the place in Roman history, but it developed into a considerable rival to Milan in the early Middle Ages. The Milanese destroyed it in 1111, but Frederick Barbarossa rebuilt the town on its present location on the right bank of the Adda in 1158.

Lower Sea (281, Mare Inferum): this term was more commonly used to refer to the sea west of Italy than the Tyrrhenian Sea.

Lucca (175, Luca): first attracted history's notice in 56 BC as the site of the famous meeting of Julius Caesar, Pompey, and Crassus (the first "Triumvirate"). In the Middle Ages, under the rule of Castruccio Castrancani (1316–1328), Lucca won supremacy in western Tuscany, but later fell under the control of Pisa (1343–1368).

Lucrine Lake (294, Lucrinus): shallow salt water lagoon, situated at the innermost point of the bay between Pozzuoli and Baia and separated from the bay by a narrow bank of sand which Julius Caesar fortified to protect oyster beds in the lake. Later Agrippa undertook major new construction involving Lucrinus and Avernus, resulting in a new harbor called Portus Julius. A volcanic eruption in 1538 reduced the size of Lucrine Lake in half. Petrarch mistakenly identified the Lucrine Lake with Mare Morto. See Porto Miseno.

Luni (158, Luna): founded as a Roman colony in 177 BC as a base of operation against the Ligurians, Luni was an important place in antiquity and was still thriving in the early Middle Ages. It gradually succumbed to the flooding of the Magra River and the consequent plague of malaria in the early thirteenth century. It serves Petrarch as an *exemplum* of what results from illicit sexual passion.

Lycia (457, Licia): mountainous country in the southwest corner of Asia Minor, to the west of anc. Cilicia. Perhaps Petrarch mentions Lycia because of the epic associations of the name. Sarpedon, Lycia's legendary chieftain, was a distinguished ally of the Trojans (Troy mentioned in 445) and two of Sarpedon's brothers fought with Aeneas in Italy (Virgil, *A.* 10.125–126).

Magna Graecia (358): collective name for Greek cities on the coasts of southern Italy but, generally speaking, not those of Sicily.

Magra (156, Macra): a considerable river, about 40 miles long; it marked the boundary between Liguria and Tuscany in antiquity, as it did in the Middle Ages.

Malea (432): a cape at the extremity of the eastern peninsula of the Peloponnese, a proverbially dangerous stretch of sea (as in Propertius, 3.19.7–8).

Mantua (356): 75 miles southeast of Milan on the Mincio River. It was ruled in Petrarch's day by the Gonzaga family and was flourishing as a brilliant center of art and culture. In the very cold December of 1354, Petrarch was invited here from Milan to meet Emperor Charles IV, who was pausing at Mantua on his circuitous route to Rome to be crowned by the Pope's representative. Petrarch's dream of the Pope and the Emperor ruling in Rome jointly took wings but soon fluttered to the ground. Only a few months earlier Petrarch had received word that Cola di Rienzo had been killed by a Roman mob, reminding Petrarch of his disappointed hopes in that direction.

Mare Morto (298): inner basin of Porto Miseno (q.v.).

Massa (168): situated about 5 miles south of Carrara on the Frigido amid marble-producing hills. Mentioned for the first time in 882 in ecclesiastical records, it was fortified in the eleventh century (Massa Vecchia). The Visconti had ambitions here as they did throughout Liguria and Tuscany. This place is not to be confused with Massa Marittima farther down the coast.

Massa Marittima (200): located 24 miles north-northwest of Grosseto about 12 miles from the coast. Ammianus Marcellinus (c. 330–395) is the first author to mention this town, citing it as the birthplace of Gallus, son of the emperor Constantius and his appointed successor (14.11.27). The place was of no particular interest to Petrarch, except for its possible relationship to ancient Populonia. He once believed that Massa was the modern name of the ancient city. The Chigi Manuscript used by Lumbroso for his edition of the *Itinerarium* reads "Populonia quae nunc Massa Maritima dicitur" (1889.18, n.1); see Pellegrin's description of the manuscript, 1975.96–98. Petrarch eventually realized his mistake (de Nolhac 1907.2:29).

Ammianus's history was unknown in Italy until Poggio brought it to Florence from Germany in 1407. The work's digressions on Egyptian obelisks and hieroglyphs stimulated humanistic interest in these subjects, preparing the way for the reception of Horapollo's *Hieroglyphica* a few years later. See Egypt.

Matarea (631–639): a suburb about 6 miles northeast of Cairo. It covers part of the ancient site called Heliopolis (City of the Sun) by the Greeks and On by the Hebrews, an approximation of the ancient Egyptian name Yunu. The place is distinguished today by a red granite obelisk and the fresh water spring to which

Petrarch assigned miraculous qualities. It was a favorite stop for pilgrims on their way to or from Mt. Sinai.

The obelisk, which stands behind the Metropolitan Museum of Art in New York, one of a pair called "Cleopatra's needles," once stood in the ancient city before the Temple of the Sun, a gift of Thutmosis III. Its mate now stands in London on the Thames Embankment. In Petrarch's day, the two obelisks were still in Alexandria, where they had been brought by Augustus Caesar to adorn the temple built to honor the deified Julius Caesar.

Meliora (189): vulgar spelling of Meloria. This fortified rock, site of the disastrous Pisan defeat of 1284 in a naval battle with Genoa, lies between the island of Gorgona and Livorno on the mainland.

Meroë (143): refers to Pliny's Meroë Insula (*Nat.* 5.53). It is not really an island, but the large area between the White Nile, the Blue Nile and the Atbara rivers. It was famous for its wine, as Petrarch says, but it was even more famous to ancient and medieval geographers as one of the fixed points on the north / south meridian, which began in the south with Meroë and passed through Syene (Aswan), Alexandria, Rhodes, Byzantion and the Borysthenes (Dnieper). South of Meroë was *terra incognita* on medieval maps (see Brown 1949.42, 49, 52 and 69).

Messina (382, Messana): in northeast Sicily on the Strait of Messina. Originally a Greek settlement of the eighth century, Messina became a free city and Roman ally after the First Punic War. Under the Normans, it became famous for monastic learning and important as a crusader port. After Sicily threw off Angevin control in 1282, the city flourished.

Milan (254, Mediolanum): when Petrarch took up residence here in the summer of 1353, it came as a shock to his friends, especially those in Florence. Many considered the Visconti, who had been in firm control of the city for 40 years, to be tyrants. Archbishop Giovanni Visconti, sole lord of Milan since the death of his brother Luchino in 1349, treated Petrarch well until his death in 1354, when the power passed to his three nephews. In June of 1361, Petrarch left Milan, returning frequently for friendly visits.

Modon (433, Mothona): ancient town of Methone in the southwest corner of the Peloponnese. The Venetians controlled it from the early thirteenth century and used it as a major port of call on the way to the Holy Land. In 8.337–339 of the *Africa*, Petrarch confuses this Methone with another city of the same name in Macedonia, where Philip, father of Alexander the Great, lost an eye in battle (see notes in Corradini 1884.461 and Fera 1984.376).

Monastery of St. Catherine (610): built between AD 548–565 by Justinian, at an altitude of 5,000 feet, close to the southern tip of the triangular Sinai peninsula, the monastery was originally dedicated to the Holy Virgin, but was known from the ninth century as St. Catherine's. Even before the monastery existed, there were many holy places for the Christian pilgrim to visit here, as Petrarch's narrative indicates. Egeria, a pious aristocrat from Spain who visited here in 381, has left the best earliest account. It took Egeria 22 *mansiones* (*mansio* = a day's journey) to travel from Jerusalem to Mt. Sinai, via the coastal road linking Syria and Egypt (*Egeriae Itinerarium*, 17.2 in Franceschini 1965 and Wilkinson 1971).

Monte Circeo (226–227): promontory 30 miles south of Anzio. Homeric tradition (*Od.* 11.135) makes Circe's home an island, but later tradition, represented by Apollonius of Rhodes (*Argon.*, 3.312), calls her home a "promontory of the Tyrrhenian mainland." Virgil and Ovid follow Apollonius's example.

Motrone (173, Mutro): established as a landing place for ships in the twelfth century by the Lucchese, Motrone is a few miles north of Viareggio.

Naples (328, Neapolis): Greek colony founded c. 600 BC, with the original name of Parthenope (Pliny, *Nat.*, 3.62) and subsequently Palaeopolis. A new settlement of c. 450 BC was called Neapolis (New Town). In the fourth century, Naples became a Roman ally and remained loyal throughout the Pyrrhic and Punic Wars. In the late Republican period, it became a fashionable resort for Romans (such as Virgil) who were attracted by the Greek ambience. Naples retained some of its Greek flavor even in Petrarch's day, though it had passed from Roman hands to the Byzantines, Saracens, Normans, Hohenstaufens and Angevins in turn. Petrarch recommends the following for Mandelli's inspection:

1. Crypta neapolitana
2. S. Maria di Piedigrotta
3. S. Maria delle Hydrie
4. Tomb of Virgil
5. Royal chapel in Castel Nuovo to see paintings by Giotto
6. Monastery of San Martino
7. Church and monastery of S. Chiara
8. Districts of (Porta) Capuana and Nido

Petrarch does not recommend a visit to the Castel dell'Ovo because of the silly stories that associated Virgil with the place.

Nile (618, Nilus): river in east and northeast Africa, flowing generally north through Uganda, Sudan and Egypt. It is the world's longest river from its remotest source (4,160 miles), and from Lake Victoria to the Mediterranean, it is 3,473 miles. See Don.

Olives, Mt. of (522): highest point in the range of hills to the east of Jerusalem, rising above the city by some 300 feet and separated from it by the Valley of Jehosaphat. The Garden of Gethsemane and the Tomb of the Virgin are at its foot. It was believed that Jesus ascended from the Mount into heaven and would return to its western slopes for the Final Judgment.

Ostia (214): name of the ancient town 15 miles from Rome at the mouth of the Tiber but now 4 miles upstream. According to a legend repeated by Petrarch after Florus, Romans founded it in the seventh century BC as their first colony, but the surviving remains are no older than the fourth century. Ostia's harbor was superseded in the first and second centuries AD by those of Claudius and Trajan, but the town remained an important business center until the third century, when it began its slow decline. In the fifth and sixth centuries, piratical raids quickened its decline, but the site was not abandoned until the ninth century.

Otranto (421, Hydrus): port city at the mouth of the Adriatic Sea; the point of Italy nearest Greece. It superseded Brindisi in the Byzantine period, and in the time of the crusades became the chief embarkation point for pilgrims and traders on their way to the Holy Land. The Turkish fleet destroyed it in 1480, and it never recovered its importance.

Parthenope (347): original name of the Greek colony sent from Cuma to the modern site of Naples. The name is said to have been derived from one of the Sirens. When the clever Ulysses escaped their alluring and deadly song, the Sirens drowned themselves in vexation. The body of one, Parthenope, was washed ashore in the Bay of Naples and this event gave her name to the new city. The ancient sources for the connection of the name with Naples are conveniently gathered in D'Arms 1970.230–231. Petrarch often uses this name to refer to Naples in his letters, as do others of his contemporaries. Like Trinacria (for Sicily), Parthenope seems often to be used with added contemporary meaning. When French revolutionary forces took Naples in 1799, they proclaimed a Parthenopean Republic.

Peloro (397): cape on the northeast extremity of Sicily (mod. Punta del Faro). According to a legend accepted by the Romans, Hannibal, suspecting treachery, killed his helmsman Pelorus and buried him here.

Pharus (660): name of a small island off the coast of Alexandria, later linked to the mainland by a causeway. The first two Ptolemies (late fourth and early third centuries BC) constructed a famous lighthouse there and named it after the island. When Ibn Battuta visited the Pharus in 1349, he found it in so ruinous a condition that he could not enter it (Clayton 1988.155).

Pietrasanta (169): Located about 6 miles south of Massa and 16 miles northwest of Lucca, the city is often said to have been founded by the Milanese Guiscardo da Pietrasanta while serving as *podestà* of Lucca. But there is inconsistent testimony in sources that perhaps makes Guiscardo's father, Pagano, the more likely founder. Mandelli's interest in all the places in Liguria and Tuscany mentioned by Petrarch is more than that of an ordinary tourist.

Piombino (193, Plumbinum): identified with the Roman Portus Faleriae or Falesiae, about 40 miles south of Livorno. It was a seaport with iron works, under control of Pisa until it was ceded to the Visconti in 1399. Petrarch mistakenly places Piombino north of Populonia (q.v.). See also Massa Marittima.

Pisa (176, Pisae): as a boy, Petrarch lived in Pisa for about a year (1311–1312; *Sen.* 18.1). Two of his letters, both dated 30 April 1341, were written in Pisa: *Fam.* 4.7, addressed to King Robert of Naples, and *Fam.* 4.8 addressed to Barbato da Sulmona, Robert's secretary; both speak of his recent coronation with laurel in Rome. Situated 43 miles southwest of Florence on the Arno, Pisa succumbed to Florentine efforts to control the city in 1406.

Pompeii (362): prosperous port and market town about 5 miles southeast of Vesuvius, having some 20,000 inhabitants when it was destroyed by volcanic eruption on 24 August AD 79. In AD 62 or 63, it had suffered extensive damage by an earthquake, which Petrarch mistakenly believed had wiped out the city. This town's location was never forgotten, but systematic excavations did not begin until the eighteenth century.

Ponza (230, Pontiae or Pontia): the largest of six small islands lying about 20 miles to the west of Monte Circeo. Commonly used as a place of exile in Rome's imperial period, the island fittingly played host to Mussolini for a short time after his fall.

Populonia (200): an important Etruscan city in antiquity. Petrarch's interest in this place, which had disappeared from the maps of his day, derives from his historical and geographical researches. He incorrectly places it south of Piombino. See Massa Marittima.

Port' Ercole (203, Portus Herculeus): small port on the south end of Monte Argentario. Both this port and S. Stefano are indicated on the portolan charts.

Porto Miseno (277–278): harbor built by Agrippa for Octavian's fleet between 34 and 31 BC, some 4 years after the naval works at Portus Julius were completed. The port consisted of two basins of which the inner, Mare Morto, was connected to the outer by a canal. It eventually supplanted Portus Julius, owing to the difficulties in maintaining that port in operation. Petrarch, misled by his informants, applied the name Mare Morto to the Lucrine Lake. Porto Miseno does not appear to have been in operating order in Petrarch's day.

Porto Pisano (184, Portus Pisanus): still a large and important harbor in Petrarch's day. It remained operative until it was superseded by Livorno's harbor in the early fifteenth century.

Porto Talamone (200, Thelamonis Portus): small port about half way between the Ombrone river and Monte Argentario on the west coast of Italy. It was named in antiquity after Telamon, one of the Argonauts. At *Africa*, 3.879–880, Petrarch incorrectly places Porto Talamone and the Ombrone south of Port' Ercole.

Portofino (131, Alphini Portus): small picturesque harbor on the Tyrrhenian coast south-southwest of Rapallo. Petrarch thought that its beauty merited three lines in the *Africa* (6.845–847).

Portovenere (133, Portus Veneris): this small port town is located on the south arm of the large Gulf of La Spezia. Petrarch uses the term to refer to the large gulf, as many others do, but not out of ignorance. The Virgilian resonance was too inviting for him to resist. At *Africa*, 6.856–859, he uses the term in its proper sense, to refer to the small port on the coast.

Pozzuoli (300, Puteoli): originally a Greek colony of the sixth century BC, Pozzuoli became Roman in 194 BC and Rome's chief harbor in the south. As the principal Italian port for trading with the East, it was adorned, especially by Augustus, with an impressive array of public works. Among these was a huge mole, a breakwater for the harbor, extending nearly 400 yards into the bay. It was from the end of this pier that Caligula built his famous "bridge" to Baia. Though much in decline from its ancient glory, Pozzuoli was still a considerable town in Petrarch's day and the see of a bishop.

Procida (248, Prochita): small island situated between Ischia and Cape Miseno. It is mentioned by Petrarch to provide himself with an opportunity to speak of the deeds of Giovanni da Procida.

Rapallo (132): 19 miles southeast of Genoa by road, this town is first mentioned in 964. It gives its name to the Gulf of Rapallo. Its name appears on the earliest portolan charts.

Ravenna (279): a city in the Po delta. Augustus Caesar made this town important when he established it as the permanent station of his fleet in the Adriatic or Upper Sea. The town grew in size and sophistication in the fifth and sixth centuries after Honorius moved his imperial court here. The town remained important throughout the Middle Ages.

Red Sea (603, Mare Rubrum): inland sea between the Arabian Peninsula and northeast Africa, about 1,200 miles long. What the Greeks and the Romans called the Red Sea (Gk. Erythra Thalassa) we call the Arabian Sea, and what we call the Red Sea they called the Arabian Gulf. Petrarch here means what we do when we speak of the Red Sea.

Reggio (406, Regium): on the Strait of Messina 202 miles south-southeast of Naples. Founded as a Greek colony at the end of the eighth century, Reggio became an ally of Rome in 282 BC. The city flourished throughout the Roman imperial period but was later dominated by the Ostrogoths, Byzantines, Saracens, Normans and Angevins. Often called Reggio di Calabria to distinguish it from Reggio in Emilia (North Italy).

Rhodes (452): island in the southeast Aegean Sea, 7 miles off the southwest coast of Asia Minor (Turkey); 48 miles long from north to south and 22 miles at its widest point. The famous colossal statute of the sun god Helios was erected 294–282 BC, but was toppled by an earthquake some 70 years later. The Knights of St. John (Hospitallers) took the island in 1310 and held it for the next 200 years.

Rome (219): the city whose place in secular and religious history Petrarch so admired and as one of whose citizens he counted himself since his coronation there in 1341 was in a pitiable condition in the fourteenth century. In theory an independent city-state, Rome by custom put its governance in the hands of the Pope, who appointed successive senators to conduct the city's business. In reality, the Colonna and Orsini families, neither of Roman origin, waged unending battle with one another for control. Petrarch's unheeded recommendation was to exclude these families from government and allow only Roman citizens to serve as Roman senators (*Sine Nomine,* 7). Petrarch also tried to persuade the Popes to return from their Babylonian exile (Avignon) and to urge the Roman Emperor Charles IV to return to the city of Augustan authority and peace. Petrarch's desire to revive Rome as a seat of Empire led to his uncritical enthusiasm for Cola di Rienzo's attempts at reform (1347–1354).

Salerno (370): city located on the north shore of the Gulf of Salerno (anc. Sinus Posidonius). Founded as a Roman colony in 194 BC, Salerno became an independent principality in the ninth century AD and the site of the first medical school in medieval Europe (Schola Salernitana). By the twelfth century it held a preeminent position in the medical arts, but had fallen from this glory in Petrarch's day.

Samos (443): island in the Aegean Sea off the west coast of Turkey. It is of interest to Petrarch as the birthplace of Pythagoras, c. 580 BC.

Santo Stefano, Porto (203, Sancti Stephani Portus): small port on the north end of Monte Argentario.

Sardinia (214): second largest island in the Mediterranean 115 miles from Capraia and Elba to the northeast. A Roman province by the third century BC, Sardinia was controlled in the period following Rome's collapse by Vandals, Byzantines and Arabs. In the eleventh century Pisa and Genoa carved out spheres of influence and entered into a protracted struggle for control until the issue was settled for a time by Genoa's defeat of Pisa in the battle of Meloria in 1284. In 1297, Pope Boniface VIII invested James II of Aragon as King of Sardinia, but the Aragonese did not secure their hold on the island until well into the fourteenth century. In 1326, Pisa abandoned all claim on the island and any pretense at being a maritime power.

Sarzana (165, Sarzanum): lies on the plain of the Magra river, 11 miles southeast of La Spezia. Mentioned as a fortress in 963, as a town in 1084, and as the see of a bishop in 1204, Sarzana grew as the citizens of Luni deserted their city. Petrarch's spelling of the name seems to have been an acceptable variant at this time.

Scalea (379): town about 3 miles north of the river Lao, which marked the ancient boundary between Lucania (mod. Basilicata) and Bruttium (mod. Calabria). Whether Scalea is to be identified with the ancient Greek settlement of Laus is unknown. Scalea has a good harbor, but not so good as to justify the rubication of its name on portolan charts.

Scilla (385): a promontory on the west coast of Calabria (anc. Bruttium), 15 miles north of Reggio and almost exactly at the western entrance to the Strait of Messina. Myth locates the abode of the monster Scylla on this rocky headland, opposite the whirlpool called Charybdis.

Scyros (440): an island in the Aegean Sea to the east of Euboea. The island is famous in myth as the place where Thetis concealed her son Achilles to save him from an evil fate at Troy. The story was well known in the medieval period from Statius's account, which was commonly used as a school text.

Sea of Sodom (581): salt lake between Israel and modern Jordan; 51 miles long and 11 miles wide at its greatest extent. Roman geographers regularly called it Lacus Asphaltites, but the late second or early third century Roman historian, Justin, called it Mare Mortuum (Dead Sea), the preferred name henceforth. The same designation is found somewhat earlier in the Greek authors Pausanias and Galen of the second century. The toponym Sea of Sodom is found on Angelino Dalorto's 1325 portolan chart, but it is hard to find elsewhere. The apocryphal 2 Esdras 5:7 (printed as an appendix to the New Testament in the Catholic Vulgate) has Mare Sodomiticum, but the frequency of the term's use has yet to be established. It appears to be a very rare term indeed.

Sele (370, Siler): river in southern Italy marking the boundary between Campania and Lucania. A peculiarity of this river mentioned by Pliny (*Nat.* 2.226) is that its water has the power of petrifying sticks and leaves.

Serchio (174, Serclus): named the Auser or Ausar in antiquity, this river (about 60 miles long) flowed into the Arno at Pisa until the early Middle Ages (see Rutilius Namatianus, *De reditu suo*, 1.565–570). Then it changed its course and flowed to the sea about 7 miles north of the Arno. The modern name is derived from a diminutive form of the ancient name.

Sestos (449): ancient town on the Hellespont, on the narrowest part of the strait opposite Abydos (q.v.). It was the northwest terminus of the bridge of boats built by the Persian King Xerxes for his invasion of Greece in 481 BC, a feat to which Petrarch compares Caligula's bridge in the Bay of Naples (cf. *Metr.* 3. 4, 31–43 in *Rime* 774–776 and *Itinerarium* lines 295–298).

Sestri Levante (133, Siestrum): this is the Segesta Tigulliorum mentioned by Pliny. From his reading of Virgil (*A.* 5.523–524) and of Servius' commentary *ad loc.*, Petrarch may have thought this place had some real connection with the vastly more famous Segesta in Sicily, a place with important connections with Aeneas's legend and with Roman history. Cf. Lerici and Portovenere.

Sicily (382): the largest of the Mediterranean islands, Sicily owes its ancient name (Trinacria) to its shape; the name Sicily is derived from its ancient inhabitants, the Siculi or Sicels. Colonized by Greeks in the eighth-sixth centuries BC and largely in Carthaginian hands by the third, Sicily became Rome's first province after the first two Punic Wars. Overrun by Arabs in the ninth–tenth centuries AD, the island was controlled in the eleventh by Normans who founded the kingdom of Sicily, comprising Sicily and Norman holdings as far as the Bay of Naples (Kingdom of the Two Sicilies). Conquered by Charles of Anjou from his base in Naples (1266–1268) and mistreated by him, Sicily rebelled in 1282 and allied itself with the House of Aragon, while Naples remained in Angevin control.

Sion, Mt. (522): The citadel of Jerusalem taken by David from the Jebusites c. 1000 BC. It was the smaller and eastern of two adjacent hills, now called the Temple Mount. The rock now enshrined in the famous Dome of the Rock, built by an Umayyad caliph in 691, must have been considered the foundation of the Holy of Holies of Herod's temple, which was swept away in 135 by Hadrian's temple to Jupiter. Owing to a misinterpretation of several Old Testament texts (such as Micah 3:12), Christians of the fourth century transferred the name Mt. Sion to the larger hill to the west. By the fifth century, Christians located here the scene of the last supper and the descent of the Holy Spirit at Pentecost.

Sorrento (365, Surrentum): town located on the south side of the Bay of Naples, 17 miles southeast of Naples and 7 miles from the southern boundary of the bay. It was known chiefly for its wine in antiquity.

Squillace (409, Scyllaceum): a town on the east coast of Calabria, on the "sole" of Italy's boot, situated in a large bay always regarded as dangerous to ships.

Strait of Messina (383, Pharus Messanensis): channel between southern Italy and northeast Sicily, 2-1/2 to 12 miles wide. Petrarch follows the French idiom in calling it Pharus; Romans called it Siculum Fretum.

Sur (492, anc. Tyrus): important maritime city in south Lebanon. Most famous for Alexander the Great's lengthy siege in 332 BC, the city fell subsequently under control of the Seleucids and the Romans, and, in the seventh century, it passed over to Muslims. The crusaders took it in 1124, but surrendered it to the Mamluks in 1291. Petrarch uses the name he found on his portolan chart; other forms are: Syro, Surro, Zur.

Syria (496): a toponym of fluctuating meaning, but in antiquity and the Middle Ages of much wider extension than the modern term. According to Marino Sanudo's *Liber secretorum fidelium crucis* (written 1306–1321), Syria extends from the Tigris in the east to the Mediterranean in the west and from Armenia on the north to Egypt and Arabia on the south. In Book 3.14 (Steward 1896 a. 1–4), Sanudo says that Syria is divided into ten parts. Syria the Second, also called Coele-Syria, has Antioch as its chief city. Syria the Fourth has Damascus as its capital. Sanudo's division corresponds in many important ways with the earlier account (1280) of Burchard of Mt. Sion, who also makes Antioch and Damascus the capitals of the Second and Fourth Syrias, respectively (Steward 1896. 5–8). By medieval reckoning, there would be no opposition between Antioch and Damascus as to which was capital of Syria: each is the capital of a major division of Syria. Petrarch, however, is right to describe Damascus as the more important city at this time, not because the prophet Isaiah says so, but because Mamluk geopolitical strategy has made it so. See Damascus and Antioch.

Syrtes (594): two wide gulfs on the north coast of Africa, where in antiquity navigation was considered dangerous. The Greater Syrtis (now the Gulf of Sidra) is east of Tripoli, capital of Libya; the Lesser is off the coast of Tunisia.

Taranto (414, Tarentum): excellent seaport, 156 miles southeast of Naples, couched where the "sole" and inner part of Italy's "heel" meet. A Spartan foundation of the late eighth century BC, the city figured prominently in Rome's campaigns against two of its most dangerous enemies, Pyrrhus early in the third century BC and Hannibal near the end of the same century. A Roman colony in 272 BC, Taranto's importance faded in the imperial period. In AD 927 it was destroyed by Saracens, but it was rebuilt by the Byzantines in 964, regaining much of its old glory under the Normans and Angevins, who controlled the city in Petrarch's day. It was of special interest to Petrarch as the place where the poet Ennius was born (as Petrarch thought) and where some said that Virgil died.

Tartarus (265): the name refers to an area in the underworld where the wicked suffer for their misdeeds on earth. Dante and others of the Middle Ages thought of this place as freezing cold because of an etymology supplied by Isidore (*Etym.*, 14.9.8).

Terra di Lavoro (366, Terra Laboris): in antiquity referred to an especially fertile area northwest of Naples, but in Petrarch's day commonly used to denote Campania as a whole or the Kingdom of Naples as a political entity.

Terracina (232, anc. Anxur, later Tarracina): seaport some 65 miles south of Rome and near Gaeta; a Volscian town which came under Rome's control c. 400 BC. An important stop for travelers on the Via Appia, it flourished as a royal resort in the early empire. Its fine harbor, which was in part artificial, appears on all the earliest portolan charts.

Tiber (213, Tyberis): river rising in the Tuscan Apennines, it flows south through Umbria and Latium, where it turns southwest on its journey through Rome, which is 16 miles from its mouth at Ostia on the Tyrrhenian Sea; 250 miles long.

Tortosa (491, anc. Antaradus; mod. Tartus): port city north of Tripoli, about 45 miles south of Latakia (anc. Laodicea). In the Middle Ages, it was a populous and well-fortified city, frequented by pilgrims arriving in Syria from Cyprus. The crusaders took the town and held it until the Mamluks captured it in 1291.

Trinacria (374): name of Greek origin to denote Sicily, used primarily by poets among Roman authors. In Petrarch's time there was an attempt to revive the name to refer to a new political arrangement regarding the kingdom of Sicily. At *Africa*, 1.19 Petrarch hails King Robert of Naples as "Trinacrii moderator maxime regni," supreme ruler of the Kingdom of Trinacria [Sicily]. Both sentiment and its expression reflect current political daydreaming in Naples. The Kingdom of Naples and Sicily (The Two Sicilies) were reunited, not however under the Angevins, but under King Alfonso V of Aragon.

Tripoli (491): in mod. Lebanon, a joint foundation in the seventh century BC of Tyre, Sidon and Aradus, each of which had its own walled quarter within the city. It was held by the Seleucids and Romans and passed to the Muslims in the seventh century AD. The crusaders took it in 1109, but gave it up to the Mamluks in 1289. It was often referred to as Tripoli di Soria (Tripoli of Syria), to distinguish it from several other cities of the same name, especially the "Tripolis" in Libya, which referred not to a single city, but three separated and federated cities.

Troy (162): otherwise known as Ilion or Ilium (see *Itinerarium*, line 450). Its site, 4 miles from the Aegean Sea and a couple of miles south of the Hellespont, has been located and excavated from 1870 to the present. Petrarch's Greek was not good enough to read the *Iliad* in the original, but he had read a considerable amount on the Trojan War in various Latin writers. Petrarch mentions the place for its exemplary value as the most famous city to fall because of illicit sexual conduct. The traditional date for the fall of Troy is 1184, but the city was refounded c. 700 BC by Greeks and was later taken over by the Romans under the name Ilium. This place survived in a much-reduced form until about AD 1200.

Upper Sea (280, Mare Superum): the Adriatic Sea. This was a term in very common use for the Adriatic Sea.

Venice (435): on 14 July 1361 Petrarch, while a guest of Francesco da Carrara in Padua, received word that his son Giovanni (24 years old) had died of the plague in Milan. In September of the following year, he arranged to move to Venice, perhaps to escape painful memories. In return for the use of a house for the rest of his life, Petrarch had agreed to name San Marco as the heir of his many books, which were to be the foundation of a public library (see the translation of an official Venetian document in Wilkins 1961.184–186). For reasons unspecified, Petrarch decided to leave Venice in 1368, terminating the agreement. He divided his last six years of life between Padua and Arquà, about 10 miles southwest of Padua in the Euganean hills. His son-in-law Francescuolo da Brossano inherited his books, which were in time dispersed throughout Western Europe. Venice had to wait for another 100 years for its "biblioteca publica," when the Greek humanist Cardinal Bessarion willed his library to the Republic of Venice, the foundation of the Biblioteca Marciana.

Verona (356): in northeast Italy, on the Adige river 92 miles east of Milan; under control of the della Scala family from 1260 to 1387, when it fell to the Visconti. Verona was the home of two of Petrarch's good friends: Guglielmo da Pastrengo, a scholar with interests similar to Petrarch's, and Rinaldo Cavalchini, quondam teacher of his son Giovanni. While on a visit in 1345, he found in the Cathedral library a manuscript of Cicero's letters to Atticus. It was a discovery of supreme importance to him and led him to make his own two great collections of letters: 350 prose letters on "familiar matters" and 127 letters "of old age." Further research in the same library led him to other ancient authors with whom he had not been acquainted.

Vesuvius (351, Vesevus): volcano on the east side of the Bay of Naples, about 4,200 feet in height at present. The cone is half encircled on the north side by Monte Somma, part of the wall of a large crater in which the present cone was formed, probably in AD 79 when Pompeii and Herculaneum were destroyed. Following Virgil, Petrarch uses a variant spelling admissible to hexameters.

Viareggio (173, Via Regia): established in the twelfth century by the Lucchese, this fortress had fallen into Pisan hands in Petrarch's day. It lies on the coast directly west of Lucca.

Appendix

Notes on the *Cursus* in the *Itinerarium*

The term *cursus* refers to the rhythm produced in the Latin prose of the Middle Ages by a fixed succession of stressed and unstressed syllables at the end of clauses and sentences (clausulae). In antiquity, the basis of the rhythm was the quantity of the syllables (from the time of Cicero), but by the end of the fourth century quantity had effectively given way to accented syllables. The rule was that two or four (under certain circumstances, three) unaccented syllables must separate the accented syllables of the last two (usually) words of a subordinate clause or sentence. At the beginning of the eighth century, the *cursus* fell largely into disuse until the end of the eleventh century. In 1088 Iohannes Caietanus, afterwards Pope Gelasius II (1118), developed the *cursus* under the influence of Albericus of Monte Cassino, who said in his *Breviarium de dictamine* that prose should be *sonoram et distinctam, id est quasi currentem*. Elaborate rules for the *cursus* were later drawn up by Albertus de Morra who became Pope under the name of Gregory VIII (1187). Hereafter, the *cursus* was called the *stilus Gregorianus* or the *cursus Curiae Romanae* (rival schools of thought had different names for it); see Clark 1910.6–20 and Haskins 1929. 170–192.

The three basic types of the *cursus* were named the *planus* (e.g., univérsi fidéles), the *tardus* (e.g., máter ecclésiae), and the *velox* (ómnia perdidíssent). In the strictest application of the rules, the number of syllables in the final word was limited to three (in the *planus*) or four syllables (in the *tardus* and *velox*). Other freer types were admitted especially in non-ecclesiastical writing, being viewed as acceptable variations on the three basic types. For example, a monosyllable and a disyllable might substitute for a trisyllabic final word in the *planus* (e.g., núllus est módus), where *est* is considered an unaccented proclitic; or two disyllabic words might substitute for a tetrasyllabic final word in the *velox* (e.g., véritas fàri iúbet), where the first disyllable is considered as having a minor accent. Other similar licenses were also permitted. Altogether, the writer of elegant prose had some seven or so varieties of accentual rhythms with which he might end his clauses or sentences. The freer varieties were seen by many as necessary for the avoidance of monotony, but learned controversy between Italian *dictatores* and their Gallic brothers in Orleans raged throughout the thirteenth century about the proper forms of the *cursus;* see Nicolau 1930.141–147, Schiaffini 1943.11–24, Strecker 1963.86–90, Scaglione 1972.98–105, and Janson 1975.

During the fourteenth century, the use of the *cursus* continued in official documents of church and state and, until Petrarch's innovations, in the private and secular Latin prose of the time, e.g., in the works of Dante, Cola di Rienzo, and Boccaccio. Inspired by his discovery of Cicero's *Letters to Atticus* in 1345, Petrarch began to modify the rules of the *cursus,* which he had imbibed in his youth, in favor of new accentual rhythms and the quantitative rhythms of Classical Latin. Petrarch's modifications of the *cursus,* however, did not constitute a rejection of it as it is sometimes suggested. His new practices had a discernible effect on his friend Boccaccio's style; and Coluccio Salutati (1331–1406), Petrarch's friend and admirer, became openly contemptuous of the *cursus* in his private correspondence, while he continued to ply the *cursus* with great diligence in his official capacity as Florence's Chancellor. In praise of a private letter written to him without the use of the *cursus,* Salutati says, "Benedictus deus quod sermonem unum vidimus hoc fermento [the *cursus*] non contaminatum et qui legi possit sine concentu et effeminata consonantiae cantilena" (quoted by Clark 1910.21; for the text of this and other disparaging remarks by Salutati on the *cursus* see Novati 1891.1:133, 2:78, and 3:630–633). Despite this denunciation of the *cursus,* Salutati himself sometimes used it as if by instinct in his private writings, as if unable to guard himself against ingrained habits (Witt 1976.25).

There is no doubt that Petrarch used the *cursus* in the *Itinerarium.* Some examples (all taken from the first page of the Latin text) here follow. The *planus* is labelled (P), the *tardus* (T), and the *velox* (V):

1. insperáta contíngunt (P)
2. páream cógit (P); sometimes regarded as a variety of the *medius* (5, below).
3. fortúna moderátur (P); often called the *cursus trispondaicus* and treated separately; coincides with Cicero's *esse videatur* rhythm; Petrarch is fond of this variety.
4. uncísque detíneor (T)
5. áliter áccidat (T); sometimes called the *medius* (M) and treated separately; *vítam péperit* would be considered a *medius* by Martellotti (1951.36), as well as 2 (above).
6. áliud ingemíscat (V)
7. princípia rèrum régit (V)

Items numbered 1, 4, and 6 are the standard three forms of the *cursus* and are well represented in the *Itinerarium*. Petrarch freely admits forms represented by items 2, 3, 5, and 7. The type represented by *princípia rèrum régit* (7) is a particular favorite of Petrarch's in the *Itinerarium*.

Fairly often, Petrarch combines clausulae to form compounds with two or three members (cf. a similar practice in Dante, Toynbee 1924). For example *premeditáta destítuunt , insperáta contíngunt* (line 3 of the *Itinerarium*) is a combination of a *tardus* (premeditáta destítuunt), a *velox* (destítuunt insperáta) and a *planus* (insperáta contíngunt). An example of a two-member compound is *felices facit et miseros* (lines 23–24), where a *planus* (félices fácit) is combined with a *tardus* (fácit et míseros).

The following short passage (lines 115–120) shows a high incidence of the *cursus*, with one three-member compound (italicized) with the pattern of (T) + (V) + (P). Several debatable forms of the *cursus* have been discounted.

> Hinc tu tametsi sócii próperent (M) et naute de lítore fùnem sólvant (V), <ne> tamen ánte discésseris (T) quam pretiosum illud et *insígne vas sólido* (T) *e smarágdo* (V) *quo Crístus* (P), cuius te tam procul a pátria àmor tráhit (V),

> pro parópside ùsus fértur (V), videas, devótum si síc est (P), alióquin suápte (P) spécie clàrum ópus (V).

This passage, given an almost hymnal quality by the pervasive use of the *cursus*, displays a tendency seen in many other authors whereby the rhythms of the *cursus* are extended to the internal structure of the clause or sentence. Observable too is Petrarch's fondness for the *velox*, especially the variety represented by *lítore fìnem sâlvant* (four occurrences), as though to emphasize the haste with which Mandelli must see the sights in Genoa. There are several other passages in the *Itinerarium* that approximate but do not equal this one in the high frequency of the *cursus*.

So consistent are some writers in the use of the *cursus* that modern editors feel justified in suspecting some difficulty in the text when a clausula does not achieve an acceptable rhythm. Very often, it is an easy matter to restore the *cursus* by simply transposing a word or two, but the absence of a correct *cursus* may signal a more deep-seated corruption requiring more cautious remedies (Eklund 1984.27–56). Although Petrarch's use of the *cursus* in the *Itinerarium* is unmistakable (i.e., its occurrence is not due to chance), it is not so consistent or pervasive that an editor should feel free to rearrange or emend the text to restore a correct *cursus*. For example, no reading in the *Itinerarium* is more secure than the first seven words, the ending of which provides the first clausula in the work — *rerum exitus respondent*, but it is not an acceptable *cursus*. Matters could be set to rights by transposing *rerum exitus* so that *exitus rérum respóndent* is the result, giving the *planus*, yet there would be no justification for doing so. Martellotti (1951.36) would argue that the type represented by *éxitus respóndent* is an irregular form of the *planus*. Petrarch liked the rhythm, whatever it may be called. It is not a prose-rhythm sought by any classical author known to Petrarch (see *OCD*, s.v. Prose-rhythm).

Authors whose use of the *cursus* is completely reliable are comparatively rare. Even authors who adhere closely to the rules of the *cursus* freely dispense with it in didactic, argumentative, or technical passages in which expressions are required that are not easily manipulated according to the rules. Often proper names and titles resist the *cursus*. This last point is perhaps relevant to the *Itinerarium,* whose text contains a large number of proper names. Another relevant consideration may be the fact that Petrarch composed it in some haste (at least by his standards). It could be argued, for example, that the evidence for the *cursus* in the *Itinerarium* is so strong precisely because Petrarch wrote it in such haste. The rhythms of the *cursus* simply flowed, so to speak, from his unguarded hand.

Before any firm conclusions can be made about Petrarch's use of the *cursus* in his later writing, a much larger body of statistical evidence than now available will need to be gathered for examination. Until such time, confident generalizations will be best resisted. To judge from the *Itinerarium,* however, Martellotti's conclusion (1951.45), based on an analysis of samples taken primarily from the *De viris illustribus,* but with a good number from the *Familiares* and elsewhere, seems on the whole justified:

> L'armonia particolare del periodo petrarchesco risulta dal vario incontrarsi di ritmi accentuativi ben riconoscibili con il ritmo per così dire prosastico, cadenzato dal cursus. In questa sapiente mistura il Petraraca non disdegna i mezzi di ornato cari ai dettatori; soltanto ch' egli se ne serve con un certo eclettismo, traendoli spesso ad effetti espressivi tutti particolari.

Certainly there is no evidence that Petrarch ever discarded the use of the *cursus* entirely, but rather sought to blend its use with new accentual rhythms of his own liking and quantitative rhythms of his favorite classical authors as Martellotti says. It appears that Petrarch's rhythmical practice was in transition from the accentual to the metrical. The fourteenth century, therefore, was seeing the reversal of the trend observed in the fourth century in the work of St. Ambrose, for example, when the practice was in transition from the metrical to the accentual (Wiesner 1970.82–84).

BIBLIOGRAPHY AND ABBREVIATIONS

PETRARCH'S WORKS

I. Collections

A National Edition of Petrarch's complete works has been in progress since 1926, but the project will not be finished for some time to come. For some things one must still rely on *Francisci Petrarchae Florentin . . . opera quae extant omnia*, 3 vols. (Basel 1554). This collection was reprinted in 1581 and 1965 (Ridgewood, N.J.). Meanwhile there are two modern collections which contain on a generous scale representative texts of his Latin and Italian productions. They are:

1. Neri, F., Martellotti, G., Bianchi, E., and Sapegno, N. eds. 1951. Francesco Petrarca, *Rime, Trionfi e Poesie latine* (La letteratura italiana, storia e testi 6), Milan/Naples. This volume contains complete texts of the *Canzoniere* and the *Trionfi*, with selections from the *Africa* and the *Epistole metriche* among other things. It will be cited as *Rime*. Bigi, E. (*Opere di Francesco Petrarca*, notes by G. Ponte [Milan, 1963]) may be used as a supplemental volume.

2. Martellotti, G., Ricci, P.G., Carrara, E., and Bianchi, E. eds. 1955. Francesco Petrarca, *Prose* (La letteratura italiana, storia e testi 7), Milan / Naples. This volume contains the complete texts of the *Letter to Posterity*, the *Secretum*, and *De vita solitaria;* it prints a large part of *De sui ipsius et multorum ignorantia* and the various Invectives and much lesser amounts of the *Rerum memorandarum libri*, the *De remediis utriusque fortune*, the *De otio religioso*, the *De viris illustribus*, and the two large collections of letters (*Familares* and *Seniles*). Although A. Bufano's *Opere latine di Francesco Petrarca*, 2 vols. (Turin, 1975) inevitably contains many of the same texts as *Prose*, it prints some others not at all repre-

sented in the earlier collection. Both *Rime* and *Prose* are well annotated and supply a facing Italian translation when the original is Latin; both volumes contain succinct essays on the current (then) status of each individual text. Unless otherwise indicated, the texts of *Rime* and *Prose* have been used whenever possible.

II. Individual Works

The following individual works call for special attention.

1. The *Africa.*
   a. Festa, N. ed. 1926. *L'Africa* (Edizione Nazionale). Florence. This is the standard text of Petrarch's unfinished epic poem, but since Martellotti's text in *Rime* often improves on it (if only in the matter of orthography), his version will be cited whenever possible.
   b. Bergin, T. and Wilson, A. eds. 1977. *Petrarch's "Africa."* New Haven. This careful translation has very helpful notes.
2. *Epistolae familiares (Fam.)*
   a. Rossi, V. and Bosco, U. eds. 1933–42. *Epistolae familiares, Le familiari,* 4 vols. (Edizione Nazionale). Florence. This is the standard edition of the 350 letters that constitute the *Epistolae familiares.* Vol. 4 contains a superb two-part index. Rossi edited the first three volumes, Bosco the last. Twenty-five of the most famous letters may be found in *Prose.*
   b. Dotti, U. ed. 1974–78. *Le familiari [libri I–XI]*, 2 vols. Urbino. This edition has an Italian translation facing the Latin text and is supplied with an excellent introduction and notes. It is always worth consulting. Cited as Dotti.
   c. Bernardo, A. ed. 1975–1985. *Letters on Familiar Matters: Rerum familiarum libri I–XXIV*, 3 vols. Baltimore. Bernardo has rendered a welcome service especially for English speakers by producing this scholarly translation. The letters are dated only by day and month; there is no index.

3. *Seniles (Sen.)*

a. *Librorum F. Petrarchae impressorum annotatio* (Venice, 1501). This scarce edition (reprinted in 1503) is considered the most reliable text of the *Seniles*.

b. *Francisci Petrarchae . . . opera quae extant omnia,* vol. 2. (Basel, 1554) 812–1070. This is the most accessible text of the *Seniles* (cited as *Opera*). If this edition is used to consult the Latin text, the reader must be aware that its numbering system of the 128 letters differs from that of the 1501 edition. To sort out the discrepancies, one may consult E. Wilkins, *The Prose Letters of Petrarch: A Manual* (New York, 1951) 6–8. Eleven of the *Seniles* are contained in *Prose.*

c. Bernardo, A., Levin, S., and Bernardo, R. eds. 1992. Francis Petrarch, *Letters of Old Age: Rerum senilium libri I–XVIII,* 2 vols. Baltimore. Bernardo's translation of the 1501 edition of the *Seniles* is especially valuable in view of the inaccessibility of the Latin text. It has a helpful index.

Other individual works will be cited as required.

Note on Ancient and Medieval Authors

On a number of occasions, specific editions are cited for individual authors of the classical period, but to do so for all of them would have greatly enlarged the Bibliography to no good purpose. They all have serviceable editions (and translations) available in one or another collection of texts such as the Oxford Classical Texts, the Teubner series, the Loeb Classical Library, or the Budé series. Some major authors of the later classical or early Christian periods, such as Cassius Dio or Augustine, are treated in the same way. However, for lesser-known writers of the late classical period and for medieval authors like Liudprand or Gervase of Tilbury, it has been assumed that bibliographical information would generally be required.

The titles of these authors' works usually are abbreviated in the manner prescribed by such authorities as the *Oxford Latin Dictionary (OLD)* or the *Oxford Classical Dictionary*, 3rd ed. 1996 *(OCD)*. The *Barrington Atlas of the Greek and Roman World*, with separate 2 vol. *Map-by-Map Directory*, ed. by R. Talbert (Princeton, 2000) is very useful for scholars of the later periods.

WORKS CITED

Aerts, W. et al. eds. 1978. *Alexander the Great in the Middle Ages: Ten Studies on the Last Days of Alexander in Literary and Historical Writing.* Nijmegen.

Allmand, C. 1988. *The Hundred Years War: England and France at War c.1300–c.1450.* Cambridge.

Almagià, R. 1929. *Monumenta Italiae Cartographica.* Florence.

———. 1944–55. *Monumenta Cartographica Vaticana*, 4 vols; vol. 1: *Planisferi carte nautiche e affini dal secolo XIV al XVII.* Vatican City.

Altamura, A. ed. 1974. *Cronaca di Partenope.* Naples.

Amalfitano, P., Camodeca, G., and Medri, M. eds. 1990. *I campi flegrei: un itinerario archeologico.* Venice.

Angelini, C. ed. 1944. *Viaggi in Terra Santa.* Florence.

Armour, P. 1989. *Dante's Griffin and the History of the World.* Oxford.

Arnaud, P. 1984. "L'image du globe dans le monde romain," *Mélanges de l' École Française de Rome: Antiquité* 96.53–116.

Ascoli, R. 1991. "Petrarch's Middle Age: Memory, Imagination, History, and the 'Ascent of Mount Ventoux,'" *Stanford Italian Review* 10.5–43.

Ashtor, E. 1984. Review of Cardini 1982 in *Rivista storica italiana* 96.214–218.

———. 1985. "Venezia e il pellegrinaggio in Terrasanta nel basso medioevo," *Archivio Storico Italiano* 143.197–223.

Atiya, A. 1938. *The Crusade in the Later Middle Ages*, 2nd ed. 1965. London.

———. 1975. "The Crusade in Fourteenth Century," 3–26 in Hazard 1975. Madison, Wis.

Avena, A. ed. 1906. *Il "Bucolicum Carmen" e i Suoi Commenti Inediti.* Padua.

Bacchi della Lega, A. ed. 1945. Niccolò da Poggibonsi, *Libro d' Oltramare or A Voyage Beyond the Sea* (1346–1350), 2nd ed. B. Bagatti

(Studium Biblicum Franciscanum 2), 2 vols. Jerusalem. (Vol. 2 is an English translation by T. Bellorini and E. Hoade.)

Bagatti, B. ed. 1948. *Visit to the Holy Places of Egypt, Sinai, Palestine, and Syria in 1384*, trans. T. Bellorini and E. Hoade, with preface and notes by Bagatti (Studium Biblicum Franciscanum 6). Jerusalem.

Balbi, G. ed. 1975. Giorgio Stella, *Annales genuenses* (Rerum italicarum scriptores N.S. 17, part 2). Bologna.

Baldwin, M. ed. 1969. *A History of the Crusades*, vol. 1: *The First Hundred Years*, 2nd ed.; general ed. K. Setton 1969–89, q.v. Madison, Wis.

Ball, J. 1942. *Egypt in the Classical Geographers*. Cairo.

Balsdon, J. 1934. *The Emperor Gaius*. Oxford.

Banks, M. ed. 1904. *An Alphabet of Tales* (Early English Text Society), 2 vols. London.

Barber, J. ed. 1991. Francesco Petrarca, *Rime disperse* (Garland Library of Medieval Literature, series A, 75). New York.

Barlow, C. 1938. "Codex Vaticanus latinus 4929," *Memoirs of the American Academy in Rome* 15.87–124.

Baron, H. 1962. "The Evolution of Petrarch's Thought: Reflections on the State of Petrarch Studies," *Bibliothèque d'Humanisme et Renaissance* 24.7–41.

———. 1985. *Petrarch's "Secretum": Its Making and Its Meaning*. Cambridge, Mass.

Barrett, A. 1990. *Caligula: The Corruption of Power*. New Haven.

Barthelémy, A. 1935. *Dictionnaire Arabe-François, Dialectes de Syrie*. Paris.

Baxandall, M. 1971. *Giotto and the Orators: Humanist Observers of Painting in Italy and the Discovery of Pictorial Composition, 1350–1450*. Oxford.

Baynham, E. 1998. *Alexander the Great: The Unique History of Quintus Curtius*. Ann Arbor.

Beazley, C. 1897–1906. *The Dawn of Modern Geography: A History of Exploration and Geographical Science from the Conversion of the Roman Empire to AD 900*, 3 vols. London.

Becker, J. ed. 1915. Liudprand, *Liudprandi Episcopi Cremonensis opera* (Monumenta Germaniae historica, Scriptores). Leipzig.

Bell, A. Jr. 1977. "An Historiographical Analysis of the *De excidio Hierosolymitano* of Pseudo-Hegesippus." Diss. U. of North Carolina, Chapel Hill.

Benedetto, F. di 1969. "Leonzio, Omero e le *Pandette*," *IMU* 12.53–112.

Benedetto, L. ed. 1928. Marco Polo, *Il Milione*, Florence.

Benoit, W. 1980. "Aristotle's Example: The Rhetorical Induction," *Quarterly Journal of Speech* 66.182–192.

Bergdolt, K. 1992. *Artz, Krankheit und Therapie bei Petrarca: Die Kritik an Medizin und Naturwissenschaft in italienischen Frühhumanismus.* Weinheim.

Berghoff, W. ed. 1967. Palladius, *De gentibus Indicae et Bragmanibus.* Meisenheim.

Bergin, T. 1970. *Petrarch.* New York.

———. ed. 1974. *Petrarch's "Bucolicum Carmen."* New Haven.

———. ed. 1983. "Petrarch's *Epistola metrica* II.10: An Annotated Translation," 183–229 in *Dante, Petrarch, Boccaccio: Studies in the Italian Trecento in Honor of Charles S. Singleton,* eds. A. Bernardo and A. Pellegrini. Binghamton, N.Y.

Bernardo, A. 1955. "Petrarch's Attitude Toward Dante," *Publications of the Modern Language Association* 70.488–517.

———. 1962. *Petrarch, Scipio, and the "Africa": The Birth of Humanism's Dream.* Baltimore.

———. 1976. *Concordance to the "Epistolae familiares" by Francesco Petrarca .* New York. (Microfiche.)

———. ed. 1978. E. Wilkins, *Studies on Petrarch and Boccaccio* (Studi sul Petrarca 6). Padua.

Berschin, W. 1988. *Greek Letters and the Latin Middle Ages: From Jerome to Nicolas of Cusa,* rev. and trans. by J. Frakes. Washington, D.C.

Bertolini, V. 1968. "Le carte geografiche nel *Filocolo,*" *Studi sul Boccaccio* 5.211–225.

Beugnot, A. and Prévost, A. eds. 1844. William of Tyre, *Historia rerum in partibus transmarinis gestarum. RHC, Occ.,* vol. 1 (2 pts.). Paris. (Translation in *A History of Deeds Done Beyond the Sea,* edited by E. Babcock and A. Kreg [Records of Civilization 35] 2 vols. New York 1943.)

Billanovich, G. ed. 1943. *Rerum memorandarum libri iv* (Edizione Nazionale). Florence.

———. 1946. *Petrarca e Cicerone* in *Miscellanea Giovanni Mercati* (Studi e Testi 124). Vatican City.

———. 1947. *Petrarca letterato,* I: *Lo scrittoio del Petrarca.* Rome.

———. 1948. "La tradizione del *Liber de dictis philosophorum antiquorum* e la cultura di Dante, del Petrarca e del Boccaccio," *Studi petrarcheschi* I. 111–123.

———. 1951. "Petrarch and the Textual Tradition of Livy," *Journal of the Warburg and Courtauld Institutes.* 14.137–208.

———. 1952. "Autografi del Boccaccio nella Bibilioteca Nazionale di Parigi," *Rendiconti della Accademia nazionale dei Lincei: Classe di scienze morali, storiche e filologiche,* series 8, 7:376–388.

———. 1956. "Dall' antica Ravenna alle biblioteche umanistiche," *Aevum* 30.319–353. (Reprinted in *Annuario della Università Cattolica del Sacro Cuore* 1955–57 [Milan, 1957] 73–107.)

———. 1960. "Nella biblioteca del Petrarca. II. Un altro Suetonio del Petrarca (Oxford, Exeter College, 186)," *IMU* 3.28–58.

———. 1966. "Petrarca e il Ventoso," *IMU* 9. 389–401.

———. 1981–85. *La tradizione del testo di Livio e le origini dell'umanesimo*, 2 vols. (Studi sul Petrarca 9). Padua. (Vol. 2 is a complete facsimile of Petrarch's Livy, British Lib., Harley 2493; Part 2 of vol. 1 is still to be published.)

Birks, P. and McLeod, G. eds. 1987. *Justinian's "Institutes,"* with Latin text by P. Krueger. Ithaca, N.Y.

Bisanti, A. 1994. "Petrarca, Virgilio e Inarime: In margine all' *Itinerario* e ai *Triumphi*," *Sileno* 20.333–341.

Bischoff, B. 1966. "Die lateinischen Übersetzungen und Bearbeitungen aus den Oracula Sibyllina," 150–171 in his *Mittelalterliche Studien: Ausgewählte Aufsätze zur Schriftkunde und Literaturgeschichte,* vol. 1. Stuttgart.

———. 1990. *Latin Palaeography: Antiquity and the Middle Ages*, trans. D. Ó Crónín and D. Ganz. Cambridge.

Bishop, M. 1963. *Petrarch and His World.* Bloomington, Ind.

Blatt, F. ed. 1958. *The Latin Josephus*, vol. 1: *Introduction and Text: The Antiquities, Books I–V* (Acta Jutlandia, 30.1, Hum. Ser. 44). Aahus and Copenhagen.

Bloomer, W. 1992. *Valerius Maximus and the Rhetoric of the New Nobility.* Chapel Hill.

Boase, T. 1977. "Ecclesiastical Art in the Crusader States in Palestine and Syria," 69–116 in Hazard 1977.

———. ed. 1978. *The Cilician Kingdom of Armenia.* Edinburgh / London.

Boer, E. ed. 1961. *Claudii Ptolemaei Opera,* vol. III. 2, 2nd ed. (Bibliotheca Teubneriana). Leipzig.

Boitani, P. and Torti, A. eds. 1986. *Intellectuals and Writers in Fourteenth-century Europe* (The J. A. W. Bennett Memorial Lectures, Perugia 1984). Tübingen.

Bolgar, R. 1954. *The Classical Heritage and Its Beneficiaries.* Cambridge.

Bongars, J. ed. 1611. Marino Sanudo, *Liber secretorum fidelium crucis super Terrae Sanctae recuperatione. . .*, vol. 2.1–288 in *Gesta Dei per Francos.* Hanover. (Separate reprint with intro. by J. Prawer, Jerusalem 1972.)

Bonnard, G. ed. 1961. *Gibbon's Journey from Geneva to Rome: His Journal from 2 April to 2 October 1764.* Edinburgh.

Bonneau, D. 1971. "Liber Aristotelis de inundatione Nili," *Éudes de papyrologie* 9.1–33.

Branca, V. 1976. *Boccaccio: The Man and His Works*, trans. R. Monges. New York.

Brandt, S. ed. 1890. L. Caelius Lactantius, *Divinarum institutionum libri vii* (Corpus scriptorum ecclesiasticorum latinorum 19). Vienna. (Translation in M. McDonald, *The Divine Institutes* [Fathers of the Church 49] Washington, D.C. 1964.)

Braudel, F. 1972. *The Mediterranean and the Mediterranean World in the Age of Philip II*, 2 vols., trans. by S. Reynolds. New York.

Bremond, C., Le Goff, J., Schmitt , J.–Cl. 1982. *L' "exemplum."* Turnholt.

Briscoe, J. ed. 1998. Valerius Maximus, *Factorum et dictorum memorabilium libri ix*, 2 vols. (Bibliotheca Teubneriana). Leipzig.

Brodersen, K. 1992. *Reiseführer zu den Sieben Weltwundern: Philon von Byzanz und andere antike Texte*. Frankfurt / Main and Leipzig.

———. 1995. *Terra Cognita: Studien zur römischen Raumerfassung* (Spudasmata 39). Hildesheim.

Brown, L. 1949. *The Story of Maps*. Boston. (Reprinted New York 1979.)

Brown, V. 1981. "Portraits of Julius Caesar in Latin Manuscripts of the Commentaries," *Viator* 12.321–354.

Bruère, R. 1961. "Lucan and Petrarch's *Africa*," *Classical Philology* 56.83–99.

Brundage, J. 1962. *The Crusades: A Documentary Survey*. Milwaukee, Wis.

Bryer, A. 1967. "The Great Idea," 100–117 in *Universal Rome*, ed. by A. Birley. Edinburgh / London.

Budge, E. 1911. *Cook's Handbook for Egypt and the Egyptian Sudan*, 3rd ed. London.

Burgalassi, S. 1984. "Il tabù della Meloria ed altri stereotipi negativi," 68–74 in Danielli and Borghini 1984.

Burkert, W. 1972. *Lore and Science in Ancient Pythagoreanism*, trans. by E. Minar. Cambridge, Mass.

Burns, R. 1980. "Piracy as an Islamic-Christian Interface in the Thirteenth Century," *Viator* 11.165–178

Butzmann, H. ed. 1970. *Corpus Agrimensorum: Codex Acerianus A der Herzog-August-Bibliothek zu Wolfenbüttel* (Codices graeci et latini photographice depicti 22). Leiden.

Byrne, E. 1930. *Genoese Shipping in the Twelfth and Thirteenth Centuries*. Cambridge, Mass.

Cachey, T. 1991. "Petrarch, Boccaccio, and the New World Encounter," *Stanford Italian Review* 10.45–59.

———. 1995. *Le Isole Fortunate: Appunti di storia letteraria italiana*. Rome.

Cameron, P. 1988. *Crete*, 5th ed. (Blue Guide). London / New York.

Campbell, A. 1931. *The Black Death and Men of Learning.* New York.
Campbell, J. 1982. "To Hell and Back: Latin Tradition and Literary Use of the 'Descensus ad Inferos' in Old English," *Viator* 13.107–158.
Campbell, T. 1986. "Census of Pre-sixteenth-century Portolan Charts," *Imago Mundi* 38.67–91.
———. 1987. "Portolan Charts of the Late Thirteenth Century to 1500," 371–463 in Harley and Woodward 1987.
Canzanella, C. 1999. *La Madonna di Piedigrotta: il culto, il mito, la storia.* Naples.
Capasso, M. 1983. *Il sepulcro di Virgilio.* Naples.
Cappelli, A. 1886. "La biblioteca estense nella prima metà de secolo XV," *Giornale storico della letteratura italiana* 14.1–30.
Caputo, P., Morichi, R., Paone, R., and Rispoli, P. eds. 1996. *Cuma e il suo parco archeologico: un territorio e le sue testimonianze.* Rome
Cardini, F. ed. 1982. *Toscana e Terrasanta nel medioevo.* Florence.
———. 1986. "Three Florentine Travellers to the Holy Land in 1384–1385: The Synoptic Texts of Their Accounts," 191–203 in Boitani and A. Torti 1986. Tübingen.
Caretta, A. and Samarati, L. 1958. *Lodi: profilo di storia medievale.* Lodi.
Carozza, D. and Shey, H. eds. 1989. *Petrarch's 'Secretum,"* with notes and critical anthology (American University Studies, series 17, 7). New York.
Carrara, E. 1932. *Da Rolando a Morgante.* Milan.
Carson, T. ed., 1994. *Barbarossa in Italy: A Verse Translation of the 'Carmen de gestis Frederici I imperatoris in Lombardia."* New York.
Cary, G. 1950. "Petrarch and Alexander the Great," *Italian Studies* 5.43–55.
———. 1954. "A Note on the Medieval History of the *Collatio Alexandri cum Dindimo,"Classica et Mediaevalia* 15.124–129.
———. 1956. *The Medieval Alexander,* ed. D. Ross. Cambridge.
Casson, L. 1971. *Ships and Seamanship in the Ancient World.* Princeton.
Castagnoli, F. 1975–76. "L'orientamento nella cartografia greca e romana," *Rendiconti della Pontificia accademia romana di archeologia* 48.59–69.
Cesareo, G. 1904. "La carta d'Italia del Petrarca," in *Da Dante al Leopardi, Raccolta di scritti critici . . . per le nozze Scherillo-Negri,* 219–225. Milan.
Cheney, C. 1961. *Handbook of Dates for Students of English History.* London.
Chiapponi, L. 1960. "Il *De architectura* di Vitruvio nel primo umanesimo," *IMU* 3.59–99.
Chibnall, M. 1975. "Pliny's *Natural History* and the Middle Ages," 57–78 in *Empire and Aftermath: Silver Latin II,* ed. T. Dorey. London.

Chiovenda, L. 1953. "Die Zeichnungen Petrarcas," *Archivum Romanicum* 17.1–61.
Clagett, M. 1963. *Greek Science in Antiquity*. New York.
Clark, A. ed. 1907. *Q. Asconii Pediani orationum Ciceronis quinque enarratio.* Oxford.
———. 1910. *The 'Cursus" in Mediaeval and Vulgar Latin* . Oxford.
Clark, R. 1969. "Christ's Resurrection at Avernus: a Virgilian Influence," *Classica et Mediaevalia* 30. 300–307.
———. 1977. "Virgil, *Aeneid*, 6, 40 ff. and the Cumaean Sibyl's Cave," *Latomus* 36. 482–495.
———. 1996. "The Avernian Sibyl's Cave: From Military Tunnel to Mediaeval Spa," *Classica et Mediaevalia* 47. 217–243.
———. 1996a. "Conrad of Querfurt and Petrarch on the Location of the Virgilian Underworld," *Papers of the British School at Rome* 64. 261–272.
Claussen, M. 1991. "*Peregrinatio* and *Peregrini* in St. Augustine's *City of God*," *Traditio* 46.33–75.
Clayton, P. and Price, M. 1988. *The Seven Wonders of the Ancient World.* London.
Clogan, P. ed. 1968. *The Medieval "Achilleid" of Statius.* Leiden.
Cluver, P. 1624. *Italia antiqua*, 2 vols., paginated consecutively. Leiden.
Coarelli, F. 1985. *Italia centrale* (Guide archeologiche Laterza). Rome / Bari.
Cochin, H. ed. 1892. *Un ami de Pétrarque: lettres de Francesco Nelli à Pétrarque.* Paris.
Cognasso, F. 1955. *L'unificazione della Lombardia sotto Milano*, vol. 5 in *Storia di Milano*, 16 vols. (Fondazione Treccani degli Alfieri). Milan.
———. 1966. *I Visconti.* Milan.
Colker, M. ed. 1964. "A Medieval Pilgrim's Guide," 100–143 in vol. 2 of Henderson 1964.
———. ed. 1978. Walter of Châtillon, *Alexandreis* (Thesaurus Mundi: Biblotheca Scriptorum Latinorum Mediae et Recentioris Aetatis, 17). Padua.
Comparetti, D. 1941. *Virgilio nel medio evo*, 2 vols., 3rd ed. G. Pasquali. Florence. (See the English translation of the second edition [1895] of Comparetti by E. Benecke, *Virgil in the Middle Ages*, 2nd ed. [London, 1908]; reprinted Hamden, Conn., 1966; Princeton 1997.)
Contini, G. 1980. "Petrarca e le arti figurative," 115–131 in *Francesco Petrarca: Citizen of the World*, ed. by A. Bernardo. Padua / Albany, N.Y.
Cook, A. 1914–1940. *Zeus: A Study in Ancient Religion*, 3 vols. Cambridge.

Copenhaver, B. and Schmitt, C. 1992. *Renaissance Philosophy* (A History of Western Philosophy 3). Oxford.

Corradini, F. 1874. *Africa Francisci Petrarchae nunc primum emendata* in *Padova a Francesco Petrarca nel quinto centenario della sua morte.* Padua.

Cosenza, M. 1913. *Petrarch: The Revolution of Cola di Rienzo*, new ed. by R. Musto 1986. Chicago.

Crane, T. 1890. *The Exempla or Illustrative Stories from the Sermones Vulgares of Jacques de Vitry.* London.

Critchley, J. 1992. *Marco Polo's Book.* Cambridge.

Cunningham, M. ed. 1966. Aurelius Prudentius Clemens, *Carmina* (Corpus Christianorum, series latina 126). Turnout. (Translation by M. Eagen, *The Poems of Prudentius*, 2 vols. [Fathers of the Church 43/52], Washington, D.C. 1962–65.)

Curtius, E. 1953. *European Literature and the Latin Middle Ages*, trans. W. Trask. New York.

D'Amato, J. 1975. "Prolegomena to a Critical Edition of the Illustrated Medieval Poem *De balneis Terre Laboris* by Peter of Eboli." Diss. Johns Hopkins U., Baltimore.

———. 1996. "The *Turris Pharo* at Capo Miseno: A Monument of Medieval Scholarship," *Viator* 27.215–264.

D'Ancona, A. 1889. "La leggenda di Maometto in Occidente," *Giornale storico della letteratura italiana* 13.199–281.

Daniel, N. 1975. *The Arabs and Medieval Europe.* London/Beirut.

———. 1989. "Crusade Propaganda," 39–97 in Hazard and Zacour 1989. Madison, Wis.

Danielli, F. and Borghini, G. eds. 1984. *1284: l'anno della Meloria* (Circolo filatelico numismatico iconografico Pisano). Pisa.

D'Arms, J. 1970. *The Romans on the Bay of Naples.* Cambridge, Mass.

Datillo, V. 1963. *Castel dell'Ovo: Storie e leggende di Napoli*, 2nd. ed. Naples.

Davis, C. 1957. *Dante and the Idea of Rome.* Oxford.

———. 1984. "Dante's Italy," 1–22 in *Dante's Italy and Other Essays.* Philadelphia.

———. 1993. "Dante and the Empire," 67–79 in *The Cambridge Companion to Dante*, ed. by R. Jacoff. Cambridge.

De Frede, C. 1967–78. "Da Carlo I d' Angio a Giovanna I (1263–1382)," vol. 2.9–354 in *Storia di Napoli*, 10 vols. Naples.

Degenhart, B. and Schmitt, A. 1973. "Marino Sanudo und Paolino Veneto," *Römisches Jahrbuch für Kunstgeschichte* 14.1–137.

De La Mare, A. C. 1973. *The Handwriting of Italian Humanists*, vol. 1, pt. 1. Oxford.

Delfiol, R. 1982. "Su alcuni problemi codicologico-testuali concernenti le relazioni di pellegrinaggio fiorentino del 1384," 139–176 in Cardini 1982. Florence.

Deluz, C. 1987. "Le livre Jehan de Mandeville, autorité géographique à la renaissance," 205–220 in J. Céard and J.-C. Margolin, *Voyager à la Renaissance*. Paris.

Demartre, L. 1987. "Medicine, Schools of," in *Dictionary of the Middle Ages*. New York.

Der Nersessian, S. 1969. "The Kingdom of Cicilian Armenia," 630–659 in Wolff and Hazard 1969.

Destombes, M. ed. 1964. *Mappemondes, AD 1200–1500 : Catalogue préparé par la Commission des Cartes Anciennes de l'Union Géographique Internationale*. (Monumenta cartographica vetustioris aevi 1). Amsterdam.

Deycks, F. ed. 1851. Ludolph von Suchem [Sudheim], *De itinere Terrae Sanctae liber* . . . (Bibliothek des litterarischen Vereins in Stuttgart 25). Stuttgart.

Dilke, O. 1967. "Illustrations from Roman Surveyors' Manuals," *Imago Mundi* 21.9–29.

———. 1971. *The Roman Land Surveyors: An Introduction to the Agrimensores*. Newton Abbot.

———. 1985. *Greek and Roman Maps*. Ithaca.

———. 1987. "The Growth of an Empirical Cartography in Hellenistic Greece," 148–160 in Harley and Woodward 1987.

———. 1987a. "Itineraries and Geographical Maps in the Early and Late Roman Empire," 234–257 in Harley and Woodward 1987.

Dimock, J. ed. 1867. Giraldus Cambrensis, *Opera*, vol. 5 (Rerum britannicarum medii aevi scriptores 21). London.

Doblhofer, E. ed. 1972–77. Rutilius Claudius Namatianus, *De reditu suo sive Iter gallicum*, 2 vols. Heidelberg.

Dols, M. 1977. *The Black Death in the Middle East*. Princeton.

Dopp, P. 1950. "Le Caire vu par les voyageurs occidentaux du Moyen Age," *Bulletin de la Société Royale de Géographie d' Égypte* 23.117–149.

Doren, A. 1922-23. "Fortuna in Mittelalter und in der Renaissance," *Vorträge der Bibliothek Warburg* 2.71–144.

Dostourian, A. ed. 1993. Matthew of Edessa, *Armenia and the Crusades, Tenth to Twelfth Centuries: The Chronicle of Matthew of Edessa*. Lanham.

Dotti, U. 1992. *Vita di Petrarca*, 2nd ed. Rome / Bari.

Du Cange, C. ed. 1883–87. *Glossarium ad scriptores mediae et infimae Latinitatis*, 5th ed. by L. Favre, 10 vols. Niort (reprinted in Paris 1937–1940 and Graz 1954).

Duff, J. and Duff, A. eds. 1935. *Minor Latin Poets* (Loeb Classical Library). Cambridge, Mass.

Dunn, R. 1986. *The Adventures of Ibn Battuta: A Muslim Traveler of the 14th Century*. Berkeley.

Durling, R. ed. 1976. *Petrarch's Lyric Poems: The "Rime sparse" and Other Lyrics*. Cambridge, Mass.

Dutschke, D. 1981. "The Anniversary poems in Petrarch's *Canzoniere*," *Italica* 58.83–101.

———. 1986. *Census of Petrarch Manuscripts in the United States* (Censimento dei codici petrarcheschi 9). Padua.

Ehrenberg, V. and Jones, A. 1955. *Documents Illustrating the Reigns of Augustus and Tiberius*, 2nd ed. Oxford.

Eisenhut, W. ed. 1958. *Dictis Cretensis Belli Troiani Libri* (Bibliotheca Teubneriana). Leipzig.

Eklund, S. 1984. "The Use and Abuse of Cursus in Textual Criticism," *Archivum Latinitatis Medii Aevi* 43.27–56.

Elliott, J. ed. 1993. *The Apocryphal New Testament: A Collection of Apocryphal Christian Literature in an English Translation*. Oxford.

Engels, D. 1985. "The Length of Eratosthenes' Stade," *American Journal of Philology* 106.298–311.

Ernout, A. and Meillet, A. 1959. *Dictionnaire étymologique de la langue latine*, 4th ed. Paris.

Ewald, M. ed. 1952. *Early Christian Biographies*, ed. R. Deferrari (Fathers of the Church 15). Washington, D.C.

Farmer, D. 1987. *The Oxford Dictionary of Saints*, 2nd ed. Oxford.

Feder, T. 1978. *Great Treasures of Pompeii and Herculaneum*. New York.

Feldman, L. 1984. *Josephus and Modern Scholarship (1937–1980)*. Berlin.

Feo, M. 1974. "Inquietudini filologiche del Petrarca: il luogo della discesa agli inferi (storia di una citazione)," *IMU* 17. 115–183.

———. 1977. "Un Ulisse in Terrasanta," *Rivista di cultura classica e medioevale*, 19.383–388.

———. 1988. "Petrarca, Francesco," in *Enciclopedia Virgiliana*, vol. 4. Rome.

Fera, V. 1984. *La revisione petrarchesca dell' Africa*. Messina.

Fernández-Armesto, F. 1987. *Before Columbus: Exploration and Colonization from the Mediterranean to the Atlantic 1229–1492* . London.

Ferrante, J. 1984. *The Political Vision of the "Divine Comedy."* Princeton.

Finegan, J. 1992. *The Archeology of the New Testament: The Life of Jesus and the Beginning of the Early Church*, 2nd. ed. Princeton.

Finke, H. ed. 1910–22. *Acta Aragonensia: Quellen aus der diplomatischen Korrespondenz Jaymes II, 1291–1327* , 3 vols. Berlin and Leipzig.

Fleischman, S. 1983. "On the Representation of History and Fiction in the Middle Ages," *History and Theory* 22.278–310.

Flint, V. 1991. *The Rise of Magic in the Early Middle Ages.* Princeton.

Foresti, A. 1977. "Peregrinazioni di Francesco Petrarca fanciullo: ove gli fu fatto conoscere Dante," 1–7 in *Aneddoti della vita di Francesco Petrarca,* ed. A. Benvenuti. Padua.

Forsyth, G. and Weitzmann, K. 1973. *The Monastery of St. Catherine at Mount Sinai: The Church and Fortress of Justinian.* Ann Arbor.

Foster, K. 1984. *Petrarch: Poet and Humanist.* Edinburgh.

Foulet, A. 1989. "The Epic Cycle of the Crusades," 98–115 in Hazard and Zacour 1989. Madison, Wis.

Fracassetti, G. ed. 1863. Francesco Petrarca, *Epistolae de rebus familiaribus et variae,* vol. 3.309–488. Florence.

Franceschini, A. and Weber, R. eds. 1965. *Itinerarium Egeriae,* 29–90 in *Itineraria et alia geographica* (Corpus Christianorum, series latina 175). Turnhout.

Fraser, P. 1972. *Ptolemaic Alexandria,* 3 vols. Oxford.

Frasso, G. 1974. *Itinerari con Francesco Petrarca,* with introduction by G. Billanovich and photos by L. Capellini. Padua.

Frazer, R. ed. 1966. *The Trojan War: The Chronicles of Dictys of Crete and Dares the Phrygian.* Bloomington, Ind.

Frederiksen, M. 1984. *Campania,* ed. with additions by N. Purcell. Oxford.

French, R. and Greenaway, F. eds. 1986. *Science in the Early Roman Empire: Pliny the Elder, His Sources and Influence.* Totawa, N.J.

Fridh, A. ed. 1973. Cassiodorus, *Magni Aurelii Cassiodori Variorum libri xii* (Corpus Christianorum, series latina 96). Turnhout.

Friedman, J. 1981. *The Monstrous Races in Medieval Art and Thought.* Cambridge, Mass.

Fubini, R. ed. 1964. Giovanni Francesco Poggio Bracciolini, *Opera omnia,* vol. 3: *Poggii epistolae.* Turin. (Fubini reprints the three-volume edition of T. de Tonellis, Florence 1832–61.)

———. 1968. "Biondo, Flavio," in *Dizionario biografico degli Italiani.* Rome.

Galbiati, G. ed. 1930. *Francisci Petrarcae Virgilianus Codex.* Milan. (Biblioteca Ambrosiana MS S.P. 10/27, once A. 79 inf.)

Gardiner, E. ed. 1991. E. Bacco, d' Engenio Caraccioli, C., et al., *Naples: An Early Guide,* with essays by C. Bruzelius and R. Musto. New York.

Gardner, E. 1930. *The Arthurian Legend in Italian Literature.* London / New York.

Gautier, L. 1883. *La chevalerie.* Paris.

Geffcken, J. ed. 1902. *Die Oracula Sibyllina* (Die griechischen christlichen Schriftsteller der ersten Jahrhunderte 8). Leipzig. (The only reliable complete translation in English is that of J. Collins in *Old Testament Pseudepigrapha*, vol. 1.317–472, ed. by J. Charlesworth, Garden City, N.Y. 1983.)

Gelsomino, R. ed. 1967. Vibius Sequester, *De fluminibus, fontibus, lacubus, nemoribus, paludibus, montibus, gentibus per litteras libellus* (Bibliotheca Teubneriana). Leipzig.

Gelzer, M. 1968. *Caesar: Politician and Statesman*, trans. by P. Needham. Cambridge, Mass.

Gersh, S. 1986. *Middle Platonism and Neoplatonism: The Latin Tradition*, 2 vols. Notre Dame, Ind.

Ghinassi, G. ed. 1861. Luchino dal Campo, "Viaggio a Gerusalemme di Nicolò da Este," in *Miscellanea di opuscoli inediti o rari dei secoli xiv e xv*, vol. 1.101–160. Turin.

Ghinato, A. 1951. *Fr. Paolino da Venezia, OFM, Vescovo di Pozzuoli (+1344).* Rome.

Gilson, E. 1936. *The Spirit of Medieval Philosophy*, trans. A. Downes. London.

Giulini, G. 1854–57. *Memorie spettanti alla storia, al governo ed alla descrizione della cittàe della compagna di Milano ne' secoli bassi*, 7 vols., new ed. with supplemental notes. Milan. (Reprinted Milan, 1973–75; first edition published Milan, 1760–1771.)

Godi, C. 1965. "L'orazione del Petrarca per Giovanni il buono," *IMU* 8.45–83.

Golding, A. 1587. *The Excellent and Pleasant Worke of Iulius Solinus Polyhistor*. London. (Facsimile ed. with introduction by G. Kish, Gainesville, Fla. 1955.)

Golubovich, G. ed. 1909–26. *Biblioteca bio-bibliografica della Terra Santa e dell' Oriente francescano*, 5 vols. Quaracchi (near Florence).

Gordan, P. ed. 1974. *Two Renaissance Book Hunters: The Letters of Poggius Bracciolini to Nicolaus de Niccolis* (Records of Western Civilization, Sources and Studies 91). New York.

Gormley, C., Rouse, M., and Rouse, R. 1984. "The Medieval Circulation of the *De Chorographia* of Pomponius Mela," *Mediaeval Studies* 46.266–320.

Gottfried, R. 1983. *The Black Death: Natural and Human Disaster in Medieval Europe*. New York.

Graesse, J. ed. 1890. *Legenda aurea, vulgo Historia Lombardica dicta*, 3rd ed. Dresden. (Reprinted Osnabrück, 1969.)

Grandgent, C. ed. 1972. Dante Alighieri, *La divina commedia*, revised by C. Singleton. Cambridge, Mass. (Singleton prints the text of G. Pe-

trocchi, *La commedia secondo l'antica volgata*, 4 vols. Milan 1966–67.)
Grant, E. ed. 1974. *A Source Book in Medieval Science*. Cambridge, Mass.
Gribaudi, P. 1907. "Sul nome di 'Terra di lavoro,'" *Rivista Geografica Italiana* 14.193–210.
Griffin, N. ed. 1936. Guido delle Colonne, *Historia Destructionis Troiae* (Medieval Academy of America). Cambridge, Mass.
Gryson, R. et al. 1994. *Biblia sacra iuxta vulgatam versionem*, 4th rev. ed. Stuttgart.
Gryting, L. ed. 1952. *The Oldest Version of the Twelfth-Century Poem 'La Venjance Nostre Seigneur"* (University of Michigan Contributions in Modern Philology 19). Ann Arbor.
Guarnieri, G. 1931. *Il porto di Livorno e la sua funzione economica dalle origini ai tempi nostri*. Pisa.
Guasti, C. ed. 1880. Ser Lapo Mazzei, *Lettere di un notaro a un mercante del secolo XIV*, 2 vols. Florence.
Guidetti, S. 1998. "Fonti e tecniche di compilazione nella *Chronica civitatis ianuensis* di Jacopo da Varagine," 17–36 in *Gli umanesimi medievali* (Atti del II Congresso dell' "Internationales Mittellateinerkomitee" Firenze, Certosa del Galluzzo, 11–15 settembre 1993). Florence.
Guidubaldi, E. 1976. "Stabili, Francesco (Cecco d'Ascoli)," in *Enciclopedia dantesca*, 5.404–405. Rome.
Guillaumin, J.-Y., ed. 1995. Boethius, *Institution Arithmétique* (Association Guillaume Budé). Paris.
Gundersheimer, W. 1973. *Ferrara: The Style of a Renaissance Despotism*. Princeton.
Haase, F. ed. 1886. Seneca, *L. Annaei Senecae opera quae supersunt*, vol. 3. Leipzig.
Hadas, M. 1959. *Hellenistic Culture: Fusion and Diffusion*. New York.
Hägg, T. 1983. *The Novel in Antiquity*. Berkeley.
Hahn, T. 1978. "The Indian Tradition in Western Medieval Intellectual History," *Viator*. 213–234.
Hainsworth, P. 1988. *Petrarch the Poet: An Introduction to the "Rerum vulgarium fragmenta."* London.
Hankey, A. 1957. "Domenico di Bandino of Arezzo," *Italian Studies* 12. 110–130.
———. 1957a. "The Library of Domenico di Bandino," *Rinascimento* 8.177–207.
———. 1960. "Successive Revisions and Surviving Codices of the *Fons Memorabilium Universi* of Bandini," *Rinascimento* 11.3–48.

Hanly, M. 1996. "An Edition of Richart Eudes's French Translation of Pietro da Eboli's *De balneis puteolanis*," *Traditio* 51.225–255.

Hardie, C. ed. 1957. *Vitae Virgilianae antiquae*, 2nd ed. Oxford.

Harley, J. and Woodward, D. eds. 1987. *A History of Cartography*, vol. 1: *Cartography in Prehistoric, Ancient, and Medieval Europe and the Mediterranean*. Chicago.

Harvey, P. 1987. "Local and Regional Maps in Medieval Europe," 464–501 in Harley and Woodward 1987.

———. 1991. *Medieval Maps*. Toronto.

Haskins, C. 1929. "The Early *Artes dictandi* in Italy," 170–192 in his *Studies in Mediaeval Culture*. Oxford.

Hatzfeld, A. and Darmesteter, A. eds. 1964. *Dictionnaire général de la langue française*. Paris.

Hazard, H. ed. 1975. *A History of the Crusades*, vol. 3: *The Fourteenth and Fifteenth Centuries*, general ed. K. Setton 1969–89. Madison, Wis.

———. ed. 1977. *History of the Crusades*, vol. 4: *The Art and Architecture of the Crusader States*, general ed. K. Setton 1969–89. Madison, Wis.

———. and Zacour, N. eds. 1989. *A History of the Crusades*, vol. 6: *The Impact of the Crusades on Europe*, general ed. K. Setton 1969–89. Madison, Wis.

Healy, J. 1978. *Mining and Metallurgy in the Greek and Roman World*. London.

Hebel, J., ed. 1933. Michael Drayton, *Poly-Olbion*, vol. 4 in *The Works of Michael Drayton*, 5 vols. Oxford.

Heitmann, K. 1958. *Fortuna und Virtus: Eine Studie zu Petrarcas Lebensweisheit*. Köln.

Helm, R. ed. 1898. *Fabii Planciadis Fulgentii opera* (Bibliotheca Teubneriana). Leipzig.

Henderson, C. Jr., ed. 1964. *Classical, Mediaeval, and Renaissance Studies in Honor of B. L. Ullman*, 2 vols. Rome.

Hennecke, E. ed. 1963. *New Testament Apocrypha*, ed. W. Schneemelcher, with English trans. R. Wilson et al., 2 vols.; vol. 1: *Gospels and Related Writings*. Philadelphia.

Henschel, A. 1846. "Petrarcas Urtheil über die Medizin und die Ärtze seiner Zeit," *Janus* 1.183–223.

Herlihy, D. 1958. *Pisa in the Early Renaissance: A Study of Urban Growth*. New Haven.

Hibbert, C. 1982. *Africa Explored: Europeans in the Dark Continent 1769–1889*. London.

Hinks, A. 1929. *Portolan Chart of Angellino de Dalorto 1325 in the Collection of Prince Corsini at Florence, with a note on the Surviving Charts and Atlases of the Fourteenth Century*. London.

Hoffman, D. 1990. "The Arthurian Tradition in Italy," 1.170–188 in V. Lagorio and M. Day, *King Arthur Through the Ages,* 2 vols. New York.
Housley, N. 1982. *The Italian Crusades: The Papal-Angevin Alliance and the Crusades against Christian Lay Powers, 1254–1343* . Oxford.
———. 1986. *The Avignon Papacy and the Crusades, 1305–1378.* Oxford.
Housman, A. ed. 1926. *M. Annaei Lucani Belli civilis libri decem.* Oxford.
Howard, D. 1980. *Writers and Pilgrims: Medieval Pilgrimage Narratives and Their Posterity.* Berkeley.
Hugen, D. 1974. "Small Birds of Cyprus," *Paideuma* 3.229–238.
Hyde, J. 1982. "Real and Imaginary Journeys in the Later Middle Ages," *Bulletin of the John Rylands Library* 65.125–147.
———. 1993a,b,c,d. *Literacy and Its Uses: Studies on Late Medieval Italy,* ed. D. Waley. Manchester. This volume contains:
———. a. "Medieval Descriptions of Cities," 1–33.
———. b. "Navigation of the eastern Mediterranean in the 14th and 15th centuries according to pilgrims' books," 87–111.
———. c. "Italian Pilgrim Literature in the Late Middle Ages," 136–161.
———. d. "Ethnographers in Search of an Audience," 162–216. (The first three essays are reprints.)
Imperiale di Sant' Angelo, C. ed. 1923. *Annali genovesi di Caffaro e de' suoi continuatori,* 5 vols. (Fonti per la storia d' Italia 3). Rome.
———. ed. 1926. This is the fourth vol. in the Fonti series (preceding item).
IMU= Italia medioevale e umanistica.
Irwin, R. 1986. *The Middle East in the Middle Ages: The Early Mamluk Sultanate, 1250–1382.* London.
Iversen, E. 1961. *The Myth of Egypt and Its Hieroglyphs in European Tradition.* Princeton.
Jackson, W. 1985. "The Progress of Parzival and the Trees of Virtue and Vice," 218–225 in his *The Challenge of the Medieval Text: Studies in Genre and Interpretation,* ed. by J. Ferrante and R. Hanning. New York.
Jacob, W. and Hanslik, R. eds. 1952. Cassiodorus-Epiphanius, *Historia ecclesiastica tripartita: Historiae ecclesiasticae ex Socrate, Sozomeno et Theodorito in unum collectae nuper de Graeco in Latinum translatae libri numero duodecim* (Corpus scriptorum ecclesiasticorum latinorum 71). Vienna.
Jacoby, F. ed. 1958. *Die Fragmente der griechischen Historiker, vol. 3.C.2: Geschichte von Städten und Völker: Autoren über einzelne Länder.* Leiden.

Jacono, L. 1937. "Il Porto Julio," *Reale Accademia d'archeologia, lettere ed arti: Rendiconti* n.s. 18.31–59.

Jal, A. 1848–1850. *Glossaire nautique: Répertoire polyglotte de termes de marine anciens et modernes,* 2 vols. Paris.

Jal, P. ed. 1967. L. Annaeus Florus, *Tableau de l' histoire du peuple romain, de Romulus à Auguste,* 2 vols. (Association Guillaume Budé). Paris.

James, M. ed. 1924. *The Apocryphal New Testament.* Oxford.

Janson, T. 1975. *Prose Rhythm in Medieval Latin from the 9th to the 13th Century.* Stockholm.

Jarry, E. 1896. *Les origines de la domination française à Gênes, 1392-1402.* Paris.

Jensen, R. ed. 1973. *Domenico Silvestri: The Latin Poetry.* Munich.

Jones, H. ed. 1917–32. *The Geography of Strabo,* 8 vols. (Loeb Classical Library). Cambridge, Mass.

Jung, E. and von Franz, M. 1970. *The Grail Legend,* trans. by A. Dykes. New York.

Katzenellenbogen, A. 1939. *Allegories of the Virtues and Vices in Medieval Art from Early Christian Times to the Thirteenth Century,* trans. by A. Crick. London. (Reprinted Nendeln, Liechtenstein 1968.)

Kauffmann, C. 1959. *The Baths of Pozzuoli: A Study of the Medieval Illuminations of Peter Eboli's Poem.* Oxford.

Kedar, B. 1976. *Merchants in Crisis: Genoese and Venetian Men of Affairs and the Fourteenth-Century Depression.* New Haven.

Keen, M. 1984. *Chivalry.* New Haven / London.

Kibre, P. 1975. "Hippocrates Latinus: Repertorium of Hippocratic Writings in the Middle Ages," *Traditio* 31.99–126.

Kibre, P. and Siraisi, N. 1978. "The Institutional Setting: The Universities," 120–144 in D. Lindberg 1978. Chicago.

Kieckhefer, R. 1990. *Magic in the Middle Ages.* Cambridge.

Kleinhenz, C. 1986. "Italian Arthurian Literature," 293–299 in *The Arthurian Encyclopedia,* ed. N. Lacy. New York.

Knott, B. ed. 1969–88. Desiderius Erasmus, *De duplici copia verborum ac rerum commentarii duo,* vol. 1, 6 in *Opera omnia Desiderii Erasmi Roterodami.* Amsterdam.

Kratz, D. ed. 1991. *The Romances of Alexander.* New York.

Kretschmer, K. 1909. *Die italienischen Portolane des Mittelalters: Ein Beitrag zur Geschichte der Kartographie und Nautik* (Veröffentlichungen des Instituts für Meereskunde und des Geographischen Instituts an der Universität Berlin 13). Berlin. (Reprinted Hildesheim 1962).

Kristeller, P. 1945. "The School of Salerno: Its Development and Its Contribution to the History of Learning," *Bulletin of the History of Medicine* 17.138–194.

———. and Randall, J. eds. 1948. *The Renaissance Philosophy of Man*. Chicago.

———. 1961. "The Aristotelian Tradition" and "Renaissance Platonism," 24–47 and 48–69 in *Renaissance Thought: The Classic, Scholastic, and Humanist Strain*. New York.

———. 1963. *Iter Italicum: A Finding List of Uncatalogued or Incompletely Catalogued Humanistic Manuscripts of the Renaissance in Italian and Other Libraries*, vol. 1: *Italy: Agrigento to Navaro*. London.

Kroll, W., Skutsch, F., and Ziegler, K. eds. 1897–1913. *Iulii Firmici Materni Matheseos libri viii*, 2 vols. (Biblioteca Teubneriana). Leipzig. (Translation in J. Bram, *Ancient Astrology: Matheseos libri viii by Firmicus Maternus* [Park Ridge, N.J., 1975].)

Krueger, H. 1969. "The Italian Cities and the Arabs before 1095," 40–53 in Baldwin 1969. Madison, Wis.

Labarge, M. 1982. *Medieval Travellers: The Rich and the Restless*. London.

Lacaita, G. ed. 1887. Benvenuto da Imola, *Benvenuti de Rambaldis de Imola, Comentum super Dantis Aldigherii Comoediam*, 5 vols. Florence.

Laistner, M. 1948. "The Value and Influence of Cassiodorus' Ecclesiastical History," *Harvard Theological Review* 41.51–67.

Lanman, J. 1987. *On the Origin of Portolan Charts* (H.D. Smith Center for the History of Cartography 2). Chicago.

Lappenberg, I. ed. 1869. Arnold of Lübeck, *Cronica Slavorum a. 1172–1209* (Monumenta Germaniae historica: Scriptores 21). Hanover.

Laurent, J. ed. 1873. *Peregrinatores medii aevi quatuor: Burchardus de Monte Sion, Ricoldus de Monte Crucis, Odoricus de Foro Julii, Wilbrandus de Olenborg* . . . 2nd ed. Leipzig.

Leclercq, H. 1924. "Gênes," in *Dictionnaire d' archéologie chrétienne et de liturgie*, 6A, colls. 900–903. Paris.

Le Goff, J. 1980. *Time, Work, and Culture in the Middle Ages*, trans. by A. Goldhammer. Chicago.

Legrand, L. ed. 1895. "Relation du pélerinage à Jerusalem de Nicolas de Martoni, notaire italien (1394–1395)," *Revue de l'Orient latin* III.566–669.

Lemut, M. 1984. "I Pisani prigionieri a Genova dopo la battaglia della Meloria: la tradizione e le fonti documentarie," 75–87 in Danielli and Borghini 1984.

Leone de Castris, P. 1987. *Arte di corte nella Napoli angioina*. Florence.

Lerner, R. 1986. "Petrarch's Coolness Toward Dante: A Conflict of 'Humanisms,'" 204–225 in Boitani and Torti 1986. Tübingen.

Leutsch, E. and Schneidewin, F., eds. 1839. *Corpus Paroemiographorum Graecorum*, 2 vols. Göttingen. (Reprinted Hildesheim 1965).

Lewis, B. 1993. *The Arabs in History*, 6th ed. New York.

Levi, E. ed. 1914. *Fiore di leggende: cantori antichi*. Bari.

Liburnio, N. ed. 1978. Giovanni Boccaccio, *Dizionario geografico: De montibus, silvis, lacubus, stagnis seu paludibus, et de nominibus maris*, preface by G. F. Pasini. Turin.

Liebrecht, F. ed. 1856. *Des Gervasius von Tilbury "Otia Imperialia" in einer Auswahl neu herausgegeben*. Hanover.

Lietzmann, H. 1910. *Lateinische altkirchliche Poesie*. Berlin.

Lindberg, D. ed. 1978. *Science in the Middle Ages*. Chicago.

———. 1978. "The Transmission of Greek and Arabic Learning to the West," 52–90 in D. Lindberg 1978 (see preceding entry). Chicago.

Lindsay, W. ed. 1911. *Isidori hispalensis episcopi Etymologiarum sive Originum libri xx*, 2 vols. Oxford.

Little, A. 1908. *Liber exemplorum ad usum praedicantium* (British Society of Franciscan Studies). Aberdeen.

Lo Monaco, F., ed. 1990. Francesco Petrarch, *Itinerario in Terra Santa 1358*. Bergamo.

———. 1993. "L' *Itinerario in Terrasanta* di Francesco Petrarca," 363–378 in *Relazione di viaggio e conoscenza del mondo fra Medioevo e Umanesimo* (Atti del V Convegno internazionale di studi dell' Assoc. per il Medioevo e l'Umanesimo latini, Geneva, 12–15 Dec. 1991), ed. by S. Pittaluga. Geneva.

Lumbroso, G. ed. 1889. "La guida compilata dal Petrarca ad uso d' un pellegrino," in his "*Memorie italiane del buon tempo antico*," 16–49. Turin. (Reprinted from "L'*Itinerarium* del Petrarca," *Atti della Reale Accademia dei Lincei*, series quarta, 4 [1888] 390–403.)

Luttrell, A. 1975. "The Hospitallers at Rhodes, 1306–1421," 314–339 in Hazard 1975.

Lyons, J. 1989. *Exemplum: The Rhetoric of Example in Early Modern France and Italy*. Princeton.

Macadam, A. 1991. *Blue Guide: Northern Italy*, 9th ed. New York.

MacKail, J. 1921. "The Italy of Dante and the Italy of Virgil," 105–131 in *Dante: Essays in Commemoration 1321-1921*. London.

MacKendrick, P. 1952. "A Renaissance Odyssey: The Life of Ciriaco of Ancona," *Classica et Mediaevalia* 13.131–145

———. 1960. *The Mute Stones Speak: The Story of Archaeology in Italy*. New York.

Mailler, C. 1979. "La tradizione medievale dei bagni flegrei," *Puteoli: Studi di storia antica* 3.141–153.

Maiuri, A. 1963. *The Phlegraean Fields: From Virgil's Tomb to the Grotto of the Cumaean Sibyl*, 4th ed., trans. V. Priestley. Rome.

Mann, N. 1975. "Petrarch Manuscripts in the British Isles," *IMU* 18.139–527.

———. 1984. *Petrarch.* Oxford.

Manzoni, L. 1894–95. "Fratre Francesco Pipino da Bologna," *Atti e memorie delle R. Deputazione di storia patria per le Provincie di Romagna,* ser. 3. 13.273–281, 316–332.

Martellotti, G. 1949. "Linee di sviluppo dell' umanesimo petrarchesco," *Studi petrarcheschi* II.51–93.

———. 1951. "Clausole e ritmi nella prosa narrativa del Petrarca," *Studi petrarcheschi* IV.35-46. (Collected in *Scritti petrarcheschi,* eds. M. Feo and S. Rizzo [Padua, 1983] 207–219.)

———. ed. 1954. Francesco Petrarca, *La Vita di Scipione l'Africano.* Milan / Naples.

———. ed. 1964. "La *Collatio inter Scipionem Alexandrum Hanibalem et Pyrrum,*" 145–168 in vol. 2 of Henderson 1964. (Collected in *Scritti petrarcheschi,* Padua 1983.)

———. ed. 1964a. *De viris illustribus,* vol. 1 (Edizione Nazionale). Florence.

Marti, M. ed. 1969–72. Giovanni Boccaccio, *Opere minori in volgare,* 4 vols. Milan.

Martini, P. 1972. "Un carme di Lorenzo Vitelli sulle origini di Corneto," *IMU* 15.347–354.

Mazzanti, M., Pasquinucci, M., and Drioli, U. 1984. "Il sistema secche della Meloria-Porto Pisano: geomorfologia e biologia marina in relazione ai reperti archeologici," 5–53 in Danielli and Borghini 1984.

Mazzino, E. 1961. "L'organizzatione urbanistica del porto e del molo di Genova nel Medioevo," 172–184 in *Miscellanea in onore e memoria di U. Formentini* (Memorie dell' Accademia Lunigianese di Scienze, 32). La Spezia.

Mazzoni, F. 1970. "Benvenuto da Imola," in *Enciclopedia dantesca* 1.593–596. Rome.

McGinn, B. 1973. "Joachim and the Sibyl," *Citeaux* 24.97–138.

McGovern, J. 1972. "The Documentary Language of Medieval Business, 1150–1250," *Classical Journal* 67.227–238.

McKay, A. 1972. *Cumae and the Phlegraean Fields: Ancient Campania,* 2 vols. Hamilton, Ont.

———. 1997. "Review Article: The Monuments of Cuma," *Virgilius* 43.78–88.

McVaugh, M. 1987. "Medicine, History of," in *Dictionary of the Middle Ages*. New York.

Meek, C. 1980. *The Commune of Lucca under Pisan Rule, 1342-1369*. Cambridge, Mass.

Meek, M. ed. 1974. Guido delle Colonne, *Historia Destructionis Troiae*. Bloomington, Ind.

Meiggs, R. 1973. *Roman Ostia*, 2nd ed. Oxford.

Meister, F. ed. 1873. *Daretis Phrygii De Excidio Troiae Historia* (Bibliotheca Teubneriana). Leipzig. (Reprint 1991).

Merkle, S. 1996. "The Truth and Nothing but the Truth: Dictys and Dares," 563–580 in *The Novel in the Ancient World*, ed. G. Schmeling. Leiden / New York.

MGH, SS = Monumenta Germaniae Historica, Scriptores. Berlin, 1877– .

Milner, N. ed. 1996. *Vegetius: Epitome of Military Science*, 2nd. ed. (Translated Texts for Historians 16). Liverpool.

Minio-Paluello, L. 1972. "Il *Fedone* latino con note autografe del Petrarca," 107–113 in *Opuscula: The Latin Aristotle*. Amsterdam. (Reprinted from *Accademia Nazionale dei Lincei: Rendiconti della Classe di scienze morali*, series 8, 4, 1–2 [1949]: 107–113.)

Miskimin, H. 1978. *The Economy of Early Renaissance Europe, 1300-1460*. London / New York.

Momigliano, A. 1974. "Polybius' Reappearance in Western Europe," 347–372 in *Polybe* (Fondation Hardt: Entretiens sur l' antiquité classique 20). Geneva.

Mommsen, T. ed. 1895. C. Iulius Solinus, *Collectanea rerum memorabilium*, 2nd ed. Berlin.

Mommsen, T. ed. 1957. *Petrarch's Testament*. Ithaca.

Monga, L. 1996. "Travel and Travel Writing: An Historical Overview of Hodoeporics,"*Annali d'Italianistica: L'Odeporica/Hodoeporica* 14.6–54.

———. 1996a. "Renaissance Hodoeporics: A Bibliography of Theoretical Texts on *Methodus apodemica* (1550–1700)," *Annali d'Italianistica: L'Odeporica / Hodoeporica* 14.645–684.

Monleone, G. ed. 1941. Jacopo da Voragine, *Chronica civitatis ianuensis ab origine urbis usque ad annum MCCXCVII*, 3 vols. (Fonti per la storia d' Italia 84–86). Rome.

Monneret de Villard, V. ed. 1949. Ricoldo da Montecroce, *Il libro della peregrinazione nelle parti d'Oriente di frate Ricoldo da Montecroce* (Institutum historicum Fratrum Praedicatorum, Dissertationes historicae 13). Rome.

Montet, P. 1957. *Géographie de l'Égypte ancienne*, vol. 1: *La Basse-Égypte*. Paris.

Monti, R. 1991. "The Topographical and Literary Evidence for the Identification of the Sibyl's Cave at Cumae," *Virgilius* 37.39–59.

———. 1994. "The Identification of Virgil's Cave of the Cumaean Sibyl in *Aeneid* 6," *Virgilius* 40.19–34.

Moore, E. 1896. *Studies in Dante, First Series: Scripture and Classical Authors in Dante.* Oxford.

Moorehead, A. 1971. *The White Nile.* New York.

Moos van, P. 1988. *Geschichte als Topik: Das rhetorische* Exemplum *von der Antike zur Neuzeit und die historiae im 'Polycaticus' Johanns von Salisbury* (Ordo: Studien zur Literatur und Gesellschaft des Mittelalters und der frühen Neuzeit). Hildesheim.

Morgan, A. 1990. *Dante and the Medieval Other World.* Cambridge.

Morisani, O. ed. 1972. Benedetto di Falco, *Descrittione dei luoghi antiqui di Napoli a del suo amenissimo distretto.* Naples.

Mosshammer, A. 1976. "Geometrical Proportion and the Chronological Method of Apollodorus," *Transactions of the American Philological Association* 106. 291–306.

MR = *Missale Romanum,* 7th ed. New York 1949.

Müller, K. and Schönfeld H. eds. 1954. Curtius Rufus, *Geschichte Alexanders des Grossen.* Munich. (Latin and German translation in Tusculum edition; English translation with good notes by J. Yardley and W. Heckel in Penguin edition 1984.)

Müller, R. 1993. "Überlegungen zur *Hiera Anagraphe* des Euhemeros von Messene," *Hermes* 121.276–300.

Muoni, D. 1877. *Famiglie notabili milanesi.* Milan.

Murphy-O'Connor, J. 1998. *The Holy Land (Oxford Archaeological Guides),* 4th ed. Oxford.

Musa, M. ed. 1996. Francesco Petrarch, *The Canzoniere or Rerum vulgarium fragmenta.* Bloomington, Ind.

Musto, R. 1985. "Queen Sancia of Naples (1286–1345) and the Spiritual Franciscans," 179–214 in *Women of the Medieval World: Essays in Honor of John H. Mundy,* ed. J. Kirshner and S. Wemple. Oxford.

Mynors, R. ed. 1937. *Cassiodori senatoris institutiones.* Oxford. (Translated by L. Jones, *An Introduction to Divine and Human Readings* [Records of Civilization, Sources and Studies 40] New York 1946.)

Nardis, M. de 1992. "Aristotelismo e doxografia antica (ancora sul *Perì toûNeîlou anabáseos),"Geographia antiqua* 1.89–108.

Newett, M. 1907. *Canon Pietro Casola's Pilgrimage to Jerusalem in 1494.* Manchester.

Newton, A. ed. 1926. *Travel and Travellers of the Middle Ages.* London.

Nicolau, M. 1930 *L'origine du "cursus" rhythmique et les débuts de l'accent d'intensitéen latin.* Paris.

Nissen, H. 1883. *Italische Landeskunde*, vol. 1: *Land und Leute.* Berlin.

Nolhac, P. de 1907. *Pétrarque et l'humanisme,* 2nd ed., 2 vols. in one. Paris.

Norden, E. 1957. P. Virgilius Maro, *Aeneis Buch VI*, 4th ed. Darmstadt.

Novati, F. ed. 1891–1911. *Epistolario di Coluccio Salutati,* 4 vols. (Fonti per la storia d'Italia 15–18). Rome.

———. 1890. "Donato degli Albanzani alle corte Estense," *Archivio Storico Italiano* 5, 6.365–385.

———. 1904. "Il Petrarca ed i Visconti," 11–63 in *F. Petrarca e la Lombardia*. Milan.

———. 1909. "Di un *Ars puctuandi* erroneamente attribuita a Francesco Petrarca," *Rendiconti del Reale Istituto Lombardo di Scienze e Lettere,* ser. 2, 42.83–118.

O'Conner, M. 1986. "The Etymology of *Saracen* in Aramaic and Pre-Islamic Arabic Contexts," 603–632 in *The Defense of the Roman and Byzantine East*, 2 vols. Oxford.

ODCC = *Oxford Dictionary of the Christian Church,* 3rd ed. by F. Cross and E. Livingstone. Oxford 1997.

Ohler, N. 1989. *The Medieval Traveller,* trans. by C. Hillier. Woodbridge, Suffolk.

Omont, H. 1882. "Les sept merveilles du monde au moyen âge," *Bibliothèque de l' école des Chartes* 43.40–59.

Önnerfors, A. ed. 1995. Vegetius, *P. Flavii Vegeti Renati Epitoma rei militaris* (Bibliotheca Teubneriana). Stuttgart.

Ormerod, H. 1924. *Piracy in the Ancient World.* Liverpool.

Ostrow, S. 1979. "The topography of *Puteoli* and *Baiae* on eight glass flasks," *Puteoli: Studi di storia antica* 3.77–140.

Ottone, T. da 1940. *La leggenda di Santa Caterina vergine e martire di Alexandria*. Genoa.

Paccagnini, G. 1958–68. "Martini, Simone," *Encyclopedia of World Art*, vol. 10, cols. 502–508. New York.

Padoan, G. 1964. "Petrarca, Boccaccio e la scoperta delle Canarie," *IMU* 7.264–277.

———. ed. 1965. Giovanni Boccaccio, *Esposizioni sopra la Comedia di Dante,* vol. 6 in *Tutte le opere di Giovanni Boccaccio,* ed. by V. Branca. Milan.

Paget, R. 1968. "The Ancient Ports of Cumae," *Journal of Roman Studies* 58.159–169.

———. 1969. "Portus Julius," *Virgilius* 15.25–32.

———. 1971. "From Baiae to Misenum," *Virgilius* 17.22–38.

Paolella, A. 1992. "Petrarca e la letteratura odeporica del medioevo," *Studi e problemi di critica testuale* 44.61–85.

———. ed. 1993. *Volgarizzamento meridionale anonimo di Francesco Petrarca, Itinerarium breve de Ianua usque ad Ierusalem et Terram Sanctam*. Bologna.

———. 1996. "Petrarca: *peregrinus an viator?*" in *Annali d'Italianistica: L'odeporica / Hodoeporics* 14.152–176.

Paoletti, L. 1966. "Benvenuto da Imola," in *Dizionario biografico degli Italiani* 8.691–694. Rome.

Paris, P. ed. 1879. *Guillaume de Tyr et ses continuateurs*, 2 vols. Paris.

Parke, H. 1988. *Sibyls and Sibylline Prophecy in Classical Antiquity*, ed. B. McGing. London.

Parkes, M. 1993. *Pause and Effect: An Introduction to the History of Punctuation in the West*. Berkeley.

Patch, H. 1927. *The Goddess Fortuna in Medieval Literature*. Cambridge, Mass.

———. 1950. *The Other World According to Descriptions in Medieval Literature*. Cambridge, Mass.

Paton, J. 1951. *Chapters on Medieval and Renaissance Visitors to Greek Lands*. Princeton.

Pearson, L. 1960. *The Lost Histories of Alexander the Great*. New York.

Pease, A. ed. 1955–58. *M. Tulli Ciceronis De natura deorum libri*, 2 vols. Cambridge, Mass.

Pecoraro, C. ed. 1954. Domenico Silvestri, *De insulis et earum proprietatibus* in *Atti della Accademia di Scienze, Lettere e Arti di Palermo*, 4th Series, Part II, Fasc. II, 14.1–320.

Peebles, B. 1964. "The *Ad Maronis Mausoleum*: Petrarch's Virgil and Two Fifteenth-Century Manuscripts," 169–190 in vol. 2 of Henderson 1964.

Pegna, M. 1967. *L'origine di Livorno* (Quaderni di studi storici toscani, series 4, 2). Florence.

Pellegrin, E. 1975. *Manuscrits de Pétrarque à la Bibliothèque Vaticane: Supplement au Catalogue de Vattasso* (Censimento dei codici petrarcheschi 5). Padua.

Pertusi, A. 1964. *Leonzio Pilato fra Petrarca e Boccaccio: Le sue versioni omeriche negli autografi di Venezia e la cultura greca del primo Umanesimo* (Civiltà veneziana, Studi 16). Venice / Rome.

Petrucci, A. 1963. "Aspetti del culto e del pellegrinaggio di san Michele Arcangelo sul Monte Gargano," 145–180 in *Pellegrinaggi: Pellegrinaggi e culto dei santi in Europa fino alla 1a crociata* (Convegni del Centro di Studi sulla Spiritualità Medievale 4). Todi.

———. 1967. *La scrittura di Francesco Petrarca* (Studi e testi 248). Vatican City.

Petrucci, L. 1979. "Le fonti per la conoscenza della topografica delle terme flegree dal XII al XV secolo," *Archivio Storico per le Provincie Napoletane* 3.99–129.

Pfister, F. ed. 1911. *Kleine Texte zum Alexanderroman*. Heidelberg.

PG = *Patrologia cursus completus, series Graeca*, ed. J.-P. Migne, 162 vols. Paris, 1857–1886.

Philipp, H. 1942. "Padus," *RE* col. 2180.

Phillips, E. 1953. "Odysseus in Italy," *Journal of Hellenic Studies* 73.53–67.

Phillips, J. 1988. *The Medieval Expansion of Europe*. Oxford.

Pinto, G. 1982. "I costi del pellegrinaggio in Terrasanta nei secoli xiv e xv (dai resoconti dei viaggiatori italiani)," 257–284 in Cardini 1982. Florence.

Piur, P. 1925. *Petrarcas "Buch ohne Namen" und die päpstliche Kurie.* Halle.

PL = *Patrologiae cursus completus, series latina*, ed. J.-P. Migne, 217 vols; indices 218–221. Paris, 1844–1864.

Podestà, F. 1913. *Il porto di Genova, dalle origini alla caduta della Republica genovese*. Genoa.

Podossinov, A. and Chekin, L. 1991. "Extended Review" of Harley and Woodward 1987 in *Imago Mundi* 43.112–123.

Porcaro, G. 1958. *Piedigrotta: storia, leggenda, folklore*. Naples.

Porena, M. 1952. "Il *Mons Falernus* secondo Francesco Petrarca," *Rendiconti della (R.) Accademia di Archeologia, Lettere e Belle Arti di Napoli* N.S. 27.75–81.

Porro, G. ed. 1855. Pietro Casola, *Viaggio a Gerusalemme.* Milan.

Porta, G. ed. 1990–91. Giovanni Villani, *Nuova Cronica*, 3 vols. (Bibliotheca di Scrittori Italiani). Parma.

Postan, M., Rich, E., and Miller, E. eds. 1963. *The Cambridge Economic History of Europe*, vol. 3: *Economic Organization and Policies in the Middle Ages.* Cambridge.

Pound, E. 1975. *The Cantos*. London.

Powell, J. ed. 1990. *Moslems under Latin Rule, 1100–1300.* Princeton.

Prawer, J. 1972. "Pilgrims, Pilgrimages and the 'Holy Geography,'" in his *The Latin Kingdom of Jerusalem: European Colonialism in the Middle Ages.* London.

Price, B. 1975. "Paradeigma and Exemplum in Ancient Rhetorical Theory." Diss. U. of California, Berkeley.

Purcell, N. 1995. "On the Sacking of Carthage and Corinth," 133–148 in *Ethics and Rhetoric: Classical Essays for Donald Russell*, ed. by D. Innes, H. Hine, and C. Pelling. Oxford.

Quaglio, A. ed. 1967. Giovanni Boccaccio, *Filocolo*, in *Tutte le opere*, vol. 1, ed. by V. Branca. Milan.

Quintavalle, A. and Povoledo, E. 1960. "Giovan Battista Aleotti," *Dizionario biografico degli Italiani*. Rome.

Raban, A. and Holum, K. 1996. *Caesarea Maritima: A Retrospective after Two Millennia*. Leiden.

Rackham, H., Jones, W., and Eichholz, D. eds. 1938–63. Gaius Plinius Secundus, *Natural History* (Loeb Classical Library). Cambridge, Mass.

Rahlfs, A. ed. 1935. *Septuaginta*. Stuttgart.

Rahner, H. 1963. "The Christian Mystery of Sun and Moon," 89–154 in *Greek Myths and Christian Mystery*, trans. by B. Battershaw. New York.

Rand, E., Savage, J. et al. eds. 1946. *Servianorum in Virgilii carmina commentariorum editionis Harvardianae volumen II, quod in Aeneidos libros I et II explanationes continet*. Lancaster, Pa.

Randall, J. 1961. *The School of Padua and the Emergence of Modern Science*. Padua.

Rashdall, H. 1936. *The Universities of Europe in the Middle Ages*, ed. by F. Powicke and A. Emden, 3 vols. Oxford.

Rawski, C. ed. 1967. *Petrarch: Four Dialogues for Scholars*. Cleveland.

———. ed. 1991. *Petrarch's "Remedies for Fortune Fair and Foul": A Modern English Translation of "De remediis utriusque fortune," with a Commentary*, 5 vols. Bloomington.

Rawson, E. 1969. *The Spartan Tradition in European Thought*. Oxford.

———. 1985. *Intellectual Life in the Late Roman Republic*. London.

Raymond, A. 1975. "La population du Caire de Maqrizi à la *Description de l'Égypte*," *Bulletin d'Études orientales* 28.201–215.

RE = A. Pauly, G. Wissowa, et al. *Realencyclopädie der klassischen Altertumswissenschaft*, 84 vols. Stuttgart, 1893–1980.

Redi, F. 1984. "Il fervore edilizio di Pisa dopo la Meloria: consistenza e interpretazione," 93–127 in Danielli and Borghini 1984.

Reeve, M. 1989. "The 'vetus Carnotensis' of Livy Unmasked," 97–112 in *Studies in Latin Literature and its Tradition in Honour of C. O. Brink*, eds. J. Diggle, J. Hall, and H. Jocelyn (Cambridge Philological Society, suppl. vol. 15). Cambridge.

Reeves, M. 1969. *The Influence of Prophecy in the Later Middle Ages: A Study in Joachimism*. Oxford.

Reifferscheid, A. ed. 1860. C. Suetonius Tranquillus, *Praeter Caesarum libros reliquiae*. Leipzig.

Rennie, N. 1995. *Far-Fetched Facts: The Literature of Travel and the Idea of the South Seas*. Oxford.

Renzi, S. de ed. 1854. *Collectio salernitana*, III. Naples.

Reynolds, L. ed. 1986. *Texts and Transmissions: A Survey of Latin Classics*, 2nd ed. Oxford.

RHC, Occ. = *Recueil des historiens des croisades: Historiens occidentaux*, ed. by the Académie des inscriptions et belles-lettres, 5 vols., Paris 1844–95.

Ricci, P. G. 1943. "L'interpunzione del *De ignorantia* petrarchesco," *Rendiconti dell' Accademia d'Italia, Scienze Morali*, ser. 7, 3. 401–408.

———. 1950. "Per una monographia su Domenico Silvestri," *Annali della Scuola Normale Superiore di Pisa: Lettere, Storia e Filosofia*, ser. II, 19.13–24.

———. ed. 1978. Francesco Petrarch, *Invective contra medicum, testo latino e volgarizzamento di Ser Domenico Silvestri*, with appendix by B. Martinelli (Studi e testi 32). Rome.

Rico, F. 1974. *Vida u obra de Petrarca, I: Lectura del "Secretum"* (North Carolina Studies in the Romance Languages and Literatures 33). Chapel Hill. (Also published in *Studi sul Petrarca* 4, Padua 1974.)

———. 1984. "Sobre la cronologia del *Secretum:* Las viejas leyendas y el fantasma nuevo de un lapsus biblico," *Studi petrarcheschi* N.S. 1.51–102.

———. 1986. "Philology and Philosophy in Petrarch," 45–66 in Boitani and Torti 1986.

Riddle, J. 1974. "Theory and Practice in Medieval Medicine," *Viator* 5.157–170.

Riese, A. ed. 1878. *Geographi latini minores*. Heilbronn. (Reprinted Hildesheim 1964.)

Riley-Smith, J. 1987. *The Crusades: A Short History*. New Haven.

———. ed. 1991. *The Atlas of the Crusades*. New York.

Robbert, L. 1985. "Venice and the Crusades," 379–451 in Zacour and Hazard 1985.

Robbins, F. ed. 1940. Claudius Ptolemy, *Tetrabiblos* (Loeb Classical Library). Cambridge, Mass.

Rogers, P. 1995. *Johnson and Boswell: The Transit of Caledonia*. Oxford.

Rohde, E. 1966. *Psyche: The Cult of Souls and Belief in Immortality among the Greeks*, 8th ed. (1925) trans. by W. Hillis, with intro. by W. Guthrie, 2 vols. New York.

Röhricht, R. ed. 1884. Ricoldo da Montecroce, "Lettres sur la prise d'Acre, 1291," in *Archives de l'Orient latin* II. 2.258–296.

———. 1890. *Bibliotheca geographica Palaestinae: Chronologisches Verzeichnis der von 333 bis 1878 verfassten Literatur über das Heilige Land . . .*, ed. with supplements by D. Amiran 1963. Jerusalem.

———. ed. 1895. Giacamo da Verona, *Liber peregrinationis*, in *Revue de l'Orient latin* III. 155–302.

Roncioni, R. 1844. *Istorie pisane*, in *Archivio storico italiano*, ser. 1, vol. 6, pt. 1.

Rose, H. ed. 1934. *Hygini fabulae*. Leiden.

Rose, V. ed. 1886. *Aristotelis qui ferebantur librorum fragmenta* (Biblioteca Teubneriana). Stuttgart. (Reprinted 1967.)

Ross, D. 1988. *Alexander Historiatus: A Guide to Medieval Illustrated Alexander Literature*, 2nd ed. Frankfurt am Main.

Ross, J. 1927. "On the Early History of Leontius' Translation of Homer," *Classical Philology* 22.341–355.

Ross, W. 1970. "Giovanni Colonna, Historian at Avignon," *Speculum* 45. 533–545.

Rothschild, E. and Wilkins, E. 1928. "Hell in the Florentine Baptistery Mosaic and in Giotto's Padua," *Art Studies* 6:31–35.

Rotondi, G., ed. 1958. *Il "De otio religioso" di Francesco Petrarca*, ed. G. Martellotti (Studi e testi 195). Vatican City.

Runciman, S. 1958. *The Sicilian Vespers: A History of the Mediterranean World in the Later Thirteenth Century*. Cambridge.

———. 1969. "The Pilgrimages to Palestine Before 1095," 68–78 in Baldwin 1969.

Russell, J. 1958. "Late Ancient and Medieval Population," *Transactions of the American Philosophical Society*. N. S. 48, pt. 3.5–152.

Rzach, A. 1923. "Sibyllinische Orakel" and "Sibyllen," *RE* colls. 2073–2183.

Sabbadini, R. 1905–14. *Le scoperte dei codici latini e greci ne' secoli xiv e xv*, 2 vols. Florence. (Reprinted with author's additions and corrections in 1967.)

Saffrey, H. 1968. "ΑΓΕΩΜΕΤΡΗΤΟΣ ΜΗΔΕΙΣ ΕΙΣΙΤΩ: Une inscription légendaire," *Revue des études grecques* 81.67–87.

Saffron, M. 1975. "Salernitan Anatomists," 12:80–83 in *Dictionary of Scientific Biography*. New York.

Sahas, D. 1972. *John of Damascus on Islam: The "Heresy of the Ishmaelites."* Leiden.

Salomon, R. 1936. *Opicinus de Canistris: Weltbild und Bekenntnisse eines Avignonesischen Klerikers des 14. Jahrhunderts* (Studies of the Warburg Institute, vols. 1A and 1B, text and plates). London.

———. 1953. "A Newly Discovered Manuscript of Opicinus de Canistris," *Journal of the Warburg and Courtauld Institutes* 15.45–57.

Salt, H. 1814. *A Voyage to Abyssinia and Travels into the Interior of That Country*. London.

Santini, C. ed. 1979. Eutropius, *Breviarium ab urbe condita* (Bibliotheca Teubneriana). Leipzig. (Translation and commentary may be found in H. Bird's *The "Breviarium ab urbe condita" of Eutropius*, Liverpool 1993.)

Sarton, G. 1959. *A History of Science: Hellenistic Science and Culture in the Last Three Centuries BC*. Cambridge, Mass.

Savage, H. 1977. "Pilgrimages and Pilgrim Shrines in Palestine and Syria after 1095," 36–68 in Hazard 1977.

Scaglione, A. 1972. *The Classical Theory of Composition from Its Origins to the Present*. Chapel Hill.

Scandurra, E. 1972. "The Maritime Republics: Medieval and Renaissance Ships in Italy," 205–224 in *A History of Seafaring Based on Underwater Archaeology*, ed. G. Bass. New York.

Scanlon, L. 1994. *Narrative, Authority, and Power: The Medieval Exemplum and the Chaucerian Tradition*. Cambridge.

Schein, S. 1991. *Fideles Crucis: The Papacy, the West, and the Recovery of the Holy Land*. Oxford.

Scheiwiller, V. ed. 1956. *De moribus Brachmanorum liber Santo Ambrosio adscriptus*. Milan.

Schiaffini, A. 1943. *Tradizione e poesia nella prosa d' arte italiana dalla latinità medievale a G. Boccaccio*. Rome.

Schmitt, C. 1971. "Theophrastus in the Middle Ages," *Viator* II. 257–270.

———. and Knox, D. 1985. *Pseudo-Aristoteles Latinus: A Guide to Latin Works Falsely Attributed to Aristotle before 1500* (Warburg Institute Surveys and Texts 12). London.

Schoene, A. ed. 1967. *Eusebi Chronicorum libri duo*, 2 vols. Zürich. (A reprint of the edition of 1866–75.)

Schreckenberg, H. 1972. *Die Flavius-Josephus-Tradition in Antike und Mittelalter* (Arbeiten zur Literatur und Geschichte des hellenistischen Judentums 5). Leiden.

———. 1977. *Rezeptionsgeschichtliche und textkritische Untersuchungen zu Flavius Josephus* (Arbeiten zur Literatur und Geschichte des hellenistischen Judentums 10). Leiden.

Scott, J. 1972. "La contemporaneità Enea-Davide [*Convivio*, IV v 6]," *Studi danteschi* 49.129–134.

Seel, O. ed. 1972. M. Iunianus Iustinus [Justin], *Epitoma Historiarum Philippicarum Pompei Trogi*, 2nd ed. (Bibliotheca Teubneriana). Leipzig, (A translation of Justin may be found in J. Watson, *Justin, Cornelius Nepos, and Eutropius* [London, 1853] and in J. Yardley, *Epitome of the "Philippic History" of Pompeius Trogus* [Atlanta, 1994].)

Segrè, C. 1903. "Chi accusò il Petrarca di magia?" 99–124 in his *Studi petrarcheschi*. Florence.

Setton, K. 1948. *Catalan Domination of Athens, 1311–1388*. Cambridge, Mass.

———. ed.-in-chief 1969–89. *A History of the Crusades*, 2nd ed. in 6 vols.; see Baldwin 1969, Wolff and Hazard 1969, Hazard 1975 and 1977, Zacour and Hazard 1985, and Hazard and Zacour 1989. Madison, Wis.

———. 1992. *Western Hostility to Islam and Prophecies of Turkish Doom* (American Philosophical Society 201). Philadelphia.

Seymour, M. 1967. *Mandeville's Travels*. Oxford.

Sforza, G. 1922. "La distruzione di Luni nella leggenda e nella storia," 3–139 in *Miscellanea di storia italiana*, 3rd series, 19. Turin.

SHA = *Scriptores Historiae Augustae*, 3 vols. ed. D. Magie (Loeb Classical Library). New York 1932.

Shackleton Bailey, D. ed. 1988. M. Annaeus Lucan, *De bello civili libri* x (Biblotheca Teubneriana). Stuttgart.

Sherwin, W. ed. 1973. *Deeds of Famous Men (De viris illustribus): A Bilingual Edition*. Norman, Okla.

Sigurdsson, H. et al. 1982. "The Eruption of Vesuvius in AD 79: A Reconstruction from Historical and Volcanological Evidence," *American Journal of Archeology* 86.39–51.

Silberman, A. ed. 1988. Pomponius Mela, *Chorographie* (Association Guillaume Budé). Paris. (An English translation, the first in over 400 years, may be consulted in F. Romer, *Pomponius Mela's 'Description of the World,"* Ann Arbor 1998.)

Simon, M. 1966. "Zur Abhängigkeit spätrömischer Enzyklopädien der *artes liberales* von Varros *Disciplinarum libri," Philologus* 110.88–101.

Simone, F. 1965. *Il Rinascimento francese*, 2nd ed. Turin. (Translated by H. Hall as *The French Renaissance* [London, 1969].)

Siraisi, N. 1990. *Medieval and Early Renaissance Medicine: An Introduction to Knowledge and Practice*. Chicago.

Smalley, B. 1981. "Jean de Hesdin O. Hosp. S. Joh," 345–392 in *Studies in Medieval Thought and Learning*. London. (Reprinted from *Recherches de Théologie ancienne et medievale* 7 [1961] 285–330.)

Smith, D. 1968. *A History of Sicily*, 3 vols.; vol. 2: *Medieval Sicily, 800–1713*. New York.

Sottili, A. 1971. "I codici del Petrarca nella Germania occidentale," *IMU* 14.313–402.

Southern, R. 1956. *Western Views of Islam in the Middle Ages*. Cambridge.

———. 1992. *Robert Grosseteste: The Growth of an English Mind in Medieval Europe*, 2nd ed. Oxford.

Spargo, J. 1934. *Virgil the Necromancer: Studies in Virgilian Legends* (Harvard Studies in Comparative Literature 10). Cambridge, Mass.

Spillenger, P. 1991. "Dante's *Arte* and the Ambivalence of Retrospection," *Stanford Italian Review* 10.241–268.

Stahl, W. ed. 1952. *Macrobius: Commentary on the Dream of Scipio* (Records of Civilization, Sources and Studies 48). New York.

———. 1962. *Roman Science: Origins, Development, and Influence to the Later Middle Ages.* Madison, Wis.

Stahl, W., Johnson, R., and Burge, E. eds. 1971–77. *Martianus Capella and the Seven Liberal Arts*, 2 vols. (Records of Civilization, Sources and Studies 84). New York.

Stanford, E. 1935. "Propaganda and Censorship in the Transmission of Josephus," *Transactions of the American Philological Association* 66.127–145.

Starn, R. 1982. *Contrary Commonwealth: The Theme of Exile in Medieval and Renaissance Italy*. Berkeley.

Starr, C. 1960. *The Roman Imperial Navy,* 2nd ed. Cambridge.

Stelten, L. ed. 1990. Flavius Vegetius Renatus, *Epitoma rei militaris* (American University Studies, series 17.2). New York / Bern.

Stewart, A. ed. 1896. Ludolph von Suchem, *Description of the Holy Land and the Way Thither* (Palestine Pilgrims' Text Society 12). London. (Reprinted New York, 1971.)

———. ed. 1896. Burchard of Mount Sion, *A Description of the Holy Land.* Contained in the same vol. as the preceding; paginated separately.

———. ed. 1896a. Marino Sanudo, *Secrets for True Crusaders to Help Them to Recover the Holy Land*. Contained in A. Stewart 1896; paginated separately.

Stewart, H. and Rand, E. eds. 1918. Anicius Manlius Severinus Boethius, *The Theological Tractates and the Consolation of Philosophy* (Loeb Classical Library). Cambridge, Mass. (Partly revised by J. Tester 1973.)

Stocchi, M. 1959. "Il *De Canaria* boccaccesco e un *locus deperditus* nel *De Insulis* de Domenico Silvestri," *Rinascimento* 10.143–156.

———. 1963. *Tradizione medievale e gusto umanistico nel "De montibus" del Boccaccio.* Padua.

———. ed. 1998. Giovanni Boccaccio, *De montibus, silvis, fontibus, lacubus, fluminibus, stagnis seu paludibus et diversis nominibus maris*, 1817–2122 in *Tutte le opere*, vol. 7–8, pt. 2 ed. by V. Branca. Milan.

Stoneman, R. ed. 1994. *Legends of Alexander the Great*. London.

——. 1995. "Naked Philosophers: The Brahmans in the Alexander Histories and the Alexander Romance," *Journal of Hellenic Studies* 115.99–114.

Strayer, J. 1969. "The Crusades of Louis IX," 487–518 in Wolff and Hazard 1969.

Strazzullo, F. 1968. "Il *Privilegium fundationis Carthusiae Neapolitanae* della regina Giovanna I (14 luglio 1347): Nel VI centenario della consacrazione della chiesa di S. Martino (26 febbraio 1369)," *Atti dell' Accademia Pontaniana di Napoli* N.S. 17.179–200.

Strecker, K. 1963. *Introduction to Medieval Latin,* revised and trans. by R. Palmer. Berlin.

Stuart, D. 1917. "The Sources and the Extent of Petrarch's Knowledge of the Life of Virgil," *Classical Philology* 12.364–404.

Stummer, F., ed. 1935. *Monumenta historiam et geographicam Terrae Sanctae illustrantia* (Florilegium Patristicum 41). Bonn.

Suerbaum, W. 1981. "Von der Vita Virgiliana über die Accessus Virgiliani zum Zauberer Virgilius: Probleme, Perspektiven, Aufgaben," *Aufstieg und Niedergang der rånischen Welt* 31(2).1156–1262.

Sumption, J. 1975. *Pilgrimage: An Image of Medieval Religion.* Totowa, N.J.

Symonds, J. 1912. *Renaissance in Italy: The Revival of Learning,* 2nd ed. London.

Tabacco, G. 1989. *The Struggle for Power in Medieval Italy: Structures of Political Rule,* trans. by R. Jensen. Cambridge.

Tabulae codicum manu scriptorum praeter Graecos et Orientales in Bibliotheca Palatina Vindobonensi asservatorum, vol. 6: *Cod. 9001-11,500* , 1873. Vienna.

Tangheroni, M. 1984. "Perché i Pisani combatterono alla Meloria?" 57–67 in Danielli and Borghini 1984.

Tarn, W. 1933. "Alexander: The Conquest of Persia," 352–386 in *The Cambridge Ancient History,* vol. 6. Cambridge.

Taylor, E. 1956. *The Haven-Finding Art: A History of Navigation from Odysseus to Captain Cook.* London.

Taylor, J. 1993. *Christians and the Holy Places: The Myth of Jewish-Christian Origins.* Oxford.

Temkin, O. 1991. *Hippocrates in a World of Pagans and Christians.* Baltimore.

TeSelle, E. 1996. "Looking for Home: Travel as Metaphor in Augustine," *Annali d'Italianistica: L'odeporica/Hodoeporics* 14.103–120.

Tester, S. J. 1987. *A History of Western Astrology.* Woodbridge, Suffolk.

Thackeray, H. et al. eds. 1926–65. Flavius Josephus, *Life, Against Apion, Jewish War, Antiquities,* 10 vols. (Loeb Classical Library). Cambridge, Mass.

Thilo, G. and Hagen, H. eds. 1881–87. *Servii grammatici qui feruntur in Virgilii carmina commentarii*, 3 vols. Leipzig. (Reprinted Hildesheim, 1961.)

Thomas, E. ed. 1960. *The "Philobiblon" of Richard de Bury, Bishop of Durham, Treasurer and Chancellor of Edward III*, new ed. by M. Maclagan. Oxford. (Latin text and translation.)

Thorndike, L. 1923–58. *A History of Magic and Experimental Science*, 8 vols. New York.

———. 1928. "Sanitation, Baths, and Street Cleaning in the Renaissance," *Speculum* 3.192–203.

———. 1944. *University Records and Life in the Middle Ages*. New York.

———. 1946. "More Light on Cecco d'Ascoli," *Romanic Review* 37.293–306.

———. ed. 1949. *The Sphere of Sacrobosco and Its Commentators*. Chicago.

Tischendorf, K. von ed. 1876. *Evangelia Apocrypha*, 2nd ed. Leipzig. (Reprinted Hildesheim, 1966.)

Tobler, T. ed. 1859. Francesco Pipino, *Tractatus de locis terrae sanctae*, 400–412 in *Dritte Wanderung nach Paläｓtina in Jahre 1857* . Gotha.

Toynbee, P. 1924. "The Bearing of the *Cursus* on the Text of Dante's *De vulgari eloquentia*,"*Proceedin gs of the British Academy* 10.359–377.

———. ed. 1920. *Dantis Alagherii epistolae: The Letters of Dante*, 2nd ed. 1966. Oxford.

Tozzi, P. 1990. *Opicinus e Pavia*. Como.

———. 1992. "Il *Mundus Papie* in Opicinus," *Geographica antiqua* 1.167–174.

Trapp, J. 1984. "The Grave of Virgil," *Journal of Warburg and Courtauld Institutes* 47.1–31.

———. 1986. "Virgil and the Monuments," *Proceedings of the Virgilian Society* 18.1–17.

Traube, L. ed. 1896. Sedulius Scottus, *Carmina*, in *Monumenta Germaniae historica, Poetae latini aevi Carolini*, vol. 3.151–240. Berlin.

Trinkhaus, C. 1979. *The Poet as Philosopher: Petrarch and the Foundation of Renaissance Consciousness*. New Haven/London.

Tristano, C. 1974. "Le postille del Petrarca nel Vaticano Lat. 2193 (Apuleio, Frontino, Vegezio, Palladio)," *IMU* 17.365–468.

Tritton, A. 1930. *The Caliphs and their non-Moslem Subjects*. Oxford. (Reprinted London, 1970.)

Trompeo, P. and Martellotti, G. 1943. "Cartaginesi a Roma," *Nuova Antologia* CDXXX 11–12.254–264.

Tubach, F. 1969. *Index Exemplorum: A Handbook of Medieval Religious Tales*. Helsinki.

Ullman, B. 1928. "Tibullus in the Mediaeval *Florilegia*," *Classical Philology* 23.128–174.

———. 1960. *The Origin and Development of Humanistic Script*. Rome.

———. 1964. "Geometry in the Mediaeval Quadrivium," 263–285 in *Studi di bibliografia e di storia in onore di Tommaso de Marinis*, vol. 4. Verona.

———. 1973. "Petrarch's Favorite Books," 113–133 in *Studies in the Italian Renaissance* (Studi e testi 51), 2nd ed. Rome.

———. 1973a. "Petrarch's *De vita solitaria*," 135–175 in preceding entry.

Upson, H. 1943. "Medieval Lives of Virgil," *Classical Philology* 38.103–111.

Usener, H. and Radermacher, L. eds. 1892–1929. *Dionysii Halicarnasei quae extant opera;* vol. 6, 2: *Opuscularum volumen secundum*. Stuttgart. (Reprinted in 1965.)

Ussani, V. ed. 1932. *Hegesippi qui dicitur historiae libri V*, vol. 1: Text; vol. 2 (1960): *Preface* by C. Mras and *Indices* by Ussani (Corpus scriptorum ecclesiasticorum latinorum). Vienna.

———. 1943–44. "Il Petrarca e Flavio Giuseppe," *Rendiconti della Pontificia accademia romana di archeologia* 20.447–467.

Vasoli, C. and de Robertis, D. eds. 1988. Dante Alighieri, *Convivio*, vol. 1, pt. 2 in *Opere minori*. Milan / Naples.

Vattasso, M. 1908. *I codici petrarcheschi della Biblioteca Vaticana*. Rome.

Vessereau, J. and Préchac, F. eds. 1961. Rutilius Namatianus, *Sur son retour* [De reditu suo] (Association Guillaume Budé). Paris.

Walbank, F. 1957–79. *A Historical Commentary on Polybius*, 3 vols. Oxford.

Waley, D. 1988. *The Italian City-Republics*, 3rd. ed. New York.

Ward-Perkins, B. 1978. "Luni: the decline and abandonment of a Roman town," *Papers in Italian Archaeology I: The Lancaster Seminar* (British Archaeology Reports) 41.313–321.

Warner, G. ed. 1889. *The Buke of John Maundeuill*. Westminster.

Waszink, H. ed. 1962. *Timaeus a Calcidio translatus commentarioque instructus* (Plato latinus 4). London.

Weikert, H. 1987. "Plankton and the Pelagic Environment," 90–111 in *Red Sea*, ed. by A. Edwards and S. Head. Oxford.

Weisheipl, J. 1978. "The Nature, Scope, and Classification of the Sciences," 461–482 in Lindberg 1978.

Weiss, R. 1964. "Petrarch the Antiquarian," 199–209 in vol. 2 of Henderson 1964.

———. 1969. *The Renaissance Discovery of Classical Antiquity*. Oxford.

Welter, J.-Th. ed. 1926. *La Tabula exemplorum secundum ordinem alphabeti*. Paris / Toulouse.

———. 1927. *L'exemplum dans la littérature religieuse et didactique du moyen âge*. Paris. (Reprinted Geneva, 1973.)

White, K. 1984. *Greek and Roman Technology*. Ithaca, N.Y.

Whitfield, J. 1943. *Petrarch and the Renascence.* Oxford.

———. 1971. "Machiavelli's Use of Livy," 73–96 in *Livy*, ed. by T. Dorey. London.

Wiesner, W. ed. 1970. *S. Ambrosii De bono mortis: A Revised Text with an Introduction, Translation, and Commentary* (Patristic Studies 100). Washington, D.C.

Wilcken, U. 1967. *Alexander the Great*, trans. G. Richards with notes by E. Borza, New York.

Wilkins, E. 1951. *The Making of the "Canzoniere" and Other Petrarchan Studies.* Rome.

———. 1955. *Studies in the Life and Works of Petrarch* (The Mediaeval Academy of America 63). Cambridge, Mass.

———. 1958. *Petrarch's Eight Years in Milan*. Cambridge, Mass.

———. 1959. *Petrarch's Later Years.* Cambridge, Mass.

———. 1961. *Life of Petrarch.* Chicago.

———. ed. 1962. *The Triumphs of Petrarch.* Chicago.

———. 1978. "On Petrarch's *Ep. Fam.* VI 2," in Bernardo 1978. (Reprinted from *Speculum* 38 [1963] 620–622.)

———. 1978a. "On Petrarch's Appreciation of Art," in Bernardo 1978. (Reprinted from *Speculum* [1961] 299–301.)

———. 1978b. "An Introductory Boccaccio Bibliography," in Bernardo 1978. (Reprinted from *Philological Quarterly* 6 [1927] 111–122.)

———. and Billanovich, G. eds. 1978. "Miscellaneous Letters of Petrarch," in Bernardo 1978. (Reprinted from *Speculum* 37 [1962] 226–243.)

Wilkinson, J. 1974. "L' apport de St. Jérôme à la topographie," *Revue biblique* 81.245–257.

———. 1977. *Jerusalem Pilgrims before the Crusades.* Warminster, Eng.

———. 1981. *Egeria's Travels to the Holy Land.* rev. ed. Warminster, Eng.

Wilkinson, J., Hill, J., and Ryan, W. eds. 1988. *Jerusalem Pilgrimage 1099–1185* (The Hakluyt Society, 2nd series 167). London.

Williman, D. ed. 1982. *The Black Death: The Impact of the Fourteenth-Century Plague* (Medieval and Renaissance Texts and Studies 13). Binghamton, N.Y.

Willis, J. ed. 1963. Ambrosius Theodosius Macrobius, *Commentarii in Somnium Scipionis*, vol. 2 (Bibliotheca Teubneriana). Leipzig.

Wilpert, P. 1960. "The Fragments of Aristotle's Lost Writings," 257–264 in *Aristotle and Plato in the Mid-fourth Century*, eds. I. Düring and G. Owen (Studia graeca et latina gothoburgensia 11). Göteborg.

Wilson, N. 1992. *From Byzantium to Italy: Greek Studies in the Italian Renaissance.* London.
Witt, R. 1976. *Coluccio Salutati and His Public Letters* (Travaux d' humanisme et Renaissance 151). Geneva.
Wittkower, R. 1942. "Marvels of the East: A Study in the History of Monsters," *Journal of the Warburg and Courtauld Institutes* 5.159–197.
Wolff, R. 1948. "Romania: The Latin Empire of Constantinople," *Speculum* 22.1–34.
———. and Hazard, H. eds. 1969. *A History of the Crusades,* vol. 2: *The Later Crusades,* 2nd ed.; general ed. K. Setton 1969–89. Madison, Wis.
Wölfflin, E. 1892. "Zur Psychologie der Völker des Altertums,"*Archiv für lateinische Lexikographie und Grammatik* 7.140–146.
Wood, F. 1995. *Did Marco Polo Go to China?* London.
Woodward, D. 1987. "Medieval *Mappaemundi,*" 286–370 in Harley and Woodward 1987.
Wright, J. 1925. *The Geographical Lore of the Time of the Crusades: A Study in the History of Medieval Science and Tradition in Western Europe* (American Geographical Society Research series 15). New York.
Wright, J. ed. 1975. *The Life of Cola di Rienzo* (Pontifical Institute of Medieval Studies). Toronto.
Zaccaria, V. ed. 1967. Giovanni Boccaccio, *De mulieribus claris,* in *Tutte le opere,* vol. 10, ed. by V. Branca. Milan.
Zacher, C. 1976. *Curiosity and Pilgrimage: The Literature of Discovery in Fourteenth-Century England.* Baltimore.
Zacour, N. 1973. *Petrarch's "Book without a Name"* (Pontifical Institute of Medieval Studies). Toronto.
———. and Hazard, H. eds. 1985. *A History of the Crusades,* vol. 5: *The Impact of the Crusades on the Near East:* general ed. K. Setton 1969–89 Madison, Wis.
Zangemeister, K. ed. 1889. Paulus Orosius, *Historiarum adversum paganos libri vii* (Bibliotheca Teubneriana). Leipzig. (Translated as *The Seven Books of History against the Pagans,* by R. Deferrari [Fathers of the Church 50] Washington, D.C., 1964.)
Zeigler, P. 1969. *The Black Death.* New York.
Zeitlin, J. ed. 1924. Francesco Petrarca, *The Life of Solitude.* Urbana.
Ziada, M. 1975. "The Mamluk Sultans, 1291–1517," 486–512 in Hazard 1975. Madison, Wis.
Ziadeh, N. 1953. *Urban Life in Syria under the Early Mamluks.* Beirut.

INDICES

INDEX OF BIBLICAL NAMES

INDEX OF PLACE NAMES

INDEX OF PERSONAL NAMES

The index includes the names of ancient, early Christian, and early modern authors cited or alluded to in the *Itinerarium* and mentioned or cited in the Introduction and Commentary.

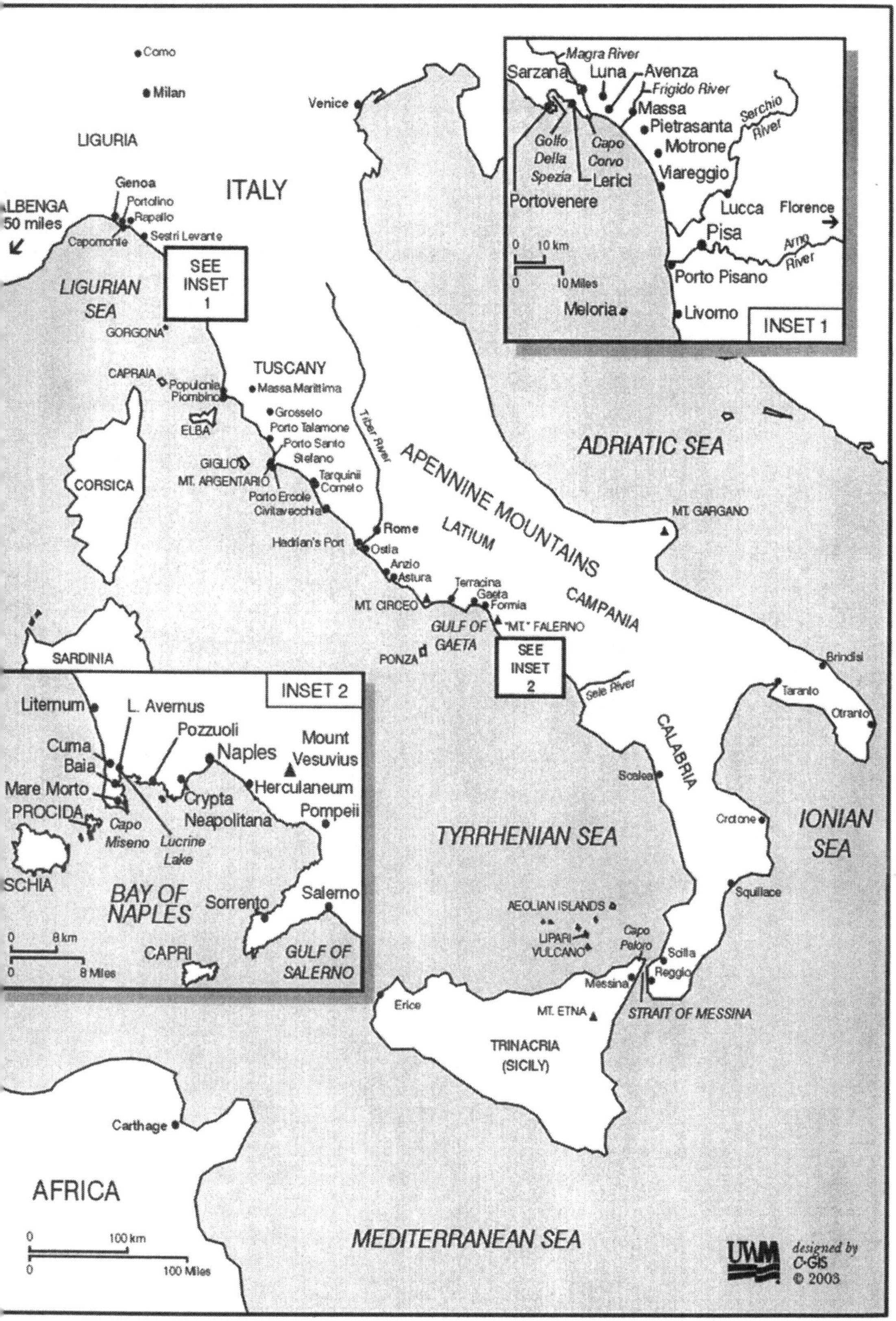
Como
Milan
Venice
LIGURIA
ITALY
Genoa
Portofino
Rapallo
Sestri Levante
Capomonte
ALBENGA
50 miles
SEE INSET 1
LIGURIAN SEA
GORGONA
CAPRAIA
Populonia
Piombino
ELBA
TUSCANY
Massa Marittima
Grosseto
Porto Talamone
Porto Santo Stefano
GIGLIO
MT. ARGENTARIO
Porto Ercole
Tarquinii
Corneto
Civitavecchia
CORSICA
Tiber River
APENNINE MOUNTAINS
LATIUM
Rome
Hadrian's Port
Ostia
Anzio
Astura
MT. CIRCEO
Terracina
Gaeta
Formia
GULF OF GAETA
"MT." FALERNO
PONZA
SEE INSET 2
CAMPANIA
SARDINIA
ADRIATIC SEA
MT. GARGANO
Sele River
CALABRIA
Brindisi
Taranto
Otranto
Scalea
Crotone
IONIAN SEA
TYRRHENIAN SEA
Squillace
AEOLIAN ISLANDS
LIPARI
VULCANO
Capo Peloro
Scilla
Reggio
Messina
Erice
MT. ETNA
STRAIT OF MESSINA
TRINACRIA (SICILY)
Carthage
AFRICA
MEDITERRANEAN SEA
0 100 km
0 100 Miles
designed by C-GIS © 2003
Magra River
Sarzana
Luna
Avenza
Frigido River
Massa
Pietrasanta
Serchio River
Golfo Della Spezia
Capo Corvo
Lerici
Motrone
Viareggio
Portovenere
Lucca
Florence
Pisa
0 10 km
0 10 Miles
Arno River
Porto Pisano
Meloria
Livorno
INSET 1
INSET 2
Liternum
L. Avernus
Pozzuoli
Mount Vesuvius
Cuma
Baia
Naples
Mare Morto
Herculaneum
PROCIDA
Crypta Neapolitana
Pompeii
Capo Miseno
Lucrine Lake
SCHIA
BAY OF NAPLES
Sorrento
Salerno
0 8 km
0 8 Miles
CAPRI
GULF OF SALERNO

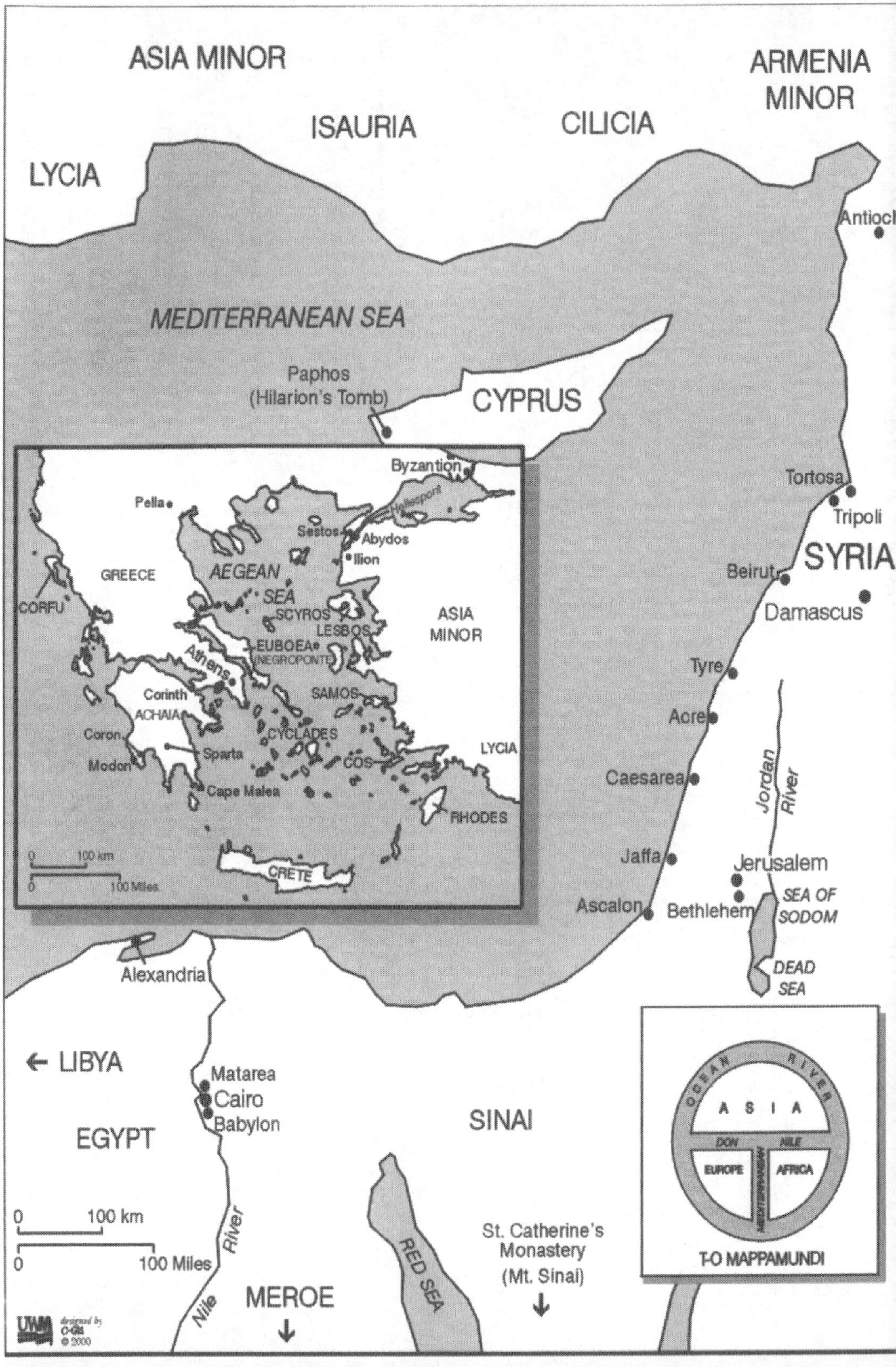

ASIA MINOR
ARMENIA MINOR
ISAURIA
CILICIA
LYCIA
Antioch
MEDITERRANEAN SEA
Paphos (Hilarion's Tomb)
CYPRUS
Byzantion
Pella
Hellespont
Sestos
Abydos
Ilion
GREECE
AEGEAN SEA
CORFU
SCYROS
LESBOS
ASIA MINOR
EUBOEA (NEGROPONTE)
Athens
Corinth
ACHAIA
SAMOS
Coron
CYCLADES
Sparta
LYCIA
Modon
COS
Cape Malea
RHODES
0 100 km
0 100 Miles
CRETE
Tortosa
Tripoli
SYRIA
Beirut
Damascus
Tyre
Acre
Caesarea
Jordan River
Jaffa
Jerusalem
Ascalon
Bethlehem
SEA OF SODOM
DEAD SEA
Alexandria
LIBYA
Matarea
Cairo
Babylon
EGYPT
SINAI
OCEAN RIVER
ASIA
DON
NILE
EUROPE
AFRICA
MEDITERRANEAN
T-O MAPPAMUNDI
0 100 km
0 100 Miles
Nile River
St. Catherine's Monastery (Mt. Sinai)
RED SEA
MEROE
designed by C-GIS © 2000